CONTAINING THE ARMS RACE

Written under the auspices of
THE CENTER FOR INTERNATIONAL AFFAIRS
Harvard University

CONTAINING THE ARMS RACE
Some Specific Proposals

Jeremy J. Stone

THE M.I.T. PRESS
Massachusetts Institute of Technology
Cambridge, Massachusetts, and London, England

To
I. F. STONE

FOREWORD

WE ARE COMPLETING twenty years of the greatest arms race the world has ever witnessed; a period in which both American and Russian technologists have worked intensively to develop new weapons that might provide a military advantage. Concurrently, to this same end, military intellectuals on both sides have formulated strategies for the use of the new weapons and influenced plans for their purchase.

This process has been a confusing and frightening one for the average citizen to watch. Lacking classified information, available only to government officials, about either the characteristics of our weapons or about Soviet activities, the spectator citizen has generally concluded that it is impossible for him to form any responsible judgment concerning the major policy battles of which he has caught glimpses in newspaper "leaks," in speeches by military leaders, or in parts of Congressional testimony that are made public. Told that it is vital for him to understand and express himself on these issues and those of disarmament he has often asked, "How can we get enough facts and a good enough understanding of the choices to have a conscientious position?"

There was a time when the answer to that question had to be, "You can't," but that is hardly the case today, and this book is one of several available to which the serious spectator, intent upon understanding contemporary military and arms control debates, can turn.

In the 1950's new military technology was being introduced so rapidly that existing strategic concepts were obsolete. Not even the experts understood adequately the implications of the revolutionary increases in fire power and speed of delivery that thermonuclear bombs, ballistic missiles, and electronic computers — employed together — had made possible. Nor did they possess sufficient information about Soviet military achievements to reach a consensus on the potential threat that U.S. weapons had to counter. Furthermore, during that period of very rapid technological change, great military advantage accrued to a policy of secrecy that withheld new developments from the competitor, and hence from the American public, for as long as possible.

However, the situation is very different today. For the moment, weapons technology and strategic thinking have reached a plateau. New weapons developments of the past several years have been primarily refinements leading to greater reliability, greater fire power, higher efficiency, and greater economy; they have hardly been of a sort to make either side fear that any one development would disrupt, even partially, the established nuclear stalemate. At the same time the increased openness of the Soviet society and our improved ability to obtain information by other means have provided a much more realistic assessment of Soviet capabilities than existed in the 1950's. With these developments has come a sufficient diminution of fears on both sides to permit a serious search for means to halt the arms race. This, in turn, has focused professional interest on alternatives to the present "quiet arms race" with its inherent costs and dangers.

A major consequence of the new conditions has been a willingness, almost an anxiety, on the part of the Department of Defense officials to explain to the public and to Congress the reasoning by which they have arrived at their weapons decisions. In Congressional testimony and speeches, Mr. McNamara, Dr. Harold Brown, and other Defense Department officials have provided comprehensive discussions of our current military strategy and the weapons plans to support it. The exhaustive hearings in 1962 on the Nuclear Test Ban Treaty made available a vast amount of information about contemporary military problems, particularly those related to the prospects of achieving an adequate defense against attack by ballistic missiles.

Similarly, one can find much information in the reports of Congressional hearings on strategic bombing and bombers, on civilian defense, on air defense, and on many other military subjects. Although published proceedings of Congressional investigations are often couched in general terms, much technical information can be found in the aerospace journals that vie with one another to be the first to disclose such details.

In this book, Dr. Stone has brought together much of this publicly available information on strategic military systems — bombers, missiles, and antimissile defenses — as well as much information pertinent to the problems of their control. The book examines in considerable depth the arguments for and against two of the most important current arms control proposals — the freeze of strategic delivery systems, and agreements between the United States and the Soviet Union not to deploy missile defense systems. The unique characteristic of this book is that it musters the facts and arguments pertinent to current and emerging public debates; in a real sense, it is a textbook for persons with a genuine desire to understand the contemporary arguments. Though specialists with access to secret information will, I am certain, believe that some technical issues are treated inadequately, and even completely disagree with some of the author's judgments, the book provides nonetheless a thoroughly adequate basis for understanding current strategic problems. With this book available no person need feel that he lacks the information required for a sound judgment on these issues. With it, he can identify the basic assumptions and uncertainties that underlie the debates; he will be able to see why reasonable people using the same basic data can come to very different conclusions concerning proposals for controlling the strategic weapons arms race.

The chapters on the antiballistic missile defenses are particularly timely. Technical developments seem to be forcing the leadership of both the United States and the Soviet Union to face continuously the decision to purchase, or to defer the

purchase of, full-scale antiballistic missile systems — a decision that will be both costly and fateful. Many observers believe that an affirmative decision to deploy substantial missile
defenses will signal a new round in the arms race, leading
almost certainly to a massive civil defense program, and the
procurement of many more ballistic missiles by both sides.
The cost of these actions will be measured in tens of billions
of dollars. Furthermore, the present strained, but real, calm
and the prospects for any reduction in armaments are almost
certain to be casualties of these actions. These decisions could
determine much of the course of U.S.-Soviet relations for the
next decade, until a new stable position is achieved. And such
is the power of offensive weapons that, when this round is
over, it is likely that the ability of each side to inflict damage
on the other will have been increased rather than curtailed.

In attempting to evaluate the feasibility and acceptability
of arms control proposals, it is necessary to make assumptions
regarding the perspective from which an opponent, whose real
attitudes and objectives are unknown, will view the measure.
Dr. Stone's analysis of real Soviet interests and their possible
reactions to U.S. moves seems generally sound; in fact, his attempt to be a neutral observer in judging the reactions of
both sides to the various proposals for arms control is an outstanding feature of this book. Even so, he sometimes clearly
fails to take into account important aspects of the proposals
that will probably make at least one of them unacceptable to
Russian leaders. For example, in the discussion of heavy-bomber
disarmament, Dr. Stone excludes the new U.S. fighter-bomber,
the F-111, from the list of bombers that would be destroyed.
Distinguishing heavy bombers from fighter-bombers is consistent with the U.S. draft proposal for a freeze on nuclear
delivery systems, but is rather difficult to justify from a military viewpoint. True, the F-111 was planned for use as a
tactical and fighter aircraft. But the global nature of U.S. commitments placed a high premium on an aircraft that could be
deployed quickly from one point to another. This dictated a
large, fast, well-instrumented aircraft, which turns out to be

a very satisfactory bomber. In fact, in the short interval since the book was completed, Secretary of Defense McNamara has announced his intention to purchase 250 modified F-111's as future replacements for B-52 bombers.

How should these problems of categorizing weapons systems be handled? If the F-111 is regarded as a strategic aircraft and included in bomber disarmament or a freeze, U.S. tactical forces will be required to use a smaller, less satisfactory, aircraft. If it is excluded, the United States will be permitted to build a bomber force of major proportions (plans have been discussed for the purchase of about 1,500 F-111's by the Air Force and the Navy). On the whole, however, Dr. Stone's discussions are well balanced, and I should guess that Soviet military planners would agree with as much of the author's analysis as would Americans.

Since Soviet acceptance of arms control proposals is no less important than our own, it would be especially useful if this book, and others like it that throw light on the underlying choices in the arms race, were generally available in the Soviet Union, as well as in the West. Maybe the Russians will translate and publish it.

JEROME B. WIESNER

December 16, 1965

ACKNOWLEDGMENTS

THIS BOOK was conceived in January 1964 when I was working at the Hudson Institute. An early version of Chapter One, entitled "Should the Soviet Union build an Antiballistic Missile System?," had been written. It was increasingly apparent that the main arms control problems and opportunities could be discerned by reading the open literature. A book of studies seemed indicated.

After leaving Hudson Institute, I completed Chapter Two.* At this point, thanks to the sponsorship of Thomas C. Schelling, I had the splendid opportunity to complete this volume at the Harvard Center for International Affairs.

Since I knew nothing of strategy or arms control before entering Hudson Institute in March 1962, a certain amount of the blame or credit for this volume attaches to it, and to its director, Herman Kahn. From him, like so many others, I learned a great deal despite my best efforts to avoid it. Some time after my appointment, Donald G. Brennan became Hudson's president; I was thus privileged to work for, and with, this extraordinarily diligent, tenacious, and talented arms controller. For much of my education in this subject I am indebted to him.

At the Harvard Center for International Affairs, I had the pleasure of enjoying the wit and wisdom of Tom Schelling. To Mort Halperin I am especially indebted for a gentle treatment of my residual misconceptions, for encouragement, ad-

* It is here reprinted, much as it appeared in *World Politics*, to whose editors I am grateful for the right of republication.

vice, and comradeship. And to Ina Halperin I owe the index to this volume.

At one time or another, the chapters got a fairly wide circulation in Cambridge and Washington; it is difficult to thank all who have commented on them so I shall thank none by name, but I am grateful to all. Finally, this book has benefited from Bob Erwin's cheerful editing; and I am obliged to him for shepherding it through the shoals of publication.

I add, as is customary, that I am solely responsible for the book's contents and form and for the opinions expressed within.

JEREMY J. STONE

January, 1966

CONTENTS

CONTENTS

INTRODUCTION

THE MOST dramatic and fearsome aspect of armaments production in the United States and the Soviet Union has been the procurement of long-range strategic nuclear forces —bombers and missiles. Parallel to the construction of the forces have been the attempts to procure strategic defenses against them: bomber defenses, missile defenses, and defenses against submarines.

This volume considers the important arms control and disarmament issues that involve these U.S. and Soviet strategic weapons. It attempts to consider, from a technical and political point of view, how the United States and the Soviet Union might reach various arms control agreements.

The book is composed of five chapters that are closely related. Two are devoted to bombers, and one each is given to missile defense, to missile reductions, and to a proposal to limit strategic force levels. Every chapter puts forth a policy suggestion and argues for it. For this reason, the chapters are in a sense studies of, or briefs for, particular policy proposals. On the other hand, the existing problems do not present a wide range of quite different policy alternatives. Hence, by revealing the basic political and technical issues that are involved in any proposal concerned with a certain weapon system, the chapters allow the reader to consider for himself what other policy might be followed.

The chapters are closely related in their subject matter even when they refer primarily to different strategic weapons. The question posed by one strategic weapon generally involves others. For example, if we are to build a defense against one strategic weapon, must we build defenses against others lest we leave a weak link in our posture? Must a treaty to halt the procurement of offensive weapons include provisions to halt the procurement of defensive weapons so as to maintain the existing balance? If an agreement called for the dismantlement of heavy bombers, would the missiles targeted on airfields become surplus to the needs of the major powers and hence themselves become ripe for reductions? Has the construction of missiles made bombers of sufficiently little use to permit their destruction by a treaty or by informal agreement?

The book is organized in the following way. Perhaps the most important arms control issue at the present time is whether to encourage or discourage the construction of missile defenses in our own country or in the Soviet Union. The first chapter sets forth the situation and argues that missile defenses should be avoided.

The second chapter discusses heavy-bomber disarmament and argues that the elimination of heavy bombers from the armories of both major powers should be considered. It sets forth the underlying considerations, as of early 1964.

By late 1964 it was becoming possible to see how the problem of dismantling heavy bombers would be handled by the major powers in the absence of a formal treaty. The third chapter describes the situation and suggests that informal bomber disarmament agreements are more likely to be implemented than formal ones.

In Chapters One, Two, and Three, discussion of bomber disarmament and missile defenses can be set forth without a very close analysis of the character of modern missiles. Chapter Four, however, which treats the problem of missile reductions, requires and supplies a good deal more such information. It is suggested here that a Soviet proposal calling for "reductions to strictly limited and agreed numbers" of missiles might be accepted in principle.

Chapter Five discusses the problem of "freezing" numbers and characteristics of strategic weapons, and rests upon the information introduced in Chapter Four. A proposal is made in

Chapter Five that the United States should consider a freeze of strategic weapons: a "pause" that would last for five years and would be renewable.

In short, each of the five chapters supports a specific policy goal. Each treats arms control and disarmament in concrete rather than in general terms. Each assumes that there is *mutual* interest in arms control. None attempts to conceal those one-sided advantages that we may find in disarmament. An agreement based on such deception is neither likely to be achieved nor likely to be maintained.*

In general, we in the United States must endeavor to seek the Soviet interest just as we seek our own. And the Soviets must be persuaded to agree not only to what is good for us but also to what is good for them. Their misunderstanding of their interests is no less an obstacle than our misunderstanding of our own. Persuading the one side is no less important than persuading the other.

While we have a greater right to presume to advise our own government there are questions for which American analysts may find the Soviets a more logical audience. Much of arms control involves considering the impact of the decisions of one side on those of the other. To this extent the Soviets are an important audience for those predictions of U.S. reactions that may forestall miscalculation on their side.

Reasons for believing that there is merit in the actions suggested are set forth in the course of the discussion. These are not restricted to those advantages that seem especially desirable to me; included also are those arguments that appeal to others of a different turn of mind. No nation, no group of men, has a single motivation for action. If some analysts are, by and

---

* Ware Adams put it this way: "There is however a tendency at times to think of international agreements as devices for one party to get an advantage over the other, either by imposition or trickery, or sleight-of-hand or just plain out-smarting him, as a device to compel a nation to undertake something contrary to its own interest. This is foolish. No nation keeps such agreements, not even we. Even if achieved such an agreement would be dangerous not merely for one, but for both parties, because of its inherent instability, resting on false premises." [1]

large, obsessed with irrelevant calculations, I have not hesitated to describe the benefits of my proposals in them. If others ignore strategic computations to a greater extent than would I, I have nonetheless been willing to describe the consistencies between their point of view and these proposals.

This approach produces a set of arguments that will often seem improper, if not inconsistent, to those who argue for arms control and disarmament for any one particular reason. For example, if someone believes that the central purpose of agreements is to reduce destruction if war occurs, what is he to make of the argument that, under a particular agreement, our forces would increase in destructive capacity? Or, if he believes that security is paramount, what is he to make of a great emphasis on the saving of resources?

In fact, these proposals do not stem from any single overriding concern to modify the strategic context in some particular way. They are not discussed from a consistent philosophy or viewpoint. Nor has there been any particular reason to sort out exactly on which grounds these proposals most appeal to me. I have been their lawyer and not their judge.

There is some controversy over the utility of posing "solutions," and of doing so in a spirit of advocacy. But it can be useful in generating interest, in furthering the discussion, and in instructing if not in solving the problems — which it may also do in some cases. And it tends to overcome one of the main obstacles to the study of such low probability events as a comprehensive arms control agreement: the inability of the analyst to do more than conclude that the agreement is, on the whole, unlikely. That analysts are often unable to supply a plausible explanation of how the agreement will be achieved — considering de Gaulle, the rate of fatigue of aircraft, and the statements of Senator Russell — is not very interesting. Many problems will turn out not to matter, and the policies advocated will only take effect after many conditions have changed. These discussions therefore concentrate on the most important technical and political issues.

Such discussions would slight the "other side" of the argument if there were one. But, in fact, there is no "other side," only a variety of different positions, the proponents of which argue different courses of actions for different, often wildly different, reasons. It is not possible to do justice to all of these from a public vantage point. The information available, somewhat surprisingly, permits an interesting and often a cogent case for given policies. It does not provide a comprehensive, certainly not a decisive, case. It can be used to prove that something should be studied but not that it should be done.

Most readers will find disturbing the extent to which computations made in this volume concern destruction of people and cities; and well they may. It is surprising, as well as disturbing, that decisions should be made upon a weapon, or a defense, because it can take or save X million lives if an unimaginable catastrophe descends upon us. Those who accept the necessity to make such decisions may yet be appalled that these are so delicately influenced by cost. And those who appreciate the extent to which we habitually determine by cost our capacity to destroy or protect may be disturbed, in turn, by the impact of these strategic computations on disarmament. If the world becomes safer, future generations will find it hard to believe that the calculations involved in this kind of reasoning could have influenced defense and disarmament policy.

Working from Public Sources

It is surprising how little unofficial work attempts to deal with the policy problems of arms control measures involving specific strategic weapon systems. The problem is difficult, the analysts are often unfriendly to the subject, many are frustrated by the problems of getting the government to take action, and the Soviet attitude is not encouraging. Many who are sympathetic to arms control have tended to discuss other than concrete problems. The difficulties of attaining sufficient public information are inhibiting. The number of articles that present a problem, propose a solution, and make some attempt to discuss its political and strategic implications for both U.S. and Soviet policy are very few.*

For example, it is revealing to note that until the United States proposed a freeze on strategic weapon procurement the very sizable literature on arms control studies had not dealt in a significant way with this alternative to disarmament. To have proposed this possibility, and to have sketched its implications, would have been a contribution both to arms control and to defense thinking. A large part of what follows is meant to "stretch" arms control thinking in much the same way. Thus, the discussions of bomber disarmament are designed in part to anticipate the obsolescence of the B-52's and to stimulate thinking about their disposal. The discussion of a "freeze" presents the idea of a "pause" in procurement. The chapter on antiballistic missile systems argues on arms control grounds against a *defensive* system. These chapters deal with issues that deserve a great deal more public and governmental attention than they are likely to get.

These chapters attempt to predict policies. It is not possible to study arms control without such predictions. If the government is soon to cease funding new missile silos, and one wants this act to be accompanied by a resounding announcement, it is necessary to predict the event in time to advocate the choice. Similarly, if one wants to influence whether bombers are destroyed unilaterally — or bilaterally through an agreement — U.S. plans to phase down the B-52 force must be anticipated. And it is only if one perceives that antiballistic missile systems are unlikely to be highly desired by governments that one can see an opportunity for restraint based on arms control grounds. Part of the problem is to be sufficiently ahead of government thinking to add something new and yet not so far ahead that everyone believes nothing can be done. Of course, being somewhat ahead of the thinking of one agency may mean being a good deal ahead of the thinking of

---

* The Test Ban has received such treatment in "Policy Considerations of a Nuclear Test Ban," by D. G. Brennan and M. H. Halperin.[2] There are some other examples.

another. Where the government position is when no position has yet been fought out is often very hard to say. For this reason, the exact extent to which these chapters are "unrealistic" is sometimes difficult to estimate.

Nothing is discussed that could not reasonably be considered by a President who felt deeply the need for progress. By the same token, however, many Presidents might see no purpose in seeking any formal restraints whatsoever on missiles or bombers. What is a "workable, acceptable" plan often depends, perhaps most often depends, upon the President himself and his most private assessment of the political forces at work, the chances for success, the risks of trying, and the obligation to take them. As no less an authority than a Presidential Adviser on National Security Affairs, McGeorge Bundy, said:

> It is only the American President who can carry the American Senate and the American people in any agreement on arms control, and it is only with American participation that any such agreement can have meaning for the Soviet Government.
> Unless a President uses these powers with energy, arms control agreements are improbable.[3]

The contentions concerning strategy have been documented with relevant quotations. In some cases this may be misleading, even within the restraints of public information. But the elementary details of the strategic situation are for the most part accurately reflected in the public literature; this has been the consensus of many observers. However, the possibility certainly remains that large gaps exist in the literature.

The present Secretary of Defense is one of the most common sources and, of course, one of the most authoritative, for establishing simple facts or for documenting agreed national doctrines or estimates. His testimony has been used for these purposes, as well as for his judgments. This has sometimes given an exaggerated impression of the extent to which the chapters depend upon the Secretary of Defense's preferences among policy alternatives; but that I have a high degree of sympathy with Secretary McNamara's record is undeniable.

Mr. McNamara is not the first Secretary of Defense to have emphasized, both by direct comment and by the depth of his disclosures, how important it is that potential adversaries appreciate the extent and nature of our strength. This has provided a good deal of information to the public, but several other sources have also. It is well known to the community of defense analysts, and to the Soviets, that such journals as *Aviation Week and Space Technology* and *Missiles and Rockets*, in combination with Congressional hearings, reveal the broad outlines of the strategic situation. The reports of the Institute for Strategic Studies, and the military commentators of *The New York Times* and the *Washington Star* are also useful sources of information that can hardly be overlooked by interested parties.

Is the U.S. government right to release so much information? Should it be used for estimating the likelihood of arms control agreements and the forms that they might take? I, personally, am sympathetic to the government efforts and believe that they might go somewhat further than they do. The missile gap is an excellent example of the unfortunate consequences of classifying information too highly. Until quite recently, the government never gave even upper estimates on the number of missiles constructed by the Soviets. This maintained a climate in which it was difficult to object to U.S. procurement of (I believe) a disproportionately large number of intercontinental ballistic missiles. An informed electorate might at least have understood the issues, if not encouraged still better explanations, had this information been available.* In any case, the information exists and can be found in sources

---

* My general view is not too dissimilar to that of former Deputy Secretary of Defense, Roswell Gilpatric. For example, under the title "Gilpatric Asks Defense Facts for the Public," *The Christian Science Monitor* quoted the former Deputy Secretary of Defense as saying: "I don't feel we should put as high a barrier on strategic information. . . . In the end, those in positions of authority will have to make the final decisions. . . . But, nevertheless, there should be enough understanding of public affairs in the public sector to provide support for (or condemnation of) basic national policies." [4]

which, according to the testimony of defecting Soviet spies, are carefully examined by Soviet authorities.† There seems no cost to our consideration of it; the question is what we might be able to do with it.

The Strategic Context

The strategic situation changes so rapidly and the action of the major powers in procurement and dismantlement proceeds so steadily that the information is rapidly outdated. Indeed, over a few years the nature of the problems and the best approach to them can change. If we watch closely, we discover that disarmament proposals, like "old soldiers," tend only to fade away. Those most hostile to them tend to ignore them. Those most sympathetic are unlikely to consider their time well spent in destructive criticism. Hence the proposals simply get less and less attention as the technological and political presuppositions become less favorable, until even the most sympathetic arms controller avoids them in his considerations.

The strategic context has been changing especially rapidly over the last few years. For those concerned with arms control, even the plans and hopes of 1961 seem hopelessly outdated. And the speed with which these plans have become implausible is itself an important consideration in assessing the chances for present plans.

Control of strategic weapons is now pursued in an environment in which both powers are incredibly well armed. In the last five years, the United States has deployed approximately 1,000 land-based intercontinental missiles, about 500 sea-based strategic missiles, and innumerable tactical nuclear weapons, many of which are larger than the Hiroshima bomb. We have, in addition, continued to maintain a force of several hundred strategic bombers. There are a variety of ways of describing

† The former Chief of the Central Intelligence Agency, Allen Dulles, gives an interesting discussion of this situation in his widely read book.[5]

the unprecedented power of this force. It is sufficient to say that these weapons are capable, indeed are designed to be capable, of destroying a sizable portion of the world's population. The United States has built these forces at a cost measured in tens of billions of dollars. It has deployed submarine-launched missiles in the Atlantic and the Pacific oceans and in adjoining seas. Intercontinental missiles have been installed on the continental United States. The tactical nuclear weapons are largely in Europe or on ships on the surface of the sea. It is generally believed, but difficult to verify, that the nuclear force is under close control, and that it is not very susceptible to accidental or inadvertent launching or unauthorized behavior.

The Soviet Union has the second largest strategic nuclear force in the world — a force of a few hundred intercontinental missiles and a few hundred intercontinental bombers. It has several hundred shorter-range strategic missiles targeted on Western Europe and many hundreds of bombers capable of following up any attack. It has a small but growing fleet of missile-launching submarines. Like the United States, the Soviet Union has procured a force capable of destroying, and designed to be capable of destroying, a sizable portion of the world's population. While the Soviet force is much smaller, much less sophisticated, and procured at somewhat greater cost to the Soviet economy, it holds hostage much the same number of civilians in the United States and the allied countries as we ourselves hold hostage in the Soviet Union. Except for a number of submarines deployed on the high seas, the Soviet force is based in the Soviet Union. Like the American strategic force, it is believed to be under careful and prudent control; but, as with ours, it is difficult to know precisely what this will mean in practice over the years.

The strategic forces of the two sides have emerged from a race. What kind of race has been involved is not completely clear. In part there has been competition in particular weapons. In part there has been competition for the political power that can be gleaned from nuclear weapons. This race has proceeded with unexpected swiftness. By and large, the perspective of those concerned with arms control has been too short, changes in weapons too rapid, and the general situation too unprecedented and too broad in scope to be grasped completely.

A few years ago there was much discussion on measures that would discourage surprise attack. Since that time both major powers have made such progress toward diminishing the vulnerability of their forces that much of the motivation for these measures has been lost. Moreover, the rapid changes from aircraft to missile have removed many of the technological presuppositions of the discussion. Aircraft, but not missiles, gave hours of warning of attack as they were readied for a mission. And again, aircraft, but not missiles, could be moved to safety in the warning time that might have been provided.

In 1961, we sought to limit stockpiles of bombs. Now we think in terms of cutting off the production of fissionable materials, production which is only tenuously related to the limitation of a destructive capability that has already reached enormous heights. Fissionable material cutoffs have become arms control measures in form and political measures in fact.

We used to speak of "no-first-use" of nuclear weapons policies that would encourage and reflect strengthened conventional NATO forces in Europe. But it is doubtful whether the situation could ever have been brought to that point of conventional adequacy sufficient to induce a no-first-use policy by the United States.

The prospects for substantial reductions in strategic forces have decreased as weapons have been built. The problems of proliferation have changed as France and China have built nuclear weapons. The prospects for halting wars once begun or for restricting attacks to military targets seem to have increased with changes in U.S. doctrine that have responded to this possibility. Virtually every aspect of arms control problems has changed over the last few years.

An Approach to Arms Control

At the present time, there seem to be three related functions for arms control measures pertaining to strategic weapon systems. The first and most general is simply to reach a better understanding with the Soviet Union on a range of arms race problems. The second, and more specific, goal is to achieve a "freeze" in procurement of certain strategic weapon systems either by informal understanding or by agreement. Third, the achievement of a somewhat larger number of arms control agreements of almost any nature between the two powers would seem useful.

The most fundamental and lasting arms control achievement that could be constructed between the Soviets and ourselves would be a suitable understanding of the problems that face us. By suitable is meant an understanding that would diminish rather than exacerbate differences and would encourage the generation of feasible solutions. Such an understanding need not exist. In principle, greater understanding could lead to greater differences, to heightened awareness of inequities, to diminished confidence and increased suspicion. Certainly in particular cases — for example, in discussion of certain very sensitive issues — it is easy to create more misunderstanding than one can immediately resolve. But it is hard to believe that this would be the case in general and for the indefinite future. I hold the view, on strategic matters, that a great increase in the U.S.-Soviet strategic dialogue, if handled with care, would ultimately be to our advantage as well as to that of the Soviets. This dialogue should be accompanied by personal contacts. These, more than any increase in transmitted words, are likely to erode the suspicion that has accumulated.

In any case, in the absence of a carefully conceived dialogue we shall have a continuing less formal conversation. Our Congressional testimony, our action in procuring and deploying weapons, our reaction to Soviet volumes on strategy, and so on, all speak for us. The question may be whether we shall leave discussions with the Soviets to air shows, to tough or friendly talk in speeches, and to trade magazines sympathetic to the procurement of strategic weapons.

In a more concrete vein, our goal should be to control the procurement of strategic weapons. It is much easier, though still difficult, to prevent the procurement of further strategic weapons than to arrange for the reduction of existing systems. Until that reduction has gone a very long way, the capacities for destruction will not be very significantly changed. Nor will reductions have very substantial effects on the likelihood of war. This likelihood is now very small: the reductions are not directly related in strategic terms to the probability of war, and the political effects of reductions can be gained, in large measure, by agreements to halt procurement. More generally, it may be a mistake at present to attempt to link most arms control measures to the probability of war and the destruction that will follow if it occurs. Most of the feasible measures at the present time are not portrayed realistically by rationalizations of this type.

It is true that a significant motivation for arms control remains the desire to prevent nations from achieving a still greater capacity for destruction. There are, presumably, types of very destructive and undesirable weapons that either side could build but that neither has yet built. And the United States has an interest in limiting the growth in numbers of the Soviet force so as to limit its capacity for destruction. (The converse is not true. The U.S. force is now so large that a further increase in numbers would not significantly increase its capacity to destroy Soviet population and industry.) But the desire to forestall any increase in destructive capacity is now simply one reason among others for limiting major-power procurement of strategic weapons. Depending upon the weapon system, motivations of comparable importance can be the waste involved in buying the weapons, the political or strategic instability caused by them, and their tendency to induce further procurement.

This last point is especially important: since the procurement of strategic weapons tends to breed further procurement of strategic weapons, it may be well even to halt the procurement of some strategic weapons that would not in themselves be highly undesirable. The case against antiballistic missile defenses is the most important instance of this principle. But, in general, it may be worth while to slow the rate at which procurement proceeds simply because a few developments that are especially undesirable may be forestalled in this fashion. The case against individual procurement of particular weapons is thus part of a general interest in slowing "progress" in weapon development.

Strategic weapons have more than strategic consequences. They also impinge upon the national consciousness in a variety of ways and have political consequences. Programs of procurement with strategic consequences may have almost as much impact upon domestic politics or upon the prospects for a U.S.-Soviet *détente* as a war in Vietnam, a severely divided electorate, or disarray within the Alliance. In this sense, agreement on limiting procurement represents a political opportunity. Since a great many political problems underlie the arms race, the proper short-term goal for arms controllers may be to keep weapon procurement from interfering with better political relations. Most of the time this will mean restraining ourselves and the Soviets either from procuring more strategic weapons or from provoking the procurement of more.

If we increase the dialogue with the Soviets, if we make attempts to halt procurement of strategic weapons, we shall, I think, be doing much that arms control of strategic weapons should now be doing. But, in addition, I think we should try to secure a number of minor or innocuous *formal* arms control agreements of whatever nature. The political impact of minor agreements will, during this period, almost invariably outweigh their strategic impact. To this extent there is likely to be some gain involved in such agreements if the will is there to sign them. Indeed, it is the reflection of this will to sign agreements that gives the agreement its importance as a political signal.

Containing the Arms Race

Considering the speed of weapons development and the predilections of policy makers, it is quite possible, of course, that no single one of the proposals made here can be achieved in the form discussed. Neither reductions of missiles, nor bonfires of heavy bombers, nor even tacit or formal halts in further procurement of offensive or defensive weapons may be possible. It therefore behooves us to consider carefully the course to be followed in the event that the major-power arms race continues to spiral.

Obviously we must stand ready to achieve whatever agreements and understandings seem to us useful. Equally clearly, we must have a philosophy with which to deal with the spiraling process itself. Most of the time treaties and understandings will not be feasible for one reason or another. If arms control can usefully influence the form and nature of the spirals, then obviously considerable effort should be devoted to this goal.

The answer to these problems may be to seek the course that seems most likely to *contain* the competition. We need not pursue this goal because we see in any simple-minded way how a course of containing the arms race will reduce the probability of war or diminish its destructiveness. We should be mature enough to recognize the desirability of discouraging continued strategic weapon expenditures for reasons both more direct and more indirect. On the one hand, there should be motivations arising from such (direct) implications of strategic weapon procurement as we have mentioned, for instance, their cost and potential political implications. On the other hand, there should be motivations arising from a responsible concern for the long-run risks of a continuing arms race.

These reasons do not constitute a case for following a course of "containment." Other approaches to the arms race are possible, and there are arguments for them. We could try to "win," to stay ahead, to reshape the competition, or to turn it back, and there are other possibilities as well. This volume makes no attempt to grapple with issues on the level of abstraction that such a comparative discussion would require. But it may be useful to describe in some detail what containing the arms race means.

A policy of containing the arms race is one that strives to slow the rate, and influence the kind, of procurement of strategic weapons in each major power and throughout the world. It is a policy in which we buy or avoid buying weapons in part so as to inhibit later buying.

What does this mean in practice? Consider some examples. If the Soviets discover some novel way of destroying a large number of U.S. land-based (Minuteman) missiles, we shall feel obliged to take some counter action. One choice would be to build more Minuteman missiles; another would be to protect Minuteman missiles; a third might be to buy more Polaris submarines or to replace Minuteman with mobile missiles. Whatever response we chose would have an effect on the Soviet posture, which might, in turn, again require modifications of our own course. A policy of containing the arms race would reflect upon these possibilities quite as much as it would upon the relative cost effectiveness of the initial response by the United States.

Another case would be one in which the Soviets made efforts to build an antiballistic missile system. Should our response to it be one of building offensive weapons that would negate the effectiveness of the Soviet defense? Or should our response be to build a defense of our own? These different responses have very different implications.

On the one hand, we could build a defense. It could lead to the purchase of larger numbers of Soviet ICBM's to improve the Soviet capacity to attack us despite the defenses. But a relatively larger number of Soviet ICBM's might begin to threaten the future of the existing U.S. land-based missiles. This might, in turn, precipitate the rearrangement of our own land-based missiles or the purchase of additional missiles. Both alternatives would be expensive. Each might give rise to further adjustments and to another spiral of activity.

On the other hand, the procurement of additional offensive weapons designed to negate the Soviet defense might add only marginally to our threat against Soviet land-based missiles and might pose no problem for Soviet penetration of our defenses. Hence it might lead to only a few extra Soviet missiles and thus add only marginally to the vulnerability of our land-based missiles. In this case, the impact of the Soviet action in procuring defenses would tend to die out.

In fact, our response to a Soviet defense would probably lie somewhere between these two illustrative reactions, and what would be open to influence might only be nuances. Nevertheless, we can, in principle, achieve some control over the spiraling of arms procurement.

Clearly, even if it were determined that one response led to a new spiral while the other did not, many other considerations would be involved in determining which course to take. The prominent difference between the two responses outlined is that in the first we would have a better active defense, which might (or might not) function sufficiently well to save some people if war occurred. But, if we bought offensive weapons, we might save resources — offenses are likely to cost less — and achieve a more satisfactory retaliatory force.

The question here may be, as it often is, how much we are to emphasize the short-run response and how much the relatively longer-run implications.

Because it is difficult to know all the implications of specific strategic weapon policies and because these decisions involve a host of uncertainties, there is room for argument over the emphasis to be given to future problems and future potential costs. Those who argue for containing the arms race are arguing that these problems should be given greater emphasis and greater consideration. They are also arguing that little of significance is likely to be gained by continuing to engage in spirals of action and response, even if these spirals are slow and quiet.

In any case, in the long run only a sensible procurement policy can contain the arms race, can decelerate, check, curb, confine, and restrain the pressures in both powers to reinstitute an arms spiral.

Such a policy of restraint would have many facets. If we adopted it, we would not telegraph punches that we had no intention of throwing; we would not pointlessly startle or frighten; we would not boast or bluff. Thus we would not exaggerate the likelihood of our buying a missile defense; we would not distort the capability of newer offensive weapons; we could be sober in determining what to do in the future. We *would* telegraph what we intended to do, and we would encourage the adversary to reciprocate; we would seek no short-run advantage in surprise.

A policy of restraint would not tinker with the existing capabilities in an effort to achieve purposeless marginal improvements. Such a policy presents an impression of quiet sufficiency. It suggests that the procurement race is, if not over, at least much less important.

A policy of restraint avoids significant enlargements of the competition. It does not procure, without very good reason, the weapons that will lead arms competition into a new spiral or dimension. It seeks to avoid competition in outer space, in cheaper weapons, or in novel defensive schemes. It neither builds "super" weapons nor makes strenuous efforts to add greatly to the destructive power of present ones. It is not eager to exploit novel weapons effects. Such a policy is conscious of the rapidity with which our new weapons developments reach the hands of adversaries who then arm themselves with them.

A policy of restraint seeks to induce or persuade competitors to refrain from enlarging the arms race; in particular it seeks to deter them from pushing ahead, if this is possible. Such a policy places less emphasis on beating adversaries to the punch than on avoiding an exchange of "blows." Self-restraint becomes a corollary to success in inducing restraint.

A policy of restraint does not emphasize the short-term advantage over the long-run disadvantage. It does not "cross bridges when it comes to them." Instead, it gives full measure in advance to the possibility of adversary actions. It considers the illogical response as well as the logical. And it encourages decision makers to view with some skepticism the possibility that such significant advantages could be maintained indefinitely that they would justify upsetting the *status quo*. It puts relatively little emphasis on spurts of effort that are likely, after a few years, to find the rival steadily closing a gap whose creation has left both sides poorer, in greater danger, or in greater opposition.

A policy of restraint emphasizes, in its doctrine and in the corresponding actions, that economy is sought and that the probability of nuclear war is low. Both attitudes are catching: if one side takes this view, it is far more likely that its opponent will. Each judges the likelihood of war, in part, by assessing the other's fears. Each judges the feasibility of making savings, in part, by the willingness of the other to curb expenses.

A policy of restraint would attempt to justify restraint by emphasizing the finality of the situation, the inevitability of retaliation, the pointlessness of further efforts, and the extent of our break with the past: we have reached a level of weapons development where further preparation for general war is very unlikely to be of any significance.

Finally, a policy of restraint would try to arrange rules and methods for policing and inducing restraint. If weapons must be improved, perhaps their number can remain fixed for such periods as will make this "rule" a tradition that can be depended upon. A policy of restraint would make use of treaties, U.N. resolutions, understandings, or coordinated announcements. It would value token reductions and a variety of other signals that further procurement was being halted.

Finally, a policy of restraint would be careful not to procure systems that are so vulnerable as to encourage an opponent to take advantage of them. The pressures to maintain an advantage are already strong enough. Vulnerable or slow-reacting systems may provide built-in rationalizations that would induce an opponent to prepare to exploit them if war should occur. Each side should strive to get the most "survivability," lest it tempt the other to spend rubles or dollars to neutralize the expenditures. If the longer-term goal is to slow down procurement, each may be more afraid of the other's mistakes than of his sensible efforts. Unfortunate policies can tempt a renewal of the competition that each seeks to avoid.

What does all this mean in practice? It means that the instructions given to the Defense Department should now be quite similar to those that could be given to the Arms Control and Disarmament Agency. Each is now seeking to confine the competition. While in the past the interest in stability and the interest in achieving a secure posture in the arms race may have seemed to conflict, this conflict has now diminished with the virtual completion of our missile force buildup. If, in the past, it was argued that arms control policy was a part of military policy, it may now be argued that strategic weapon policy is an adjunct to arms control efforts. If, in the past, arms control seemed more urgent, it now seems more feasible and, in the long run, no less vital. This is a time for renewed, subtle, and coordinated efforts to keep the competition within bounds.

ANTIBALLISTIC MISSILES AND ARMS CONTROL

Introduction

THIS CHAPTER is devoted to certain problems of anti-ballistic missile (ABM) procurement and their relation to arms control. But these problems immediately raise far more fundamental questions concerning the relationship between active defense and the strategic balance in which we find ourselves. It seems useful to describe some of these fundamental questions because they are of very great importance and also because they have influenced the approach and tone of this chapter.

We live in a world in which active defense seems impotent compared to the powers of the strategic offense. It would be surprising if this peculiar and, in many ways, unprecedented strategic context did not have surprising and unprecedented corollaries for the stability of the strategic balance of forces. One such corollary, in my view, affirms that the development of a very effective defense is likely to be pernicious, destabilizing, and dangerous. Moreover, this corollary suggests that the procurement of less effective defenses may have correspondingly reduced, but still significant, drawbacks of an unusual nature.

We are only now being delivered from some serious instabilities associated with vulnerable weapons as an era unfolds in which an ever more stable "balance of terror" is developing. As Secretary of Defense Robert McNamara put it: "We are approaching an era when it will become increasingly improbable that either side could destroy a sufficiently 'large' portion of the other's strategic nuclear force."[1] This situation has obvious disadvantages, but it seems fairly stable. What could cause this stability to be lost if it continues to be possible to provide weapons with a high order of invulnerability? Speaking in the abstract, the answer is clear: the invention of an effective defense. This has been noted by many analysts, in particular by the famous Soviet physicist, P. Kapitsa, who wrote in 1956:

> In the struggle for the prevention of atomic war, it is essential to take into account the possibility that there will be found a reliable defense against nuclear weapons. If this is achieved by a country with aggressive intentions, then being itself protected against the direct effects of nuclear weapons, it can much more easily decide to launch an atomic war.[2]

Speaking very generally, it seems that if we want the stability associated with defense, we must make the effective use of nuclear weapons impossible. And if we want the stability of deterrence, we must avoid the construction of effective defenses. Between these two extremes, there can only be a continuing contest between offensive and defensive strategic weapons.

What would this contest be like? What would happen if each major power proceeded to buy ballistic missile defenses? If the defenses were ineffective, there would be great waste because defenses against missiles are very expensive even by present standards. What if the defenses became effective? In this case each power would redouble its efforts to procure offensive strategic weapons. In sufficiently extreme cases, there would be political repercussions inside countries as the responsibility for the loss or impairment of the "deterrent" was fixed. In relations between major powers, and in their alliances, there would be repercussions associated with a perceived shift in the major-power balance. In the United States, which is still politically committed to maintain a capacity to destroy the entire Communist bloc in a retaliatory blow, the political impact of even partly successful Soviet defenses would be especially substantial.

It should not be difficult to persuade either the Americans or the Russians of the existence of the phenomenon just described. There is a strong analogy between, on the one hand, a race in which each power attempts, or is thought to be attempting, to maintain a capacity to *strike* the other's forces and, on the other hand, a race in which each attempts or is thought to be attempting to achieve the capacity to *defend against* the other's forces. And, to our dismay, we have already seen the former situation unfold.

In the late fifties, we in the United States believed that the Soviets might be attempting to achieve the capacity to destroy all U.S. forces on the ground. Whether or not there might have been a "delicate balance of terror," the political impact of that possibility cannot be denied. The fear among strategists, the "missile gap" debates of the Kennedy-Nixon campaign, the efforts of the Strategic Air Command to disperse bombers and to develop an airborne alert were all very real. If the Soviets had seemed to be developing a *defense* as effective in neutralizing our retaliatory force as a surprise missile attack, the fears would have been no different.

The Soviets must understand even better than we do what it means to maintain a retaliatory capacity against an adversary who seeks to undermine it. In the early sixties we bought enough missiles to target virtually all Soviet missiles simultaneously. In principle, an effective defense would have been as unsettling.

Thus we can ask about such a race to achieve defenses, as we can about the race to achieve the capacity to disarm adversaries, whether both competitors can achieve their goal while each maintains the capacity to retaliate effectively. In both cases, there is an essential incompatibility from which practical difficulties flow. By contrast, attempts by the two sides to achieve only the ability to retaliate are highly compatible. In these cases, defense departments are not charged with the problem of obstructing each other from achieving the goal. If a race occurs to install a new weapon, each side races only to the completion of the task. In short, two sides can both seek a retaliatory capability without a contest, but they cannot both so easily seek to deter *and* to defend, just as they cannot *both* effectively deter and threaten.

What has this meant in practice? So far it has meant that both have been satisfied primarily to deter. Neither has attempted to procure an expensive defense against missiles with its concomitant need for improvements in civil defense, bomber defense, and antisubmarine defense. This effort has been largely too difficult and too expensive. Nevertheless, in view of the long "lead times" involved in developing offensive weapons and the uncertainties of defensive actions by the adversary, even the prospect of defenses has already encouraged offensive weapon procurement.

What would happen if the race got started now? Some analysts in the United States think we could have our cake and eat it too. We would construct a fairly effective defense at considerable cost, and by constructing suitable offensive weapons would neutralize the Soviet defenses. The Soviets would then hold *relatively* few Americans hostage (a few tens of millions), while we would continue to be able to destroy the Soviet Union outright. Western casualties — those involving the allies as well as ourselves — would remain high (many tens of millions). For this reason and because the Soviets seem to have been willing to acquiesce in this situation so far, they might be satisfied with it. And this situation might obtain for some time. This is the most favorable view of the outcome.

But there are other possibilities. Our missile defense might be a tremendous waste (as many believe our bomber defenses have been), either because the Soviet capacity to destroy Americans could not be reduced, when Soviet countermeasures were taken into consideration, or because the likelihood of war was so low. Or, in the long run, the Soviets might develop an especially effective defense.

Hence, the two extreme possibilities for a race involving defenses are, on the one hand, waste and, on the other, political and strategic uneasiness. In between these two extremes, of ineffective defenses and strategic imbalance, lies the possibility of accelerated procurement or of replacement of offensive and defensive strategic weapons.

Therefore if the probability of war is sufficiently low and the cost of defenses sufficiently high, if the value placed on a stable strategic situation is sufficiently high and the need for further improvement in our strategic superiority sufficiently low, it might be well to consider ways of preventing or inhibiting, by treaty or otherwise, the development or procurement of defenses. This is the position adopted in this chapter.

There are three reasons why this point of view receives less recognition than it should. First, present-day defenses are only just beginning to be effective, and, as a result, the potential political and strategic effects of their bilateral deployment and further development are obscured. Second, the historic role of defense and even the general connotation of the word make it difficult to argue against it. Third, and most important, there is little understanding or discussion about the possibility of controlling the development of defense on *both* sides. It will help neither side to control defenses — if it helps at all — unless this control is bilateral. Therefore arms controllers must take up the subject; others may have no immediate interest in it.

Can bilateral control over defenses be achieved? Technically, the problem may be relatively easy. First, defenses are at present expensive, and no one expects them to be very effective. Hence the motivation for their installation is reduced. Second, for the foreseeable future it will be far easier to inspect for defenses than for offensive weapons. For example, with present defenses the very idea of a clandestine defense problem is ludicrous. By contrast, the clandestine weapon problem, at low levels of weapons, looks insoluble. Third, effective defenses will take several years to install. The length of this lead time will be reassuring so long as the procurement decision is likely to be detected.

Indeed, at the present time if we are undecided between the

stability of very effective defense and the stability of mutual deterrence, we would probably be well advised to try for the latter. This effort would act *with* the forces of technology — as they are presently perceived — rather than against them. But even if we were to try to return to a world of defense, through disarmament, we would surely have to control defenses just as carefully as we limited armament — at least until the treaty required each side to have no second-strike capability at all. Hence the decision to control defenses *now* does not require a choice between disarmament and mutual deterrence. Either will find this control necessary.

The control of defense is not as inappropriate as it may seem. If it is true that "we must either live together or die together," then there can be no more fundamentally appropriate agreement than one which, by controlling defenses, emphasizes the fundamental vulnerability of each side to the weapons of the other.

If the speculations of this chapter are borne out, the situation is both hopeful and urgent for the control of defenses. It seems (a) that the United States is uncertain about procuring ABM defenses, for doctrinal and economic reasons; (b) that Soviet procurement of ABM systems would probably lead to U.S. procurement; (c) that bilateral procurement of ABM systems would not serve the real interest of either major power; (d) that restraint in procurement of ABM systems can be arranged to entail little risk for either major power; and therefore (e) that both powers should give consideration to such restraint. And it may also be that U.S. procurement would give rise to the otherwise avoidable Soviet procurement of ABM systems. Obviously, it is difficult for an American analyst to discuss this question because there is no suitable Soviet source material available. For this reason, the following analysis shows considerable lack of symmetry.

In any case, the chain of reasoning may be wrong, on one or several counts. But it deserves careful study because it is likely to be relevant to future problems involving the procurement of defenses that will plague arms controllers in the coming years. In the present strategic context, it may be the defense, and not the offense, to which the attention of arms controllers should be drawn. For this reason, we must reach a consensus on these issues as soon as possible.

Of course, these general propositions do not decide concrete cases: in particular, the ABM problem has its own special characteristics, which are discussed in this chapter.

Progress in the United States

Antiballistic missile systems are only beginning to show any significant effectiveness. The first substantial U.S. attempt at such a system was the proposed Army Nike-Zeus system designed, essentially, to shoot down only a single incoming missile at a time.[3] In the late fifties, the Army proposed the development of this system but did not receive the support of the other members of the Joint Chiefs of Staff or of the Secretary of Defense.[4] The system would have cost $8 or $9 billion and would have been operational in 1963–1964.[5] However, Secretary McNamara pointed out in 1962 that this money would have been effectively wasted, considering the requirements of 1963–1964. And even General Taylor, a long-time supporter of Nike-Zeus, was in substantial agreement: testifying immediately after the Secretary, he could only argue in defense of its procurement that

> One, we would now be learning by doing. As far as my experience goes with new weapons, that is the only way you can make any great progress. It takes a considerable amount of actual employment of weapons systems to get the best out of them. . . .
> The other point is that we would have had a technological triumph over the Soviets. Some day there will be a great bally-hoo that the Soviets have an antiballistic missile and we do not. The claim may be largely sham and propaganda, but we face that possibility of a cold war defeat.[6]

Over the years the Nike-Zeus technology has improved; nevertheless, in 1963 the Secretary of Defense decided not to procure an operational system of this type or two alternative modifications of it. His reasoning was, in part, that he could deploy a Nike-Zeus type of system (with two improvements) by 1968 but that he was "certain they could introduce into their warheads, if they have not already done so, the capability to penetrate such a system by 1966." [7] Further improvements were indicated, and it was decided to wait, at least until these could be made.

These improvements were to constitute a new system, Nike-X, which would have an enhanced capacity to distinguish decoys from actual missiles. A year later, in January 1964, the Secretary of Defense was more optimistic concerning the effectiveness of the system. He stated:

> The continued testing of the NIKE-ZEUS and preliminary studies of the NIKE-X system's characteristics and effectiveness provide grounds for believing that the technical problems of at least a partial defense against a ballistic missile attack may be solved within the next several years.[8]

The basic philosophy behind Nike-Zeus and Nike-X was to attack incoming missiles at the lowest possible altitudes consistent with safety. In this way, we would buy time and permit the atmosphere to "screen" out decoys, that is, permit atmospheric effects such as "drag" to affect the perceived motions of incoming objects.[9] Partly because of this low-level, terminal-intercept approach, civil defense preparations have become an important complement to ABM systems. Some believe that shelters will be required to protect against the blast effects of the detonating ABM warheads. Thus *Air Force and Space Digest* states: "Department of Defense studies show that persons on the ground in the target area would have to be in shelters to prevent their being injured by the blasts from the nuclear-warhead Sprint missiles." [10] Whether or not this is correct, the fact that larger enemy warheads could be detonated at the intercept height probably indicates a need for blast shelters.

In any case, fallout shelters will be required to prevent an adversary from attacking unprotected rural areas in such a way as to kill urban residents with fallout. The Secretary of Defense maintained in 1963 that he "will never recommend an anti-ICBM program unless a fallout program does accompany it." [11]

The cost of the presently proposed Nike-X ABM system, for deployment alone, around "20-odd metropolitan centers, containing some 35 percent of the population" is projected to be about $14 billion.[12] This would presumably be spent over a period of a few years. Nevertheless the cost is significant. There are some indications, however, that the Defense Department's strategic budget will drop for a time until presently procured missile systems require replacement. For example, Secretary McNamara pointed out in November, 1963:

> The funding for the initial introduction of missiles into our forces is nearing completion. We can anticipate that the annual expenditure on strategic forces will drop substantially, and level off well below the present rate of spending. This is not to rule out the possibility that research now in progress on possible new technological developments, including the possibility of useful ballistic missile defenses, will require major new expenditures.*

And Senator Symington reports being told that our expenditures for strategic forces will drop from around 16 per cent of the budget to 7 per cent (that is, a decline of $4 to $5 billion).[15] About three or four years of such "saving" would provide approximately $15 billion. This would procure the system just discussed. Hence the cost of an ABM system might, in part, be absorbed in the budget.

But the lifetime of the system is uncertain. Most people be-

---

* These remarks were substantiated by pointing out that "The U.S. force now contains more than 500 operational long-range ballistic missiles — ATLAS, TITAN, MINUTEMAN, POLARIS — and is planned to increase to over 1,700 by 1966. There is no doubt in our minds and none in the minds of the Soviets that these missiles can penetrate to their targets. In addition, the U.S. has Strategic Air Command bombers on air alert and over 500 bombers on quick reaction ground alert." [13] The Secretary argued elsewhere in 1963 that "our second strike would exceed the weight of the first strike that was directed against us." [14]

lieve that the offense can install countermeasures more rapidly than the defense can prepare to defeat them. Thus Harold Brown in his capacity as Director of Defense Research and Engineering said

> Major changes in deployed ABM systems will generally take more time than major changes in penetration aid systems. Remembering that wide deployment of an ABM system will take several years, that our intelligence should give us information of its development even before then, that we can carry out very extensive development and deployment of still more advanced penetration aids in only a few years, and that a substantial increase in the numbers of our offensive forces can also be made relatively quickly, it appears that our retaliatory capability can be preserved with a large margin of safety. . . .[16]

And the costs to the offense are likely to be much lower than those of the defense. For example, if the $14-billion system referred to above covered 25 areas, and assuming that strategic missiles could be procured by the Soviet Union at about $4 million apiece — as they are by us — then 140 missiles of the Minuteman type (in their silos) could be purchased by the Soviet Union for *each* defended area at a total cost equal to that of the proposed system. Polaris-type missiles (in submarines) cost somewhat more — $9 to $10 million each — but would permit 56–62 missiles per metropolitan area.[17]

Against salvos or even repeated firings of such numbers of missiles, the ABM system would surely fail to protect the area from substantial destruction. Moreover, improvement of existing missiles to give them penetration advantages against deployed systems is probably much cheaper and somewhat quicker than buying new missiles. Other possibilities might include techniques for destroying defended areas without penetration, for instance, the use of fallout from bombs exploded in rural areas. This does not necessarily indicate that ABM defense is hopeless or even that it is not worth buying. It does indicate that active defense is relatively expensive in an arms race where the offense applies resources to nullify it and strikes with a substantially undamaged force.

The Likelihood of U.S. Procurement

For reasons such as these, it is uncertain, at the moment, whether the presently proposed Nike-X system will or will not be procured. The Secretary of Defense has recognized the reasons for procuring even a limited capability, and has maintained that every effort should be made to design an effective system even if no decision is made to procure and deploy it.[18] He said in 1963: "Would it be wise to deploy the NIKE-X system? I think the question is open." He further affirmed that, although the point had not been reached where a production decision could properly be made, "were we at that point today, I do not know what I would recommend to you, because it would be a very, very difficult decision." [19]

By 1964, the Secretary of Defense was carefully linking a variety of other defensive measures to the decision to procure Nike-X. It was argued that a decision to go ahead with Nike-X would commit us "to continue and perhaps improve" our defense against manned bombers and to build a system of fallout shelters costing "perhaps $3 to $6 billion." Hinting at a need for blast shelters or further protection, he suggested that a decision to procure a ballistic missile defense would require us to "carefully consider what additional civil defense measures might be required for the population." Procurement cost estimates of the type given earlier were made, but it was noted that these "may prove to be low." [20] Maintenance costs were quoted at "maybe a billion and a half a year to operating expenses." [21] Over-all, the Secretary suggested that

> the cost to the Soviets of adding additional missiles to their force or augmenting their missiles with penetration aids would probably be but a fraction of the cost to us of offsetting these additional missiles or increased penetration capability with additional defense measures.[22]

It was widely believed that the time was still not ripe for a final decision while further improvements and tests were pending. Many reports suggested a final decision in January

1965, but in that month the President's defense statement to Congress called only for a continuation of research and development. It suggested that "we must always be alert" to the possibilities for limiting destruction, noted that "many proposals have been advanced" to this end, and went on to emphasize the complexity of the decision and the many costs as follows:

> Shifting strategy and advancing technology make the program of building adequate defense against nuclear attack extremely complex.
>
> Decisions with respect to further limitation of damage require complex calculations concerning the effectiveness of many interrelated elements. Any comprehensive program would involve the expenditure of tens of billions of dollars. We must not shrink from any expense that is justified by its effectiveness, but we must not hastily expend vast sums on massive programs that do not meet this test.
>
> It is already clear that without fall-out shelter protection all defense weapons lose much of their effectiveness in saving millions of lives. . . . We will continue our existing programs. . . .
>
> We shall continue the research and development which retains the options to deploy an anti-ballistic missile system, and manned interceptors and surface to air missiles against bombers.[23]

Evidently, the Department of Defense was still not ready to procure a system.*

Among the important considerations that may determine whether currently conceived systems will be procured are

---

* As this book goes to press in December 1965 a high-level citizen's panel report on arms control — associated with the International Cooperation Year activities — has proposed a three-year moratorium on the production of ballistic missile defenses in the United States and the Soviet Union. The resulting stir — already three editorials have appeared in *The New York Times* — brought to light the unanimity of the Joint Chiefs of Staff behind a decision to deploy. However, an article by Jack Raymond suggests that the decision will be put off for another year, with the possible purchase of some long-lead-time items that would not commit the later choice. The common public argument for a defense continues to be the possibility of conflict with a nuclear-armed China; the possibility of on-going Soviet preparations for a defense has figured in a few articles without much public impact on the recent debate.

our perception of Soviet progress in developing or deploying antimissile systems; the extent to which the need for complementary civil defense may dampen enthusiasm for procurement; the ease with which the system can be quickly neutralized; the likelihood that the system will have an Achilles' heel; and, especially, the political climate.

Particularly important is the progress, or apparent progress, of the Soviet Union. Many informed persons in our government seem to think that the United States is at least on a par with, if not slightly in advance of, the Soviet Union in ABM development. For instance, Harold Brown said in 1963: "I think that we are roughly comparable. If I were forced to say one side or the other is ahead on knowledge, I would say that we were, but I don't think that is a very firm statement on my part." [24] However, the Soviet Union was for a time evidently following a course of proclaiming its progress somewhat prematurely.* And, according to several public reports, the Soviet Union has established an ABM battery around Leningrad that can shoot down the Polaris missile, if not the Minuteman missile.[26]

The relative vulnerability of Polaris or, more generally, of IRBM's, as opposed to ICBM's, is due to the angles and speed of re-entry.[27] This claimed progress has caused concern of several kinds. For instance, repeated references to the Leningrad installation have been made in Congressional testimony. Congress has always been very sensitive to the problems of matching the Soviet Union in procurement of individual weapons, whether or not this has been indicated from a purely logical point of view. Thus, a bomber gap in the fifties generated more interest in the rate of bomber production than in

* See, for example, the volume edited by Sokolovskii.[25] A note by the American translators points out that Soviet authors have been more sober in their assessment of the effectiveness of antimissile defense than have public Soviet claims. Public claims have ranged from, "The problem of destroying missiles in flight has been successfully solved," to the assertion that Soviet antimissile missiles could "hit a fly in outer space," and, finally, to the more recent and repeated announcement that the Soviet Union has prepared "complexes of numerous means for the defense of our country against enemy missile attacks."

defense against Soviet bombers. Concern could well arise over a "defense gap" similar to the earlier bomber and missile gaps.* Congress is not the only decision-making element that wishes to maintain at least a parity in each separate area of importance. For example, in discussing the U.S. need to test in response to Soviet tests, allegedly with the aim of *developing* an antimissile defense system, President Kennedy said: "Were we to stand still while the Soviets surpassed us — *or even appeared to surpass us* — the Free World's ability to deter, to survive and to respond to an all-out attack would be seriously weakened." [29] (Italics added.) Certainly the Soviet Union would seem to some to be overtaking us if it *built* a defensive capability while we had none.

Whether or not "matching" plays an important role in determining the likelihood that U.S. ABM systems would be procured, Soviet ABM systems may be a source of more than psychological concern. For instance, Governor Rockefeller, in giving his views on the Test Ban Treaty, stated:

> The possession by the Soviets of large missiles and warheads together with their aggressive development of anti-missile defenses in fact opens up somber prospects about Soviet intentions. The possibility must not be ruled out that large Soviet explosions or use of multiple warheads may jeopardize our hardened Minuteman sites, while the Soviet ballistic missile defense may deal with the counterblow launched from our Polaris submarines. [30]

These fears and speculations would not affect U.S. procurement of ABM directly, if that decision were to be made both on the basis of cost effectiveness and in the absence of a perceived increase in the risk of war. Instead it would lead to

---

* Take, for example the words of Senator Thurmond: " . . . by rejecting the alternative of initial deployment of an anti-missile missile system until after the perfection of the NIKE-X the United States is faced with a period in which there may be a defensive gap which would be more dangerous than a substantial missile gap. . . ." [28] While there is relatively little such talk at present, there is also little evidence, or fear, that the Soviet Union is *procuring* the ABM systems necessary to exploit any such gap visibly. Soviet procurement of many batteries would give rise to considerably more concern.

the procurement of penetration capability and invulnerability. If, however, Governor Rockefeller and others can argue that the Soviet system will lead to increased Soviet risk taking, much less to a surprise attack, then the cost effectiveness of an ABM system will be influenced by a perceived increase in the risk of war. And, in any case, there are political problems associated with failing to procure an ABM system if the Soviets do so, as illustrated by Governor Rockefeller's statement. The Democrats attacked the Eisenhower administration for a missile gap during the 1960 campaign, and they are presumably well aware of the ammunition that any semblance of a "defense gap" would hand to the Republican Presidential candidate in 1968. Here, particularly, Soviet procurement is an important factor in U.S. decision making.

On the other hand, if the Soviet Union does not procure its own system, there may be a reluctance on the part of some within the Johnson administration to procure a system that seems to be the start of another "round" in the arms race. Thus Secretary of State Dean Rusk sees "mounting defense budgets that go beyond anything now contemplated if the qualitative arms race proceeds on the basis of weapons in outer space, antimissile missiles, and missiles to penetrate those. . . ." Rusk argued for the test ban as an act that might "put some . . . lid" on this qualitative race.[31]

U.S. restraint would be further encouraged by certain relatively new strategic doctrines or attitudes that might make it easier to avoid procuring active defenses. First, recent government statements have tended to acquiesce in Soviet second-strike capabilities. Thus the Secretary of Defense said:

A very large increase in the number of fully hard Soviet ICBM's and nuclear-powered ballistic missile-launching submarines would considerably detract from our ability to destroy completely the Soviet strategic nuclear forces. It would become increasingly difficult, regardless of the form of the attack, to destroy a sufficiently large proportion of the Soviets' strategic nuclear forces to preclude major damage to the United States, regardless of how large or what kind of strategic forces we build. Even if we were to double and triple our forces we would not be able to destroy quickly all or almost all of the hardened ICBM sites. And even if we could do that, we know no way to destroy the enemy's missile-launching submarines at the same time. We do not anticipate that either the United States or the Soviet Union will acquire that capability in the foreseeable future. Moreover, to minimize damage to the United States, such a force would also have to be accompanied by an extensive missile defense system and a much more elaborate civil defense program than has thus far been contemplated. Even then we could not preclude casualties counted in the tens of millions. *What we are proposing is a capability to strike back after absorbing the first blow.*[32] (Italics added.)

This kind of statement indicates that the nation may be led to accept as unavoidable the absence of a true defense against the effects of nuclear weapons. It is no isolated remark. The Secretary of Defense has spoken mostly of maintaining "a superior strategic nuclear power" or "over-all U.S. superiority."[33] While statements indicating that the absence of a defense may be unavoidable tend to encourage U.S. restraint in response to Soviet restraint, the Secretary's claim to "over-all" superiority, to which these admissions seem to be linked, will encourage U.S. procurement in response to Soviet procurement. Both of these effects increase the potential impact of Soviet decision making on our own decisions.

Next it should be noted that U.S. policy increasingly attempts to resolve the problem of European defense by viewing allied European territory as an extension of our own, to be defended without consideration of outcome. President Kennedy, in a speech in Bonn, on June 23, 1963, stated: "So long as our presence is desired and required, our force and commitments will remain. For your safety is our safety, your liberty is our liberty, and an attack on your soil is an attack upon our own."[34] And Secretary McNamara has indicated that we would back up our commitment in Europe without regard to consequences:

The term "unacceptable damage" is a relative one. . . . For example, we have made it quite clear that the defense of Western Europe is as vital to us as the defense of our own continent and that we are prepared to back up our commitments there with our strategic nuclear power *no matter what degree of damage might result* should the deterrent aspect of this policy fail.[35] (Italics added.)

Other remarks by the Secretary have indicated that strategic response to invasion of Europe might even be inevitable, or at least feared as inevitable, and hence our threats might even have an automatic quality. He has argued that

. . . the Soviet Union is deterred from a massive attack on Western Europe by the size of our strategic force and the recognition that we are so intertwined in the defense of Western Europe that that force would be brought to bear against the Soviet Union should they engage in any massive attack on Western Europe.[36]

These positions all make it less necessary to procure ABM to support strategic threats. They imply that a credible threat to defend Europe does not depend upon a defense designed to reduce expected American casualties. A "defenseless" posture is still further encouraged by re-evaluations of ground forces that indicate the United States is stronger and the Soviet Union weaker than was formerly believed.[37]

The position of the Joint Chiefs of Staff must also be considered. In the past they failed to achieve unanimity on ABM procurement, and such uncertainty increases the potential impact, on our decision, of a Soviet decision to procure. For instance, in 1963 the Secretary of Defense reported that the Chiefs had been "uncertain" about deploying an ABM system.[38] In General Taylor's word, they were "split." The Army Chief of Staff, General Wheeler, testified that he had received "pretty unanimous" support for his Nike-Zeus program. The Chief of Naval Operations testified that he favored the "early deployment of the improved Nike-Zeus, contingent upon successful progress in system demonstration tests." However, Chief of Staff of the Air Force, General Curtis E. LeMay, said that we were "not quite ready" actually to put Nike-Zeus into operation. He questioned the advisability of "expending that much money for such poor results." He argued for the continuation "at full speed" of development, and ventured the belief that "eventually we can arrive at an acceptable solution to the problem." [39] But by November 1965, *The New York Times* was pointing out that the Joint Chiefs were unanimously in favor of deployment.

In short, it would seem that an antiballistic missile program had far more support from the Chiefs than had been the case when General Taylor wrote of their deliberations from a position of temporary retirement in 1959. He indicated then that all the other Chiefs "viewed NIKE-ZEUS as a rival for defense funds" and that he was the sole advocate of procurement funds for it. [40]

The Chiefs have undoubtedly been influenced by the possible Chinese threat, the U.S. slowdown in offensive weapon procurement — which diminishes competition for funds — and the extent to which expenditures on bomber and submarine defenses have been tied with ABM.

But certainly the most important consideration in this decision is the international atmosphere and the perceived risk of nuclear war. In one political climate, the expenditure of tens of billions of dollars for a missile defense can seem to high government officials to be the most incredible nonsense and a pointless waste. But after a few incidents in Berlin, a Soviet ultimatum, and some troop movements, there will be years when nothing will seem more natural than to complement our offensive weapons with defensive ones. In this sense, the ultimate decision whether or not we should buy a defensive system is likely to be made by the Soviets.

This discussion of the likelihood that we shall procure an ABM system is not systematic, but, in the present situation, no very complete appraisal is possible. In 1963 and before, analysis of the question would have been complicated by the absence of any consensus, even in the Department of Defense, on the rationale for a defense of such marginal effectiveness as provided by the then foreseeable terminal-intercept systems.

In 1964, the Defense Department position became fairly firm in associating active defenses with "the limitation of damage upon the United States should war occur." Thus the most obvious justification for the defense was simply prudence, much as it has been the main justification for civil defense programs in the last few years. However, some in the Defense Department undoubtedly believed that the defense would improve the credibility of our threats to risk nuclear war and would impress the Soviets with our technical superiority. Finally in 1965, the Chinese threat became the Defense Department's rationale for ballistic missile defense.

In other agencies and interested departments there might be different attitudes toward ballistic missile defense, for instance, in the Arms Control and Disarmament Agency, The Bureau of the Budget, the President's Science Advisory Committee, and the Department of State. All of these would have a substantial interest, if modest influence, in the outcome of the debate on the building of a defense, if the Secretary of Defense proposed one; with the possible exception of the Department of State, they could be expected to be opposed. It seems, however, that the Secretary of Defense is sufficiently disinclined to rush ahead with defenses to avoid proposing them unless both the political atmosphere and the technical case for them clearly warrant such action. In this situation, considering his extraordinary influence in these matters, he might well get his way for at least a few years.

The Likelihood of Soviet Procurement and the Soviet National Interest

It is, of course, very difficult to determine what the Soviet Union might do. As noted earlier, their progress is thought to be comparable to our own, though some of their statements boast of much more. And their actions may be as dependent upon ours as our actions may be on theirs. The alleged ABM activity near Leningrad has been mentioned; and it should also be noted that interceptors, apparently for an ABM system, have rolled through Red Square.[41] Probably the most important question is whether or not the Soviet Union will procure and deploy batteries to a sizable number of cities, that is, to more than two or three. Lesser deployment is probably more symbolic than it is strategically or politically significant.

In considering this question, it is useful, on the one hand, to examine past experience of Soviet behavior and existing statements of Soviet scientists and decision makers and, on the other hand, to ask ourselves whether, as nearly as we can tell, Soviet procurement of ABM systems is justified in our eyes by Soviet interests. While it is easier to answer the latter question than it is to predict Soviet behavior from past events, that answer may not be very useful for the prediction of future Soviet actions. Not only are we likely to fail to perceive certain valid Soviet concerns, we may also fail to take into account many invalid concerns that are nevertheless strongly motivating.

Nevertheless, this point of view is useful. In discussions with the Soviet Union in which we try to point out "mutual interests," we must make an assessment of what we think is, and is not, in the interests of the Soviet Union. When *their* assessment of *their* interest coincides with our own, we need do nothing. But when this is not the case, and when our assessment of Soviet interest coincides with our own interest, then we must be aware of it and be prepared to persuade the Soviet Union to our view.

Consider an example: it is likely that the Soviet Union procures and deploys defenses as if even highly inadequate and expensive defenses were very necessary to its interests. From our point of view, such defenses seem easily neutralized and a waste of Soviet resources. If we believe that it is in our interest to have the Soviet Union waste its resources, then we need say nothing — the Soviets' perception of their interest would coincide with our own. However, if the attempt to procure inadequate defenses can lead to such unfortunate consequences that this attempt is neither in our interest nor, on balance, in the Soviet interest (as we see it), then we must be prepared to persuade Soviet decision makers to review their policy.

Do the Soviets see even quite inadequate active defenses as being in their interest even in the nuclear age. The answer to this question is probably yes. For example, General LeMay testified that "they are spending a greater portion of their resources by far than we are on defenses." [42]

Among the factors that are sometimes adduced to explain Soviet defense expenditures are: a desire for defense induced by two world wars; a feeling of being surrounded; and Soviet bureaucratic vested interests. [43] Other explanations are even simpler. When asked by Senator Frank Lausche, in apparent reference to the purported Leningrad installation, why the Soviet Union had "deployed an ABM system" if it were not effective, Herbert York, former Director of Defense Research and Engineering, replied: "Some of their scientists or engineers sold them a bill of goods. That happens here, too. I mean, the situations are not all that asymmetrical." Later he added: "Well, there is plenty of evidence that the Soviets have been very strongly defense minded for years. I mean, you know with respect to certain other things they have done. They try very hard in this area. Trying is not enough." [44]

Evidence of this Soviet interest appears in the "authoritative" Soviet work, edited by Marshal Sokolovskii:

> The rapid development of nuclear-armed missiles and their adoption as the basic means for delivering nuclear blows to targets deep within the country have sharply posed the problem, for all states, of creating an effective antimissile defense capable of destroying enemy ballistic missiles in the air. In principle, a technical solution to this problem has now been found. In the future this form of defense must be perfected. [45]

Interestingly, the second edition of this work deleted the final two sentences of this quotation. The implications of this change are controversial. But we must concede a very great Soviet tendency to procure defense.

Consider the Soviet national interest as it might be viewed by an American analyst. We assume that Soviet procurement would trigger an otherwise avoidable procurement by the United States. This is very possibly the case, as indicated previously. But even if it were not, this assumption would be the proper one for us to consider for two reasons. First, Soviet decision makers surely cannot assume that their procurement will *not* be matched. There is too much contrary evidence for this to be a reasonable hope. Hence, putting ourselves in their position, we should assume "matching." Second, it is useful in the present circumstances to consider the case in which the United States wishes to deter Soviet procurement of ABM rather than to procure our own system. This is at least one of the most interesting arms control cases.

If Soviet procurement led to U.S. procurement, would the Soviet Union find its posture improved or degraded by its decision to procure ABM? It would probably be degraded relative to the United States — though not relative to France. This conclusion follows from considering, first, the effect of U.S. deployment; second, the small utility of current Soviet ABM systems; and, third, the corresponding reduction of Soviet efforts to improve their second-strike posture and to maintain their momentum in space exploration.

First, from the Soviet point of view, U.S. first-strike capabilities are large and may already be frightening. ABM systems that defend cities will further strengthen our ability to threaten Soviet forces. In a confrontation between the U.S. President and the Soviet Premier, the President can hint that even some highly invulnerable Soviet missiles will not deter the United States if its vital interests are threatened: ABM batteries will simply shoot down Soviet retaliatory attacks. A U.S. President would certainly feel less compelled to admit, as was done during the Cuban crisis, that "American citizens have become adjusted to living daily on the bull's-eye of Soviet missiles located inside the U.S.S.R. or in submarines." [46] An ABM program is likely to save more lives than a fallout-shelter program alone against city-directed attacks.*

---

* Studies of potential urban-area casualties from attacks on cities generally show that one-half to three-quarters of the fatalities would be

Although this effect may yet seem small to Americans, it ought not to seem so to responsible Soviet decision makers. If the Soviet Union is afraid that the United States may retain a capacity to strike Soviet forces without risking total devastation, then the Soviets should seek to prevent, not to encourage, our ABM deployment.

Second, if Soviet deployment is the stimulus for U.S. deployment, there would probably be little advantage from the Soviet point of view in balancing the U.S. gain in counterforce capability. Soviet ABM batteries deter virtually nothing. They certainly do not deter attacks upon Soviet forces if those attacks try to avoid cities — one of the options indicated by the Secretary of Defense.* And it is the opinion of Secretary McNamara that ABM systems will not prevent retaliatory attacks on Soviet cities. Thus he argued in 1963 much as he has done more recently:

> But, regardless of the design of any Soviet ABM system, in view of the warhead improvements we can make under the treaty, of the massive U.S. force available to saturate their defenses, and of the array of penetration aids which are being developed and will continue to be developed and improved, by underground

induced by blast, and the remainder would result from fallout.[47] Thus, without ABM or blast shelters, expected casualties from attacking Soviet weapons would remain high independent of fallout protection; with some kind of ABM program that avoids or minimizes blast effects this is no longer necessarily true.

* "In talking about global nuclear war," McNamara pointed out, "the Soviet leaders always say that they would strike at the entire complex of our military power including government and production centers, meaning our cities. If they were to do so, we would, of course, have no alternative but to retaliate in kind. But we have no way of knowing whether they would actually do so. It would certainly be in their interest as well as ours to try to limit the terrible consequences of a nuclear exchange. By building into our forces a flexible capability, we at least eliminate the prospect that we could strike back in only one way; namely, against the entire Soviet target system including their cities. Such a prospect would give the Soviet Union no incentive to withhold attack against our cities in a first strike. We want to give them a better alternative. Whether they would accept it in the crisis of a global nuclear war, no one can say. Considering what is at stake, we believe it is worth the additional effort on our part to have this option." [48]

testing where necessary, the United States will continue to have the capability, and . . . the Soviets will know that we will continue to have the capability — to penetrate and to devastate the Soviet Union if a retaliatory blow is required.[49]

To Soviet decision makers who do not anticipate an attack on American cities or an invasion of Western Europe, the risks of such attacks upon their own cities should appear quite small. In short, ABM batteries deter little and provide protection only against fairly unlikely contingencies.

Third, by comparison to ABM batteries, Soviet retaliatory missiles probably provide the Soviet Union with more substantial strategic advantages, while Soviet space achievements probably provide more substantial propaganda benefits. It is appropriate to compare these three potential enterprises because they require the same limited resources, and probably cannot all be funded in quantity.*

Consider the relationship between ABM and retaliatory missiles. While apparently admitting that a secure Soviet second-strike capability is inevitably forthcoming, Secretary of Defense McNamara nowhere admits that our retaliatory forces are not, at present, capable of disrupting them to a significant degree. He said in 1963:

> In planning our second strike force, we have provided, throughout the period under consideration [1964–1968], a capability to destroy virtually all of the "soft" and "semihard" military targets in the Soviet Union and a large number of their fully hardened missile sites, with an additional capability in the form of a protected force to be employed or held in reserve for use against urban and industrial areas.
>
> We have not found it feasible, *at this time*, to provide a capability for insuring the destruction of *any very large* portion of

---

* John P. Hardt argues that three priority areas — offensive missilery, missile defense capability, and space exploration programs — "must draw on the same limited military-space supporting industries. The costs of each of the programs must be calculated in terms of the alternative programs. How many ICBM's is a missile defense system for Moscow worth to Soviet leaders? Or will a program to land a man on the moon justify retarding their offensive and defensive missile programs? These are presumably the type of difficult decisions that must be faced by Soviet leaders. . . ."[50]

the fully hard ICBM sites, *if* the Soviets build them in quantities, or of missile launching submarines. . . . Our ability to destroy these submarines before they fire their missiles will be limited *once* the Soviet Union places any large number of them on station.[51] (Italics added.)

That same year, Harold Brown, Director of Defense Research and Engineering, stated: "I do not think it is possible for them to destroy all of our retaliatory capability or for us to destroy all of theirs, *providing that both sides plan carefully*." [52] (Italics added.)

In 1964, the Secretary of Defense was similarly conjectural. In denying that we could achieve a "full first-strike" capability that would reduce Soviet retaliatory capability to "acceptable" levels, he referred to it as unattainable "on the basis of our estimates of the Soviet nuclear strikes forces in the fiscal year 1967–69 period. . . ."

But the United States is not restraining its procurement to assist the Soviet Union in maintaining a second-strike capability. Evidently, Soviet expenditures on relatively invulnerable retaliatory forces would not be wasted from a purely strategic point of view and would probably be more useful than would analogous additions to our retaliatory forces.

In the past the preponderance on our side has permitted the United States to threaten strategic responses to other than strategic attacks. Our statements have threatened "massive retaliatory power." * We have spoken of "some circumstances" in which we would take the "initiative." [54] In the case of Cuba, President Kennedy stated that "it shall be the policy of this nation to regard any nuclear missile launched from Cuba against any nation in the Western hemisphere as an attack by the Soviet Union on the United States requiring a full retaliatory response upon the Soviet Union." [55] Our superiority has also made it somewhat less difficult to affirm, with conviction, that we will prevent a massive Soviet invasion with such responses. Thus an official White House statement of

---

* "The basic decision," said Secretary of State John Foster Dulles, "was to depend primarily upon a great capacity to retaliate, instantly, by means and at places of our choosing." [53]

March 27, 1962, reads: "It has always been clear that in such a context as a massive conventional attack on Europe by the Soviet Union, which would put Europe in danger of being overrun, the West would have to prevent such an event by all available means. This has been United States policy since the late Nineteen Forties and it represents no change." [56] Secretary McNamara stated more concretely that "it is our policy to utilize whatever weapons are needed to preserve our vital interests. Quite clearly, we consider access to Berlin a vital interest." [57]

Such pronouncements indicate that the decision to defend Europe is, like a similar decision to defend our own country, not a matter to which computations of risk apply. Nevertheless, all things being equal, the Soviet Union would presumably prefer to make any computations concerning these threats look very sobering.

The Soviet choice between retaliatory weapons and ABM defenses should also be influenced by the probable U.S. response. As indicated earlier, the United States generally seems prepared to see the Soviet retaliatory capability grow without responding by the procurement of more and more U.S. missiles — assuming that these missiles do not threaten us; in any case, it is not clearly U.S. policy to try to maintain an ability to strike Soviet forces. However, substantial numbers of ABM batteries would, at least in principle, provoke the most serious efforts to maintain our all-important retaliatory capability. This might, of course, be done largely with further improvements in penetration aids, but it might also lead to larger warheads and more numerous weapons.

The Soviet decision between offensive missiles and defensive missiles should also be influenced by costs. As noted earlier, a very considerable number of retaliatory weapons can be purchased for the price of an ABM system covering only about twenty metropolitan areas. And defending fewer cities is somewhat pointless, for strategic purposes, when faced with thousands of missiles.

Finally, the entire construction of ABM batteries for twenty or fifty cities could be a complete waste of money in terms of protection provided if war actually occurred. For instance, the United States might build a missile that could elude defenses. Or we might learn exactly how the Soviet system worked and use tactics that nullified it. These and simultaneity of arrival, streamlined (and hence faster) re-entry vehicles, smaller radar cross sections, nonradar reflecting nose cones, and so on, are all being considered.[58] The offense could easily leave the defense hopelessly far behind.

By comparison, several hundreds or thousands of Soviet missiles procured in place of a defense would provide additional deterrent value in any general war. In fact, they would threaten to reduce the critical postwar problems of U.S. passive and active defense to ultimate problems of economic recovery and recuperation. It has been argued, for example, that economic viability of the postwar economy would be an obstacle to recovery after an attack upon the United States of 1,000–4,000 megatons of which 750–2,000 were exploded on nonmilitary targets. This would "create serious to insuperable obstacles to the achievement of [economic viability] . . . unless extensive pre-attack preparations were made to avoid this. Much would depend on whether the attacker did, or did not, attempt to maximize the economic difficulties created by the nonmilitary portion of the attack."[59] Note that even the upper limit requires only 1,000 missiles, with 2-megaton warheads, devoted to urban targets. Threatened by numerous additional missiles, we should probably find that our problems became as insoluble as those that now presumably would face the Soviet Union in an unlimited war.

Next, we should consider the relative propaganda benefits of constructing ABM systems, on the one hand, and achieving space "firsts," on the other. In the long run, there seems to be much wider scope for the latter than for the former. Presumably, space achievements will follow each other for some time to come. By comparison, a deployed ABM system is likely to exhaust its potential for propaganda quickly. And there is a high probability, as indicated earlier, that a one-shot Soviet propaganda achievement in defense would be nullified by the construction of a system by the United States. By contrast, continuing space "firsts" may be possible despite the best U.S. efforts.

From the Soviet point of view, the case for ABM defenses seems stronger as protection against new nuclear powers (Nth countries) than against the United States. The Soviet military establishment probably views the possibility of a future ballistic missile threat from France or Germany as a strong motivation for a defense. Without questioning the legitimacy of these fears — which are naturally of more concern to the Soviet bloc than to ourselves — we may question the legitimacy of an ABM response to the danger. Must a great power, with the capability for complete destruction of a lesser power, take defensive steps to prevent "small" attacks from that country? Or can a great power simply put its trust in deterrence? Finally, is a defense against smaller powers worth an acceleration of the arms race with respect to the other major power? These are some of the questions an American analyst would expect a Soviet specialist in arms control to be concerned with.

Would Soviet Restraint in Procurement Be Risky?

There seems relatively little Soviet risk of "falling behind" in the procurement of ABM systems, and little strategic risk of actually doing so. U.S. procurement requires authorization by Congress, and hence warning is given of our intentions. While the exact period between procurement decisions and various stages of projected deployment may not be known, Soviet decision makers can probably predict these lead times at least roughly. Furthermore, any propaganda advantage that might arise from a first announcement that ABM systems were to be procured by the United States — the "technological triumph" anticipated by General Taylor in an earlier quotation — could probably be nullified by Soviet statements concerning their (possibly fictitious) achievements. Without intelligence information, and possibly even with it, we could not easily determine who procured first: it would be a matter of years between the first completed installation for a city and the twentieth or fiftieth such installation. Neither power can catch the other by surprise, or even credibly claim to have done so, in such a situation.

A more serious problem is the risk that war will occur and, in the absence of defenses, wreak greater destruction than would have occurred otherwise. This assumes that the defenses will actually work and envisions an uncontrolled war or one fought to the bitter end. But it is becoming ever more likely that the destruction caused by the United States in a future strategic war would be determined more by our intentions than by our capability, which for practical purposes is "unlimited." Thus a strategic reserve would probably be maintained, and Soviet cities would be spared to whatever extent American cities had been spared. Such an evolution in doctrine further diminishes the likelihood that defenses would play a significant role. Defenses around cities to be attacked might be overwhelmed with weapons from a large reservoir of such forces, and other defenses might be ignored. (However, a war that involved a spasm of destruction is still possible — especially if Soviet plans provide for no other options. On the other hand, in such a war the Soviet Union might find present and projected defenses of only very, very marginal assistance, if U.S. statements quoted in the previous section are to be believed.)

Would U.S. Restraint Be in the U.S. Interest?

Should we try, as Secretary Rusk wishes, to put some "lid" on a new qualitative arms race? Or should we argue that the only firm basis for our policy is to exploit technology by procurement in old and new areas alike? Shall we seek security through attempts to stay ahead of arms race developments or through attempts to slow them down? Should we discourage Soviet procurement of defenses by threatening to purchase our own in response or encourage it by purchasing them first?

Obviously these decisions involve a host of political issues. Attempts continually to press ahead in the procurement of strategic weapons can be argued to have either good or bad effects on the U.S.-Soviet political relationship. Certainly the decision to press ahead with ballistic missile defenses can be expected to have significant political effects in comparison with other weapons developments.

Undoubtedly, however, a lot depends on the surrounding political climate and the statements issued to accompany the decision. If, as might seem likely, the decision to buy a ballistic missile defense were made in a period of international tension, then the defense would signal precisely what motivated it — increased risk, and fear, of war. If the defense, despite its great expense, were procured in a period of low tension, built slowly, or built in response to a Chinese threat, and if it were combined with increasingly close U.S.-Soviet relations in other spheres, little political harm might be done.

The strategic issues involved in restraint are perhaps somewhat easier to describe. We have at present two alternative methods of limiting damage upon the United States if war occurs. The first involves the construction of a variety of defenses. The second involves the negotiation, or quiet encouragement, of a halt in offensive missile procurement; this is discussed in Chapter Five.

But there is probably little point to restraint in procuring antiballistic missile systems if there is to be no serious effort to establish either an informal or a formal halt in missile procurement. In the absence of such an effort, U.S. ballistic missile defense systems will probably be procured as soon as any one of a variety of events occur over the years. These include a Soviet ballistic missile defense, a new administration more receptive to defense, defensive batteries of higher efficiency, political pressure upon the current U.S. government to do "more," further Chinese progress in weapons development, and so on. In short, restraint, if not pursued vigorously, may not be effective in the long run. Of course, the desirability of restraint depends on the likelihood that it will be effective. If we do not believe that missile defenses can be restrained by treaty, understanding, or unwillingness to make the necessary expenditures, then there is that much less point in trying.

Undoubtedly, the prospects for bilateral restraint in procuring ballistic missile defenses depend first and foremost on the very large expenditures associated with them and on their low expected efficiency. If either one of these factors "improved," the prospects for restraint could be substantially diminished. Second, the prospects for restraint depend upon the perceived risk of war. Third, and considerably less important as a motivating force in either government, is the belief that effective restraints might become possible by treaty or otherwise.

At present, the prospects for success in an attempt to achieve restraint are fairly good in the short run. Both sides probably perceive more clearly than ever before how high the costs of a successful defense might be. This is in part because of experience with large, expensive, and ineffective air defenses. Second, the perceived risk of war is at present low. Many believe that the Cuban crisis was the high-water mark in the risk of nuclear war. Finally, with the U.S. suggestion at Geneva that both parties should consider the possibility of a "freeze" of strategic weapons, the prospects for either informal or formal halts in offensive weapon procurement seem to be improved. In short, restraint might well achieve its objective for a time at least.

What are the strategic objectives of this restraint? We might begin to freeze our present advantage — whatever it may be. We might save tens of billions of dollars required in building defenses and more billions required to achieve the necessary confidence that we could neutralize Soviet defenses. (This last requirement may already have cost us a few billion dollars for the advance development of improvements in Minuteman and Polaris missiles that would otherwise have been unnecessary.)

We might begin to build a relationhip with the Soviet Union that permitted restraint to operate — or deterrence to work — in forestalling other weapon developments, not yet fully perceived, which might become a source of future prob-

51

lems — strategic and political. We might develop a consensus for trying to solve these problems, confidence that the problems could be solved, and some sophistication and expertise as to how this might be done. Many of the subtler of these advantages depend on the way in which the restraint is effected; this is discussed at greater length in the treatment of a freeze in Chapter Five.

A common and somewhat annoying issue is sometimes raised. Should we welcome or fear Soviet prosperity? Most people have resolved this issue in their own minds, but as a nation our position is still uncertain. During the Test Ban hearings, the following exchange occurred:

> *Senator Hickenlooper:* Therefore, if it comes to spending and economic threats we can outspend them and we can go on and really drive them to a position of economic distress if we want to continue with our scientific advancement.
> Therefore, who gets what out of this treaty? The Russians — don't they get relieved here from those further tremendous expenditures and charges on their economy, while we abandon that particular advantage . . . ?
>
> *Secretary Rusk:* Senator, I think we could do it but I don't think we could enjoy it.[60]

Should we welcome the possibility that both sides will spend great quantities of money on ABM because we are better at it? Or, as Secretary McNamara argues, should we maintain that "it is very much in our interest to have the Russians expand their educational system and consumer goods distribution. . . ."[61] There is also the possibility that the Soviet Union will procure defenses even if we do not. If they do this for invalid reasons, should we explain the issues to them and try to discourage their waste of resources?

Related Arms Control Issues

There are a number of topics that relate the ABM problems to arms control. Some of these are referred to briefly in turn.

Research and Development in ABM

It is certainly very difficult and not necessarily desirable to prevent research and development in missile defense problems. Antiballistic missilery represents an important area of military interest, and it is only natural that both sides should want to stay on top of development problems. Furthermore, work on defense is necessary for work on offense problems. Many are beginning to believe that this is its main function. During the Test Ban hearings the following exchange occurred.

> *The Chairman* [Senator Fulbright]: If I understand him [Herbert York] correctly, the value of the ABM system is largely in testing the penetrability of our own weapons, and that we should pursue the ABM, but this is its main function.

> *Dr. Kistiakowsky:* Yes Sir.[62]

And, in any case, the pressure to continue research is very substantial. For example, in explaining the personal attention which he gives to missile defense, the Secretary of Defense said:

> I do this for a variety of reasons, but among them is to assure myself that every possible action is being taken to accelerate the development. I know of absolutely nothing that was cut back from which we could benefit. I know of no action that could have been taken that wasn't taken during the past year. . . . I met with one of the heads of Bell Labs. . . . on this specific point, to ask him whether there was anything we could do that we had not done to accelerate the program.
>
> He assured me that all the resources that they could profitably employ were being profitably employed. No additional amount of money could expedite the program.[63]

And of course the Secretary is not merely responding to pressure. Elsewhere he has said:

> Whether we will be successful, I can't predict. But I am not prepared to say that there can be no defense against intercontinental ballistic missiles.[64]

This attitude is entirely appropriate. The development of highly effective ABM systems would not be far more surprising, judged from the vantage point of the parties involved, than the development of ICBM's themselves.

Nevertheless, research and development (R & D) in these areas by *both* powers does not *necessarily* serve our nation's interest. Though it is difficult to know how to prevent or slow it, or even whether we should want to try, several things can be said against R & D. First, the research continues to provide uncertainties and chances for strategic imbalance. Second, if both sides eventually achieve equal chances of making a breakthrough in defense, each will anticipate being at a substantial disadvantage: each may anticipate that it will not itself exploit its periods of defense superiority, but may fear that the other will. Third, whatever breakthroughs are made by either major power are likely to be duplicated, with some time lag, by the other. This has been the course of technology in the past, and it means that each power is, to some extent, working for the other and hence, possibly, working against itself.

A No-First-Procurement Policy

The decision to procure ABM systems is a most important threshold. This is probably the place to hold the line, if arms control considerations argue for restraint. This is because (a) the lead time required for procurement will act as a kind of "firebreak" between a period of no defense (associated with relative strategic security) and a period of defense (associated with possible destabilization of certain weapons systems); (b) the procurement decision is expensive enough to be given full consideration; and (c) present defenses are quite inadequate and leave at least the United States, if not the Soviet Union, very undecided about their effectiveness.

The "firebreak" aspects of a no-first-procurement policy are especially important. A deployed system, unlike a system under development, may suddenly increase in usable effectiveness, or such improvement may be feared. For example, it is clear at the present time that it will take several years to procure *any* system whether it is to defend against one, three, five, ten, or a hundred missiles fired at it simultaneously. Once the system is deployed, however, its capability may be increased, in relatively short periods of time, from being adequate to defend against, say, three missiles to being adequate against ten. This possibility will accelerate the arms race by encouraging procurement of certain nonballistic missiles such as low-altitude cruise missiles. At present, with a "firebreak" of several years, the procurement of such new types of missiles can be continually deferred, so long as major Soviet procurement of missile defense is deferred. In other words, deployment of ABM systems could be expected to accelerate the race by encouraging production and improvement of missiles to cope with offense-defense interactions that would otherwise be considered academic.

Verification for No-First-Procurement Policies

It may be possible merely by using intelligence information to verify that the Soviet Union is not building missile defense batteries. In other words, the United States may be able unilaterally to "police" the Soviet compliance with a no-first-*procurement* understanding. However, some inspection in industrial areas may be required to ensure nonproduction. On the other hand, the verification only of the *nondeployment* of terminal-intercept systems should be simpler and can presumably be done by unilateral U.S. methods.

Advances over Terminal-Intercept Systems

The most important arms race dangers, and the most significant possibilities for protection, will arise from improvements over terminal-intercept systems. The present systems can absorb large amounts of money and encourage further expenditures, but they are unlikely to limit expected casualties to very low absolute numbers or to protect society. Even if the defense drew ahead in terminal-intercept ABM systems, it would still be possible for each side to threaten agriculture, small towns, and so on. But with systems that destroyed enemy missiles in mid-course or immediately after firing, more serious imbalances might arise. Such schemes are always under consideration:

> *Chairman Russell:* You said that we had no alternative to the NIKE family in a defense against missiles. There was a plan at one time, I do not know how far it got, to have some huge missile shot up into the skies [deletion in original]. . . . BAMBI would get all of the decoys and everything else if it would function as it was planned to do.

> *Secretary McNamara:* I think we found that the sky was bigger, perhaps, than we anticipated.[65]

Neutralizing these systems may require nonballistic methods of delivery. But a Bambi-type system might be realized at a time when strategic aircraft did not exist in large numbers. While other methods of delivery exist, and some are undoubtedly under development, one side might not be as prepared for such a defense as it would have liked, especially if it had been built quickly. In many ways the real threat to stability of ABM is its potential for just this kind of technological surprise. Some publicly discussed possibilities for such a surprise in ABM systems include the use of cannons for ABM defense and the use of novel offensive weapons effects for the destruction of missiles in their silos.[66] Other notions that Soviet authorities claim to have found in our press include the possibility of throwing up a screen of fine metal fragments in front of missiles, the use of a stream of high-speed neutrons to detonate nuclear warheads of incoming missiles, and the use of electromagnetic energy to destroy or deflect them.[67]

The Arms Race after Deployment

Once terminal-intercept or more advanced systems are deployed, the arms race may very possibly take on a different quality. Each country will be forced, by its opponent's secrecy, to "game" the offense-defense race within its own establishment. This is done to some extent at present. Thus, Dr. Brown testified:

> The United States decided not to deploy the Nike-Zeus because its effectiveness was inadequate against U.S. penetration aids programed for entry into the U.S. inventory before a Nike-Zeus system could be deployed, and we assume the same would be true of Soviet penetration aid capability.[68]

Thus, once deployed, improvements in our missile defense capability would be sought to keep pace with our improving offensive capability, and vice versa; the buying of strategic weapons would be accelerated.

Progress Toward General Disarmament

The procurement of ABM systems may, all things being equal, impede progress toward arms limitation or reductions. We have mentioned the reasons why these systems may accelerate the arms race, and these reasons lend support to our conclusion. There are further reasons, however. Negotiated arms control is complicated by ABM systems. Their effectiveness provides another unknown — an unknown that is particularly hard to assess without very detailed inspection.

We have only just begun to think in concrete terms of the problems of "equalizing" missile capabilities on each side. Should the treaty refer to retained megatonnage, numbers of missiles, gross vehicle weights, or what? But this balancing of missile capabilities may be child's play compared to the problems of balancing defensive capabilities and their relations to penetration mechanisms. The ability of the defense will depend on its tactics, as well as on its radar, computers, types of interceptors, "hardness," complementary civil defense capabilities, and so on. The most detailed inspection and the most complicated negotiations would be necessary to reach a consensus on the comparative utility of a U.S. and a Soviet ABM system — even if measured against a given type of missile. Missiles have many different penetration properties and may be fired in many ways — in salvos, with decoys, with electronic countermeasures, and so on. Again the most detailed inspection would be necessary to ascertain the penetration properties of the adversary's missiles. By comparison, the disarmament problems of balancing the retaliatory capabilities of both sides against undefended cities seem trivial. There will never be any defensive balance as suitable for arms control as no defense at all, so long as mutual deterrence is used to prevent general war.

It is useful to consider defenses as a *form* of disarmament if only to see their disadvantages in a better light. The process of defending one's own country can be viewed as akin to disarming one's opponents. If both sides build efficient defenses, a kind of disarmament will result; but this disarmament would be desired by neither side (at least as concerns its own disarmament), would be unregulated by any control organ, would be subject to the caprices of technology, and would be unrelated to political progress in resolving underlying conflicts. Most important, it would probably be resisted by the defense community in each major power, which has become accustomed to deterring potential enemies with an enormous capacity for retaliatory destruction.

Accidents

One commonly mentioned arms control virtue of ABM systems is their capacity to protect against accidental missile firings. This advantage is generally overstated, however, for two reasons. First, the likelihood that a Soviet or U.S. armed missile will be fired accidentally at a city is very, very small. There has been, as far as I know, no instance of a single missile being fired accidentally. And even if one were fired, the missile might not fire reliably or accurately, and might not be targeted on a defended site. Second, to protect against this threat, scores of ABM batteries would have to be kept on an alert that permitted firing with only a very few minutes warning.

It seems unlikely that the U.S. Department of Defense or the Soviet Defense Ministry would permit so many nuclear warheads to remain on a sustained alert of this kind in noncrisis periods. These short-range missiles, on high alert, probably pose a greater threat to cities than accidental enemy firings — even though their warheads are smaller. The warheads may not be small by the standards of the Hiroshima bomb; hence, an accidental detonation over an urban area, or in a silo, could be very destructive and could possibly trigger actual attacks. Probably, therefore, the defenses would be activated only in crises and would defend only against crisis accidents.

Nth-Country Deterrence

Another argument for ABM systems is that they would be useful for defense against ballistic missile threats from Nth countries. Communist China is generally taken as an example of such a country. Persuasive examples of such a threat in the next decade are harder to find for the United States, though perhaps not so hard to find for the Soviet Union. It is often further argued that while ABM systems may not be sufficient to cope with the threat from one of the two major powers they ought to be capable of effective defense against primitive weapons from less advanced powers. This argument depends upon details.

It might or might not be true that the penetration methods used by a major power would be expensive or complicated. If these methods required small, efficient, light warheads — perhaps to permit large numbers of bombs to be delivered by a single missile — then the necessary techniques might be too advanced for China in the seventies. On the other hand, if penetration could be effected by easily achieved techniques for eluding interception, such as cheap decoys, a country with a few missiles might penetrate quite as easily as one with a large quantity. Since presently foreseeable systems admittedly only "raise the price" to the offense, and since a Chinese threat might concentrate on a few cities, it is possible that an advanced ABM system might be vulnerable to fairly primitive Chinese missiles.

Whether or not the defensive system can protect against a few Chinese missiles or force the Chinese to build twenty missiles rather than two to hold hostage a few defended cities, there will probably remain a large number of undefended sites ranging from cities with a population of a few hundred thousand to such installations as dams, nuclear laboratories, and the RAND Corporation. Hence, the Chinese capacity to destroy probably cannot be denied.

More important, however, than the technical nature of the offense-defense race is an assessment of the situations in which Sino-American relations could call for threat and counterthreat on a level of nuclear violence. Most Asian sources of conflict will either permit direct U.S. defense or involve a low level of violence, with which nuclear threats are not likely to be associated. Thus, we can defend against invasions of Formosa or Japan and, more often than not, will find nuclear strategy irrelevant to guerrilla action in Southeast Asia. As a result, it is difficult to imagine plausible situations in which the United States and China would trade nuclear threats.

Even were these threats to be traded, it is again difficult to imagine situations in which our willingness to take action would depend on the extent to which we had procured a defense against Chinese ballistic missiles. The very best defense would be untried and of uncertain effectiveness. Hence, the President would not be able to depend upon it. The targets that the Chinese selected for their missiles would be unknown in advance, and potential casualties in the United States would be very large in absolute numbers, at least after the initial stages of procurement of intercontinental missiles by the Chinese. Our pattern of action would probably be similar to that of past actions and policies in which we determined the course to be followed relatively independently of detailed calculations of consequences. For some things, we would act as if we would fight to the last man. For others, we would not even take the political risks of adopting a posture of determined resistance. There are probably very few situations in which Presidents calculate the costs sufficiently carefully (and have sufficient confidence in the defense) to make these calculations relevant.

Moreover, whatever the calculated cost to ourselves, the potential cost to our allies will be large. The Chinese cannot fail to perceive the feasibility of directing their threats against our allies in the Far East. Hence, computations of potential cost will be complicated, and our own potential costs will become still less relevant.

It seems that the argument for decreasing expected U.S. losses in order to deter further the Communist Chinese is an application of the now-discredited principles that were applied earlier to the deterrence of Soviet aggression in Europe. As noted then, we do not any longer consider it necessary to have a "credible first-strike capacity" based on our ability to reduce Soviet retaliatory capability to "acceptable" levels in order to deter Soviet threats. These principles of nuclear blackmail are likely to be even less applicable in Asia than in Europe.

Especially important in considering the problem of China is timing. The existence of a Chinese intercontinental ballistic missile threat may be far distant, or it may occur in ten years. At this point it is very difficult to tell. We can build some kind of antiballistic missile system in a few or several years. Since the procurement of defenses is an especially sensitive problem in the development of U.S.-Soviet strategic relations, there is much merit in waiting until the danger is clearly perceived before introducing this potentially disturbing issue. We should avoid being panicked into defenses by the Chinese bomb.

Hard-Point Defense of ICBM's

The discussion has concentrated on the impact of urban defense ABM systems. But ABM's might, in principle, be useful for defending ICBM's. Because ICBM's can more easily be hardened, they are more easily defended with an ABM system than are cities. Nevertheless, such a defense is now considered more expensive than the more efficient multiplication of missile sites. Defense of missile sites would not so definitely encourage offensive weapon procurement as would defense of cities.

Separation of Forces from Urban Targets

Related to the problem of reducing destruction if war occurs is that of keeping or redeploying forces away from urban areas. This might be part of a unilateral or bilateral arms control measure. Point-defense ABM systems (protecting only a city and its surroundings) might discourage this separation by providing a degree of protection for whatever forces might be in or near the city. For example, the deployment of B-58 or F-111 bombers to civilian airfields, as a dispersion operation, could be encouraged in crises by the knowledge that the ABM system defending the nearby city would also defend the airport. However, low-level interception of missiles may not protect delicate aircraft parked in the open or in ordinary hangers.

Destabilization

It is possible that missile defense systems might turn out to be better able to defeat Polaris-type missile systems than ICBM's. This means that a Soviet or U.S. ABM system would have its greatest impact on what has, until now, been considered the most secure part of the strategic force. The effect of such an "undermining" of the strategic posture was indicated in the words of Governor Rockefeller that were quoted earlier in this chapter. By contrast, without ABM, Polaris-type systems would probably guarantee for the present a second-strike capability to whoever builds them.

Inspection

It could be as important to keep secret the locations and workings of ABM systems as it is to keep secret the locations of missile sites. An adversary might want to attack ABM installations or to know which targets are not protected by them. And it certainly would be useful for an enemy to know specific characteristics of the system if it is to neutralize it. Therefore, Soviet procurement of ABM systems might encourage, and seems likely in no significant way to discourage, Soviet secrecy. This has implications for many other disarmament agreements.

Nuclear Diffusion and the Denuclearization of Europe

If ABM systems become efficient, particularly against IRBM's, there may be some interest in deploying them around European cities. Whether or not the warheads of interceptor missiles could be kept under U.S. control is not clear. If the weapons were maintained on alert and the systems were owned by the European powers, it might be necessary to relinquish control of the warheads. Conceivably, this difficulty might be avoided, but if it were not, it would constitute nuclear diffusion. In either case, denuclearization policies would be defeated by European ABM systems unless special provision were made for ABM interceptor warheads. While there is no particular theoretical reason why this exception cannot be made, the matter would probably be, at the least, a source of difficulty in negotiation.

Qualitative Acceleration of the Arms Race

At the present time, efforts to neutralize the defenses of terminal-intercept systems emphasize the saturation of the defense with decoys or the simultaneous arrival of missiles. This need not remain the case, and it is certainly conceivable that new weapon effects or large warheads of some kind might be found very effective for overcoming defenses. In this case the procurement of ABM systems could have unfortunate collateral effects on the arms race. The *kind* of effect to be feared could be an increased relative effectiveness of weapons in orbit. Depending on technical details, weapons in orbit might or might not be able to penetrate systems that were designed to counter a ballistic missile trajectory from a particular continent. If these weapons turned out to be cost effective against deployed ABM systems, there would be a temptation to abrogate the present U.S.-Soviet understanding not to put weapons of mass destruction in outer space. Another example might be "dirty" bombs designed to be exploded in rural areas and to cover defended cities down wind with long-lasting fallout.

Catalytic War (Or Unauthorized Behavior)

The procurement of ABM systems seems to decrease the probability of a war initiated by a third party because it makes it more difficult to destroy an urban target in either the United States or the Soviet Union. However, although the catalytic attack itself need not be successful it can cause dangerous strains and hasty actions, and, of course, an attack need not necessarily be on city targets — an airfield might do as well. If malevolence is assumed, as opposed to inadvertence, it may be reasonable to expect an attack sufficiently concerted to achieve penetration. Probably the major benefit of a deployed system is the increased likelihood that Moscow and Washington, viewed as command posts, would survive.

Nuclear Materials Cutoff

There has been discussion of a nuclear materials cutoff. While we cannot be certain without reference to classified information, it seems that the procurement of ABM systems would probably require such large amounts of fissionable material, either here or in the Soviet Union, that a bilateral cutoff would become impossible. After all, thousands of interceptors may be procured.

Test Ban Treaty

It is generally believed (and the Secretary of Defense has so testified) that the United States can procure an ABM system without abrogating the Test Ban Treaty to conduct relevant tests. This may also be true for the Soviet Union. However, it is possible that the Soviet Union would find tests useful to develop an efficient interceptor warhead, and both powers could be tempted to test the system against certain nuclear effects. For instance, the Director of the Los Alamos Scientific Laboratory, Norris E. Bradbury, testified that, although tested warheads existed "on the shelf" for ABM interceptors, "we could look to making better ones . . . ," and General Taylor has stated: "Both sides could achieve an antiballistic missile, but one with less desirable characteristics than would be the case if additional atmospheric tests were conducted." [69]

Classified information should be available to determine whether the development of interceptor warheads can be carried out easily underground. In any case, this problem has obvious interactions with an extension of the Test Ban Treaty to underground tests. Whether a major power might some day announce that its security required it to test an ABM system against atmospheric nuclear effects, it is obviously impossible to say. But certainly the decision to procure and deploy a large-scale system must tempt decision makers to fill any gaps in their knowledge of its effectiveness. Again, classified information may make it possible to determine the significance of such gaps.

What Is to Be Done?

It is quite evident that there is a case for attempting to avoid, rather than to build, ballistic missile defenses and the complementary types of defense that they may require. This case depends, of course, on certain values and estimates. One must decide what one believes about the risk of war, the value of resources, the nature of the U.S.-Soviet competition, and so on. But there is a case worth considering, and it raises the question of what might be done to induce restraint.

There are two quite different ways of avoiding the procurement of ballistic missile defenses and some intermediate possibilities. First of all, we could resort to formal or informal agreement.

A formal agreement prohibiting ballistic missile defenses would almost surely have to prohibit as well an increase in the number of offensive missiles. While it might be possible to imagine an agreement to freeze defenses without an agreement to engage in actual disarmament of missiles, it is very difficult, for political reasons, to imagine an agreement to avoid defenses without even a *freeze* of offensive weapons.

The role of antiballistic missile systems in the context of formal agreements is discussed in Chapters Four and Five. It seems necessary to include restraints on antiballistic missile systems in either a freeze or reduction agreement since, otherwise, the strategic presuppositions of the agreement would change so drastically as to imperil the agreement. However, in some cases, the avoidance of missile defenses could be based on a tacit understanding underlying the treaty. In any case, the restraints on antiballistic missile systems are likely to be the most important and valuable aspects of either the freeze or the reduction agreement in terms of resources saved and strategic stability ensured.

Leaving the discussion of formal agreements for later, the question arises as to whether there are useful ways for maintaining tacit restraints on deployment and procurement. Whether or not these restraints could be effective for a long period, they might well be useful in the short run.

The most important way of discouraging the procurement of ABM defenses is to make them unlikely to work. We should spend the money necessary to ensure, so far as we can, that the Soviets will think ballistic missile defenses are ineffective. And we should emphasize the impact of their actions on our own.

For example, it might be of interest for the Secretary of Defense to discuss, in open testimony, his estimates of (*a*) Soviet costs to procure an ABM system of a type being considered by them; and (*b*) the costs to the U.S. strategic system to ensure penetration. It is quite possible that the Secretary of Defense is better able to compare these costs than any person in the Soviet Union. The comparison may be revealing — and it may be observed by important members of the Soviet bureaucracy who would otherwise not be shown such discouraging information.

It might also be useful to point out that very large systems are required to guarantee the recovery of a country. In particular, we should not permit a Soviet defense ministry to persuade relevant civilian decision makers that it is useful and significant to protect ten or twenty large cities, if in fact it is not. In other words, we might indicate that the costs are going to be quite high if anything is to be gained.

It seems that there is sometimes a very serious doctrinal lag in the Soviet system. This might be documented and discussed publicly by U.S. officials. Such discussion could discredit Soviet authorities and Soviet departments responsible for procuring useless defenses in the past. Although existing documentation would be classified, it might be declassified at little "cost" on the authority of high civilian officials in the Department of Defense. The policy of documenting Soviet procurement mistakes might be extended into a policy of ridiculing Soviet defenses and emphasizing their inadequacy. Our statements might be as specific or unspecific as seemed desirable. (This tactic could of course have undesired consequences, and should be considered with much more care than we have yet given it.)

Still stronger action might call for explanation in general terms of the penetration capabilities necessary to avoid the Soviet defense. For instance, if our missiles have very advanced techniques, we might point out that certain decoys will easily saturate the Soviet system, clearing the way for U.S. missiles with even more advanced capabilities. Some Congressional testimony is already close to this. And these statements would increase the credibility of our assertion.

Another method for deterring Soviet procurement is to threaten action that will more than re-establish our existing advantage. We could point out that Soviet procurement might just tip the scales toward U.S. procurement. This would degrade the Soviet offensive missiles or require the Soviets to expend additional resources to keep up. If it were clearly U.S. policy to "match" Soviet procurement of ABM missiles for a substantial number of cities, this inevitable response could be passed along. In fact, if it were our policy *not* to procure the present ABM systems under any circumstances, it might even be useful to say this forcefully, as it would presumably underscore any accompanying statements attesting to the worthlessness of Soviet procurement. Another way to threaten dramatically to maintain an advantage is to propose procurement of a substantial number of nonballistic missiles in response to a Soviet ballistic missile system.

It might also be useful to describe the arms race in terms that indicated the incompatibility of defense and deterrence. We might point out that another "round," once started, would continue and lead to risks and costs for the Soviet Union that cannot be clearly visualized at present. Space-based systems might be pointed out as a destabilizing possibility.

Finally, most of the methods just described for discouraging Soviet procurement could also be used by the Soviet Union to discourage procurement by us. Thus, the Soviet Union could threaten to match our procurement, offer to restrain their own, warn that bilateral procurement would assist their posture, and so on. In addition, the Soviet Union could, by offering various kinds of inspection, very substantially increase the feasibility, from the American point of view, of a no-first-procurement policy. Such inspection might only have to take place in or around urban areas. This would minimize its conflict with the demands of Soviet military secrecy.

Current Prospects

A year after the reports appeared of Soviet missile systems around Leningrad, there seemed to be little further indication of Soviet progress. The rumors of such defensive systems may have been of the kind that periodically sweep the defense community. For example, in January 1965, John A. McCone, Director of the Central Intelligence Agency, briefed Congressional committees that dealt with defense, foreign policy, and atomic energy, and a UPI report expressed the change in emphasis like this:

> Some Congressional leaders expressed concern about Russia's progress on a missile killer when the limited nuclear test-ban treaty was debated nearly two years ago.
> At that time there were reports that antimissile-missiles were being deployed near Leningrad. The concern has not abated, but it now involves possible Russian progress *in the art* of intercepting and destroying ballistic missiles.[70] (Italics added.)

Evidently, the risk has diminished that the Soviets would greatly encourage our procurement of a missile defense by a premature attempt to claim that their own system existed.

In part for this reason, but also for reasons about to be described, the crucial question seemed to have become whether the United States would, without such provocation, set about building some kind of missile defense anyway. The growing likelihood that we might initiate such a new round in procurement was given credence by a variety of signals.

When the fiscal 1965 budget was introduced (in early 1964), the Secretary of Defense began to justify our rather large missile force by emphasizing its capacity to "limit damage" by striking Soviet forces after our own had been attacked. This doctrine seems to have been shaped by a desire to deny our capacity to strike Soviet forces first — the much debated "counterforce capability" — while justifying an otherwise apparently excessive number of missiles. This was the first time since the civil defense controversy that the United States was thinking in terms of limiting damage if war occurred and it had some unexpected aftereffects. It was immediately obvious to the cost-conscious Defense Department that there were a variety of competitive and complementary methods for limiting damage. If one was to be tried, others also had to be considered. Perhaps civil defense was more effective than the use of missiles to attack Soviet residual forces. If so, civil defense would have to be given a higher priority. More generally, missile defense, bomber defense, and antisubmarine defense had to be considered closely and in relation to one another.

The effect of this perception was to give some impetus to the idea of ballistic missile defense but also to undermine the damage-limiting notion itself. If damage limiting implied ballistic missile defense, then the latter seemed more reasonable and the former potentially more expensive than had been formerly believed.

As a result, many studies were evidently done on ballistic missile defense. When the Secretary of Defense testified on the fiscal 1966 budget, he discussed damage-limiting capability at some length. The main impression given by the testimony is that the degree to which we should aim to protect ourselves against the possibility of war is still very much undecided. The testimony shows an increased awareness of the ability to buy different amounts of defense; this tends to increase the likelihood that some will eventually be bought and hence that more will be procured later.

One of the most interesting parts of the testimony was the following table, which depicts the results of a Soviet attack in the early seventies. The "Early Urban Attack" assumes that cities are attacked at the outset. The "Delayed Urban Attack" assumes that attacks on cities are sufficiently delayed to permit us to attack Soviet forces effectively. The table illustrates the effects, in reducing casualties, of successively larger expenditures in initial investment. The first $5 billion would be

ESTIMATED EFFECT ON U.S. FATALITIES OF ADDITIONS TO THE
APPROVED DAMAGE-LIMITING PROGRAM
(BASED ON 1970 POPULATION OF 210 MILLION)

Additional Investment	Millions of U.S. Fatalities	
	Early Urban Attack	Delayed Urban Attack
0	149	122
5	120	90
15	96	59
25	78	41

spent for fallout shelters. The $15 billion investment would add some ballistic missile defense and some bomber defenses, and the $25-billion investment would add more of each.

The emphasis on damage-limiting seems to have changed somewhat in its rationale from the previous year. In 1964, the Secretary of Defense had claimed that studies continued to show the utility of attacking Soviet forces after we had ourselves been attacked. These were described as residual forces that could not be launched at once. In the more recent testimony, the use of missile attacks for effective damage limiting seemed to depend primarily on a Soviet delay in attacking American cities, a delay that was described parenthetically as "an unlikely contingency." [71] Part of this change of emphasis stemmed from the fact that the more recent testimony considered Soviet forces in the early seventies, while the previous discussion was associated with Soviet forces in the late sixties. For whatever reason the change was made, it tended to diminish the justification for damage-limiting expenditures.

As for the central item in the defense package, Nike-X, the Secretary planned to "reexamine the question of production and deployment of the NIKE-X system again next year." He noted:

Considering the vast amount of development, test and evaluation work still to be accomplished, deferral of this decision to the FY 1967 budget should not delay an initial operational capability by many months beyond what we could expect to achieve if we were to start production in FY 1966.[72]

Thus the situation remained quiescent, but the United States could hardly be expected to avoid a decision forever. It is particularly important to appreciate the fact that figures based on Soviet capabilities in the early seventies could be most misleading if our estimates were too high. In the absence of a treaty prohibiting, among other things, procurement of ballistic missile defenses, the United States could eventually find that its reasons against procurement had been undercut by a Soviet decision to relax their efforts.

Among the arguments for buying a missile defense, one achieved especial prominence in 1964. The Chinese explosion of a bomb encouraged the argument that an ABM system was required for defense against a possible forthcoming Chinese intercontinental missile. However, Secretary McNamara noted that studies showed "the lead time for additional nations to develop and deploy an effective ballistic missile system capable of reaching the United States is greater than we require to deploy the defense." [73]

There is another level on which the prospects for ballistic missile defenses can be dimly perceived. This is in the dialogue between the two major powers, which invariably contains echoes of the changing likelihoods that one side or the other will push ahead. This dialogue is carried on through articles, papers, and pronouncements of various kinds. In early 1965, two interesting Soviet commentaries appeared.

The first, an article by General N. Talensky on "Anti-missile Systems and Disarmament," appeared in the Soviet journal *International Affairs*. It referred to Western writing and considered many of the themes just presented. General Talensky minimized the danger that an effective antimissile system in the hands of an aggressive state could intensify the danger of an outbreak of war. In this he was in agreement with a variety of American strategists who did not believe that the literal "stability" of the situation was imperiled by prospective defenses. General Talensky went even further and argued that stability might be *enhanced* by the resultant shifts in emphasis between defensive and deterrent weapon systems.

The Soviet officer conceded that the possibility could not be ruled out that "the side lagging" in the construction of defensive systems might build up its attack capabilities, thus accelerating the arms race. This is probably the crucial point to be communicated to Soviet decision makers (as well as to our own — but they know it). Somewhat illogically, however, he maintained that the side which made a "spurt" in the means of attack as a response to defensive measures would instantly expose its aggressive intentions and stand condemned as the aggressor. The general further maintained that the early implementation of general and complete disarmament was the one reasonable alternative to a race between antimissile systems.

In short, this declared Soviet view seemed to reserve its position on defensive systems, to assert its right to push ahead, and to deny our right to respond with further procurement of offensive weapons. It did not rule out the possibility, however, that it would respond in this way to our procurement of defensive systems. Perhaps most interesting, it did not contain the usual Soviet assertion that a Soviet defense already existed.

The possibility of a race in the procurement of antiballistic missiles is conceded; the implementation of general and complete disarmament is held out as an alternative to the procurement race. If such progress is put off "indefinitely," while the means of nuclear attack are built up, then a peace-loving state could not forgo the creation of its own defense.

All in all, this Soviet approach is a considerable step forward over other Soviet positions. Although it denies most of the Western premises at least once, it also concedes most of them at one time or another, and it obviously understands them.

A second Soviet scientist, Academician V. Emelyanov, also

devoted some space to this topic in an interesting paper, "What Scientists Say," in *New Times*. Most of the paper is devoted to conversations that Emelyanov had with Americans.

In these conversations, one American says that antimissile systems will not work and goes on to add that "if the whole thing is taken over by Big Business, arms spending will grow to monstrous proportions." Emelyanov's self-quoted remarks show him to be fiercely skeptical of the possibility of avoiding defense. But comments interspersed into the reported conversation say approvingly:

> The problem of anti-missile missiles has been the cause of much concern among the American scientists. If Big Business comes into the picture it will be hard to stop their production. For it is a profitable business and no capitalist is likely to forfeit his profits.

It is possible, therefore, that Soviet spokesmen may become sober and responsible in their statements on ballistic missile defense. Premier Khrushchev referred to the Soviet ability to hit a "fly in the sky," but the days for such words from Soviet leaders may be over. Spokesmen such as Marshal Sokolovskii continue to say: "We have successfully solved the complex and extremely important problem of intercepting and destroying enemy rockets in flight." [74] But in February 1965, an editorial in *Kommunist* declared that forces in the United States "want to exhaust the Soviet Union economically by imposing a new arms race on Moscow." [75] These apprehensions may well inhibit Soviet statements and actions that would encourage such forces.

BOMBER DISARMAMENT:
UNDERLYING CONSIDERATIONS, 1964

Introduction

THIS CHAPTER deals with bomber disarmament as a partial measure that might be agreed upon by the two major powers in the absence of more general progress toward disarmament.

The conclusions are simple and can be summarized here. The U.S. proposal for reciprocal destruction of obsolescent B-47's and outdated Soviet Badgers does not go far enough.* Such an agreement might well prevent further bomber disarmament for political reasons and would, from a strategic point of view, do little more than would result from a few more years of obsolescence. On the other hand, the Soviet suggestion that all airforce bombers throughout the world should be destroyed seems — if taken literally — to be both ill-defined and unworkable.† This chapter proposes instead something that is likely to be desirable on strategic grounds, although it may be politically infeasible either here or in the

---

* William C. Foster, Director of the U.S. Arms Control and Disarmament Agency, and Secretary of State Dean Rusk broached this possibility informally to Soviet officials on the occasion of the signing of the Test Ban in Moscow.[1]

† The Soviet proposal was contained in a memorandum presented to the Eighteen Nation Disarmament Conference on January 29, 1964. The Soviet Union has since suggested that there is a possibility of "agreeing to start with the major powers," has promised to be "flexible" in negotiating, and has indicated that it will come forward with a series of proposals.[2]

Soviet Union. Both sides might simply phase out (and destroy) B-47's and Badgers and begin proportional (heavy) bomber disarmament by phasing out (and destroying) Soviet Bears and Bisons along with U.S. B-52's over the next few years. The U.S. case for heavy-bomber dismantlement is surprisingly strong. It would not only eliminate the Soviet bomber threat, but it would also free missiles now tied down by the need to target Soviet bomber bases and air defense installations. Savings would result from smaller air defense efforts and from the elimination of bomber maintenance costs. And bombers are playing an ever more marginal role in U.S. strategy — hence their dismantlement is not a great loss.*

U.S. Bombers and Soviet Air Defenses

Composition of the U.S. Bomber Force

The United States has several thousand planes capable of dropping nuclear weapons. Since very small tactical nuclear weapons exist, almost any plane could in principle deliver a nuclear weapon if no penetration or range problems existed. Moreover, carrier- and European-based fighter-bombers carrying nuclear weapons could reach targets at varying distances within the Soviet Union. With the procurement of the F-111

---

* As of late 1965, some of the U.S. B-52's are being used for conventional attacks in South Vietnam against areas under Viet Cong control. This and related uses of B-52's for conventional attacks (such as for bombing China, if need be) are of controversial utility. For those who are persuaded of their merit, the following further arguments for dismantlement of bombers should be considered. First, bilateral destruction of heavy bombers would preclude analogous Soviet actions in support of North Vietnam or China. Second, the agreement itself might influence Soviet ability and willingness to push for a termination of the war in Vietnam. Third, other aircraft might substitute for the B-52's (unless one assumes that their maintenance is required for strategic purposes, which this chapter rejects, the costs of using B-52's in Vietnam are very high). Fourth, a limited number of B-52's might be retained, for example, 200 instead of 700.

It should also be noted as this book goes to press, that the B-47's are no longer in the operational inventory. This has little effect on the argument, which can refer to destruction of mothballed B-47's instead.

(TFX), the distinction between fighters and strategic bombers will be still further clouded. This plane will be capable of flying to Europe without refueling. It is known to have a non-stop ferry range of 3,300 miles and a bomb load capability of 10,000 lb.[3] It will cost "less than $3 or 3½ million per plane," according to Harold Brown, Director of Defense Research and Engineering.[4] It will be capable of aerial refueling.

There is little likelihood of eliminating these tactical bomber capabilities from the U.S. arsenal in any agreement that does not simultaneously have far-reaching implications for many other weapon systems. Such planes are designed for limited war, particularly for limited war in Europe. There is relatively little uncertainty in the Department of Defense concerning their utility. This is in sharp contrast to the controversy over strategic aircraft. For instance, Dr. Brown testified:

> In the case of tactical aircraft, Senator Thurmond, I think that the need will continue, so far or as far forward as I can see, 10 years, 20 years, indefinitely.
> For strategic aircraft it is harder to say. I am pretty sure the strategic aircraft will be important and useful as bombardment vehicles for at least another 5 years. They may be important for another 10 years, but I am not so sure about what happens then or after then.[5]

Therefore, while it is highly likely that tactical aircraft would be treated in detail in a general disarmament agreement, it seems equally clear that any partial measures or first steps that are to involve bombers *alone* should emphasize strategic aircraft.

As of 1964, the U.S. force of strategic bombers fell into three fleets:

1. About 630 subsonic B-52 (Stratofortress) heavy bombers. These planes have a best range of 10,000–12,500 miles and are capable of aerial refueling. Some carry only multimegaton free-fall bombs, but others, alternatively or in addition, carry two Hound Dog (4 megaton) missiles capable of traveling a distance of about 600 miles (gross weight: 450,000–488,000 lb;

typical performance: 600 mph at 50,000 ft). These planes became operational in the period 1955–1962.

2. About 700 subsonic B-47 (Stratojet) medium bombers. These planes can be refueled in flight. They have a best range of 3,200 miles (gross weight: 200,000 lb; typical performance: 600 mph at 40,000 ft). These planes became operational in the period 1952–1957.

3. About 80 supersonic B-58 (Hustler) medium bombers. These planes can be refueled in flight and have a range of more than 5,000 miles at their cruising speed (gross weight: 160,000 lb; for short distances they can travel at twice the speed of sound. These planes became operational in 1960.[6]

The B-52 subsonic heavy bombers make up the largest and the most important element in the strategic bomber force. A B-52 can fly from the United States to the Soviet heartland with a 10,000-pound bomb load and return without refueling.[7] These bombers are *not* being phased out of the existing force, and decline in their numbers projected by the Defense Department for the period 1964–1968 is based on expectations of attrition. In all, 744 of these aircraft have been procured. No further procurement is planned, and it is estimated that 630 will be in the force in 1968.[8] (Since there are 45 planes in a wing, this represents 14 wings of B-52's.) However, the last B-52 was procured in 1962, and the production lines have been closed down. There are no serious advocates of further procurement of B-52's, although there is some uncertainty concerning their expected lifetime. For instance, the Air Force Chief of Staff was asked how long the B-58's and B-52's could be kept in operation. He replied:

> This is very difficult to answer . . . ; everyone assumes that these airplanes are going to go on indefinitely, that we will be able to fly them indefinitely. This may not be the case. They may wear out sooner than we think they are going to wear out.
>
> There is a lot that we don't know about fatigue in these modern high-performance airplanes. So this bothers me, that we may have to discard these airplanes sooner than we think.[9]

Part of the problem relates to the difficulties that the airplanes are expected to have in penetrating Soviet defenses, should war occur. Expensive modifications (retrofitting) in the B-52 structures have been undertaken in anticipation of these problems. Through 1964, retrofitting had already cost $1.6 billion, with an additional $306 million requested for the fiscal year 1965.

The aging B-47's are gradually being phased out of service on a schedule that has not changed since fiscal year 1962. The schedule called for the last B-47 to leave active service in 1966. In early 1964, there were still about 700 such planes in the operational force.

The B-58 bombers are not being phased out of the force, but no more are likely to be procured. It is estimated that, as a result of attrition, there will be 72 B-58's in the force in 1968. These bombers have had problems of reliability, as evidently all bombers do. For example, in 1955, three years after the first procurement of B-47's, they had an in-commission rate of only 65 percent.[10] Secretary McNamara recalls being at Omaha on a day when "almost literally all of our B-58 bombers were unavailable for alert status because of mechanical failures." Later testimony indicates that these reliability problems have eased. But the unit cost of B-58 bombers has been high ($10 to $12 million), and since B-58's have a smaller bomb-load capability and shorter range than a B-52, they are not especially favored.[11] The generals LeMay, Power, and White would all prefer to buy additional B-52's rather than B-58's, and Secretary of Defense McNamara concurs with this judgment.[12]

U.S. Attitudes Toward Bombers

One school of opinion in the United States is concerned that the manned bomber will disappear, and believes that a new fleet of bombers would be useful. In part this belief seems to stem from a conservative view of what constitutes utility in strategic weapons. For instance, General Maxwell Taylor explained in 1959 that the other Joint Chiefs did not agree with him that we then had "an excess number of strategic weapons and weapons systems in the atomic retaliatory force." They felt, according to him, that "there are so many incalculable factors that you can never overinsure in this field." [13]

But the urge to maintain bombers also arises from other factors, not all of which are especially subject to strategic analysis. Bombers are tried and true, but missiles are not, in the eyes of their supporters. Often there are evident personal attachments to bombers. The top Air Force generals and even some of the senators most concerned about bombers have had long personal experience in flying or directing them. Their concern is associated almost invariably with the "flexibility" that would be lost if there were no manned strategic system. Evidently any manned system will do, no matter what its purpose.*

Perhaps a more fundamental obstacle to bomber disarmament, however, lies in the accumulated influence of the Strategic Air Command (SAC) and its bomber forces as a result of its prime responsibility for deterrence during the fifties. For instance, in *On Thermonuclear War*, Herman Kahn compares the British Empire's dependence on the British fleet with the U.S. dependence on the SAC bomber fleet.[15] Those who once molded this all-important force are naturally reluctant to see it disbanded. And the apparent efficiency of the Strategic Air Command officers in discharging their responsibilities has, over the years, heightened their influence both in Con-

---

* Secretary of the Air Force Eugene Zuckert testified: "We believe that as the general [LeMay] has pointed out, that our proper strategic posture demands some kind of a manned system because of the flexibility it gives you. If the B-70 proves to be a blind alley for any reason, we have to explore all the other methods because we have to come up with a manned system, in our opinion." He then referred to B-70 (a 2,000-mph supersonic bomber devoted to reconnaissance), Dromedary (a long-endurance, large, slow airplane designed to fly up to 48 hours, but not to penetrate defenses at all), and a low-altitude penetrator.[14]

gress and elsewhere. This only begins to indicate the political obstacles to bomber disarmament.

The Strategic Role of U.S. Bombers

The strategic role of our bombers is severely limited by four characteristics. Bombers are vulnerable on the ground, slow to target, of uncertain penetration capability, and they must be committed at a very early stage in a war.

First, the bomber force cannot be depended upon for a high rate of survival from a surprise enemy attack because of its great vulnerability on the ground. In normal periods, in order to minimize this vulnerability, half of the SAC bomber force is maintained on a fifteen-minute ground alert with a small number on airborne alert. The fifteen-minute warning is supposed to be provided by BMEWS (Ballistic Missile Early Warning System) stations in Clear, Alaska, Thule, Greenland, and Fylingdales, Great Britain.[16] Such notice would not be given if missiles were fired over the Antarctic — a widely discussed possibility that was mentioned by Premier Khrushchev (but which would be expensive in accuracy and in pay load) — or if submarine-launched missiles were used. Similarly, the Cuban missiles would have "outflanked" the warning system.*

The submarine-launched missiles, especially, pose a potential threat to ground-based bombers. Secretary McNamara believes that "toward the latter part of this decade . . . we must anticipate that submarine-launched missiles or others coming with very little, if any, warning will very probably destroy the majority of aircraft on the ground." [17]

Against such problems the Department of Defense has maintained the capability to fly one-eighth of the B-52 force

* If there had been no heavy bombers in the U.S. force, the strategic concern over Soviet missiles in Cuba would have been diminished since the missiles would have had no highly profitable targets. This indicates one of the ways in which bomber disarmament will have a stabilizing effect.

on airborne alert for about one year. (The Air Force had asked for one-fourth.)[18] And the number of SAC bases has steadily grown in number. SAC now presents 55 domestic air-base targets and 13 foreign targets, and, in times of immediate emergency, the force can be dispersed to 100 fields.*

Even after such dispersal, however, SAC would still provide a first-priority target. Consider, for instance, the situation in 1964. General Maurice Preston testified in 1960 that SAC's ultimate goal was one squadron (one-third of a wing of 45 bombers) of B-52's per base and one wing of B-47's per base. Since, in 1964 figures, there are about 15 wings of B-47's remaining (the 700 planes noted earlier), 42 squadrons of B-52's (the 14 wings noted earlier), and about 6 squadrons of B-58's (the 80 planes noted earlier), this would require 63 bases. Since the 55 domestic and 13 foreign bases referred to exceed this number, the goal has evidently been effectively achieved. Nevertheless, the "bonus" to enemy attack that catches the bombers on their bases would be somewhere between 15 to 1 (heavy-bomber bases) and 45 to 1 (medium-bomber bases), even assuming that the bombers carry nothing more than the single H-bomb that Secretary McNamara indicated would destroy every bomber on its base.[20] With 100 fields, the average bonus would be at least 14 to 1 since there are about 1,400 bombers. It should be emphasized that the bombers with their expected BMEWS warning would not represent an adequate deterrent in the absence of protected missile systems. In this sense, they do not provide adequate backup protection for a situation in which our missiles could be successfully attacked.

---

* Such dispersal plans were described to Congress as far back as 1956.

"*Colonel Nichols:* Now we have a dispersal plan in SAC. It works like this: Each one of our bases, let's take the base at Fairchild, we have two wings there, each wing will have a plan and the plan will have the aircraft say take off from Fairchild and come down to these green areas. They are what we call orbit areas.

"At that position the aircraft will circle. He will await then instructions from his home base if it is not destroyed or from another source if his home base is destroyed, and then he will either land at what we call our dispersal base or go back to Fairchild, depending on what he is told." [19]

The second limitation of bombers is that they are slow to target. If a bomber has a top speed of 500 mph and must travel 2,000, 4,000, or 6,000 miles, it will take 4, 8, or 12 hours to reach its target. Several different missile salvos can take place in this time. This means that bombers are especially unsuited to the "damage-limiting" strategy advocated by the Department of Defense. Only a "very, very, very, low percentage" of the effective forces will be bombers, despite the fact that they are capable of carrying a much larger number of megatons than are existing missiles. This was discussed by Secretary McNamara:

> *Secretary McNamara:* What percentage of the force that destroys the Soviet Union is delivered by bombers? The answer to that is a very, very, low percentage. . . .
>
> *Mr. Ford:* If that is the case . . . why do you keep bombers in the force at all until 1968?
>
> *Secretary McNamara:* Because they add some insurance and because certain targets may be more effectively destroyed by bombers assuming the bomber can get there before the targets have been launched against the United States, *and that is quite an assumption.*[21] (Italics added.)

The third limiting characteristic of bombers is a "substantial range between the optimistic and pessimistic estimates" of the number that will penetrate the Soviet air defenses. (This uncertainty is itself undesirable since we should prefer to have our deterrent capability unequivocal.) And in both cases, "a higher proportion of the Minuteman force than of the B-52 force can be counted upon to reach targets in a retaliatory strike." Bombers are also rated lower in "systems dependability," by which is meant that the uncertainties associated with them are harder to estimate. Thus the Secretary of Defense has noted that "we can predict the results of a missile attack with greater confidence than those of a bomber attack." [22] The extent of these uncertainties has been indicated by General Thomas White, who asserted, a few years ago, in reference to U.S. bombers: "All might get through in one case and then there might be a great loss in another." [23]

Speaking more generally of free-fall bombing, the Secretary of Defense termed it "nearly impossible" by the end of the sixties.* This means that planes would have to be dependent upon their own guided missiles which would permit an attack from a distance. But a missile of this type, Secretary Mc-Namara noted in canceling one (the Skybolt),

> . . . could not make a worthwhile contribution to our strategic capability since it would combine the disadvantages of the bomber with those of the missile. It would have the bomber's disadvantages of being soft and concentrated and relatively vulnerable on the ground and the bomber's slow time to target. But it would not have the bomber's advantageous payload and accuracy, nor would it have the advantages usually associated with a manned system. It would have the lower payload and poorer accuracy of the missile. . . .[25]

The Secretary of Defense indicates as a fourth limitation that bombers must be "committed . . . very early" in a war and cannot be used "in a controlled and deliberate way." [26] In particular, the widely used argument that bombers can be "recalled" is quite misleading: invulnerably based missiles do not need to be fired in advance and hence the ability to be recalled is not an issue with them. Furthermore, recalling bombers is dangerous and difficult. They are not, in fact, very "recallable." The recalled fleet has tired, if not exhausted, crews, and somewhere in the system there must be low, if not empty, fuel tanks. If the recall is a mistake, the bombers may have been effectively neutralized. Bombers are, for this reason, not even very capable of accepting an enemy surrender —

---

* "*Secretary McNamara:* . . . we will be in serious difficulty by the end of the decade if at that point our strategic force is dependent upon free-fall bombs as the primary weapon of attack, because no one in a responsible position at the Pentagon that I am aware of believes that free-fall bombs can be placed over the prime targets in the Soviet Union at the end of this decade.

"*Senator Stennis:* Why?

"*Secretary McNamara:* Because by that time the air defense systems of the Soviet Union will be such as to make it nearly impossible for an airplane to advance to a position over the target so that it would be in position to launch free-fall bombs against that target." [24]

the risk of recalling them to vulnerable bases (if there were no missiles) could make it impossible. Most important, the time for recall is limited. Congress has been told that civilian decision makers would have to make some (recalling) decision within one and a half hours of the time the bomber force was launched toward its targets.[27] (Obviously this does not refer to an airborne alert which might be maintained for relatively long periods.)

As a result of these restrictions, the utility of bombers is limited to certain special uses as "supplementary devices to the main force." * What are these supplementary uses? *Air Force and Space Digest* complained that

> No mention is [being] made of the position that manned strategic aircraft greatly enhance operational flexibility by allowing: recall of an attack; unmistakable displays of resolve, through stepped-up airborne alerts and large-scale maneuvers, such as were used in the Cuban crisis; wartime assessment of target damage; location and destruction of mobile targets; a close matching of the weapon to the target; and, when the occasion calls for it, the use of very-high-yield warheads.[29]

We have discussed recall of an attack. The threatening nature of a fleet of bombers on airborne alert is a more plausible but still quite dubious consideration. It has received wide attention.† In answer to a written question from Senator Margaret Chase Smith, Secretary McNamara said that the SAC bomber

---

* This comment of the Secretary of Defense was reinforced by the assertion that "There is no plan in the Air Force that I know of, or no thought of any plan to substitute air launch for sea and land launch for the great bulk of the megatonnage." [28]

† "*Senator Cannon:* When we get to the point that we are practically phased out without manned bombers under our present program we would have no method of making a visible display of strength insofar as SAC's posture is concerned, would we?

"*General LeMay:* With missiles you cannot do anything except to say, 'I will shoot my missiles,' that is all.

"*Senator Cannon:* You cannot very well take a picture of a man with his thumb about 6 inches above the trigger and say, 'He is going to put it on down if you don't do such and such.' That doesn't give you much of a bargaining point, does it?

"*General LeMay:* That is correct." [30]

fleet's advanced state of readiness during the Cuban crisis was meant both "to avoid the possibility of surprise" and to "impress upon the Soviets our seriousness and determination." [31] In this latter effort it was presumably successful, although this was most clearly only one element among other considerations. In speaking to the Supreme Soviet of the U.S.S.R., Chairman Khrushchev reported on the Cuban crisis as follows:

> Events developed at a swift pace. The American command put all its armed forces, including troops stationed in Europe as well as the Sixth Fleet, in the Mediterranean, and the Seventh Fleet based in the Taiwan area, in a state of complete combat readiness. Several paratroop, infantry and armored divisions, numbering some 100,000 men, were allocated for the attack on Cuba alone. In addition, 183 warships, with 85,000 sailors on board, were moved toward the shores of Cuba. Several thousand warplanes were to cover the landing on Cuba. About 20% of all U.S. Strategic Air Command planes carrying atomic and hydrogen bombs, were kept aloft around the clock. Reserves were called up. [32]

While analysts who emphasize air power tend to argue that the "20 per cent of SAC" was an important consideration leading to Soviet concessions, it is obviously impossible for anyone to say — perhaps even for Premier Khrushchev himself. It should be noted, however, that Soviet attitudes toward such displays of force are somewhat peculiar from an American analyst's point of view. For instance, during the Paris Summit Conference in 1960, Secretary of Defense Thomas S. Gates ordered the Joint Chiefs to institute an alert. This alert involved both the Continental Air Defense Command and the Strategic Air Command. It lasted for seven hours and was said to be justified by the need to check the ability of the President, while abroad, to keep in touch with U.S. forces. [33] (Nevertheless the action seems to have been most provocative. President Eisenhower argued that international negotiations had sometimes been used to conceal preparations for a surprise attack. This tends only to reinforce the seriousness of his act.) The reaction of American strategists, had they been in policy-making positions in the Soviet Union, would have been to put Soviet forces on alert to decrease Soviet vulnerability. Instead, at a Paris press conference, Malinovsky volunteered: "We have not declared any military alert." And Khrushchev added: "Correct. We have not declared an alert and will not declare one. Our nerves are strong." [34]

Whatever the psychological impact of airborne bombers, it can hardly fail to decline rapidly. Our bombers, even from airborne alert stations, can hardly be within one half hour of their targets as our missiles are at all times.* Hence they do not add significantly to whatever threat of surprise attack exists. And even the implied threat deliberately to initiate a nuclear war will wear very thin in the face of the increasing invulnerability of Soviet forces.

The merits of most of the remaining arguments for bombers — wartime assessment of target damage, location and destruction of mobile targets, use of very-high-yield warheads, and so on — depend in part on U.S. strategy and in part on a host of cost-effectiveness considerations. The present strategy is a "damage-limiting" one.† The intention is to preserve the option of striking at many Soviet forces, after being attacked ourselves, so as to limit the size of a follow-on attack. Secretary McNamara argues, without giving details, that "comprehensive studies" show "under a wide variety of circumstances . . . forces in excess of those needed simply to destroy Soviet cities could significantly reduce damage to the U.S. and Western Europe." It can be assumed that the studies are based, in particular, on the assumption that a nuclear war will be fought to a finish. (For instance, the Secretary intends to attack weapon *storage* sites with bombers. This "limits" damage only if the war is not likely to be terminated quickly.) On

---

* Congressman George Mahon, hypothesizing a situation in which war occurred after the bombers were approaching their targets, suggested that "probably the missile would hit its target before the bomber." General Curtis LeMay replied: "Under most circumstances, yes." [35]

† "Thus, a 'damage-limiting' strategy appears to be the most practical and effective course for us to follow. Such a strategy requires a force considerably larger than would be needed for a limited 'cities only'

the assumption that the Soviet Union achieves secure second-strike capabilities — a widely heralded expectation — these studies will become outmoded. The emphasis must then turn, in one way or another, to "war-termination strategies." If our enemy has secure second-strike forces, we will not be able to justify plans to eliminate quickly the residual forces of an aggressor. The tendency to do so now is reinforced by Soviet relative weakness, which permits the Secretary of Defense to state that "today, following a surprise attack on us, we would still have the power to respond with overwhelming force, and *they would not then have the capability of a further strike.*" [37] (Italics added.)

When the Soviet Union can retain the "capability of a further strike," two different tendencies will discourage the use of bombers even if they exist. First, it will become relatively less likely that a Soviet attack would include American cities — since the Soviets would want and be able to hold these cities hostage with their secure force. (Our own policy takes this form.)* Hence an unrestrained U.S. response to attack would not be in order. But bombers are difficult to use in a restrained fashion primarily because of penetration problems.

Second, there would be far less motivation to maintain the capability for such "bitter end" activities as assessment of target damage, destruction of weapon sites, location and destruction of mobile missiles, use of very-high-yield weapons, and so on.

Finally, there is the question of a "proper mix" in our offensive weapons. While such a mix is highly desirable, it is in-

---

strategy. While there are still some differences of judgment on just how large such a force should be, there is general agreement that it should be large enough to ensure the destruction, singly or in combination, of the Soviet Union, Communist China, and the Communist satellites as national societies, under the worst possible circumstances of war outbreak that can reasonably be postulated, and, in addition, to destroy their warmaking capability so as to limit, to the extent practicable, damage to this country and to our Allies." (Secretary McNamara) [36]

* See Secretary McNamara's Ann Arbor speech: *The New York Times,* June 17, 1962.

evitably going to be a mix of missiles in the view of the Secretary of Defense.* But missile-carrying bombers do not provide an especially good way to vary our missiles systems, for the reasons given previously.

In short, I believe that clearly foreshadowed changes in defense thinking will further reduce the utility of bombers, as Soviet second-strike capability increases. But in any case, it is clear that bombers are, by far, the most expendable portion of the strategic forces, whether judged by existing or anticipated doctrine. The bombers are simply insurance of a highly generalized kind. They have some unusual properties, which are not especially impressive. None of these calls for the approximately 700 bombers that will be in the force even after the B-47's have been phased out. From a strategic point of view, the United States should definitely be asking, "What can we get in return for dismantling our bombers?"

Future Manned Bombers

Among the considerations involved in bomber disarmament negotiations will be the likelihood that the United States will wish to procure a new manned bomber or more bombers of an existing type. This likelihood is small if it refers to a new type of bomber procured in large numbers, but not so small if the bomber is to be procured in relatively small numbers — for instance, three. Already in 1963 journalists were reporting that "even the Air Force is said to be losing faith" in the

* "I do not believe it is proper to infer . . . that I am sponsoring for all time a mix that includes missiles and manned bombers launching gravity bombs. Rather, I am talking about a mix of systems. It could be a mix of missile systems. As a matter of fact, I believe it will have to be a mix of missile systems under any circumstances, each system with characteristics different from the other systems and, therefore, adding in total to the problem of the defense." Elsewhere he remarked: "No other airborne vehicle that I have heard described for us in the 1970's depends on anything other than a missile for its striking power. So it seems to me that all of the technical developments point to the use of missiles, and it is simply a question of what kind of missile and how many and where they should be located." [38]

manned bomber furthest along in development, the B-70.*

B-70's were due to be produced for about $50 million each. For each such plane, it would be possible to procure and install about 12 Minutemen in hardened silos. Similarly, a wing of 45 B-52's procured and operated for 5 years costs at least as much (well over $1 billion) as 250 hardened and dispersed Minutemen.[40] This illustrates the unfavorable cost effectiveness of new or existing expensive bombers and emphasizes how unlikely it is that they will be procured in large numbers. No new procurement of any such bombers is now planned.

In addition to the low-level penetrator (LAMP) noted earlier, there is the Dromedary. It is also in too early a stage of development to be of concern in any disarmament negotiations. After he described its long endurance, slow speed, and stand-off characteristics, General LeMay was asked whether we had not been studying this aircraft "for at least a decade." He admitted that it had been discussed "off and on" but argued that the Air Force was taking "another look . . . because of what has been brought about by the cancellation of the B-70." However, this plane was to stand off and fire "14 to 17" improved Hound Dog missiles from as much as 1,000 miles away.[41] Probably the cancellation of Skybolt has discouraged the development of the required missile.

In short, it seems very unlikely that large numbers of any manned bomber will be procured under the Johnson administration.† However, there is always the possibility of very substantial changes in technology which, when coupled with a specific use for a bomber, could make its procurement feasible.

---

* See Jack Raymond, "New Strategic Bomber Gains Favor in Pentagon," *The New York Times*, December 26, 1963. The *new* strategic bomber referred to is a low-level penetrator, but it developed in a later column that the "favor" which it had gained was simply a $5-million research contract. This plane is apparently the LAMP (Low Altitude Manned Penetration aircraft) designed to fly at supersonic speed a few hundred feet off the ground below the beams of defensive radar.[39]

† Other administrations might well be different. Barry Goldwater said that one reason he was running for President was to maintain a proper "mix" of bombers and missiles.[42]

Such advances might be in variable-sweep wings, engine developments, penetration aids, and laminar-flow control. (The last is a method of changing the lift/drag ratio of aircraft and permits substantial reductions in size for fixed performance.)[43]

Nevertheless, this having been said, it is relatively feasible on technological grounds to argue for, or tacitly accede to, a cutoff in the production of "fleets" of new bombers. Such a cutoff would not be very restricting with present technological expectations.

Soviet Air Defenses

Soviet defenses have been characterized as "tremendously increased" in effectiveness since 1960. They are thought to include both high-altitude (SAM-II's) and low-altitude (SAM-III's) surface-to-air interceptor missiles around key points in Russia. The number of persons engaged in air defense activities is thought to be very large. In 1956, there were 550,000 people in Soviet air defense, or about four times the number engaged in U.S. defenses at that time.[44]

It is impossible, but perhaps unnecessary, to be very precise about the extent and costs of Soviet air defenses. There would apparently be great savings in defense costs to the Soviet Union if all U.S. bombers could be dismantled in a disarmament agreement. More limited agreements, such as a trade of Badgers for B-47's, would *not* permit this saving. And, to the extent that the Soviet Union intends to maintain air defenses against a growing French, and possible future German, threat, the savings would also be diminished. However, only a part of the present Soviet air defense operation would probably be necessary as a defense against French bombers. For instance, force targets, of whatever nature, and cities deep in the Soviet Union might not need protection if the U.S. bomber threat were removed. (We assume that British bomber disarmament would be part of any U.S.-Soviet agreement to scrap all strategic bombers.)

Soviet Bombers and U.S. Air Defenses

Composition of the Soviet Bomber Force

As is the case with the United States, a great many Soviet aircraft could carry nuclear weapons of one kind or another for varying distances. Again, it seems appropriate, in considering bomber disarmament as a separate measure, to restrict our attention to the Soviet strategic bomber force. This is thought to consist of the following:[45]

1. Seventy turbo-prop Bears (Tu-20), range about 7,000–8,000 miles, capable of carrying two short-range air-to-ground missiles or one large winged missile with range about 1,000 miles (gross weight: 330,000 lb; maximum speed: 580 mph). Became operational in 1956.

2. The supersonic delta-wing 4-jet Bounder, not now in production, a possible replacement for Bison (gross weight: 300,000 lb; maximum speed: 700 mph).

3. One hundred and twenty 4-jet Bisons (M-4), range about 6,000 miles, equipped for aerial refueling, capable of carrying a winged missile (gross weight: 250,000 lb; maximum speed: 600 mph). Became operational in 1956.

4. An emerging twin-engined supersonic medium bomber, Blinder, similar to the U.S. B-58, capable of aerial refueling, with a long-range air-to-ground missile. Possibly a strike/reconnaissance aircraft (gross weight: 150,000 lb; maximum speed: 1,000–1,030 mph). Became operational in 1962.

5. One thousand twin-jet medium-bomber Badgers (Tu-16), range about 3,500 miles, capable of carrying a single air-to-ground missile like the U.S. Hound Dog with range about 450 miles (gross weight: 150,000 lb; maximum speed: 610 mph). Became operational in 1955.

The Secretary of Defense has announced that "latest national intelligence estimates indicate there will be a decline in the Soviet bomber force and one far earlier than a decline in our force." [46] The Defense Department has also estimated the bombers which the Soviets "could place over this country, on two-way missions," as "no more than approximately 120 heavy bombers plus perhaps an additional 150 medium bombers, the targets for which would be limited to Alaska and the northwest areas of the United States." [47] Discussion of *two-way* missions indicates a doctrinal lag and underestimates Soviet capabilities for a first strike.

Soviet Attitudes Toward Bombers

Khrushchev stated, with the launching of Sputnik in 1957, that the era of the bomber had passed and that bombers were in the "twilight of their existence." By 1960, he stated, "Almost the entire military air force is being replaced by missiles," and he suggested that probably he would "further reduce and even discontinue the production of bombers and other obsolete equipment." During this period, the Soviet Union was, or was thought to be, ahead in missile capabilities and behind in bombers. With the development of Soviet stand-off, air-to-surface missiles, there was renewed support for the Soviet Air Force, which Khrushchev said the Soviet Union was "continuing to develop and improve." Some Soviet Air Force spokesmen — First Deputy Commander of the Soviet Air Force, Air Marshal S. Rudenko, and A. Tupolev, the Soviet aircraft designer — have spoken of the bomber in much the same terms used by U.S. Air Force spokesmen.[48]

Marshal Sokolovskii's *Military Strategy* takes a position very similar to that of our own Department of Defense. While conceding that long-range bombers are "rapidly yielding first place" to ballistic missiles, it asserts that this replacement may take "a long time" and that aircraft have not yet "completely exhausted their combat potential." Reference is made to specific missions, such as striking mobile targets, and so on.[49]

The Strategic Role of Soviet Bombers

In order to appreciate the strategic role of Soviet bombers, it is necessary to understand the general Soviet strategic posture as it has emerged over the years. This posture is exceedingly defensive in orientation — surprisingly so to many American analysts. There are various possible reasons for this of a technical, social, political, economic, bureaucratic, or other nature. They need not concern us here. But some history is appropriate.

When the United States had the only significant strategic capability, it threatened massive retaliation and built forces that were quite capable of accomplishing the destruction of the Soviet Union whether or not such an action was preceded by Soviet provocation.* Part of the Soviet response was to emphasize defenses. General LeMay testified that "they are spending a greater portion of their resources by far than we are on defenses." [51] Another part of the response was, of course, to procure strategic retaliatory forces. In fact, it was feared, especially during the missile-gap period, that the Soviet procurement of missiles would be more than sufficient to attack simultaneously all U.S. strategic weapons. Concern among strategists was genuine. For example, the present U.S. preponderance of strategic forces is precisely the reverse of the situation repeatedly anticipated in Herman Kahn's *On Thermonuclear War*. This book was written in 1959 after the author had worked for a decade at the RAND Corporation.

---

* In answer to questions which seemed to reflect on Air Force capabilities by emphasizing American casualties in a general war, General LeMay testified, somewhat petulantly: "I wish that there was some way, Mr. Chairman, I could guarantee fighting a war without getting anyone killed on our side. Unfortunately, I cannot do that at this time. There was a time when I was commanding SAC that I think we could have retaliated with the strength we then had and destroyed the greater part of Russia and the loss rate would have been the loss we would have suffered from the normal accident rate of that many hours' flying time. This situation no longer exists because they have built up their defenses and they have an atomic capability of their own." [50]

The size of the anticipated gap was enormous. The number of Soviet missiles thought to be in existence in mid-1961 was only 3½ per cent of the number that had been anticipated two years earlier for that same date. Bomber misjudgments were only slightly less dramatic.[52]

Very large numbers of relatively invulnerable missiles were ordered. Hence, when Soviet procurement ceased to be as large as anticipated, the Soviet Union's capability for attacking our enlarged forces became extremely ineffective. The U.S. capability for striking Soviet weapons became significant, however, and, as has been noted, remains sufficiently large to respond to a Soviet attack in such a way that, theoretically, no *further* Soviet attacks would be possible. (Obviously this statement is an approximation.) This "damage-limiting" capability is not shared by the Soviet Union.* Instead Soviet spokesmen emphasize 100-megaton bombs in relatively small numbers. These are better suited for an attack on urban areas than on military targets.

As a result of these considerations, the role of bombers in Soviet strategy seems to be even smaller than the role of bombers in our own strategic posture. In the first place, the relatively great capability of the United States to strike vulnerably based bombers decreases the utility of such forces to the Soviet Union. Second, the fact that the Soviet Union is not in a position to attack U.S. forces effectively at any stage in a nuclear war sharply diminishes "special purpose" reasons for retaining bombers. For instance, if the Soviet forces are insufficiently large to attack more than a small percentage of our Minutemen, what need is there for Soviet strategic reconnaissance? Similarly, a capability for attacks on U.S. land-based mobile missiles — of which there are none at this time — be-

* Secretary McNamara has said that "the relative numbers and survivability of U.S. strategic forces would permit us to retaliate against all the urgent Soviet military targets that are subject to attack, thus contributing to the limitation of damage to ourselves and our allies. . . . [This] damage-limiting capability of our numerically superior forces is, I believe, well worth its incremental cost. It is a capability to which the smaller forces of the Soviet Union could not realistically aspire."[53]

comes relatively pointless if a large number of other types of forces cannot be attacked.

These conclusions indicate that bomber disarmament of a suitably balanced kind should be quite advantageous to the Soviet Union.

Future Manned Bombers

There seems to be little public evidence of a new Soviet bomber, except for Blinder, which is thought to be a replacement for Badger.[54] However, information on Soviet research and development plans is obviously difficult, if not impossible, to come by. Hence no firm conclusions can be reached.

U.S. Air Defenses

In assessing the strategic value of Soviet bombers, the effectiveness of U.S. defenses against bombers must be considered. We should also consider those costs of maintaining defenses that might be saved under a bomber agreement.

As far as effectiveness is concerned, U.S. bomber defenses cannot be assessed unless there is a war. They were not built with a clear notion of expected effectiveness. For instance, in 1956, General Partridge, then Commander in Chief, Continental Air Defense Command, testified as follows:

> *Senator Symington:* Do you think you could knock down 50 percent of the attacking force?
>
> *General Partridge:* I would not hazard a guess.
>
> *Senator Symington:* 75?
>
> *General Partridge:* The way to evaluate our air-defense system is to try to think of it as insurance which you carry for years and hope the house will not burn down.

> .   .   .   .

> *Senator Symington:* You just don't know what you could do?
>
> *General Partridge:* No, Sir; I have no basis on which to guess, but. . . . There is a terrific difference to the enemy between

operating against some defenses and operating against no defenses.

If the enemy knows that we have no defenses, he can come in, cruise around the country, go anywhere he wants to, bomb one airplane at a time. If he does not like one approach, he can go around and make another one. He could use his fighters and just strafe up and down the streets, do anything at all.

On the other hand, if he knows we have some defenses, no matter how meager they may be, he must do many, many things which General LeMay so very effectively outlined on his chart. He must use large formations or large numbers of bombers, and he must come at night and in bad weather and so on and on and on, carry defensive weapons, perhaps carry fighters with him and so on. So his offensive capability is tremendously degraded just by the fact that there is an air defense, even if we shoot down not one bomber.[55]

The general went on to testify that it was almost impossible to get a "realistic" test of the system and that "as we build further to the North and put the sea flanks on it is going to be impossible. . . ." [56] This continues to be the case. Asked what percentage of kill our antiaircraft defenses would have, the Secretary of Defense replied that "the answer depends upon a large number of factors that are in themselves unknown." [57]

In fact the system has many inefficiencies. Herman Kahn suggested in 1960: "One way not to make a reputation as an analyst in the last five or ten years would have been to find a hole in our air defense system . . . ; people mostly think of it as being full of holes." [58] It very probably should not have been built in its present form — a form in which efforts are made to defend, essentially, the entire North American continent. And it is useful to note that this is the view of the Chairman of the Joint Chiefs of Staff, General Taylor. He suggested in 1956 that "the concept of area defense in great depth . . . has not proved feasible, in my judgment, either technically or economically." He preferred an extended "point" defense under which large urban and strategic complexes would be protected.[59] The deficiencies in our present defense should encourage attempts to negotiate bomber disarmament. At the present time, the United States plans no very strenuous efforts to improve defenses unless the Soviet Union deploys a new bomber.* Instead, the "main thrust" of our defensive efforts will be redirected to meet the rising missile threat, although so long as the Soviet Union continues to maintain a force of manned bombers capable of reaching targets in the United States, "we must continue to support a defense against them." [61] Supporting this defense costs about $2 billion each year. Not all of this could be saved even if every last Soviet intercontinental bomber were destroyed, but a fairly large proportion of it presumably could.

Third-Country Bombers

Wars involving aerial bombardment can be divided usefully into two categories. In the first category, at least one of the major powers, Communist China, the United States, or the Soviet Union, is at war. In the second category, none of these powers is directly involved. In the latter case, the conflict can be expected to involve neighboring and relatively small powers; hence, relatively small numbers of easily improvised bombers are likely to be quite suitable for bombardment. As a result, bomber disarmament is hard to define for such powers, and it is not considered further in this chapter.

Another assumption made here is that Communist China will not participate in any general dismantling of its bomber forces, because of its political posture and the fact that it has no bombers of the size discussed in this chapter. The largest bombers known to be in mainland China are Il-28 (Beagle) light bombers. Although Soviet Badgers have been sold to

---

* For instance, in discussing interceptors, Secretary McNamara stated: "We still plan to retain the existing interceptor aircraft in the force, but the number of aircraft will decline gradually because of attrition. We believe that this force will be adequate against what we presently foresee as a declining Soviet manned-bomber threat. However, if the Soviets should deploy a new long-range bomber, we would have to reconsider the size and character of our interceptor force and particularly the need for modernization." A somewhat more detailed statement was made by the Director of Defense Research and Engineering, Harold Brown. [60]

Egypt and Indonesia, apparently none were transferred to China.[62]

As a result, it seems worth considering bomber disarmament only for the United States, the Soviet Union, Britain, France, and Germany. The Federal Republic of Germany has no bombers of the size discussed here. Hence its bomber disarmament must logically await disarmament of tactical fighter-bombers.

Having made the assumption that British bomber disarmament will not become an obstacle to major-power bomber disarmament — a reasonable assumption on general political grounds — we are left with the problem of the French "Force de Frappe." This force of Mirage IV, twin-jet supersonic light-attack bombers, is supposed to grow to 22 in 1964, with another 22 delivered in 1965.* The force will hold several million Russians "hostage," assuming it is capable of penetrating Soviet air defenses: most experts agree that it can (according to Hanson Baldwin).[64]

Although the French are considering Polaris-type systems for the post-1970 period, it would be premature for them to consider even "phased" bomber disarmament schemes. Hence, without a change in French political and strategic intentions, French participation in bomber disarmament is not possible. This has, of course, far-reaching political implications for Soviet participation in a general agreement to dismantle all strategic bombers. The Soviet Union may well oppose divesting itself of types of weapons that a particular Western ally wishes to retain.† It should be emphasized, however, that there are no good *strategic* reasons for this refusal — although

---

* The planes are to be based in southwestern France, and some will be kept on air alert. The French argue specifically that an attacking Mirage IV will be detected by radar at a distance of only 1½ miles — the plane will be 100 to 300 yards above the ground — and that, at 1,500 miles per hour, a SAM-III battery will have just one, quite inadequate, second to fire at it. Other penetration aids are also envisaged.[63]

† But it is worth noting that the Mirage IV is a small 66,000-lb bomber and would not be of the size being dismantled unless and until the United States and the Soviet Union discussed tactical bomber disarmament.

there might be bargaining rationalizations. From a strategic point of view, Soviet bombers are not useful either for attack or defense against French bombers. Nor are they necessary for retaliation in response to a French bomber attack.

Conclusions

This section describes some likely effects of bomber disarmament by giving conclusions with relatively self-contained explanations. These conclusions in no case follow *directly* from the preceding material, and in all cases rest largely on the author's judgment of a variety of factors. Two different possible kinds of agreements are discussed. The first is a limited one involving the destruction of obsolescent Soviet Badgers and U.S. B-47's. The second is much more extensive and would accomplish the phasing out of long-range bombers as well.*

Two General Issues

1. *Neither limited nor extensive bomber disarmament agreements will have much direct effect on the probability of war.* Such agreements would reduce the likelihood of accidents, incidents, and unauthorized behavior, but none of these is very probable, and certainly none is very likely to cause a war on its own. Nor is reciprocal fear of surprise attack, induced by vulnerable bombers, an important possibility in the present and anticipated strategic context. However, bomber disarmament would eliminate certain kinds of fears associated with vulnerable targets — such as the "outflanking BMEWS" fears evident during the Cuban crisis. And favorable *indirect* effects

---

* The designation "long-range" is used in a technical sense defined in the 1958 Surprise Attack Conference in Geneva. It refers to aircraft with a radius of action of over 2,000 nautical miles (n.m.) and would include at least B-52's, Bisons, and Bears. Badgers and B-47's would be medium-range aircraft — those defined as having a radius of action of 750–2,000 n.m. It is not clear whether B-58's and Blinders are medium- or long-range.[65]

on the likelihood of war are quite possible, such as those that arise from the relaxation of tension.

2. *Extensive — but not limited — bomber disarmament agreements could substantially reduce destruction if war occurred.* Whether or not the total quantity of weapons that can be delivered (deliverable megatonnage) is increased or diminished after a bomber disarmament agreement depends on missile procurement and on the remaining bombers. Measured by deliverable megatonnage, extensive bomber disarmament agreements are preferable to limited agreements, all other things being equal. Limited agreements — Badgers for B-47's — would diminish deliverable megatonnage only slightly, if at all, if these planes were in fact obsolete and incapable of delivering most of their weapons. Extensive agreements would do a good deal better. However, these questions of deliverable megatonnage are less important than those of targeting and war termination. Extensive — but not limited — disarmament of bombers would remove basing or staging airfields from a military target list and hence would widen the potential separation of forces and cities. Furthermore, extensive — but not limited — bomber disarmament would substantially increase the likelihood that war could be quickly terminated, for such disarmament precludes the destabilizing possibility of committing entire fleets of bombers.

U.S. Issues

3. *A limited bomber disarmament agreement may well prevent further bomber disarmament, for domestic (and perhaps also Soviet domestic) political reasons.* It has often been stated that comprehensive agreements are no more difficult to achieve than partial agreements.* One price of the atmos-

---

* Thus, P. M. S. Blackett has said: "To justify the labor of negotiating any agreed reduction and to offset the undoubted strains and disputes that will inevitably arise from the operation of any inspection and control system, the negotiated reduction must be a major one; in fact, of

pheric Test Ban was the elimination of all immediate hope for the total Test Ban Treaty. In order to pacify the critics of the agreement, President Kennedy committed himself to a "vigorous series of tests." [67] This commitment was very explicit.* In the same way, an agreement to destroy B-47's for Badgers would probably lead to renewed assurances from Secretary McNamara that the B-52 and B-58 fleets would remain in the force indefinitely. There may be similar political problems in the Soviet system, but the available information is insufficient to determine whether or not this is so.

4. *An extensive bomber disarmament agreement would probably release considerably more "survivable" and deliverable U.S. weapons from bomber-related assignments than would be eliminated by destroying U.S. bombers.* Secretary McNamara has indicated that a few hundred Minuteman missiles have been procured for air-defense suppression to substitute for the canceled Skybolt missiles.† Furthermore it is quite evident that quick-to-target missiles rather than slow-to-target bombers must be used to attack airfields on which Soviet bombers are, or might be, based. Therefore, an extensive bomber disarmament agreement could shorten target lists by eliminating these categories. It would presumably release a few hundred missiles for other purposes. Only 315 B-52's are even on ground alert, and only about 80 of these can be kept

---

such magnitude as to change qualitatively the nature of the relative nuclear postures of the two giant powers." [66]

* The Deputy Secretary of Defense in a "Safeguards" communication drew together the commitments made by the Chairman of the Atomic Energy Commission, by the Secretary of Defense, and by the President. Among four commitments, and given first, was "The conduct of comprehensive, aggressive, and continuing underground nuclear test programs designed to add to our knowledge and improve our weapons in all areas of significance to our military posture for the future." [68]

† For instance he suggested that Skybolt would have cost "nearly $3 billion," that "incremental initial investment cost for a Minuteman missile, complete with its blast-resistant silo" was "very close" to $4 million, and that a substitution of Minuteman for Skybolt would save about $2 billion. This suggests that about 250 Minutemen were to be procured for this purpose." [69]

aloft for long periods of time.[70] In either case, many of these bombers presumably would not penetrate the Soviet air defenses.* Hence relatively few "survivable" and penetrating bombers might be lost by an agreement.

5. *The missiles released from bomber-related assignments would be more effective in the U.S. damage-limiting strategy, now and in the foreseeable future, than would the bombers destroyed.* First, consider the previous conclusion. Second, as we noted earlier, the Secretary of Defense is dubious whether our bombers can reach the Soviet weapons before these have been launched against us as part of a Soviet attack. Missiles are far more useful to exploit the raggedness in any such attack. More generally, war is not likely to occur in ways that call for all-out spasm bomber attack whether directed at forces or cities. This and the other arguments against bombers are becoming stronger as the strategic context unfolds. Thus, bombers are becoming more vulnerable, more likely to interfere with real prospects for war termination if war occurs, less likely to penetrate to targets, less likely to reach targets in time to limit damage even if penetration is successful, and less necessary as a supplement to growing missile forces.

6. *An extensive — but not a limited — bomber disarmament agreement will remove the Soviet bomber threat.* The present bomber threat cannot be adequately defended against, and can be removed in no other way than by an extensive disarmament agreement of some kind. Such an agreement is truly "defense through disarmament."

7. *An extensive — but not a limited — bomber disarmament agreement would substantially reduce U.S. costs in air defense and in maintenance and operation of bombers.* Bomber maintenance and operation costs will not be greatly reduced by destroying obsolescent bombers, since the costs would ordi-

---

* General Power has remarked that "in one weapon system, say a B-52 out of New Mexico going against the Soviet Union, if your realistic war games are thorough, you have a 50% confidence factor for destroying that target with a given weapon." [71]

narily be eliminated in any case. Nor would it be possible to diminish the annual $2-billion air defense costs if many Soviet bombers remained. However, an extensive agreement might permit a sizable reduction in air defense expenditures and also save several billion dollars in bomber costs.*

8. *An extensive, rather than a limited, bomber disarmament agreement would most improve the relative superiority of the United States over the Soviet Union as measured in existing delivery vehicles.* Recent estimates indicate that our missile superiority is about 4 to 1 or better.[73] The elimination of heavy bombers would trade about three U.S. bombers for one Soviet bomber. The elimination of B-47's and Badgers would trade approximately even numbers of bombers. Hence, according to this almost purely symbolic measure, we should eliminate bombers completely to most increase our relative superiority in delivery vehicles.

9. *There would be no important inspection problems associated with either a limited or an extensive bomber disarmament agreement.* Soviet knowledge of the size of our bomber fleet is, of course, complete. And our appreciation of Soviet bomber capabilities can be little inferior. Many public estimates of the older Soviet bombers are given to the nearest multiple of ten (for example, 70 or 120). No Soviet government could assume that bombers could be kept secret, and there would be little incentive to do so, since they are in no sense a decisive weapon.

10. *The main obstacles to extensive bomber disarmament are probably U.S. political problems, and these are substantial.* The strategic case for extensive bomber disarmament is strong, but probably only the present Secretary of Defense would have any chance of persuading Congress of it. It would take a good deal of courage in various parts of the government even to propose dismantling the SAC bomber fleet.

---

* The maintenance and operation of the B-52 force costs $820 million each year. Phasing it out steadily over three years instead of keeping all B-52's until 1969 (as the present program anticipates) would save $2.8 billion. The cost of modifying the fleet would also be saved — this is $306 million for fiscal 1965.[72]

Soviet Issues

11. *No advantages comparable to those of Conclusions 4 and 5 would accrue to the Soviet Union in an extensive bomber disarmament agreement, because Soviet force posture and strategy differ from those of the United States.* The Soviet Union would not release many missiles from bomber-base targeting, because its force is not sufficiently large to follow a "damage-limiting" strategy and is "at the present time . . . as Khrushchev has outlined it, a strategy directed primarily against our cities and our urban society," according to Secretary McNamara.[74] Similarly, it is unlikely that ICBM's from a small Soviet supply would be used to suppress partially effective air defenses to improve the penetration qualities of a 190-plane heavy-bomber force. Instead, air-to-ground missiles would probably be used. Therefore Soviet ICBM's would not be released from air-defense suppression assignments.

12. *Nevertheless, an extensive bomber disarmament agreement would be very clearly in the Soviet interest.* First, from the Soviet point of view, the Soviet Union would share in the benefits discussed in Conclusion 2 — less destruction if war occurs — and would have eliminated the potential U.S. bomber threat, at the cost of giving up vulnerable Soviet bombers. The advantages referred to in Conclusions 4 and 5 (the release of U.S. missiles from bomber-related duties) should not discourage agreement unless the Soviet Union wishes to use airfields to draw "fire" or to encourage procurement by us of additional missiles.* Conclusion 8 (increase in the relative advantage of the United States) has only symbolic significance. The dismantlement of the SAC bomber force will seem to Soviet officials to be the end of an un-

---

* The United States can be encouraged to procure additional missiles even with its present large superiority. For instance, Secretary McNamara's testimony includes the paragraph: "We have tentatively programed the funding of additional MINUTEMAN II silos after fiscal year 1965, but the actual number to be started will depend upon the situation prevailing a year or two years from now."[75]

fortunate era of American strategic dominance. Possibly they will view it as a rebuke to U.S. Air Force generals whose unauthorized behavior may have been feared in the past. A bomber agreement, even a limited one, might encourage the Soviets to attempt to dislodge the United States from overseas bases that could become superfluous in the absence of aircraft. Bomber maintenance costs would be saved. And unless French bombers and the U.S. TFX prevented it, much of Soviet air defense costs would be saved. The fissionable material in Soviet bombs could be used in Soviet missiles if it were in short supply. (A limited agreement would be of no greater assistance than obsolescence in this regard.) Bombers are not useful to the Soviets for purposes of deterrence, because they are vulnerable, as noted before, and also hard to hide and less reliable. Finally, a major disarmament agreement would represent a large part of that *détente* which is evidently the current interest of the Soviet Union. For propaganda purposes the extensive agreement could be claimed by the Soviets to be nearer to their proposal than to the U.S. informal and limited suggestion.*

What to Do?

13. *I believe it would be good disarmament strategy for either or both sides to hold out for an extensive bomber disarmament agreement.* Conclusion 3 indicates that a limited agreement might prevent further bomber disarmament. In any case the nonsymbolic results of such an agreement will soon accrue from obsolescence. (For example, the U.S. B-47's will be phased out in 1966, and the Badger force is as old.)[77] The argument that the bombers will be prevented from falling into third-country hands is not persuasive. The United States con-

---

* It would also comply effectively with the Soviet draft resolution, introduced in the Security Council on April 21, 1958, that called upon the United States "to refrain from sending its military aircraft carrying atomic and hydrogen bombs toward the frontiers of other States for the purpose of creating a threat to their security or staging military demonstrations."[76]

trols the B-47's, and if the Soviet Union wished to, it could sell light Il-28 bombers to its friends and allies. Extensive bomber agreements make much more sense than limited ones. As noted in Conclusions 2 and 7, only extensive agreements will substantially reduce destruction if war occurs and reduce U.S. air defense and bomber costs. As noted in Conclusion 6, only an extensive agreement will remove the Soviet bomber threat. And, as noted in Conclusions 4 and 5, an extensive agreement alone will *strengthen* U.S. retaliatory forces by releasing missiles from bomber-related duties. Conclusion 12 indicates a real Soviet interest also in extensive agreements. A decision to try for such extensive agreement does not create an all-or-nothing obstacle to disarmament; extensive bomber disarmament agreements will eventually become feasible, if only because the heavy-bomber fleets will get older and less desirable. In time, if nothing is done earlier, offers will be made to trade obsolete B-52's for obsolete Bears and Bisons. Are we capable only of agreeing on disarmament through obsolescence (without a freeze), or can doctrine, analysis, and an enlightened attitude toward national interest in both major powers shape the destiny of already procured, and still usable, forces? This is the question posed by bomber disarmament.

BOMBER DISARMAMENT: PROSPECTS, EARLY 1965

Introduction

IN THE FALL of 1964 the first signs appeared that B-52's were to be phased down unilaterally. These and some other observations are discussed in this chapter. It examines more closely Department of Defense bomber policy, and suggests that B-52's will decline in number as the TFX planes are phased in. This clarifies the possibilities for arms control. These include a cutoff in heavy-bomber procurement, destruction of some B-52's, Bisons, and Bears, and offers to destroy heavy bombers in conjunction with a halt in missile procurement.

A U.S. Follow-on Bomber

A new heavy bomber still seems unlikely. First of all, Harold Brown, Director of Defense Research and Engineering, testified that the Air Force had examined — in addition to multi-purpose strategic reconnaissance systems, such as B-70, and a long-range bomber that would launch stand-off missiles — "what now seems to be the most promising concept, an advanced manned precise-strike system, AMPSS." [1] The name of the system has changed frequently and now seems to be "AMSA" (Advanced Manned Strategic Aircraft), but the concept remains fairly stationary. Richard Fryklund described the leading candidate by saying that such a plane would fly toward Russia at about 600 miles an hour, descend almost to the ground as it passed Red defenses, fly at tree-top level to its target (probably at 700 or 800 miles an hour, though an all-subsonic mission is under consideration) and then cruise back to a safe base.

The AMSA would launch large numbers of small missiles (with about 200-kiloton nuclear warheads) at enemy targets 50 or 60 miles away with great precision.[2]

This plane has two serious problems. First, it would take seven years to build. General Robert Friedman testified in early 1964 that December 1971 was the "most optimistic date" that a new follow-on bomber could be expected.[3] Second, it is too expensive — $9 billion to build some 200 bombers, according to the Defense Department. And on August 24, 1964, Richard Fryklund suggested in the *Washington Star* that the fleet would cost "roughly $1.5 billion a year to maintain and operate according to rule-of-thumb experience with past bombers." (A lower estimate was given in the preceding chapter.) Hence, assuming an eight-year life, the decision to adopt such bombers involves about $20 billion in direct costs.

Of course, the procurement of a follow-on bomber depends in large part on the extent to which B-52's and other bombers can fulfill the requirement. The Secretary of Defense has asserted that they can, that

Our current research and development program will make available to us three designs, any one of which could be completed and put into production before our present bombers reach the end of their useful life.[4]

But Harold Brown noted that they might not:

The B-52 has been having structural difficulties which in one sense argues you need a new aircraft soon if you need it, and in another sense it raises the question of reliability of the aircraft. But in any event, we are trying to evaluate what is a reasonable expected lifetime for the B-52.[5]

Since the present bombers were procured over a seven-year period and have had dissimilar use and missions, calculating the expected lifetime for the fleet will be fairly complicated.* Finally in October 1964, Richard Fryklund reported:

> Existing B-52 heavy bombers will be good through 1975 according to an Air Force Defense Department–Boeing Co. study, and with continued modernization, might last into the '80's. Only 200 bombers are needed, according to the Air Force study, and more than that number of later model B-52's are available.[7]

AMSA's chances had declined.

Furthermore, Congress is gradually losing the motivation to force upon the Secretary of Defense additional funds for bomber procurement. Even influential and sympathetic Air Force supporters seem to be having doubts. Senator Richard Russell, chairman of both the Committee on Armed Services and the Subcommittee on Department of Defense of the Committee on Appropriations remarked:

> I want us to move ahead with a new manned aircraft.
> But I must confess that I have some qualms about it. What is the primary consideration in this new aircraft to replace these aging 52's and 58's? Is it speed or altitude or ability to carry long-range missiles, or are you seeking all of these things in this bomber?[8]

And significantly, a recent House Armed Services Committee minority report opposing additional bomber funds expressed disbelief "that the Congress necessarily [had] any commitment in perpetuity to long-range strategic bombers of the B-36 or B-52 type, any more than we had a commitment in perpetuity to the battleship."[9] Congress is therefore not far behind former Deputy Secretary of Defense Roswell Gilpatric who suggested that "all manned bombers" might be "retired from active deployment" in the 1970's in a suitable political environment.[10]

President Johnson is said to hope that the Air Force can find some mission for a new follow-on bomber but to believe that

---

* For example, speaking of the G and H models of B-52, General Bradley stated in 1961: "Actually the G's and H's are the ones that are in the biggest trouble. The reason is that they are carrying a much greater load in comparison to the older one."[6]

one cannot spend $10 billion for nostalgia.[11] The Secretary of Defense himself has asserted that he has not "seen or heard of anything yet that warrants development and production." [12] The *Washington Star* notes that the Air Force has recently asked again to go to the "project definition" phase of aircraft development but that civilian officials believe this "advanced design" work would commit them to "final approval" and hence they will reject it.[13] It is hard to believe AMSA has a chance.

Reductions in the Fleet of B-52's

At the same time, it seems that the B-52's will decline in number — to about 200 planes by 1971. First of all, the studies justifying an advanced bomber generally called for only 200 planes — probably because of the great expense of new bombers; but this factor may have conceded implicitly that no more than 200 planes are necessary. And the study mentioned earlier suggests that this has been accepted.

Second, additional planes are expensive in operation and maintenance costs, and in the crew, tankers, and other resources that might be used for a growing fleet of B-52's. This sort of consideration influenced the phasing out of the B-47's. In 1961, Secretary McNamara testified:

> Since the earlier B-47 medium bombers in the inventory are already approaching the end of their useful life, we propose to phase them out of the force at a somewhat faster rate than originally planned. The crews and other resources thus freed will be utilized to maintain the larger proportion of the force on the 15-minute ground alert.[14]

Third, U.S. policy is already pointing toward a verbal or actual substitution of B-52 with TFX, which will be phased in from about 1966 to the early seventies.* This is indicated

---

* It is suggested that planes "will start rolling off an assembly line in 1966." [15] Australia is to receive 24 TFX aircraft in 1967. The spending for TFX is expected to be spread over seven years, "with delivery of planes continuing into the 1970's." [16]

in responses to charges that the manned bomber will be phased out. These responses do not commit the Defense Department to B-52's in large numbers. For instance, after Senator Goldwater mentioned manned bombers in a speech to the Veterans of Foreign Wars, the Defense Department replied:

> . . . the idea that all manned bombers are to be phased out is wholly unjustified. Our forward plans now go through fiscal year 1972. Those plans include larger numbers of strategic bombers at every stage. The plans also include a bomber-deliverable megatonnage which is highly classified, but substantially greater than the Senator's statement implies.
>
> No decision has yet been made about our needs beyond 1972, but we are making ample provision: (1) for possible extension of the life of the B-52, (2) for research on new manned systems, and (3) for possible strategic uses of manned systems in production. We will have manned bombers, and plenty of them, just as long as they are needed.[17]

Indeed, the increasing reliance on TFX for a great many duties has been widely foreshadowed. Asked by Senator Mundt whether or not we would be caught short of bombers in 1969 or 1970 if the Chinese attacked India, the Secretary of Defense replied that we would have suitable manned bombers, arguing: "As you know, the TFX has a long range and a very high bomb load, and this is one of the potential missions for it." [18] Whether or not it will be possible to substitute the TFX for the B-52 in missions involving penetration of Soviet air defenses is not clear. For instance, General LeMay testified:

> The main trouble with the TFX is that it is a small airplane, and it will not carry the things you need to penetrate modern defenses and still have long enough range to do it. It is just not a big enough airplane to do this. It is going to do the job fine in a tactical role. . . .[19]

But Richard Fryklund reports:

> [TFX] could carry all of the AMSA equipment (except for an oversized antenna) and could hit almost all AMSA targets most of which are in European Russia.[20]

112

What Might Be both Feasible and Desirable?

Even though we might not be likely to buy a new heavy bomber, we probably would not be willing to say so unilaterally. Defense Department leadership tends to be unwilling to resolve hypothetical or general issues. Like the Supreme Court, it finds a certain protection in dealing with the concrete and the particular. Unless some good reason exists, the Secretary of Defense will not want to explain why *no* follow-on bomber is likely to be procured, and may not be able to.

Moreover all of our bilateral bomber proposals are likely to run into characteristic problems. Not only does the Defense Department prefer to resolve only specific issues, it also prefers to resolve them on the basis of the cost effectiveness of unilateral action. Although bilateral agreements can provide a very real additional "consideration" for actions that would be undertaken in any case, the actions are more likely to come under attack. It is easier for a hostile Congress to question an agreement than to question the application of cost effectiveness. The latter seems a relatively objective criterion, and discussions on these grounds can almost always be won by the Secretary of Defense: he has the information, the background, the staff, and the authority. By contrast, a U.S.-Soviet deal involves a possibly malevolent partner. While we can be *mistaken* in applying cost effectiveness, we can be *tricked* by the Soviets. And a U.S.-Soviet agreement raises certain political questions with which Congress feels as competent to deal as the Department of Defense. It also raises more difficult problems of coordination, since our allies, the State Department, and others must reach at least some consensus.

Such agreements, moreover, may set a dangerous precedent, arouse political pressures for unwise future agreements, mislead the Soviets as to our determination and power, and so on. Because arms control agreements raise these kinds of fears, the combination of unilateral and arms control motivations for a particular action tends to confuse the issues. To the Depart-

113

ment of Defense, it will generally seem preferable to leave the Soviets out of its arguments, lest others think that Soviet considerations dominate its deliberations. In the political process it is often the weakest, rather than the strongest, argument that influences the course of the struggle. Finally, the Defense Department would not like to make desirable unilateral actions — such as divesting itself of all bombers — contingent upon Soviet agreement.

For these reasons, Department of Defense policy makers are more likely to expect, and hence to encourage, unilateral rather than bilateral phase outs. Such expectations have certain operational consequences that generally reduce still further the likelihood of utilizing arms control mechanisms.

For example, if it were decided to try for a bilateral phase out of heavy bombers rather than for unilateral action, it would be appropriate to emphasize the strength rather than the weakness of Soviet bomber forces. It is Soviet bomber *strength* that makes a deal worth while, and it is Soviet bomber *weakness* that makes our unilateral phase down of B-52's politically possible. Hence, in the one case, Soviet bomber forces might be described in terms of their effectiveness in one-way flights; in the other case, discussions on two-way flights might be appropriate.

Other, subtler problems arise. If attempts were to be made to induce Soviet acceptance of some bargain, unilateral justifications of our action might have to be muted. Presumably, we should not emphasize too strongly to Congress that TFX can bomb European Russia just as well as B-52's can while persuading the Soviets to give up their capability to bomb the United States. (This is a question of emphasis, however, since the Soviets may understand the political need to "phase" B-52's into TFX's. Moreover, during the Test Ban hearings, they said nothing while the Secretary of Defense spotlighted the unilateral benefits of the treaty.)

These considerations limit the bilateral agreements that are possible and the forms that they may take. Three possibilities remain of interest: the destruction of heavy bombers, cutoffs of bomber procurement, and the conjunction of bomber proposals with the freeze proposal.

Destruction of Obsolescent Heavy Bombers

A central question involved in bilateral agreements to destroy obsolescent heavy bombers is "Why?" If the bombers are to be phased out anyway at much the same rate, such traditional motives for disarmament as "decreasing destruction if war occurs" are absent. Instead, the dominant motivations for heavy-bomber destruction become political. Not all of these have much to do with bombers per se. Any other strategic weapon system might do as well.

Presumably bomber disarmament agreements can help prepare for later agreements, perhaps by educating arms controllers on the two sides in the problems of justifying and drafting formal agreements and by forcing the defense analysts to think through the strategic and political issues that bomber disarmament raises.

Decision makers of the two sides would also learn. The Senate would be exposed to a thorough analysis of the advantages and disadvantages of the agreement. The principle would be firmly established that strategic computations could favor disarmament. And many of the questions raised would be relevant to any substantial agreement that might follow. A treaty would increase interest in arms control activities and would stimulate those sympathetic to further disarmament; the number of people willing to spend time on arms control would increase and the quality of their efforts might rise. Also, the Soviet "credit rating" might rise; and the successful destruction of bombers month after month might increase the political feasibility of further agreements.

This continued destruction of bombers over a period of years would probably have a desirable effect on the international atmosphere. It would periodically reassure both parties of the willingness of the other to take positive steps to maintain a treaty. This reassurance would be perceived by both as inconsistent with the kind of diplomatic pressure represented by Berlin provocations. Each would expect deteriorating relations to be signaled by a halt in the destruction of bombers and each would gain confidence from that perception.

The destruction of heavy bombers might also have favorable effects on aspects of the arms race that involve third parties, such as proliferation. At the least, in nonnuclear countries the supporters of restraint in acquiring nuclear weapons would use the prospect of progress in major-power disarmament as a debating point in their internal councils.

The treaty would be an important test of strength between those who welcomed *détente* and those who feared it. Efforts to gain a favorable consensus on both sides would provoke a great debate. And because the treaty would be strategically innocuous, it would represent a favorable "test case" for those sympathetic to arms control.* After its ratification each could accept the premise that an earnest indication of a national desire for *détente* had been given. And, from a political point of view, the treaty would announce that those interested in further procurement of strategic weapons were in the minority. This announcement could greatly enhance the prospects for a tacit freeze on the procurement of other weapons.

Of course the way in which each spoke about the treaty might influence the expectations associated with it. If the Secretary of Defense had to pacify opponents of the treaty with assurances that *additional* strategic weapons were to be built, he would retard the establishment of nonprocurement understandings. But if he linked the destruction of bombers with assurances that we had enough nuclear weapons, the tacit freeze would be encouraged.

Hopefully, the treaty would add to the U.S.-Soviet strategic dialogue, and improve the insight of each into the constraints

---

* By and large, it is not feasible in this country to argue publicly against disarmament on political grounds. The desire to achieve disarmament agreements with the Soviets, so long as the agreements are technically sound, is generally conceded in public if not in private. Hence opponents of a treaty are likely to be forced to argue their case on difficult grounds.

under which the other deals with national security and arms control policies. In the long run, this understanding will be the best guarantee of stability in strategic force procurement.

The destruction of heavy bombers by formal treaty could, for these reasons, be of significance even if very few bombers were destroyed. But assuming that 200 bombers were to be retained, and that destruction of less than one-third of the existing force would seem too inconsequential, somewhere between about 200 and 400 heavy bombers could be destroyed.

The destruction of these bombers might best be done over a period of a few years rather than a few months; it could be done weekly or monthly. Four hundred bombers could be destroyed over 4 years if 2 were destroyed each week or 8 each month. The schedule could be arranged to avoid a termination date that would be politically embarrassing to one side or the other, for example, immediately before an election in the United States.

Equal numbers of bombers might be destroyed; a two-thirds reduction of our heavy-bomber force (or 400 bombers) could be matched by a two-thirds reduction of the Soviet heavy-bomber force (or 120 bombers) coupled with the demolition of 280 medium bombers. One purpose of adding medium bombers to the destruction would be to prevent giving the impression, month after month, that the United States was destroying more than the Soviet Union. The destruction might otherwise be susceptible to politically motivated criticism. Since the medium bombers threaten our European allies quite as effectively as the heavy bombers threaten us, it is easy to rationalize the trade and useful to establish the possibility. When and if reductions are made in numbers of missiles, the same explanation would apply to bargains in which medium-range ballistic missiles were destroyed in exchange for our ICBM's.

If each side had already announced its decision to divest itself of heavy bombers, the treaty would be a "pseudo-agreement," a term used by the political scientist Fred C. Iklé to designate agreements that do not record any new settlement.[21]

117

But there would still be some strategic motives for the treaty. As in the U.S. proposal to destroy B-47's and Soviet Badgers, it could be argued that the planes might otherwise be returned to service, although, unlike the B-47's, the renovated B-52's would not be purchased by third parties; they are simply too big and expensive to be of interest to most of the world, which could make do with TFX. The return to domestic service of "mothballed" planes is a real consideration; the Air Force would probably object to burning bombers on these grounds.*

If a formal treaty is impossible, we should have to settle for portraying the separate unilateral actions of the two powers as instances of reduction by "mutual example." This would have a certain amount of political impact and might be the best we could get.

Cutoff of Heavy-Bomber Procurement

An agreement is unlikely to be negotiated formally for a cutoff in heavy-bomber procurement. It does not have the appeal of physical disarmament, the urgency of a cutoff in missile procurement or of a test ban.

But a phase down of the bomber force would eventually take the steam out of desires for a follow-on bomber. And as the focus of the debate turned from a new bomber toward the retention of old ones, the arguments for getting each side to refrain from further heavy-bomber procurement would reappear. Hence, bomber destruction agreements can encourage a tacit agreement against bombers. So also can the desire to cut back air defenses.

Once we or they dismantle air defenses, it will be that much harder to buy a new bomber. Each side would be politically embarrassed by the re-emergence of bombers after the adop-

---

* "*Mr. Stafford:* [Nominally active bombers] could be returned to active service if conditions indicate?

"*Secretary McNamara:* They could be [deletion in original]. As to their usefulness, General LeMay has asserted: 'I think the B-47 in the hand of professionals could deliver weapons in the year 2000.'" [22]

tion of a policy of phasing down air defenses. Hence for each side to engage in small decreases in air defenses may be, in some sense, to exchange political hostages.

Any Soviet leader interested in reducing air defense expenditures would probably want as many indicators as he could get of our intention not to procure a new heavy bomber. Cutting back Soviet air defense will probably run into strong opposition from the most entrenched of bureaucracies. And Soviet air defense enthusiasts would want long-range assurances of our intentions to justify their cutbacks; air defense systems are not rebuilt in a day.

We might have to avoid buying Soviet air defense by not stationing the relatively long-range TFX in Europe and Japan where it could attack the Soviet Union. And in phasing out B-52's for TFX, we would have to emphasize the irrelevance of strategic bombers in general war rather than the capacity of TFX to substitute for them.

We might also encourage the Soviets to dismantle their air defenses by phasing down our own and stressing those explanations for our action that would also apply to the Soviet Union.

Finally, we might wish to give the Soviets a political rather than a financial stake in our nonprocurement of a follow-on bomber. We could suggest to them that the question of bombers is one over which the civilian leadership in the Defense Department could lose its position. With such a loss, increased prestige, influence, and authority would accrue to those arguing for less restraint in the arms race.

Bomber Disarmament and a Halt in Missile Procurement

One important possibility is to treat bomber disarmament in the context of a halt in missile procurement such as the one discussed in Chapter Five. That proposal for a freeze contains a provision that is probably properly characterized as an error. The error reveals the extent to which the freeze proposal either was not taken seriously or was prepared hurriedly, and is related to the pressures arising from the debate over the retention of bombers.

As it stands, the freeze proposal advocates, for missiles and bombers alike, that "the immediate objective of the freeze on numbers should be to maintain the quantities of strategic nuclear vehicles . . . at constant levels," and the "objective of the freeze on characteristics should be to prevent the development and deployment of strategic vehicles of a significantly new type." [23] With respect to bombers, a prohibition of vehicles of a "significantly new type" is a prohibition on any follow-on bombers since such a bomber would certainly satisfy this description. Hence additional B-52's would have to be procured to maintain a constant level.

But maintaining the level of our present bombers by systematic replacement of old B-52's with new ones is a contingency that we are not now considering and probably never would, even under a freeze. We should have to reopen old production lines at great expense. And for what? The arguments against a follow-on bomber apply a fortiori to an older bomber not designed for the rigors of the seventies. Their lifetime would depend on the defenses of the Soviet Union.[24] Penetration problems could not be avoided by developing stand-off missiles — designed to let bombers stay outside of defenses — since a freeze would not permit their development. And, to the extent that the United States continued to use ICBM's for defense suppression (that is, to attack defenses and open a corridor for bombers), valuable missiles in a frozen force would be required for an otherwise unnecessary job.[25] The requirements for a bomber in the seventies are basically still open to question. Finally, much of the political motivation for a new follow-on bomber could not be sublimated with more B-52's. A follow-on bomber, but not more B-52's, would add to our knowledge, procure something new and exciting, and show our determination to be second to none in the aircraft development field. For all these reasons it is not likely that we would exercise our option to maintain existing levels of bombers.

If, indeed, the United States would not even exercise its option of "one-for-one replacement by externally similar vehicles" in the case of bombers, its insertion in our proposal was an error. The Soviet Union might be willing to maintain its heavy bombers indefinitely. This would have a number of unfortunate consequences. A potential Soviet bomber threat would force us to incur otherwise avoidable air defense costs and to assign missiles to Soviet air bases. And a potential Soviet bomber preponderance would have unfortunate political considerations that might induce an otherwise undesired purchase of B-52's. Finally, retained Soviet bombers would maintain a threat against our cities that could not be effectively neutralized.

In other words, the United States should have proposed, at the least, a freeze in missile procurement combined with the *nonreplacement* of heavy bombers. It would not want to buy the heavy bombers that the U.S. proposal permits. And it might have proposed an agreement more acceptable to the Russians if it had called for a phasing down of heavy bombers — a phase down that would in any case occur in a few years. Such an agreement would combine the freeze desired by the United States with the bomber disarmament proposed by the Soviets — some "arms control" with some "disarmament."

The Future

When the Soviets proposed the disarmament of all bombers in early 1964, they touched upon a sensitive nerve in Defense Department planning. Although the Soviet proposal was obviously impractical, it did reflect the relative obsolescence of heavy bombers and had the power to stir up debate over the manned bomber in the United States. The maintenance of the heavy-bomber force through the late sixties was probably the most obvious and significant deviation from cost-effectiveness considerations that existed in the entire strategic weapons program. The prospects for its phase down were relatively good.

When the Soviet proposal was made, the U.S. heavy-bomber fleet had been programed to be maintained intact until at least 1969. By the next year, in early 1965, the fiscal 1966 budget revealed that the Department of Defense planned to phase out, during that year, two squadrons containing the oldest model of B-52, the B-52B's. These were ten years old. At the same time, $300 million was requested to continue the program to extend the life and improve the capabilities of other B-52 strategic bombers. Detailed plans were not made public.

In December 1964, the Soviet Union sent to the President of the U.N. General Assembly a disarmament memorandum discussing "measures for further reduction of international tension and limitation of the arms race." It suggested eleven measures, many of them emphasizing "mutual example" and referring to agreements with political rather than strategic impact.

On the subject of bombers, the Soviets went even further than they had previously. They called the destruction of bombers "undoubtedly ready to be put into practice." The Soviet government was prepared to discuss "the phasing of the destruction of bombers *in terms of types* within an agreed over-all time limit for the destruction of all bombers." (Italics added.) The Soviets proposed that a formula be worked out under which the large powers would be the first to eliminate bombers.

Thus if a willingness on the part of both parties to reach agreement is assumed, the bargain indicated by the two positions would involve (*a*) U.S. agreement in principle to the ultimate destruction of all bombers, much like our agreement in principle to general and complete disarmament; and (*b*) U.S. and Soviet dismantlement of bombers as they were phased out. The prospects for this agreement are not especially good. Conceivably they might improve if it became obvious that a few hundred B-52's were to be phased out; this could occur in the presentation of the fiscal 1967 budget in early 1966.

Whether we or the Soviets would be willing to design a statement describing unilateral reductions as instances of mutual example is impossible to predict. But the prospects for our procuring a new heavy bomber have clearly declined still further. The testimony given in preparing the allotment of funds for fiscal 1966 argues that it would be desirable to keep open the option of developing a replacement for the B-52's when they have to be retired. But this almost admits that they might never be replaced at all.

MISSILE DISARMAMENT

Introduction

THE PROSPECTS for negotiated reductions in missiles are poor, for reasons that are discussed in the conclusions and that will become apparent in the body of this chapter. Nevertheless an examination of the problems of missile reductions can be educational in sketching the existing state of affairs in missile procurement — procurement that involves three different contests between the major powers — and in providing an appreciation of missile force computations. This chapter assumes that the problems are better understood by considering the situation than by reading arguments about it. The conclusions are mainly devoted to an analysis of the general disarmament plans. Many political issues have been ignored because the plans are so unlikely to be implemented.

If there is any over-all positive conclusion to this chapter, it is a formula, interesting at least in the abstract, whereby the United States could justify acceptance in principle of a Soviet position so as to permit more detailed discussions. The Soviets have demanded agreement in principle for a reduction to "mutually agreed and strictly limited" numbers of missiles before proceeding with technical discussions at a working level. The United States, notwithstanding its prior agreement in principle to the more radical "general and complete disarmament," has objected. Part of the disagreement stems from our general disinclination to agree in principle; there seem to be differences in attitude between ourselves and the Soviets on how bargaining is conducted. (There may also be a disinclination on one or both sides to talk in detail.)

In any case, it will be observed that the United States missile force is now improving very considerably in effectiveness per missile and that, despite these increases, the strategic force is likely over time to become incapable of attacking Soviet forces effectively. These facts provide interesting properties for a plan involving proportional missile reductions in a first stage of disarmament, and reductions to strictly limited and mutually agreed numbers of missiles in a second stage.

During the first stage, the over-all effectiveness of the U.S. force could increase, notwithstanding the reduction in numbers, because of improvements in the efficiency of the remaining missiles. Meanwhile, the Soviet threat would generally decrease. During the second stage, or thereafter, the United States would find itself gradually losing the relative advantages provided in part by the first-stage agreement and in part by its former preponderance. This may not be a fatal objection since, over the period of time required for the two stages, these advantages would probably have been lost without disarmament and would be lost under any kind of very substantial reduction.

It is difficult and unrewarding to describe the problems involved in substantial reductions. Some, but by no means all, arise from the speed with which weapons technology changes. As an introduction to present changes, it may be interesting to point out how quickly the arms race has changed in character since the end of World War II. The U.S.-Soviet arms race had just begun in 1949 when Vannevar Bush remarked:

> What would be the nature of all-out war if it came at a time when great belligerents faced each other over adequate stockpiles of atomic bombs, capable of reducing both to relative impotency soon after the storm broke? The condition may never arise. Before it can come about, there is another type of contest: the race to be prepared, in which we are now engaged. If we lose that race decisively we alone shall be devastated and there will be no atomic war between substantially equal contestants. We have to win that race. Worse than that, we have to stay well ahead at all times as the race goes on. If we do there need be no atomic war of the fully devastating sort we study.[1]

Seven years later, Admiral Robert Carney testified:

> After VJ Day, our enemies had been swept from the land, from the sea, and from the air; the scales were very steeply tilted in our favor.
>
> Later, with a monopoly on atomic weapons and a means of delivering them, we had reason to feel in any major showdown the scales were even more strongly tipped in our favor. And then came the very disconcerting realization that the U.S.S.R. was not just a land of untutored peasants; the underestimated Soviets were making technological strides which we had not been prepared to believe possible. . . .
>
> More recently, it dawned on us that our own native land could be subjected directly to attack, atomic attack.[2]

After another seven years had passed, the Secretary of Defense, Robert McNamara, felt impelled to point out that

> We are approaching an era when it will become increasingly improbable that either side could destroy a sufficiently large portion of the other's strategic nuclear force, either by surprise or otherwise, to preclude a devastating retaliatory blow.

Fifteen years after Bush's statement, it seems that the major powers will soon, if they do not now, face each other "over adequate stockpiles of atomic bombs, capable of reducing both to relative impotency," fairly independently of the course of the war. We have not lost "the race to be prepared." In fact, the Secretary of Defense would argue that "Deterrence of deliberate, calculated attack seems as well assured as it can be. . . ." Can much more than deterrence of deliberate attack be achieved unilaterally? Evidently not a good deal more. Mr. McNamara has stated, without contradiction, that "no responsible Pentagon official, certainly none of the Joint Chiefs of Staff," has proposed "a strategic force that would enable us, if we struck first, to so reduce Soviet retaliatory power that the damage it could then do to U.S. population and industry would be brought down to an 'acceptable' level. . . ."[3] The conditions that produced these admissions encourage U.S. consideration of disarmament.

These conditions have operated to improve the prospects for Soviet agreement as well. Marshal Malinovsky announced:

We have no special need for increasing the numerical strength of our rocket forces and our weapon stocks. The next stage is no longer the stockpiling of weapons, but their routine perfection and renewal of stocks.[4]

And there are domestic signs that the time is ripe to consider a halt. There are the presidential comments about "How much is enough?" There is the wide acceptance of the notion of overkill. And there are the signs of strain in the justifications of the Department of Defense for the procurement of so many weapons — the construction of which was initiated in anticipation of a missile gap that never arose. Shortly after these weapons were programed, a Congressman provoked the following exchange:

Mr. Minshall: At what point do we reach the absurd stage of these missiles? How many missiles do we have to have before we get that ridiculous?

General Irvine: I think we are going to have an interesting discussion with this committee in about 1963 on that subject.[5]

That discussion is somewhat overdue.

The Major Procurement Contests

The three major procurement contests of the mid-sixties all involve ballistic missiles. Speaking as Director of Defense Research and Engineering, Harold Brown has characterized the major contests as

one between penetration aids and ballistic missile defense, one between antisubmarine efforts and attempts to insure that ballistic missile submarines cannot be detected or attacked before they launch their missiles, and a third between hardening and missile accuracy. . . .[6]

The rate at which the contests develop surprises even the participants. In 1964, Secretary of the Air Force Zuckert evinced surprise at our own progress:

It seems to me that we too often forget that it is — it just happens to be this month — 10 years since the committee

127

headed by the great von Neumann concluded that a rapid ICBM program was practical. Today, the first generation missiles are already being replaced.[7]

And General Walsh, showing surprise at Soviet progress, suggested in 1961 that "the pace is something. You could say they have come in 5 years where we came in 10 in weapons."[8] (Another indication of this same ratio is suggested by the fact that we believe the Russians took 4½ years to build the Bison, compared with 8½ years for our construction of the comparable B-52.)[9]

There is no one in the world who knows what the shape of these contests will be twenty years hence. Without arms control and disarmament, perhaps even with them, the strategic balance facing the next generation must be assessed as highly uncertain. Neither we nor they can answer the question put to General Eisenhower by Premier Bulganin in 1957:

> First of all, who can guarantee, if the present competition in the production of ever newer types of weapons is continued and assumes still greater proportions, that it will be the NATO members who are the winners in such a competition?[10]

Ballistic Missiles

At the end of World War II, ballistic missiles were science fiction: science fiction that very much annoyed those with some grasp of the then existing capabilities. Dr. Bush told the Senate Committee on Atomic Energy in December, 1945:

> We have plenty enough to think about that is very definite and very realistic — enough so that we don't need to step out into some of these borderlines, which seem to me more or less fantastic. Let me say this: There has been a great deal said about a 3,000-mile high-angle rocket.
> In my opinion such a thing is impossible and will be impossible for many years.[11]

Even after four years had passed, Dr. Bush was still able to argue (a) that "there need be little fear of the intercontinental missile in the form of a pilotless aircraft, for it is not so effective from the standpoint of cost or performance as the airplane with a crew aboard," (b) that "we would have to pay millions of dollars for a single shot," (c) that a 2,000-mile rocket could only be "depended upon to hit within 150 miles of its target," although "perhaps within ten miles" with "sights and homing aids" and perhaps even within a mile or two if all went very well indeed, (d) that its warhead would have to be the "scarce and highly expensive" atomic bomb which could not be trusted to a "highly complex and possibly erratic carrier of inherently low precision," and (e) that even the atomic bomb would not be sufficiently powerful to permit its use with such inaccuracy.

Time has destroyed the presuppositions of these arguments, especially in the production of the hydrogen bomb warhead without which the intercontinental missile would indeed have remained science fiction. Edward Teller testified:

> . . . the development of the missiles has in actual fact, and at least to a very great extent, waited for the realization of a warhead. We did not go ahead and undertake a very vigorous program of developing long-range missiles before the time at which it was reasonably clear that a warhead was available.[12]

With an A-bomb warhead, the missile could not be of really practical use unless its precision of guidance was increased "by a factor of 100" over that required to put a satellite in orbit. With a hydrogen bomb warhead this requirement could be reduced by a factor of 10.[13]

In February 1954, after the detonation of a hydrogen bomb, a Strategic Missile Evaluation Committee headed by John von Neumann recommended an urgent "go-ahead" for the ballistic missile program and predicted, "A period of 6 to 8 years should . . . permit the attainment of the beginnings of an operational capability." [14]

Two years later, the AEC was able to advise the Department of Defense that a substantial reduction in warhead weight and size could be obtained. This made feasible a sufficiently small — hence easier to handle — solid-fuel missile. The Navy promptly sought approval for a submarine-launched

Polaris program and the right to cease participation in the Jupiter liquid-fuel program sponsored with the Army.[15] By 1956 development of both land- and sea-based ballistic missiles was underway in the forms deployed today.

Land-Based Ballistic Missiles

Three different land-based missiles have been procured or programed for strategic attack upon the Soviet Union should war occur.* The earlier of these, scheduled by the Department of Defense to be phased out in fiscal 1965 are

Atlas D: 27 missiles in 3 squadrons, liquid-fueled, 3 megaton yield hardened to 2 psi; entered service in 1959.

Atlas E: 27 missiles in 3 squadrons, liquid-fueled, 3 megaton yield, hardened to 25 psi; entered service in early sixties.

Atlas F: 54 missiles in 6 squadrons, liquid-fueled, 3 megaton yield hardened to 100 psi; completed entering service in December 1963.

Titan I: 54 missiles in 6 squadrons, liquid-fueled, 4 megaton yield hardened to 100 psi; entered service in 1961–1962.

The later missiles, to be kept in service, are

Titan II: 54 missiles in 6 squadrons, storable liquid fuel, 5 megaton yield hardened to 100 psi; evidently in the force indefinitely.

Minuteman I: 750 missiles in 5 wings, solid-fueled, 1 megaton yield of undeclared hardness; entered service between October 1962, and June 1965.

Minuteman II: 150 missiles in 1 wing, solid-fueled, funded in 1964.[16]

The missile force has become increasingly secure as the Minuteman missile has been deployed; especially important

---

* These land-based missiles are part of the Strategic Air Command (SAC) of the Air Force. Their explosive power or "yield" is measured in millions of tons of TNT equivalent, or in megatons. The hardness of their silos is measured by the number of pounds of pressure per square inch (psi) that these can withstand.

have been the efforts to disperse controls over the force. Each of the 3 squadrons in a wing has 5 launch control facilities, controlling only 10 missiles each, located peripherally around a launch center. Hence the 50 missiles in a squadron are not controlled in the final stages from a single point. Each launch facility is connected to at least one other launch facility, providing a redundant communications link to the launch center. In addition, the launch center can fire all 50 missiles.[17] The control points are protected by "extreme hardening." [18] Finally, as a further precaution, it is possible to fire Minuteman systems on the basis of a signal sent out from an aircraft. According to Dr. Brown this arrangement eliminates dependence upon "survival of the launch control centers" or "survival of their cable connections to the missile site," thus also eliminating "any effect of vulnerability of launch control centers or of control cabling." [19]

The missiles themselves are still further dispersed around the control points. They are generally 18–20 miles apart.[20] And each of them is embedded in a hardened silo "designed to withstand thermal and pressure effects and ground motion effects of typical Soviet weapons detonated at relatively close quarters." [21] It gives an idea of the degree to which the missiles are protected to note that an explosive cartridge blows the lid off the Minuteman silo before firing so that the debris that may have accumulated from the impact of a foreign missile nearby can be removed.

In short, the missile force has been built with the aim of retaining, after a nuclear attack, the capacity to achieve a retaliatory blow. It has also been designed to reduce the possibilities of accidental or unauthorized action, which has been said to be "so close to being impossible as to be of negligible importance to us."

As important as the degree of dispersal and protection of the Minuteman force may be its growing flexibility. While the first wing of Minuteman (Wing I) could carry only one target, Wings II–V will have more than one target and can be switched from one target to another by, "in a sense, pressing a button." [22] This greatly improves the strength of the force for retaliatory purposes, since one can target the missiles surviving an attack on a variety of points instead, in effect, of letting the enemy attack determine the pattern of retaliation.

The growing flexibility of the missile force will be combined with much greater efficiency as Minuteman II gradually replaces Minuteman I. Since the life of a missile is generally taken to be five years, it will presumably not be much longer than that before the force is composed primarily of the newer missiles. According to Secretary McNamara, Minuteman II "will be more than eight times as effective against the best-protected military targets as its predecessor [Minuteman I]." [23]

The missile force is presumably also gaining in reliability, but it is difficult to estimate the extent to which a high reliability of firing can be maintained. Some years ago, Secretary Donald A. Quarles noted that "very complicated" missiles that had been "in operational use for a matter of years" had achieved a reliability on the order of 70–75 percent. He suggested that "if we got to 90 percent, we would consider that very excellent engineering." [24] It is important to note that these reliability problems apply to bombers and other weapon systems as well as to missiles. Secretary McNamara has testified:

> I don't wish to leave the conclusion with the committee that these reliability problems in the missiles are any different than the reliability problems in our manned aircraft systems. They are essentially the same. They require the application of the same technology to correct, and I believe it is fair to say that many of our missile systems today are as reliable as some of our aircraft systems today.[25]

Finally, the missile force is improving in accuracy. Originally, it was estimated that Atlas and Titan missiles might fall within 5 nautical miles of their target about 50 per cent of the time, that is, have a probable circular error (CEP) of 5 nautical miles. However, by 1960, successful Atlas launches were reaching within 2 nautical miles of the predesignated target, and the President suggested that U.S. missiles had a

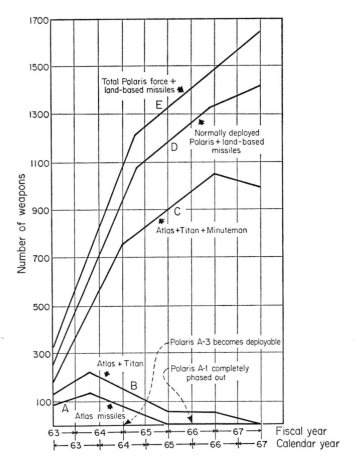

Figure 4.1. The U.S. Missile Force Growth.

Curves A and B show the Atlas, and Atlas plus Titan missile forces. They incorporate the decision of early 1965 to phase out Atlas and Titan I. The latter curve assumes that Titan II will be phased out in fiscal 1967.

Curve C adds the Minuteman force to curve B. It assumes that all Minutemen will be in place in fiscal 1966.

Curve D adds the normally deployed Polaris force to curve C.

Curve E adds the total Polaris force to curve C.

All curves are based upon the data presented either in Chapter Four or in the annual reports of the Institute for Strategic Studies.

CEP of less than 2 miles.[26] Now it has been announced that Minuteman II will have one-half the CEP of Minuteman I.[27] It is difficult to estimate the extent to which accuracies may yet improve.

The growth of the U.S. missile force is shown in Figure 4.1.

Soviet Land-Based Missiles

Presumably the Soviet force is growing in efficiency and security like our own, but information on Soviet intercontinental missiles is obviously hard to come by. The Institute of Strategic Studies suggests that there are two operational models:

1. A liquid-fueled, 10 megaton ICBM weighing 300,000 lb, capable of traveling over 8,000 miles; in service since 1955.
2. A storable liquid-fueled ICBM carrying in excess of 30 megatons; in service since 1963.

The possibility that the Soviets have lagged behind us in developing efficient solid-fueled missiles comparable to our Minuteman is corroborated by both General LeMay and Secretary McNamara, who testified that "we should recognize the [deletion in original] advantage we have in the solid propellants over the Soviets." This is a sizable advantage in simplicity of handling, speed of firing (that is, short countdown), economy, and perhaps in other ways as well. Secretary Zuckert testified that "I would rather have the solid-fueled POLARIS and MINUTEMAN than any liquid-fueled missile that I can imagine." [28]

Estimates of the numbers of Soviet intercontinental missiles have risen surprisingly slowly. In July 1962, Hanson Baldwin claimed that Soviet ICBM's "in operational readiness and in advanced stages of construction" apparently numbered considerably less than 100. Four months later, in November 1962, Stewart Alsop wrote:

"According to the current estimates, their 100th long-range missile became operational only a few weeks ago. If the current intelligence estimates are accurate—and on this score McNamara says that he is absolutely convinced.' . . ."

A year later, in November 1963, Hanson Baldwin estimated Soviet ICBM's as "one-fourth to one-fifth" of our own 500 (that is, 100 to 125). Three months later, in February 1964, he suggested that the Soviet Union had "only about 150 intercontinental ballistic missiles." [29] In April, the Secretary of Defense gave an estimate implying a force of less than 187

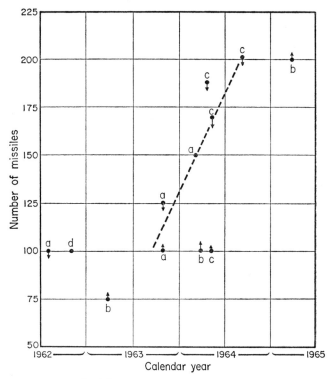

Figure 4.2.   Growth of the Soviet ICBM Force.

This chart is based upon data provided in the text. The arrows indicate upper and lower estimates. The estimates are related to their sources as follows: *a*, Hanson Baldwin; *b*, Institute for Strategic Studies; *c*, Secretary of Defense McNamara; *d*, Stewart Alsop. The dotted line indicates a plausible linear estimate of the increasing numbers of Soviet ICBM's.

135

missiles, and shortly thereafter, on April 26, Mr. Baldwin suggested the numbers 100 to 170. On August 17, Secretary McNamara gave an estimate of our superiority which implied that the Soviets had fewer than 200 ICBM's. Figure 4.2 plots these estimates. The dotted line indicates the growth that would occur if, in fact, the Soviet Union did have "about 150" on February 14, 1964, 170 by April 26, and continued to build at that rate through the next few years. This results in almost exactly 100 missiles per year.

The Soviet Union also possesses large numbers of medium-range (MRBM) and intermediate-range (IRBM) missiles deployed in the Soviet Union and aimed at targets in Western Europe. These are thought to have explosive yields measured in megatons, and to number about 800.[30]

For a variety of reasons, Soviet land-based missiles are probably relatively vulnerable if their positions are known. First, there are indications that the missiles are clustered in groups of "eight or more," sometimes with two missiles for each launch site.[31] Furthermore, in 1962, reports indicated that hardening was just beginning. It was said to be comparable to the intermediate stage of hardening for Atlas missiles, which are neither in the open nor in a silo but are set horizontally in "coffin-type" installations.[32] This suggests a hardness of approximately 25 psi, if the coffins are comparable to our own. The most recent comments by the Secretary of Defense on Soviet hardening do not indicate any very great changes, although they do indicate some.

For example, Secretary McNamara noted in early 1964, "As I pointed out last year, the Soviets are hardening some of their ICBM sites. . . ." It is possible that the very large Soviet missiles are not easy to harden. Furthermore, the liquid-fueled missiles have a slower reaction time than do solid-fueled missiles. This encourages the Secretary of Defense to believe that "it is probable that the launching of their bombers and missiles would extend over a sufficient period of time for us to receive the first blow, and to strike back not only at Soviet cities, if that be our choice, but also at the elements of their forces that had not yet been launched." [33]

A still more explicit statement of this type was made by General White:

> For years to come there are going to be a considerable number of their missiles that will not go, as there will be with ours, and it is highly useful to knock the ICBM force out. Now the trick is to find out which ones did not go.[34]

In order to protect this force, the Soviets are relying in part "on concealment and on active defence. . . ." [35] For instance, General Talensky notes:

> Most of these installations, if not all the decisive ones, are reliably concealed and consequently to hit them would require the pinpointing of a target from a launching site thousands of kilometers away. Part of the means for delivering a retaliatory blow are mobile and it would be difficult to hit them at an exact spot. Lastly, a substantial part of the means of attack would inevitably be diverted to sham targets.[36]

Vulnerability of Land-Based Missiles

Strictly speaking, land-based missiles would be much less vulnerable if they could be fired upon warning of attack but before enemy missiles had detonated. In the late fifties, when missiles were highly vulnerable, there was talk of launching missiles on warning, that is, of anticipating the arrival of Soviet missiles, indicated on a warning screen, by launching our own. But since the missiles could not be recalled or destroyed in flight, such a suggestion involved great risks of inadvertent war. Furthermore, as General White pointed out, we could not afford to fire much of our deterrent lest the warning were false and the missiles needlessly exhausted. In 1960, General Power, then Commander in Chief, Strategic Air Command, told the Economic Club of New York:

> The survivability of the missile poses a somewhat different problem from that of the bomber and must, therefore, be solved by different techniques. Since a missile cannot be recalled once

it has been launched, it would be too risky to fire it until there is incontestable proof of aggression. Therefore, our ICBM's probably would have to "ride out" the initial attack. This problem is taken into account in our later missiles which will permit launching from silos deep in the ground, thus providing good protection or "hardening" against the effects of near-misses.[37]

It is now accepted doctrine that the missiles should "ride out" a surprise attack, although the question continues to arise.* Whether the Soviets would fire missiles on warning is difficult to answer conclusively. However, the reasons given for our hesitation to fire on warning still apply to the Soviets. It should also be recognized that the Soviet system has been extensively spoofed (that is, alerted unnecessarily) by the Strategic Air Command, whether by accident or design.† After such experiences, a Soviet leader is probably loath to fire on warning. For these reasons, the invulnerability of land-based missiles must rest upon their ability to ride out an attack.

Thus, our Minutemen are likely to survive a straightforward attack in which one or more missiles are fired at each. Even the "most pessimistic view . . . suggests a vulnerability ratio for our hardened, dispersed Minuteman sites of less than two sites killed on the average by a single very-large-yield Soviet missile." [41] Hence so long as our forces are numerically superior to those of the Soviets no ordinary attack upon them could be launched. Our vulnerability problems are likely to

* For instance, in discussions of the fiscal 1965 budget this conversation occurred:

"*Chairman Russell:* What percentage of these missiles could have been launched prior to the arrival of an incoming salvo from the Communist bloc?

"*General LeMay:* I think we could launch the bulk of our missiles within the 15-minute warning time that we would allow. Our alert missiles, I think, would be launched in that time." [38]

† Thus Premier Khrushchev reported: "Take the case of General Power, who heads the U.S. Strategic Air Command. In November 1961, after a false alarm he ordered bombers stationed at all U.S. bases to head out for the Soviet Union. He did not even bother to inform the U.S. President, that is, the Supreme Commander of the country's armed forces, about it. For all of twelve and a half minutes the American Strategic Air Command was virtually in a state of war with the Soviet Union." [39] Whatever the facts of the incident reported by Khrushchev, "flushing" U.S. bombers is within the authority of the SAC Commander.[40]

arise only through esoteric methods of attack. And even these problems are diminished in significance by other weapon systems such as Polaris. In any case, a special technique would have to destroy more than one missile with each attacking weapon. One such method that has received wide publicity involves the use of "electromagnetic standing waves." Produced by the fireball of an explosion, the waves might be "of such intensity that any electrical conductors, such as wires and cables, that are strung on poles or buried in the ground in straight lines, would have currents of thousands of amperes induced in them, resulting in their destruction by melting." [42]

The Soviet vulnerability problem for land-based missiles, from a strategic point of view, may be a good deal more elemental. If the United States has learned where the smaller number of Soviet missiles are located — through reconnaissance, defectors, or spies — each such Soviet land-based missile could be attacked by several of our missiles. Thus, 300 one-megaton missiles with a CEP of three-quarters of a mile and a reliability of two-thirds could attack 100 targets of 25 psi hardness and be expected to leave less than 5 intact. [43]

In the long run, especially if the numbers of land-based missiles become comparable, increasing accuracies may become a matter of concern to both sides. One study of an arms control agreement suggests that "The problems to be encountered would be considerably alleviated if CEP's do not improve so that they are less than 3000 feet." * But in 1964 General LeMay testified that the Air Force was "optimistic" over the prospect of achieving "greatly improved accuracies with ICBM's. . . ." [45]

Sea-Based Ballistic Missiles

At the present time, most analysts would argue that the question "Can retaliatory forces survive?" may be answered in the affirmative, primarily because ballistic missiles can be

---

* This study by Air Force Brigadier General Glenn A. Kent assumes hardened and dispersed emplacement. It treats only land-based missiles under an arms control agreement. [44]

based on or under the sea. Much more attention would now be paid to the destabilizing possibility that "hard" (invulnerable) missile sites could suddenly become "soft" (vulnerable) were it not for the fact that these land-based systems are backed up by sea-based forces that are difficult to attack.

U.S. *Polaris Submarines*

Each Polaris submarine costs about $115 million, exclusive of its missiles. A submarine carries 16 missiles, and each missile must cost $3 million, since the cost of a submarine with missiles has been estimated to be $150 to $160 million.[46]

The operating cost of a Polaris submarine is somewhere between $5.5 million and $7.5 million a year.* This would indicate the costs over five years to maintain a Polaris missile on station at somewhere between $14 million and $23 million, or from three to five times that of keeping a Minuteman missile on target.†

The procurement schedule for Polaris has not changed since fiscal 1963. There were 12 Polaris submarines in June 1963, and the schedule called for the twelfth to the twenty-ninth Polaris submarines to be delivered at the rate of one a month and the thirtieth to the forty-first to be delivered one every two months.[49] In other words, about 24 by June 1964, 29 by November 1964, 33 by June 1965, 39 by June 1966, and 41 by the end of 1966.

The submarine itself should last for fifteen to twenty years if its experience is similar to that of other submarines. Its missiles are cost accounted, as are other strategic missiles, on

---

* The cost of operating the submarine may be computed as follows. Since Minuteman costs $4 million to install and $100,000 to maintain, procurement of, and operational cost for, 250 Minutemen for five years is about $1,125 million. This has been said to be comparable to the cost of operating and procuring 6 Polaris submarines for five years. Subtracting the cost of procurement gives this result.[47]

† These figures assume that half the submarines are on station, that each cost $115 million, and that the life of a missile is five years.[48] The lower figure assumes that the Polaris system will work for fifteen years; the upper figure depreciates the submarine over five years.

a five-year basis.[50] The lifetime of the system, assessed against technological breakthroughs, is also at least five years. For instance, Secretary McNamara testified:

> At the present time we see no reason to believe that the PO-LARIS will lose its invulnerability in the near future. When I say "near future," let's say 5 years. I don't see any reason to believe we will lose it after that, but I don't want to even hazard a guess as to the period after that. However, none of the techniques that might possibly cause the POLARIS to be vulnerable appear to be in the state of development so that they can be deployed within a 5-year period.[51]

The submarines each have two crews totaling 224 men, and the crews are alternated every 3 months. Of the 3 months, each submarine is in port for about 30 days and at sea for about 60.[52] It is interesting to note, especially in considering the possible growth of the Soviet submarine force, that we have been having some problem supplying the necessary crews. Personnel in the submarine force have tripled from 1960 to 1965 (from 8,000 to 25,000), and the needed men cannot be trained quickly.[53] For instance, it requires 42 months of training for men concerned with nuclear-propulsion and about 2 years for the men concerned with guided-missiles.[54]

While at sea, the submarine and its crew are highly isolated. Communication between submarine and submarine, or between submarine and surface craft, cannot be achieved "securely." [55] There is no two-way communication to shore.

Far more important, however, is the ability of the submerged Polaris submarine to receive messages from the base. However, Admiral Ignatius Galantin testified in 1962: "We still have maintained a record of 100 percent solid coverage of all traffic sent to them, and this includes numerous surprise drill messages the operations commander will send. . . ." [56] Whether or not this situation would hold during war, in particular after an attack, is not so clear. After considerable discussion of the appropriate phase, Admiral David McDonald affirmed that it was "possibly . . . but not likely" that communications with Polaris submarines could be knocked out with high-yield weapons.[57]

Not all of the Polaris submarines are maintained in a location that permits firing at once. It is often said that of the deployable submarines, we can count on "approximately 2/3 . . . being on station at all times." [58] This figure is based on the previously noted fact that each submarine is at sea only 60 days out of 90, or two-thirds of the time. However, former Secretary of the Navy Paul Nitze has remarked that the present deployment rate is "extremely high," because presently deployed ships have not yet reached their first overhaul period. Eventually, of the 41 submarines to be built, "7 would be in overhaul, 34 deployable." [59] Hence, if two-thirds of the deployable submarines were on station, about 22 submarines could be relied upon at all times. However, Admiral George Anderson has pointed out: "We also have the option of increasing the number of boats on station, if, for example, we feel that there is a particular period of tension, such as we did during the Cuban operation." [60]

When the Polaris submarine is on station, it need not be at a "fixed known location." Instead, "Each captain is free to roam at will in his area as long as he maintains his target coverage. . . ." In short, "nobody in this country knows where any one of our deployed submarines is." [61]

Since a submarine need not fire from a fixed point, it clearly has the capacity to fire at any points it wishes within its range. According to Admiral Levering Smith: "The target choices are made in the fire control system either when he receives the message or when he goes into a preselected area. As he goes from one area to another area it is current practice to shift his target." [62] Evidently the missiles are kept trained on targets which may be changed systematically as the submarine passes out of range of some points and into the range of others.

The range of the submarine-launched missiles varies. There are three different models of the Polaris solid-fuel missile. The models A-1, A-2, and A-3 have a range of 1,200, 1,500, and 2,500 nautical miles (1,380, 1,700, and 2,800 statute miles), respectively. The first five Polaris submarines are equipped with the A-1, the sixth to the eighteenth will be equipped with the A-2, and the nineteenth to the forty-first will have the A-3. Eventually, the first five submarines will have their A-1's replaced with A-3's. (The A-3 became deployable in mid-1964. The A-1 will be phased out in early 1966.) A fourth missile, the B-3, is under consideration, but according to the vice-president and general manager of Lockheed's Missile Systems Division, which would build it, the B-3 concept is still "pretty much in people's headbones." If the B-3 emerged, it would be installed in place of the A-2's.[63] (The B-3 has recently been renamed the "Poseidon.")

The significance of these ranges depends of course on the distance of Soviet (and Chinese) targets from the sea. Fairly deep penetration of the Soviet Union with a 1,200-mile missile can be achieved from the Baltic and Barents Seas and along the extended, exposed, Arctic and Pacific coast lines. With the A-2, a Polaris submarine could be on station in the Norwegian Sea (or in the Eastern Mediterranean) without being restricted to border or near-border targets. The A-3 would permit relatively deep attacks from the Atlantic off the coast of France.

Another way of looking at the situation is to note the extent to which the sea area has been increasing from which targets could be attacked. For example, the A-2 would generally double "the water area from which the submarine would fire with A-1." This has the effect of assuring for each submarine an operating area that is never smaller than "the state of Texas." (Texas has an area of 260,000 square miles; a circle with this area would have a radius of 290 miles.) The change from A-2 to A-3 will have a further impact in increasing this area. Admiral Galantin noted:

> With the A-2 missile, the area in which a submarine can be deployed and cover its important targets is about 6 million square miles. With the A-3 missile, it is going to be a little over 15 million square miles.

In fact, the A-3 missile can hit any spot on earth from the sea.[64]

Besides the range of the missiles, several other characteristics are of importance. In particular, the yield and accuracy of the missile can, in principle, determine the sort of targets for which it would be useful. There have been a variety of speculations concerning the utility of the Polaris missiles for force targets, and there has been some feeling that they are accurate enough only for city targets. In particular, their accuracy has been widely portrayed as inferior to that of the Minuteman missiles. However, in 1963, Dr. Brown said that the Polaris CEP depended "mostly on the navigation error, which is still being reduced." [65] In other words, improvements in locating the position from which the submarine would fire would improve the accuracy of the missile itself. The yield of the missiles is not thought to be smaller than that of the Minuteman missile. It is estimated at 0.7 megatons.[66] However, the B-3 or Poseidon missile will improve in yield and accuracy very substantially.

The reliability of the missile force does not seem to be in question. According to Dr. Brown, the Polaris A-2 "reached the assurance of [deletion in original] percent reliability which had been set by the Joint Chiefs of Staff as the goal," thus eliminating the need for further scheduled tests. Evidently the A-3 is following the same course. Admiral Anderson testified that its flight-test program was "on schedule" and that all indications confirmed that it would "meet or exceed the high reliability goals established for it." [67]

Finally, the readiness of the missiles is extremely high. While on patrol, all 16 missiles of each submarine have been "ready to fire on instant notice 95 percent of the time and 15, 99.9 percent of the time."

A measure of the power that these characteristics provide was given by Secretary of the Navy Nitze, who used current reliability figures for the 8 on-station submarines of an average day to conclude that these forces could eliminate most of the war-making capabilities of the Soviet urban industrial complex and kill 25 to 35 million people.[68]

The Polaris submarine is not the only possibility for hard-to-detect sea-based missiles. Although, as we have suggested, no one sees any immediate threat to the "invulnerability of Polaris," other weapon systems are being explored that would substitute for it. For instance, the Air Force is said to be exploring "Orca, a notion of constructing encapsulated, unmanned, and generally immobile missiles . . . which might be deployed at random over the earth's surface — in isolated wooded areas, arctic wastes and oceans and obscure waterways." One method of deployment might have these missiles floating "just below the ocean's surface, much like a naval mine." Lockheed has proposed "Turtle," a submerged, manned missile complex "capable of long-range mobility at very slow speed." Meanwhile, the Navy is test-firing a "Hydra" concept of launching rockets from "free-floating vertically positioned platforms at sea." Other studies refer to secreting platforms below the surface in inland or easily accessible waterways.[69]

Soviet Missile-launching Submarines

The development of nuclear submarines by the other side seems to be far behind our own in numbers and efficiency. In 1963–1964, the Soviet Union was said to have "at least" 30 missile-carrying submarines, of which 20 were nuclear powered.[70] The Secretary of Defense has asserted, "We know that the Soviets are building nuclear-powered submarines, both missile-firing and attack, but there are a number of uncertainties concerning these forces." [71]

One uncertainty seems to be the rate at which the Soviets will achieve operational status in the firing of missiles from under water. In April 1964, Secretary McNamara corroborated the fact that no Soviet missiles yet had operational firing capability under water. The key word here is probably "operational," since a Soviet Polaris-type missile named "Snark" was first displayed in Moscow as early as November 1962. And even a few months before, Hanson Baldwin had stated: "Russia's first submarines capable of launching missiles from submerged positions are just being built, and one of the first submerged missile-launchings was recently held." [72]

Until submerged firings are possible, the Soviet Union must rely on surface-launched missiles, with ranges from 100 to 400 miles, which became available in 1959. Whether or not the Soviets find this very restricting is not clear. There is some evidence that the submarine is not yet thought of as a strategic weapon. Reference to its use in Sokolovskii's *Military Strategy* is sketchy. For instance, after discussing the characteristics that Soviet submarines should possess, *Military Strategy* states: "These qualities will permit the submarine forces to engage in successful combat with an enemy navy and, if necessary, to deliver nuclear strikes to coastal targets." [73] Changes made in the second edition of this work have tended somewhat to eliminate this oversight.[74]

Surface-Deployed Ballistic Missiles

As of 1965, ballistic missiles of either major power are not at all likely to be deployed on the surface of the sea except perhaps in the proposed Western Multilateral Fleet (MLF), which may never materialize. The MLF would represent a relatively substantial barrier to missile disarmament: first, because of Soviet objection to the idea and, second, because of the increased number of parties who would be signatories to a missile reduction treaty.

Vulnerability of Sea-Based Forces

If the sea-based missiles of the United States and the Soviet Union were highly invulnerable and sufficiently numerous, the prospects for reductions in land-based missiles would be improved, assuming the absence of effective antiballistic missile defenses against sea-based missiles. The land-based forces would be unnecessary for a sure retaliatory force, and their use against other land-based targets if war broke out would be deterred by the existence of sea-based forces that could not be struck. Hence a close look at the prospects for antisubmarine warfare (ASW) is warranted. It should be mentioned that these remarks would have to be qualified if the missile defenses discussed in Chapter One were built.

It may be that both we and the Soviets would be better off if there were no effective antisubmarine defenses, since their construction could lead to renewed procurement of forces and perceived insecurity. Nevertheless, the United States sees no alternative to seeking such a defense, and, indeed, it is not clear that an effective defense could be matched eventually by an effective Soviet defense. The problem of defending against submarines is not a symmetrical one for the two major powers.

In any case, very little restraint in ASW procurement could be expected on the grounds that technology *should* be slowed. Present policy shows no uncertainty concerning the importance of ASW efforts. The Secretary of Defense has testified:

> In ASW I have one ground rule and that is that money is no limit whatever on research and development projects associated with increasing our ability to detect, track and kill Soviet submarines, including particularly Soviet missile launching submarines.[75]

Of course, procurement is another matter. In the testimony on the budget for fiscal 1965, Secretary McNamara indicated that, in view of "a number of uncertainties" concerning Soviet missile-firing and attack submarines, "the ASW force structure which we are now proposing for the latter part of the program period [1965–1969] must be considered highly tentative." Despite these uncertainties, the Secretary believes that the Soviet submarine will be "one of the major threats" by 1968.[76]

However, this threat is evidently not yet overwhelming. For example, Hanson Baldwin suggests that, during the Cuban crisis, "six Soviet submarines — all conventionally powered by diesel engines for surface cruising and electric batteries for submerged operations — were sent to the vicinity of Cuba." He viewed the possibility of other submarines as "unlikely," noted that they had been "more or less" continuously tracked "without too much difficulty," and speculated that in a state of war they "probably" could have been destroyed. This was confirmed by the Chief of Naval Operations, Admiral Anderson, who noted that the Navy had been able to identify six submarines by photographs and that "if weapons instead of camera films were employed, these submarines would surely have been 'killed.'" [77]

In addition to technical problems, the Soviets have difficulties in deploying submarines. The Atlantic and the Pacific are basically Western seas. Admiral Charles Weakley described the problems of a Soviet submarine commander in this way:

> For example, coming around the North Cape there, he has about 500 friendly miles. He has 4,000 of increasingly unfriendly miles. Coming out the other way he has about 600 friendly miles, and he has about 4,400 of increasingly unfriendly miles.
>
> Now any time he is in water[s] which are hostile to his presence, he cannot, for example, run his fathometer to check the depth of the water, he cannot use his radio for communications, he cannot do anything which reveals his presence. He must be awfully careful about charging batteries, that type of thing, because anything he does renders him liable to detection by our forces.[78]

Evidently other Western advantages exist also. Commenting on a confused newspaper article entitled, "New Submarine Finder Project Will Blunt the Role of the Polaris," Admiral William Raborn suggested:

> I think the man got himself mixed up a bit. That is designed against enemy submarines and not POLARIS submarines. I would like to point out to the writer and those who might be interested in this program that it takes friendly real estate to establish this rather comprehensive system, and the North Atlantic basin is under friendly control, and not available to potential enemies for such stations. I would think that these are facts which will become rather apparent upon thought.[79]

If future hostilities occur, a submarine fleet would probably face difficulties similar to those met by the World War II surface fleet. For instance, in 1958 Admiral Arleigh Burke described ASW efforts in time of war by saying:

> We will mine the exits and narrow channels through which the enemy submarines must pass.

We will augment the barriers.

We will have hunter-killer groups operating — constantly searching — in areas of probable enemy submarine concentrations.[80]

Of course, there is more to ASW for the United States than "bottlenecks." There are distinct problems of detection, classification, location, and destruction.

First, consider detection. The Secretary of Defense has maintained that "we are continuing a very ambitious research and development effort in the submarine detection area." At least in 1957, the Navy considered this problem "the most difficult in antisubmarine warfare . . . the one in which we have the least confidence." * In 1961, research and development efforts in submarine detection apparently emphasized the use of sound in (*a*) variable-depth sonar to provide detection ranges below the ocean thermal layer comparable to those that our new hull-mounted sonar give above the thermal layer; and (*b*) a new sonar promising further improvement in detection ranges.[84] The thermal layer referred to was described by Admiral Burke in 1959 in the following terms:

> One problem which has confronted ASW since its beginnings is that of the "thermal layer." This is a layer of water within the ocean depths where a significant change of temperature exists. This layer is usually found between the "surface" water and the water of greater depths, and forms a virtual mirror for sound waves. Sonar pings generally bounce off it. Submarines have long known this and have been hiding just below the layer. One of the major advantages of the ASW submarine is its ability also to get below the "thermal layer" and listen there where the noises travel. Surface ships have not been able to reach below "the layer." However, variable depth sonar is under development which is designed to probe at the best listening depth beneath its parent destroyer.[85]

* Admiral Burke indicated, however, that the detection range had been extended "4 to 5 times," presumably over World War II ranges.[81] By 1960, the Navy was speaking of Project Artemis, "a research program to establish the feasibility of ocean-area active sonar surveillance."[82] This would sound ambitious indeed. A year later a "closely related" program, Project Trident, was described as a research and development effort "aimed toward the development of equipment with which an effective ocean-area surveillance system can be made from shore."[83]

After detection come problems of classification and location. These call for mobility. Carriers, shore-based aircraft, helicopters, attack submarines, and so on, all play a role. They carry expendable sonars (sonobuoys) that increase "considerably the speed at which an area can be searched for submarines. These contain radios which transmit submarine information back to the parent aircraft. New sonars, planned for use on surface ships or submarines or on the sea bottom, are expected to increase substantially the distances at which submarines can be detected." [86]

The classification problem is an especially difficult one. For instance it was testified that "you have not only to distinguish a friend from a foe, but you have to distinguish the submerged object and identify it as a submarine rather than a fish, marine life, rocks, and everything else that has been classified as submarines." [87] One device used to distinguish submarines from whales, and one that indicates the kinds of subtle technical problems involved, is the magnetic anomoly detector (MAD), which senses the "distortion of the earth's magnetic field caused by the passage of a submarine." However, this device is said to have "very little growth potential" because, although accurate, it is "extremely limited" in range. [88]

After detection, classification, and location, there is the problem of destroying the target.

Many weapons are available: ASROC, an outgrowth of the rocket-assisted torpedo (RAT), used on surface ships; SUBROC, used on submerged submarines to provide them with a long-range antisubmarine attack capability (according to *The New York Times* [December 5, 1963] this range is 30 miles); and mines, delivered from the air and from submarines. [89] As progress is made in long-range detection of submarines, the demands for improved methods of destruction are increased. Admiral Lloyd Mustin pointed out that "as our sonar ranges increase, the 'time late' of target location information, longer weapon run time and opportunities for target evasion also increase, and we find that we must either provide midcourse guidance for our missiles en route to the target, or have 'weapon-carrying vehicles' that can be accurately controlled to the target and the weapon dropped within its homing range." [90]

It is clear that we have made great strides in antisubmarine warfare, a field described by the Secretary of Defense as "one of the most complex fields of development in the entire area of defense weaponry." [91] Nevertheless, the Soviet submarine threat has not diminished. Admiral Hyman Rickover has testified:

> Our antisubmarine program from its inception in 1917 has been a hit-and-miss proposition, different people coming in nearly every year. . . . I think we are no better off today relative to the Russian submarines than we were in 1941 relative to the German submarines.[92]

And in 1964, Admiral McDonald testified in these revealing terms:

> I frankly think that before we solve this problem we are going to have to come up with something that we probably are not even dreaming about now.[93]

Soviet progress in ASW seems to have been inferior to our own. The Secretary of Defense believes that "we are way ahead of the Soviet Union in this specific field." [94]

Keeping up with every submarine development is an even greater problem for the Soviet Union than it is for us, since our submarines are so much more advanced than theirs. For their part, they do not even seem to have taken the problem seriously. The editors of the RAND translation of *Soviet Military Strategy* remarked that it was interesting that the authors placed destruction of enemy carrier units ahead of destruction of missile-launching submarines.

As must be evident from the material discussed so far, no single technological breakthrough is at all likely to neutralize Polaris. It is not true, as was put so graphically by Senator Clair Engle, that, "If the Russians ever get a breakthrough on being able to see underwater, the Polaris will be just like a turtle going across a hot road." It is not "a weapons system that is wholly dependent upon one proposition: namely, you can't see underwater." [95] Even if it were easy to detect Polaris, it would still be necessary to separate the submarine's signal from that of other sources. Were this to become relatively simple, it would then be necessary to determine a relatively precise location — as indicated earlier, "kill" radii are measured in fractions of a mile. Since a submarine location can change rapidly, the destruction of even a single Polaris is not assured if it is located only at long range. Finally, the probable destruction of not one but most or all Polaris submarines relatively simultaneously would be necessary to decrease their utility as part of the U.S. military posture. And meanwhile, the range of missiles carried by our submarines increases, as we have noted. For example, since the system was initiated about eight years ago and has already doubled the range of the initial 1,200-mile missile, the range of the A-3 could easily be multiplied by a factor of 5 during the seventies, presumably in some new-model submarine. This would permit worldwide deployment in approximately 125 million square miles of ocean.

It is not necessary to discuss the vulnerability of surface-based ballistic missiles in too much detail since, with the exception of the MLF, which may never be formed, neither major power seems to be planning such a force. However, it is probably true that such a force would be highly invulnerable from a practical point of view, though vulnerable by comparison with the Polaris force. In a sense, fewer technological breakthroughs and fewer new weapon systems would be required to decrease its utility. On the other hand, new devices are always being developed to improve the security of a surface fleet.*

---

* For instance, in 1960, Secretary of the Navy William Franke suggested that aircraft carriers were considerably harder to detect than one might think. Showing a radar picture of 196,000 square miles in the Western Mediterranean, he noted that it showed "less than 25 percent of the total number of ships which were actually at sea in the area at the time." Nor was it possible from the "ideal" radar picture to pick out the two attack carriers mixed amongst other ships of the Sixth Fleet.

Ballistic Missile Defense

We have now discussed some of the elements of two of the three contests that were referred to earlier — contests between attempts to ensure survival, on the one hand, and destruction, on the other, of land-based missile systems and sea-based missile systems. Superimposed on these contests related to missile basing is another related to missile delivery. While the late fifties and early sixties posed the question, "Can retaliatory forces survive?" the late sixties and seventies could conceivably pose the question, "Can retaliatory forces penetrate?" At the present time, most believe that the offense has a substantial lead over the defense. In 1962, General Burchinal testified ". . . some scientific judgments, Dr. Von Karman's among them, . . . show we have a 2- to 4-year lead time in the offense over the defense — missile offense over missile defense." [97] But this gap may be narrowing; it is difficult to tell. This third contest was discussed in Chapter One.

Targeting

The three procurement contests under discussion culminate in the targeting of missiles and bombers on urban-industrial sites and on bomber and missile installations. The basic idea behind our strategic force targeting, if not behind that of the Soviets, is to target several weapons on each site until the probability that it would be destroyed is sufficiently high. Dr. Brown testified:

> And in every case the commander of SAC, if we are talking about strategic vehicles, and the Joint Chiefs of Staff program extra vehicles; they program extra aircraft, they program extra

---

Furthermore, if a "chance guess" located the carrier, Secretary Franke estimated that it would have moved 30 miles "before the necessary information could be collated, introduced into the launching system and the enemy missile reach the objective area." Further complications could have been introduced with the aid of "defensive electronic countermeasures." [96]

missiles, so as to raise the probability of striking the target high enough to be militarily acceptable. And, of course, that probability is different depending on what the target is.

The more important the target is militarily the higher they want that probability to be and as a consequence the more aircraft or the more missiles or the more of both they program to strike that target.[98]

Once a satisfactory likelihood of destruction of these targets has been achieved, plans are drawn up that permit selective attack. Thus General LeMay reported to Congress that the Kennedy administration wanted many options in their war plan:

We have tried to comply by producing as many as possible. I am talking about our strategic plans now. We have options now that can be exercised by the President in going to war. We also want to hold out a reserve. Whether this is desirable to do under the conditions that might exist or not remains to be seen. But I certainly have no objection to having those options.

The discussion that follows is motivated by an attempt to discern the ways in which improvements in missile efficiency might make it possible to achieve missile reductions. This theme is continued in the conclusions and should be introduced.

Improvements in the efficiency of individual types of missiles are very difficult to prevent technically and politically. And they might justify comparable reductions in missile numbers. These reductions might encourage further reductions, and the agreements might have important political effects even if the reductions themselves had little effect on force efficiency. In any case, other justification for reductions must be superimposed on that arising from improved efficiency.

Missiles improve in efficiency as they become more dependable: as the frequency improves with which a missile — surviving an initial attack — can be expected to accomplish its mission. Dependability arises from reliability (of successful firing), accuracy, yield and readiness, its ability to penetrate defenses, and such other factors as the hardness of the enemy target.

If missiles have low reliability, a great many have to be targeted on a single site. If their reliability is higher, fewer are necessary. For instance, if a missile destroyed its target whenever it was reliably fired, and if the missile has a reliability of 50 per cent, the target would be threatened with an 87 per cent probability of destruction when three missiles were fired at it. If the reliability of the missiles were increased to 70 per cent, there would be a 90 per cent probability of destroying the target with only two missiles. If reliability were 90 per cent, only one missile would be required. Evidently improvements in missile reliability can be very important for achieving high probabilities of destruction — such as 90 per cent. We do try for high probabilities of destruction. General Power has suggested that "we have a better than 90 per cent confidence factor that what we call the hard targets, important targets, will be destroyed." [99]

While an increase in missile reliability could substantially reduce the U.S. force size for fixed performance, this is not so clearly the case for the Soviet Union, if the Secretary of Defense is right that

> Given the small number of weapons they have today, the probability is they would use them primarily against urban areas. This is the theme that runs through that book on Strategy [*Soviet Military Strategy*, Sokolovskii, ed.] that you referred to.[100]

For such a countercity strategy an increase in reliability from 50 per cent to 90 per cent increases force effectiveness by .90/.50.

Of course, a single reliably fired missile may or may not destroy its target, depending upon its yield and accuracy. The effectiveness of a missile is generally assumed to improve in proportion to increases in the fraction $(\text{yield})^{2/3}/(\text{CEP})^2$. Thus, if the yield of a Minuteman went up, over the years, by a factor of 5, its efficiency as a weapon would go up by about $5^{2/3}$, or about 3. If, simultaneously, its CEP were halved, as testimony indicates would be the case if Advanced Minuteman replaced Minuteman, force efficiency would go up by an additional factor of 4, or 12 times over-all. While this does not indicate that our force could be cut by a factor of 12 — probably no target has 12 missiles aimed at it — it does indicate that substantial reductions could take place while greater probabilities of destruction were achieved.

Improvements in reliability, yield, and accuracy can have a significant impact upon the dependability of the force, but improvements in the ability of the force to be retargeted can permit more flexible planning. In particular, the ability to reassign missiles to targets for which the initial firing has failed will permit firing just one missile at a time while at the same time maintaining a small reserve. This avoids firing several missiles at each target simultaneously. These gains are somewhat complicated to characterize abstractly, and their application depends on details, but they can justify substantial reductions in force size. For example, if we want to achieve a 99 per cent probability of destruction with missiles that each have a 90 per cent likelihood of destroying their target, we would ordinarily assign two missiles to each target. If certain missiles can be retargeted, however, plans could call for firing one missile at each target and a second missile at only the 10 per cent that survived the first salvo. This would call for an average of 1.1 missiles instead of 2. It is true that there are difficulties in determining whether or not a target has survived, but if most of the uncertainty of destruction arises through the unreliability of the launch, we might simply observe the launch and estimate from its success the likelihood of destruction.

Whether or not missiles can perform their mission depends also on their ability to survive attack or, in the jargon, on their "survivability." But so long as the Soviet force is small, the survivability of U.S. land-based missiles is really very little at issue, since Soviet missiles would hardly be directed against individual Minutemen. In fact, at present, air bases would be far more attractive targets for counterforce attacks. In any case, the Secretary of Defense has noted that "the most pessimistic view . . . suggests a vulnerability ratio for our hardened, dispersed Minuteman sites of less than two sites killed on the average by a single very-large-yield Soviet missile." [101] If this average decreased from 2 to 1, then for each 100 Soviet high-yield weapons there would be an abstract gain of 100 U.S. Minutemen surviving.

Of course, such improvements in our force effectiveness could be diminished or nullified by decreases in force effectiveness arising through Soviet force improvements. Soviet forces might become better hardened, although existing Soviet forces seem to be of the type that the United States finds difficult to harden. (Our comparable first-generation liquid- or storable-fueled missiles were finally hardened, but to no more than 100 psi.) Improvements in Soviet hardening on this order would reduce the lethal radius of an attacking missile by a factor of about 2. But this could be offset, for example, by halving our CEP's or by some combination of yield and CEP in our missiles that increased the efficiency — that is, the fraction $(\text{yield})^{2/3}/(\text{CEP})^2$ — by a factor of 4.

The Soviet Union might attempt to defend force targets with active defenses. Or it might multiply the numbers of points at which targets were located. If the United States attempted to target Soviet forces, the latter would probably be the most effective thing for the Soviet Union to do, if it were not prohibitively expensive.

Conclusions

Prospects for Negotiated Missile Reductions

1. *The negotiation of general disarmament is virtually impossible in the foreseeable future.* While some kind of general disarmament under international law may be a possibility in time, nuclear weapons, the capacity to deliver them, and the knowledge required to make further nuclear weapons are a permanent part of the strategic landscape. The weapons themselves can be hidden, and the capacity to make and deliver them cannot be eradicated.

2. *The prospects for any negotiated missile reductions in*

the coming years are very poor. It is obvious from the preceding material that changes in weapons systems have been occurring so rapidly that experts are dissuaded from the necessary long-range planning. And it is not at all clear that any balanced disarmament will be perceived to be a good or fair bargain. The mutual interest in the reductions will be, for the most part, an interest in decreasing destruction if war occurs. Compared with the interest in avoiding war, this particular motivation has never found favor. If observers feel that there is any diminution whatsoever in the stability of the balance of terror, a countervailing decrease in the destructive aspect of war will not be sufficient to make the prospect attractive to them. Nor are reductions in the capacity to destroy likely to be very large unless there is substantial disarmament. A mere 50 missiles can kill 50 million people.

In any case, even if the Soviets reduced their capacity to destroy Americans, would we necessarily decide that we required anything less than a capacity to destroy every Russian citizen as a deterrent against attack? Thus, one side or the other might see no purpose whatsoever in trading reductions in capability.* Either might prefer large numbers of hostages to smaller numbers.

Some of our missiles, those targeted on Soviet missiles, could readily be given up if the same Soviet missiles were destroyed.

---

* For instance, Secretary McNamara testified: "There is general agreement that [our force] should be large enough to ensure the destruction, singly or in combination, of the Soviet Union, Communist China, and the Communist satellites as national societies, under the worst possible circumstances of war outbreak that can reasonably be postulated, and in addition, to destroy their warmaking capability so as to limit, to the extent practicable, damage to this country and to our Allies." [102] Such a goal might not be changed just because the Soviet force declined in strength.

If our goal were changed, however, it might reflect the view of former Deputy Secretary of Defense Roswell Gilpatric. In discussing the 1970 requirements for strategic retaliatory forces, he said: "Such a force, comprised of weapons systems invulnerable to surprise attack, would be *capable of destroying the centers of Soviet and Chinese Communist society.*" [103] (Italics added.) This is a much smaller requirement.

Such a trade might be called an iso-targeting reduction — permitting our targeting to remain fixed. It would probably require the power with the fewer missiles (the Soviet Union) to give up more missiles than the power with the greater number (the United States) if there were several Soviet missiles at each target point. In any case, such a trade, if prolonged to its limit, would leave the Soviets with no land-based missiles and ourselves with land-based missiles targeted on Soviet cities. Less extreme reductions along these lines would not be to the Soviet advantage either.

To the extent that a disarmament agreement saved financial resources, both sides might be interested, but, as noted below in considering existing plans, reductions themselves do not save large amounts of resources. Larger costs are involved in developing forces than in maintaining force levels. Also, by and large, the weapon systems that are more expensive to maintain tend to be replaced by less expensive ones. This reduces unilaterally the pressure for bilateral agreements to destroy armaments.

Any negotiated reductions will also raise a variety of political issues that the United States may wish to avoid. Such agreements will provide a target for both sincere and politically motivated attacks. They may be a cause of alarm to the West Germans and a source of dissension with the French. And to a far greater extent than is the case with an agreement to halt procurement, an agreement to reduce armaments raises questions concerning the nature of the relationship evolving between the United States and the Soviet Union.

It may be that the case for reductions in weapons would have to be so strong to overcome these political and strategic obstacles that any weapons satisfying the necessary conditions would be far from essential and could be disposed of unilaterally. Indeed, the agreement to coordinate reductions within the two major powers may prove a liability for attempts to persuade the U.S. electorate that we have particular missiles in excess.

Impact of Existing Plans

Largely for the reasons just sketched, neither major power has considered its plans for missile disarmament very closely. It may nevertheless be interesting to discuss the gross implications of these reasons at the present time and the ways in which U.S.-Soviet differences might be settled if serious negotiations were attempted.

There are two important issues yet to be suitably negotiated. The first concerns the degree and the nature of first-stage missile reductions. Both major powers have proposed plans for general and complete disarmament. The United States proposes proportional reductions on the order of 30 per cent.[104] The Soviet Union has suggested reductions leaving "a strictly limited and mutually agreed number of nuclear missiles which would be at the disposal of solely the Soviet Union and the United States on their national territories." *

The second outstanding disagreement concerns inspection. The United States' current attitudes on inspection are considerably more relaxed than they were previously, if discussion of the freeze is any indication. In the suggestion to limit missile stockpiles to existing levels, the United States emphasized only the monitoring of critical production steps, replacements, and launchings, although it also spoke of inspection for launching-site construction, which presumably would involve inspection that potentially pinpointed Soviet launch sites. But in a proposal to dismantle missiles, the United States might

* The Soviet Union has further stated that it would permit the retention of these missiles until the end of the third stage, that is, until the virtual completion of the disarmament process. This is regarded as a concession to Western fears. At Geneva, for example, the Soviets said: "We have agreed to the maintenance of a nuclear 'umbrella' because the Western Powers see some sort of menace to themselves if nuclear weapons were to be completely eliminated. . . ." However, it is admitted that this arrangement "would create additional guarantees for the security of States. . . ."[105] Notice that the wording of the Soviet proposal in the text prohibits both Polaris submarines and the NATO manning of U.S.-based missiles discussed in the Assembly of the Western European Union.[106]

well require greater inspection, if only for political reasons.

The Soviet plan for control over the "nuclear umbrella" would come into effect from the beginning of the second stage of disarmament and "would be established at the launching pads themselves . . . (the number of which should not be greater than the number of missiles retained)." Presumably this rules out Soviet decoy launching pads, if such exist. Both Soviet and U.S. attitudes on inspection are sketched further after Conclusion 12.

Probability of Nuclear War

3. *Either missile disarmament agreement proposed would have little, if any, direct effect on the probability of nuclear war.* The Soviet disarmament plan, to a greater extent than that of the United States, would decrease the stability of the balance of terror, but this stability itself is perhaps of less importance than political factors in determining the probability of war. On the other hand, missile disarmament would reflect, signal, and shape a significant change in major-power attitudes and would therefore have extensive *indirect* effects on the probability of war.

Destruction if War Occurs

4. *The first-stage plan for proportional reduction could reduce destruction in the United States if war occurred but would have much less effect, if any, in reducing the threat of destruction faced by the Soviet Union or Western Europe.* Reductions in the Soviet force will probably save U.S. cities if war occurs. It is, of course, possible, perhaps even likely, that the agreement would permit changes in Soviet force structure — other than numbers — which *increased* its effectiveness. For instance, increases in reliability over the disarmament period or later might increase the number of Soviet weapons that could be delivered despite the disarmament cutback. However, all important opportunities for such improvements

that are provided by the disarmament agreement are available, and at least equally likely to be acted upon, in the absence of disarmament. Hence the Soviet threat would be smaller after the agreement than without it, and perhaps smaller than at present. Notwithstanding inaccurate discussions of "overkill," this conclusion indicates, at 1965 levels of Soviet weapons, an important opportunity to defend the nation through disarmament. On the other hand, Western Europe would continue to be highly vulnerable to large numbers of Soviet weapons; even a 30 per cent reduction in Soviet missiles would leave Europe open to devastation.

The effect of the missile disarmament plan on the threat to the Soviet Union is not large. The U.S. posture emphasizes a reserve force to be withheld as a threat against cities during the course of a war.[107] The missiles dismantled under a 30 per cent decrease in the over-all force would not be taken from this most important deterrent force. And, undoubtedly, the deterrent force is now, or will soon be, quite large.

5. *The Soviet plan for reduction to specified numbers would presumably decrease destruction in both major powers and in Western Europe if war occurred.* The "minimum quantity" of weapons that would be "mutually agreed" to under the Soviet formula would limit sharply the number of cities that either side might attack. No discussion of the exact numbers has taken place. The Soviets have suggested that "if the representatives of the Western Powers would on their part like to indicate a certain figure or figures at this stage, which could be viewed in the light of the principle already mentioned, this would be considered as an indication by the Western Powers of their agreement with the matter in principle." [108]

Economic Savings

6. *Substantial economic savings would accrue to both sides as a result of almost any missile disarmament agreement; but these would result more from the "freeze" in weapons procure-*

ment associated with the agreement than from the forces dis-mantled. The real savings involved in missile disarmament do not lie in avoiding immediate procurement or in avoiding maintenance costs by dismantling missiles. They are found in stabilizing the arms race, at least for a time. Both sides could easily spend considerably more on weapons than they presently do.* Among the kinds of weapons that might be bought, the antiballistic missile systems would cost "about $16 billion in initial investment, and maybe a billion and a half a year to operating expenses. . . ." [110] The costs saved by avoiding these systems are far greater than missile-related costs at this time.†

It seems reasonable to assume that both sides will find it possible to dismantle only those land-based missiles that are well into their period of useful life. Hence one might estimate the savings associated with land-missile disarmament by computing the difference between the costs of maintaining, year after year, a missile force at two different levels. If we assume that a 30 per cent reduction would eliminate about 300 of our missiles and about 60 of theirs, this would probably save about $300 million per year for us and about $240 million for the Soviet Union.‡

With the submarine maintenance costs conjectured earlier, the "mothballing" of about 10 Polaris submarines would save $44 to $75 million per year in their maintenance, and $100

* Department of Defense Controller Hitch has estimated that Soviet expenditures on defense are about equal to our own and, in view of their smaller gross national product, that this represents 50 per cent more of their resources.[109]

† For instance, it appears that the total procurement and maintenance cost for a Minuteman per year, on a five-year accounting basis, is less than $1 million. The operating expenses alone of the ABM system are greater than could be saved by cutting back 1,500 Minutemen — about 500 more than are planned at this time.

‡ The Soviet missiles most nearly resemble our Titan or Atlas, rather than our Minuteman, and these computations have assumed our Titan II costs, simply because these were given earlier; these costs equal $4 million per year for operation and maintenance together. U.S. reductions are estimated at Minuteman costs.

million per year in procurement of the 160 missiles, assuming a five-year missile life. If submarine procurement costs can be salvaged in one way or another — for instance, by changing the submarines into nuclear-attack submarines — this would represent a saving of about $60 million per year, assuming a twenty-year life. This totals somewhat over $200 million. Soviet costs would be different but similarly irrelevant. Other direct savings could be attached to the disarmament agreement, but there is little doubt that the indirect economic savings associated with slowing down the new arms-race procurement provide the important economic benefit.

Stability with Respect to a Technological Breakthrough

7. *The U.S. — but not the Soviet — first-stage plan would increase very little the risks of a destabilizing technological breakthrough.* The U.S. proportional-reduction plan does not eliminate any weapon systems entirely. Hence it provides virtually the same protection against some new and effective method of attack. The Soviet plan, by limiting the basing of retained forces to the countries themselves, would eliminate submarine forces completely. After such a treaty an improvement in missile accuracy might be sufficient to induce fears by increasing the efficiency of attacks on land-based forces.

Either plan might have important *indirect* effects. For example, either could result in a political atmosphere in which it was more difficult to get adequate funding for research and development activities.

8. *A missile disarmament agreement would have to include a freeze, explicit or tacit, on the ballistic missile defense of cities.* The agreements under discussion might lead to further disarmament and to quite different attitudes concerning the role of urban defense. Nevertheless, at the present time, wide-scale procurement of an antiballistic missile system, no matter how ineffective, would probably be sufficient to lead to abrogation of the agreement by one side or the other. Hence a freeze on antiballistic missile defense of cities must somehow

be included with a missile disarmament agreement.* Considering the long lead time in developing and procuring antiballistic missile systems, their high cost and their low effectiveness, our control over production centers coupled with unilateral intelligence could be satisfactory in preventing clandestine ABM deployment.

Strategic Impact of Existing Missile Disarmament Plans

9. *The Soviet plan for reductions to specified numbers of missiles would — depending on the numbers — probably eliminate whatever U.S. strategic superiority remains; the Soviet plan to restrict retained forces to national territories would diminish the security of the U.S. force by eliminating Polaris submarines.* As noted in the discussion of Conclusion 7, the Soviet plan to eliminate sea-based forces would sharply decrease the invulnerability of the U.S. force. This plan would also be likely to diminish to the vanishing point whatever numerical preponderance the United States may have at present. And, while there can be no objection, in principle, to the notion of eventually restricting retained missiles to anything as vague as "strictly limited numbers" (after all, general and complete disarmament is U.S. policy), there is an objection to undertaking such drastic action in the first stage. This stems partly from common sense applied both to political and to military issues. Confidence in the disarmament process and in the other participants will have to be established first.

10. *Either the freeze of strategic weapons or the U.S. plan for proportional reductions, with or without a freeze on missile characteristics, would almost certainly be more effective in*

* As noted earlier, the U.S. plan for a freeze incorporates this point, as presumably would any of our plans for missile reduction. The Soviet plan does not. Instead, as Mr. Tsarapkin has stated: "The Soviet Union proposes to retain, as a nuclear umbrella, (i) intercontinental ballistic missiles . . . ; (ii) anti-missile missiles; and (iii) ground-to-air missiles. The two latter categories of missiles are proposed for retention in case, as the Western Powers fear, someone should try to violate the treaty and to hide a certain number of rockets or military aircraft or to utilize for an attack existing civil aircraft." [111]

maintaining our superiority than would a continuing arms race; the relative effectiveness of the other possibilities is harder to estimate. In considering missile disarmament, at least a few government analysts would, as a matter of course, consider among others the three possibilities: (*a*) that the Soviet Union strikes first (at cities); (*b*) that the United States strikes second (at forces, in an effort at "damage-limiting"); and (*c*) that the United States strikes first (after a massive Soviet invasion of Europe). In each case, the analyst would consider the effect of a freeze of missile numbers and the effect of missile reductions, both of these with and without a freeze on missile characteristics.*

Thus, the accompanying "table of preferences" summarizes the following reasoning. First, consider Column A. Assume, as is likely, that the probability of a Soviet attack is unaltered by the agreements. We are therefore concerned only with reducing its size. For any specified degree of control over characteristics, a reduction of missiles would be preferable to a freeze of missiles, since the reduction would save some U.S. targets from attack. Similarly, for any specific decision between freezing and reducing numbers of missiles, a freeze on missile and launching-site characteristics would be preferable to the absence of such a freeze. Again the freeze would save some U.S. targets by reducing Soviet force effectiveness.

* We assume that similar computations are made by Soviet strategists, but it is possible that they are not. From a U.S. strategist's point of view, it is hard to believe that the Soviet Union would be willing or able to engage in a detailed and comprehensive agreement until it has confidence in its ability to make such analyses. However, the Soviet point of view lends less weight to strategic considerations. For instance in Sokolovskii's *Soviet Military Strategy,* a statement given enough thought to be redrafted in the second edition now reads: "During a war, strategic concepts often have a reverse effect on policy. Cases even arise when the military factor acquires decisive significance." (While this may be very radical by Soviet standards, it is incredibly understated by our standards.) And sometimes Soviet spokesmen consider these considerations counterproductive, if not immoral; for example, "One cannot allow speculation on the basis of the slogan 'maintaining the balance of forces' — that is, maintaining the ratio of qualitative and quantitative indices of armed forces and their structure — because that would lead to undermining the cause of disarmament." (Mr. S. K. Tsarapkin).[112]

PREFERENCES AMONG ARMS CONTROL OPTIONS IN TWO CASES
(1 = BEST, 5 = WORST)

	A *Soviet Union strikes first** (at cities) †	B *United States strikes first** (at forces) †
I. 30 per cent reduction; no freeze on missile characteristics	3 or 2	1 or 2
II. 30 per cent reduction; freeze on missile characteristics	1	3 or 4
III. Freeze on missile numbers; freeze on missile characteristics	2 or 3	4 or 3
IV. Freeze on missile numbers; no freeze on missile characteristics	4	2 or 1
V. Continued missile force buildup	5	5

* We have noted earlier the tendency to act as if the likelihood of one's own country striking first is so unequivocally small that the adversary has no right even to consider it. The least controversial way — which we promptly embrace — to justify our consideration is that (*a*) the consideration of a Soviet first strike is the conservative military thing to do for U.S. planners, and (*b*) consideration of a U.S. first strike is desirable only because of the potential threat of a Soviet invasion of Europe that might be repulsed in no other fashion. (Neither preventive nor pre-emptive war is at issue here.)

† Obviously there are other cases to consider — for instance, a U.S. first strike at cities and a Soviet first strike at forces. But we believe our two considerations to be the most interesting from the U.S. point of view because (*a*) a Soviet attack on forces (a "rational" attack) is so well deterred and so much less threatening that a shift of attention to an irrational attack at cities is warranted, and (*b*) U.S. attacks on forces are of more interest than attacks on cities because they are more likely and also because our ability to mount such attacks is influenced far more substantially by disarmament.

Finally, agreements I–IV are clearly better than V in this regard, since the latter permits the Soviet force to improve both in numbers and in efficiency. On these grounds, II is best, and IV and V are next to last and last, respectively. The choice between I and III depends upon details (for instance, the absence of a freeze on Soviet missile characteristics might permit Soviet effectiveness — in percentage of deployed missiles deliverable — to increase by a factor of more than 1.4, thus overcoming the 30 per cent reduction.)

Column B is more complicated, and the rankings are different. Now the most important characteristics of the agreement are not those that restrict the Soviet force but those that fail to restrict our own. The ability to retrofit Minuteman I and Minuteman II (that is, turn the earlier model into the newer one) probably makes I and IV better, from the U.S. point of view, than II and III, which would presumably prevent this. V is the worst, if not in the very short run then somewhat later, as Soviet forces are hardened, based at sea, improved in efficiency, and dispersed.

11. *U.S. proposals for inspection and control, which are embodied in both the freeze and the first-stage proposal, may well be less restrictive if and when the Soviet Union can fire virtually all missiles simultaneously.** From the U.S. point of view it is highly desirable to keep Soviet missiles at a stage of effectiveness or in a state of deployment where they cannot be fired in a single salvo: this increases the ability of the United States to limit damage by striking Soviet forces even after a first salvo of Soviet missiles has struck. But such a freeze requires inspection and control of Soviet launching sites. If, on the other hand, the Soviets are at or near a stage of effectiveness, or a state of deployment, when virtually all of their missiles may be salvoed, the U.S. motivation to freeze the characteristics of launching sites and vehicles will be reduced. Quite possibly, Soviet plans do not call for making full salvos.†

---

* It is not a new idea to try to control missile characteristics. The Western experts at the Geneva Surprise Attack Conference included in their illustrative inspection system the statement: "An inspection system must be carefully evaluated and continuously re-evaluated not only in terms of present missile 'state of the art' but also in terms of the foreseeable growth potential. These changing missile system characteristics could include new vehicles and new ground support equipment greatly affecting readiness times, accuracy, preparatory activities, and over-all performance capabilities." [113]

† In the U.S., salvo characteristics generally improve — for instance, "Each Titan II squadron will be able to salvo its missiles utilizing less missile areospace ground equipment than that required by Titan I."

Where Could Agreement Be Reached
if Agreement Were Desired?

12. *The Soviet Union might not accept a proposal for a freeze that does not promise disarmament, and it might not accept a proposal that requires inspection of launching sites.* The Soviet government has consistently wished to preserve territorial secrecy during the transition period, if not after, and to permit verification only of the forces destroyed and not of those retained. Its slogan has been "control over disarmament," not "control over armaments." * Then Soviet position indicates that the control organizations would be able to send their inspection team "to any point" only after "the accomplishment of all measures relating to general and complete disarmament."

While there may be many reasons, a strategic reason for this concern is that the Soviets feel they "cannot submit information on the location of armed forces and military installations." The U.S. proposals for control "mean providing opportunities to locate targets for attack." [117] Quite obviously, from a purely strategic point of view, there are many contexts in which this could be so. And furthermore, these situations change back and forth over the years. Several U.S. strategists have tried for years to persuade the Soviet Union that secrecy is too easily

---

Therefore it is of very great interest to note a relevant change in Sokolovskii's *Soviet Military Strategy*. The second edition contains the insertion: "A nuclear missile strike consists of several simultaneous launchings of missiles with nuclear warheads by all combat-ready launching pads." [114] This is consistent with Premier Khrushchev's statements: "We are creating a system which, if one of the instruments assigned to retaliate is put out of commission, will always be able to bring duplicate instruments into play and destroy the targets from reserve positions"; and "We are locating our missiles in such a way as to ensure duplication and triplication." [115]

* Soviet statements, like our own, are carefully worded and must be read carefully. For example, the Soviet Union has announced that it is "ready to accept any proposals of the Western Powers on *control over disarmament* if those Powers accept the Soviet proposals on general and complete disarmament." [116] (Italics added.) In the Soviet view, our control suggestions are often not control over disarmament at all but control over retained weapons.

169

lost (perhaps through stealing of state documents) to be a useful defense. And because it accelerates the arms race and makes disarmament difficult, they argue that it should be given up. But this view may stem from a failure to empathize sufficiently with Soviet strategists. The Soviet problem, in Soviet eyes, has been deterrence of our attack; and deceleration of the arms race has, in their minds, been secondary to this goal. This position is quite reasonable. Furthermore, even if secrecy were not useful now, it might easily become so later as weapons and reconnaissance possibilities changed their character.

Moreover, an indefinite freeze is similarly in direct opposition to Soviet attitudes and statements. Their disarmament proposals have called for the achievement of general and complete disarmament within four years. Their speeches and rhetoric, far more than our own, view disarmament as an overriding consideration. More important, perhaps, from a "realistic" point of view is that our present missile superiority is at least 4 to 1, and without disarmament the Soviet Union would be frozen indefinitely at a level of inferiority that it might reasonably regard as unfortunate.[118]

13. *The United States is likely to enter into an agreement for missile reductions only if the agreement emphasizes proportional reductions and some inspection from the outset.* The United States has been firmly committed to proportional reductions in the past.* Furthermore, there are political and psychological arguments for inspection from the outset of an agreement.† And finally, there can be no doubt that some in

---

* At the Eighteen-Nation Disarmament Conference in Geneva, William C. Foster said: "Each side . . . presumably has designed its own defense system to meet its own needs. That is how the present balance was achieved. If every major type of armament in the defense system of each side is reduced by equal percentages at the same time, the present rough balance would be retained through the disarmament process. That is the simplest, the fairest and best way to ensure that neither side gains a military advantage over the other during the process." [119]

† With the increasingly large numbers of weapons in the hands of both major powers, it is becoming more and more common to find demands for inspection and control buttressed by such factors — plausible military arguments are more complicated and harder to discover. For in-

the U.S. government feel that Soviet secrecy is, for one reason or another, an ultimate barrier to better relations between the two powers.

14. *A missile disarmament agreement calling for inspection of production centers alone is probably the only logical compromise of U.S. and Soviet attitudes on first-stage inspection.* Conclusion 12 indicates that some limits to U.S. inspection requirements are probably necessary if agreement is to be reached. The U.S. argument for inspecting missile silos has, in the past, been based in large part on the belief that inspection was necessary to verify predisarmament weapons levels. This verification was intended to prevent the threat of surprise attack at some time during the disarmament transition. This rationalization has been a weak one for some time as the invulnerability of our own forces and our knowledge of Soviet strength have both grown. Recently two related admissions by the United States further cut the ground from under this explanation for inspection. First, the Secretary of Defense announced rather precisely the existing Soviet inventories. Second, the U.S. proposal for a freeze did not call for inspection of them. Evidently, we are not overly concerned with fears of surprise attack at the present time. And the Soviet counterforce capability is not likely to increase — independently of inspection clauses — under any agreement that we would accept.

Moreover, we should not overlook, in our emphasis on Soviet secrecy, the utility, to us, of our own secrecy. Many important and useful pieces of information concerning the vulnerability of our missiles, their performance, the performance of missiles to come, the exact locations of our missiles, and so on, may never become known to the Soviet Union. A Soviet agreement, followed by the abrogation of the treaty by one side or the other, would leave our potential adversaries with much useful

---

stance, "If disarmament is to succeed, it is essential that no country *believe* that it has been placed at a military disadvantage as the result of unbalanced reductions." [120] (Italics added.) It is revealing to reflect that a Soviet spokesman would very likely have substituted "advantage" for "disadvantage" in stating this requirement.

information that would not be, as the Soviet negotiators would say, proportional to the disarmament achieved.* Were an agreement in sight — were Soviet negotiators to indicate a willingness to discuss our proposals — these points would, I believe, be understood very rapidly in the United States.

Finally, inspection of launching sites would, in fact, pose many complicated technical and political problems. Soviet inspectors would be examining our own Minuteman missiles and Polaris submarines. Whether or not this has any strategic significance, it must surely have political significance. Disarmament agreements will be complicated enough without introducing inspection where it can possibly be avoided.

15. *A logical compromise between the U.S. and Soviet plans for reduction might call for a first-stage proportional disarmament agreement and a second-stage reduction to a strictly limited and mutually agreed number; in both cases Soviet IRBM's and MRBM's would be included in the reduction.* The phrase "strictly limited and mutually agreed" numbers can certainly be stretched to cover whatever the United States might decide it had in mind for the end of a second stage — this is a 60 per cent reduction. And, from the Soviet point of view, whether or not missile disarmament begins with a series of proportional cuts can hardly be very important. Indeed, as far as land-based missiles are concerned, both major powers have about an equal number: 1,000. The Soviets may wish eventually to destroy enough of the shorter-range missiles to change the ratio between Soviet intercontinental and other missiles. This would work in favor of our allies and would encourage them to back an agreement.

16. *Hence an indicated compromise agreement would be*

* For example, during the Test Ban hearings, George B. Kistiakowsky was able to state in discussing missile silo survivability: "We need to remember in this connection that we undoubtedly know a great deal more about the vulnerability of our sites than the Soviets do, since *we alone are well informed on the nature and structure of the silos* and have performed a number of test explosions relevant to them." [121] (Italics added.) This type of statement might become less plausible after detailed inspection.

characterized by (a) *relatively little control over, or inspection of, missile characteristics;* (b) *control and inspection of missile production facilities;* (c) *proportional reduction throughout a first stage;* (d) *reduction to specified and mutually agreed numbers during a second stage; and* (e) *a freeze on antiballistic missile deployment or procurement.* The Soviet proposal to limit retained weapons to land bases in the United States and the Soviet Union is not ultimately to the strategic advantage of either power, and we assume that the Soviet Union can be persuaded to permit sea-based forces.

The Strategic Impact of this Compromise

17. *Under the compromise agreement, the strength of U.S. missile forces would probably grow absolutely during the first stage.* Anticipated improvements in U.S. force effectiveness and increases in second-strike megatonnage during the first stage would result almost entirely from the substitution of Minuteman II for Minuteman I. In particular, Minuteman II would have increased weight-carrying capability. If the agreement contained an explicit or tacit understanding not to deploy antiballistic missile systems, it might not be necessary to use this weight for penetration aids. This would still further improve the efficiency of the force by permitting large increases in yield.* Furthermore, Minuteman II can be fired from airborne command posts and can be easily retargeted.[123] As we noted earlier, the capacity to retarget adds substantially to force efficiency.

Finally, increases in reliability might well be expected during a disarmament period. Generally speaking, all weapon systems gradually improve in reliability as they enter the force. Even if their reliabilities remain the same, the increased experience permits us to give a good estimate of that reliability. As noted earlier, increases in estimated reliability can have a

---

* If the yield were improved by a factor of 2, the efficiency of the missile would improve (against hard targets) by a factor of about 1.6. Similarly improvements in yield on the order of 3, 5, and 10 would increase efficiency by 2.1, 2.9, and 4.6, respectively.[122]

very substantial effect in reducing the number of weapons needed to target important sites (that is, those that are assigned high probabilities of destruction). The replacement of Polaris missile A-1 with A-3 will be completed in the sixties and this also will improve reliability.[124]

Therefore, it is plausible that a percentage reduction in numbers of land- and sea-based missiles might nevertheless permit an increase in force efficiency. When we add the information that Minuteman II is twice as accurate (and hence as much as four times as effective) as Minuteman I, the conclusion becomes very likely.[125] This improvement alone could, for example, permit the 150 programed Minuteman II missiles to substitute for several hundred Minuteman I and Polaris missiles in maintaining high probabilities of destroying hard Soviet targets. Since many more than 150 Minuteman I's would be replaced by Minuteman II's — there would be 750 more Minuteman I's to replace — the useful improvement in force efficiency might even be limited by the number of high-priority hard targets. This discussion makes it clear why Secretary McNamara referred to his program of "retrofitting a large number of the Minuteman I silos in the first five wings" and "integrating Minuteman I and Minuteman II squadrons into a single system" as one that "will greatly increase combat effectiveness."[126]

Of course, Soviet forces might increase their invulnerability under the agreement — negating some, but probably not all, of the U.S. advantages — but this could also occur without an agreement. The agreement is not likely to provide new ways of making the Soviet force invulnerable. And restrictions on the numbers of U.S. missiles would seem far less important, at present, than either improvements in U.S. missile efficiency — which the proposed agreement permits — or restrictions on Soviet force buildup — which the agreement prevents. Therefore, it is easy to conclude that our counterforce capability would be considerably superior under the first-stage agreement than in its absence.

18. *If the Soviet Union made appropriate efforts, then the*

U.S. counterforce and damage-limiting capabilities would be likely to decrease significantly during or after the second-stage reduction, whereupon the strategic force would revert to a counter-city retaliation function only. Soviet efforts to disperse strategic forces on land and sea would be likely to win eventually a contest against improvements in efficiency of a limited U.S. force, although even this would depend somewhat on the details of the agreement. Certainly there seems to be little opposition to a sea-based force.

19. *Under the compromise agreement, the Soviet ability to strike cities would be likely to decline during both stages; no advantages comparable to those of Conclusion 17 would accrue to the Soviet Union, because its force posture and strategy differ from our own.* The Soviet force seems designed to attack cities; its missiles have fairly large yields and, judging from Soviet space exploits, have sufficient accuracy to strike cities.[127] If this is the case, then improvements in accuracy, yield, reliability, and ability to retarget will not substantially improve the Soviet retaliatory capability. And, the U.S. missile force would still be far too large and invulnerable — some of it based at sea — to be destroyed by Soviet weapons. However, if Soviet weapons initially numbered little more than those agreed upon for the end of the second stage, there might be little change in Soviet capabilities and little U.S. interest in the plan. In that case a freeze could be more to our advantage.

Consistency with U.S. and Soviet National Interests

20. *Nevertheless, the compromise missile disarmament agreement could be in the Soviet interest.* It is quite evident that the Soviet Union does not now anticipate attacking Western Europe. Equally clearly, the Soviet Union has run far greater strategic risks of attack from the United States in the past than it would be running under this disarmament agreement. C. L. Sulzberger of *The New York Times* was quoted after an interview with Khrushchev as saying, "Quite blandly he asserts that these countries (Britain, France, Italy) are

figuratively speaking hostages to the U.S.S.R. and a guarantee against war." [128] If indeed this is the Soviet attitude, the numerical implications of intercontinental missile disarmament are much less important than they might otherwise be. Furthermore, the Soviet attitude may be one that puts less store on the numerical implications of military imbalances than do we.* And from the Soviet point of view, these strategic advantages, in which only a few of our military officers will put much faith, are of little importance. They are associated with limiting damage during a war that the Soviet Union does not intend to initiate or provoke.

Moreover, in the absence of a disarmament agreement, economic pressure on the Soviet Union will remain. The Secretary of Defense has suggested that

> . . . the Soviet leadership is confronted with a very severe resource allocation problem and must strike a balance among its various objectives: military; space; foreign aid; civilian housing; agriculture and improvement of the standard of living of the Soviet people; and so forth.[130]

By contrast the United States can more easily afford the expenses of the arms race. This was recognized by Khrushchev as, for example, when he told Walter Lippmann:

> If it comes to a war, we shall use only the biggest weapons. The smaller ones are very expensive, and they can decide nothing. The fact that they are expensive doesn't bother you because you don't care what you spend, and, what is more, many of your generals are connected with big business. But in the USSR we have to economize, and tactical weapons are a waste.[131]

In fact, it is not clear, especially to many Soviet writers, how the United States will fare economically under disarmament.

---

* For example, Tsarapkin, addressing this question in the Eighteen-Nation Disarmament Conference, said: ". . . it is one thing not to allow any State to obtain unilateral military advantages, and quite another thing to try to maintain the balance of forces with such scrupulous apothecary's precision as would not lend itself to definition in practice. After all, it is impossible to speak of disarmament measures under the pretext of maintaining the so-called military balance. Moreover, where are the yardsticks, where are the scales on which it would be possible to weigh the armaments of the two sides in order to be sure that the balance is being maintained?" [129]

And it is not only the U.S. economy but also the Western will to maintain the moral and material basis of the confrontation with the Soviet Union that may be at stake in disarmament. This is probably a common view in both major powers. Roswell Gilpatric discussed one application of this feeling when he said:

> Many of those who opposed the nuclear test ban did so not on grounds that there lay in the treaty a significant military risk to the West, but rather because they feared that any easing of tensions would soon find the Western democracies inviting disaster by letting down their guard long before a real resolution of differences between the two blocs was in sight.[132]

It seems that, from the point of view of a tough-minded Soviet "realist," the Soviet Union would do well to try to confront the West in a context of disarmament, rather than one of armament. This context might be *forced* upon the West by a determined disarmament offensive. In the course of this offensive, the Soviet Union would simply concede a series of fairly irrelevant strategic points. This is consistent at least with its declared point of view.*

Finally, many people believe that the world would, or might, be quite a different place after a significant disarmament measure had been agreed upon. The Soviet view, similar to that of some Americans, is that "as disarmament proceeds, the nature of inter-state relations will radically change, and today's tensions will give place to peaceful coexistence and broad cooperation. . . ."[134] Would it not be consistent with this view to attempt to pass quickly through a disarmament stage, in pursuit of this changed world? It seems that a wide spectrum of different Soviet views could find in missile disarmament the means to further Soviet interests.

---

* At Geneva the Soviets asserted that "in working out these measures, one should be guided not solely by the requirements of war departments or by the specific philosophy of generals concerning the maintenance of the military balance, but preference should be given to considerations for halting the armaments race, to the demands for a decisive reduction of the danger of a nuclear war, and to the interests of disarmament. In general, priority should be given to disarmament and not to any other considerations." [133]

21. *It could also be in the U.S. national interest to propose some form of the compromise agreement.* As noted in Conclusion 4, the official U.S. first-stage plan — comparable to the first stage of the proposed "compromise" agreement — would begin immediately to decrease the Soviet threat against U.S. cities. The compromise agreement could also, as noted in Conclusion 6, save billions of dollars committed to the future procurement of new weapons, and hundreds of millions of dollars for weapons dismantled. As noted in Conclusion 7, the reductions would increase little, if at all, the risks of a destabilizing technological breakthrough. And at this time, as indicated in Conclusion 10, almost any missile disarmament or missile freeze proposal would be more effective in maintaining U.S. superiority than a continuing arms race. Conclusion 12 suggests that the Soviet Union may not agree to inspection of launching sites or to a proposal that contains no significant disarmament. Finally, and most important, Conclusion 17 asserts that the relative and absolute strength of our forces, without unacceptable inspection clauses, would be likely to *increase* during the first stage of the compromise plan. Thus during the period of most concern, during which we would have least experience with disarmament, we would incur little risk. With the second stage, or thereafter, the United States would probably have to accept a situation in which both powers could effectively attack each other's cities but in which neither could effectively attack the other's forces. This situation is inherent in later stages of disarmament, and it is also inherent in later stages of the arms race. There is very little chance of avoiding it, whether by agreement or by unilateral action. What can be done is to drive the indicated bargain, in which there is initial strategic gain and little strategic risk. With this bargain, we would seek to lower the risks of national destruction if war occurred. At the same time we would try to lay the foundations for a world which would not require continuing struggles within an ever-dangerous major-power arms race.

A NEGOTIATOR'S PAUSE IN STRATEGIC WEAPON PROCUREMENT

Introduction

IN 1964 the discussions of disarmament at Geneva began to take a relatively realistic form. The United States proposed considering a freeze in the procurement of strategic weapons. This proposal envisaged freezing the numbers and characteristics of both offensive and defensive strategic weapons, including missiles of intermediate and intercontinental range, heavy bombers, and strategic antimissile missile systems.

The American representatives began by proposing that "The United States, the Soviet Union, and their respective Allies should agree to explore a verified freeze of the number and characteristics of strategic nuclear offensive and defensive vehicles." [1] They made the following points in support of the "proposal": (*a*) it should "include strategic missiles and aircraft" with the categories of weapons "defined along lines of range and weight"; (*b*) it should include antiballistic missile systems; (*c*) "the immediate objective of the freeze on numbers should be to maintain the quantities of strategic nuclear vehicles held by the East and the West at constant levels"; and (*d*) "the objective of the freeze on characteristics should be . . . to prevent the development and deployment of strategic vehicles of a significantly new type." [2] It was said that the verification system "could include the following": (1) continued inspection of declared facilities; (2) a specified number of inspections per year to check undeclared locations for possible prohibited activities; (3) the stationing of observers to verify all space launchings and all allowed missile firings; (4) observation of the destruction of — or, in case of accidents, other confirmation of — vehicles and launchers being replaced.[3]

That this proposal might conceivably be the basis for serious discussion is remarkable. But equally remarkable, despite all the discussion of arms control and disarmament over the last few years, little attention has been given to this type of proposal. It deserves more, partly because U.S. thinking about it sometimes seems to be based on a misconception about what it can be expected to achieve. Thus a discussion of the treaty's purpose is important. And since the conclusions reached are analogous to the conclusions that a similar discussion would have reached concerning the Test Ban, it may be useful to sketch that analogy first.

The Test Ban could have been an effort to halt a specific kind of research and development — testing. Many of the plans and preparations for the treaty were consistent with this purpose, if not motivated by it. When the treaty was finally negotiated, however, testing was not completely prohibited and the related research and development went forward underground. Why?

The purpose of the Test Ban, in terms of the political motivations that made it possible, was to halt pollution of the atmosphere and to achieve a "first step." Testing, in itself, meant virtually nothing. Underground testing was the most complicated part of the treaty by far; in terms of the coalition that backed the treaty, it was irrelevant. And in the end, in effect, the ban on underground tests was replaced by a willingness on both sides to continue to compete — so to speak — underground.

It is argued in this chapter that a similar evolution should take place in which the provisions of the freeze would become consistent with our real purpose. Further, it is suggested that the freeze be modified to a treaty of five years duration limiting only missile *numbers* and freezing, tacitly or formally, the procurement of missile defenses. In this no limitation would be placed on missile characteristics or on numbers of bombers. Such a freeze could be called a "negotiator's pause." During its five-year tenure, intensive negotiations with a view to achieving more substantial agreement would go forward. If further disarmament were not forthcoming, the "pause" could be renewed. In the absence of an agreement either to extend or to renew the pause treaty, the agreement would lapse and a return to unrestricted procurement would ensue.

The Purpose of the Freeze

This section discusses the *strategic* goals of the freeze, what it is supposed to achieve in terms of strategic weapons, their number, procurement, deployment, development, and control.

Many would consider this issue superfluous. Most people believe either that the freeze is a self-evidently good or a self-evidently bad idea. By contrast, at least some of those involved in deciding how great an effort the United States should make to negotiate a freeze probably have not yet made up their minds. This uncertainty is closely tied to the present ambiguity concerning its purpose.

Perhaps the best way of clarifying the strategic issues posed by the freeze is to put forth and discuss six different attitudes toward its role in controlling strategic weapons. In summary these attitudes are as follows.

First, the freeze can be viewed primarily as a step toward imminent substantial disarmament. But this view probably rests on misconceptions concerning the strategic and political feasibility of significant disarmament.

Second, the freeze can be taken at face value as an attempt to prevent further increases in levels of destructive capability. This is very much the point of view with which the notion was put forth at Geneva. This attitude toward the freeze is also misleading, partly because levels of destructive capability are so high already.

Third, a freeze treaty can be an attempt to maintain whatever U.S. strategic advantage now exists. It is this point of view that has made the freeze a relatively "realistic" proposal to the Department of Defense. However, the treaty most consistent with this approach has three disadvantages. It is complicated. It is relatively unlikely to be accepted by the Soviets. And it neither provides us with sufficiently large benefits nor resolves sufficiently pressing problems to motivate strenuous efforts in the face of the inevitable political obstacles.

Fourth, a freeze treaty can be pictured as an unnecessarily formal method of slowing aspects of the arms race — for example, growth in numbers of missiles and bombers — that can be halted by tacit agreement or that will come to a halt of their own accord. This approach seems to give insufficient attention to subtler benefits of the freeze and is too optimistic about, or too indifferent to, the perturbing impact of potential missile defenses in encouraging offensive weapon procurement.

Fifth, a freeze treaty may be justified because it is more likely to forestall future offensive weapon procurement than a tacit agreement, because it reduces incentives to procurement, and because it discourages proliferation. This point of view is, I believe, correct as far as it goes, but it may provide too diffuse a motivation to induce serious negotiation.

Finally, the freeze can be considered primarily as a method of grappling with the problems introduced by ballistic missile defenses. Indeed, it will be argued that, from the point of view of strategic weapon procurement, the freeze *must* be considered in this light; further, that this point of view leads to a resolution of the original question. In short, the chapter concludes that the strategic *purpose* of the freeze is to inhibit the procurement of ballistic missile defenses. From the point of view of narrow strategic weapon considerations, we should pursue the freeze intently if, but only if, it is our goal to avoid a round of arms race in which each major power procures expensive and unsettling missile defenses.

The Freeze as a First Step

The freeze can be pictured as a step toward substantial disarmament, and for many purposes this is a useful and proper perspective to take. Nevertheless, the mechanisms and motivations necessary to achieve disarmament are not yet apparent. Neither cost nor fear, neither social effects nor political effects of existing weapons seem sufficient to motivate the major-power political systems to grapple with the real and imagined problems of substantial reductions in weapons. In addition very substantial disarmament would be required to reduce the U.S. and Soviet capacity for destruction even to a few tens of millions of fatalities.

In any case, few people would assign a very significant probability to substantial reductions following a freeze. Rather, support for disarmament may be *diminished* following a freeze, much as the public interest in arms control diminished after the Test Ban. Still, viewing the freeze as a step toward disarmament has some validity. Disarmament without a prior freeze is especially unlikely. And even if the freeze were not likely to increase the probability of subsequent disarmament in the immediate future, it might still be proper and desirable for governments to portray the freeze as a "first step." This approach mobilizes support for arms control that might otherwise be lost because misdirected to less feasible arms control agreements.

In addition, the freeze as a step toward disarmament provides both major powers, but especially the Soviet Union, with an excuse for halting procurement. It plays the role that pollution of the atmosphere played in the Test Ban. Both the freeze and the Test Ban emphasize the long-run common interest rather than the short-run strategic interest. They provide a point around which public statements, if not private opinions, can rally without close examination of current and changing strategic realities. For the Soviet Union, which is presently behind in most aspects of strategic weapons, long-run disarmament is probably the only possible public explanation for a halt. In short, "a step toward disarmament" is a useful but somewhat misleading framework in which to place a freeze proposal. The primary immediate purpose for such an agreement must lie elsewhere.

The Freeze at Face Value

When the United States suggested that both major powers "agree to explore" the freeze, it made little reference to the prospect of later disarmament. It did describe the proposal as an "excellent point of departure for major arms reductions to follow," but it did not attempt to specify in concrete terms how these reductions might be realized. By contrast, great emphasis was placed on the rate at which the U.S. armory would continue to grow in the absence of a halt.

There are a variety of reasons for this approach. It was easy to be specific about the rate at which the destructive capability of the United States had been increasing. The Arms Control and Disarmament Agency could thus defend itself against criticism that the freeze was not "disarmament." It could assure observers, especially neutral observers, that the freeze would do something important that was comparable to disarmament.

On the other hand, the argument for the prevention of further increases in destructive capacity is not too compelling. To the Soviets, further increases in the U.S. capacity to attack their urban-industrial complex are redundant. In addition, procurement in the United States is coming to at least a temporary halt (in numbers of vehicles). In January 1965, for the first time, no new strategic missiles were programed, either land based or in submarines. Hence, interest in the freeze signifies more than our willingness to halt an increase in the numbers of offensive weapons. It reflects a prior decision to halt! Statistics quoted at Geneva to indicate how the freeze would halt increases in operational vehicles relied on a description of increases in the period 1962–1965. These figures are *not* appropriate for the coming time period.

It is true that the capacity of our force to attack Soviet land-based forces could increase significantly over the next few years. But this increase would result not from increases in numbers of operational vehicles but from changes in the characteristics of missiles as the existing force was modernized. And since these improvements are hard to control, it is not clear to what extent the treaty would restrain them.

The most important improvements are in increased yield, accuracy, and the capability to retarget. Thus, Minuteman II, destined eventually to replace Minuteman I, has been heralded as having eight times the capacity of its predecessor against hard targets; in addition it can be retargeted more easily. But its improvements in retargetability are not likely to be prohibitable, and increases in its accuracy are also difficult to prevent. Both involve internal mechanisms (or wiring) not likely to be open to inspection. Indeed, it might be that *all* of the improvements of the newer missile could be placed in its predecessor if provisions of the freeze required only that replacements be externally similar or of the same type.

Hence the force of the argument presented at Geneva — that the freeze would prevent the growth of our own strategic forces — might well be misleading on three grounds. First, the United States is not planning to increase numbers of operational vehicles. Second, it is nevertheless planning to strengthen its strategic forces considerably *without* increases in numbers of vehicles. Third, the proposed freeze on characteristics may not inhibit such increases.

In short, we may be proposing few changes in our plans for offensive weapons, but asking in return for a halt in the Soviet strategic buildup. This is not quite as bad as it sounds; our thinking might, in practice, reflect an opening bargaining position. In addition the Soviet buildup might also be due to end soon. Our estimates of it invariably turn out to be too high.

The Soviets, like ourselves, may soon be engaged primarily in qualitative rather than quantitative buildups, with the probable exception of Soviet submarine construction.

If the Soviets were not planning to halt missile construction rather quickly anyway, then the freeze would have a significant effect in limiting Soviet destructive capacity. But this effect can only be described as one that would enhance the prospects for U.S. national survival should war occur; numerical estimates of Western casualties are so dependent on the course of the war as to be misleading.

It is likely that the freeze on characteristics proposed by the United States would affect Soviet plans more adversely than would the freeze on numbers. For example, as noted earlier, such sources as the Institute for Strategic Studies portray the Soviet missile force as using liquid-fueled missiles. These are generally considered to be less efficient than our own solid-fuel rockets. If the Soviets ever changed from one type of fuel to the other, they would certainly have to change the "type" of rocket and would probably be prohibited from doing so by the present notion of a freeze.

Therefore, what can be said of the freeze taken at face value as an attempt to halt an increase in destructive capability? It may somewhat restrict the growth of Soviet destructive capacity by restricting numbers and changes in characteristics. Whether or not we could decrease the Soviet destructive capacity more substantially by avoiding the freeze and building ballistic missile defense systems is unclear — although the relative cost of achieving them in this fashion, both economically and in terms of the course of the arms race, may be considerable. As for the United States, in the form proposed the freeze would have little, if any, effect on our offensive weapon procurement. (Although the freeze in its present form seems fairly one-sided in our favor — in its restriction on offensive capacity — it may be equally one-sided in favor of the Soviets in its restriction on defensive capacity, which the United States has the economic resources to do more efficiently than the Soviets.)

Freezing Our Relative Advantage

The third approach embodies the congenial principle, "Quit while you're ahead." But freezing strategic advantages is not a simple thing to do and would require the difficult freezing of missile characteristics. In view of the complicated web of strategic and political problems, it is quite possible — maybe even likely — that no one could design a treaty that would achieve both a solid consensus in the United States and a semblance of acceptability to the Soviets. Such a treaty could be drafted to appear fair. But it would carefully have to permit those things that we wished to do and to prevent those things that we wished the Soviets not to do. The resultant treaty, complicated and tricky, would have no chance of being negotiated. And this in turn would discourage U.S. leaders from a serious effort to achieve it.

In addition, a treaty freezing Soviet modernization of their forces could not be completely successful in halting improvements. Hence it could be expected to provide a large and vulnerable target to its opponents; its proponents might be forced to admit that it could not very completely fulfill its proclaimed purpose.

More generally, the loss of our relative advantage does not provide the Defense Department with a pressing political problem comparable to that posed by the negotiation of a freeze. No one in Congress, or in the military, will object strenuously if the Secretary of Defense declines to make energetic efforts to restrain Soviet procurement through a freeze treaty.

A treaty designed merely to preserve our relative advantage is one that arouses only ambivalence and halfhearted support. Those most concerned with military advantages are least interested in treaties and most suspicious of them. Their support is characterized by a "Well, if we have to have a treaty, let's make it rough on the Soviets" attitude. Those most impressed by its rationale would be least interested in the treaty.

Those least impressed by its rationale would include important individuals in political circles, where it is often believed that we have no advantage of *strategic* significance worth preserving. In short, treating the freeze as if its purpose were to protect our strategic advantage has many problems. It can lead to failure when the freeze gets hopelessly complicated, when no one is found to support it, or when the Soviets refuse to sign. The real purpose of a freeze must lie elsewhere.

The Freeze as Unnecessarily Formal

The fourth point of view recognizes the problems and obstacles to a formal treaty of the kind just discussed and concludes that the present situation does not warrant a strong effort to achieve a freeze treaty.

Proponents of this approach realize that the strongest case for a freeze does not lie in its ability to diminish destructive capacity — to save lives in an unlikely and uncontrolled nuclear war. They put little faith in our strategic advantage over the coming years. Instead, they are concerned with managing the arms race, as part of our military-political policy, so as to produce the greatest benefits to the nation — primarily in terms of security, domestic tranquility, and solidarity with our allies. They are little concerned with the economic costs of the arms race.

According to this view, managing the arms race would now call for arranging some kind of halt, but this halt should not be purchased at too great a risk to political tranquility or future military flexibility. If a halt seems to be coming about "tacitly," without negotiation or formal treaty, and if the prospects for reaching an agreement on a formal treaty seem limited, this view would argue for not wasting the time and diplomatic effort necessary to pursue it. The temporary halt can be relied upon because the consequences of its disruption are not too serious. If each side wanted to, each could without much difficulty hold the numbers of missiles more or less fixed. Moreover, even in the context of a formal treaty, the control of many missile characteristics would require politically infeasible inspection provisions not likely to be accepted for some time by either side.

Is the freeze unnecessarily formal? There are two questions. First, would it be useful to have a treaty even if procurement of strategic weapons would halt in the major powers without it? Second, would the procurement of strategic weapons come to a halt without a treaty of some kind?

Even if we believed that strategic weapon procurement were drawing to a halt, a treaty would have three basic advantages. It would be more permanent and stable. It would affect *incentives* to procurement as well as *rights* to procurement. And it would discourage proliferation.

First, and most important, a halt in major-power procurement may be temporary in the absence of a treaty and more permanent in its presence. An unproclaimed and unnegotiated halt is not a conclusive, definitive, or solemn commitment. It is undertaken for no obvious considerations, and it is subject to pressures for further procurement of existing or novel weapons as technological, strategic, and political factors change. If our competition with the Soviets is a "long twilight struggle," then especially we must look to relatively permanent methods of containing the arms race rather than to more accidental conjunctions of intentions.

The stability of a formal treaty is enhanced by its precision. It spells out obligations, describes what is permitted as well as what is not, and reduces the likelihood that either side has misunderstood the other. Although abrogation or deception are still possible, the existence of the treaty and the solemnity with which it is negotiated tend to discourage such activities. In particular, the prospects for further comprehensive agreement would be at stake in any violation. Whatever limitations may be seen in relying upon a formal Soviet agreement, it is clear that no less deception can be practiced under a tacit agreement, and this deception need be no more than the result of a change in heart. Indeed a tacit agreement means relying upon winks rather than words and upon declarations rather than documents.

Not only is the formal treaty more stable, but it encourages future agreement to a far greater extent than does a tacit understanding. The latter has little effect in laying the groundwork for later formal agreements or even for its own continuation. A tacit agreement to show restraint is an agreement that no one, in Washington at least, will admit exists. This raises a series of problems, as gaps arise between the underlying attitudes of the highest officials and the reasons provided in public. If the effectiveness of the Nike-X ballistic missile defense improved, if the administration wished nevertheless to avoid procurement in an effort to avoid a new round of the arms race, and if it attempted to justify this restraint on the basis of cost effectiveness, these problems would certainly arise.

The formal treaty has the additional long-term benefits of building confidence that agreements can be negotiated and of building a consensus for trying to resolve strategic problems through treaties. If U.S. and Soviet force postures are to be linked by treaty during the coming years, then it would be useful to begin to accumulate the required experience in drafting, negotiating, and ratifying suitable instruments. The strategic dialogue might also be improved. At present, communications between the major powers seem too confused and ineffectual to control even minor aspects of procurement. Thus the treaty negotiations could be useful, whether or not they succeeded in producing a treaty. It is even possible that each government would give private consideration to tacit compliance with many of the restraints proposed by the other side; at least the rationalization of the restraints would be better understood. Serious negotiations could thus coordinate future actions, much as would the treaty they might produce. In addition, they could train experts on each side to understand the problems of the other.

Besides providing a more stable agreement, a formal treaty

will better diminish the *incentives* to strategic weapon procurement. Indeed, it is in recognition of this principle that opponents of arms control agreements, and cautious supporters, attempt to wrest from their governments during the ratification process commitments that "safeguard" measures will be taken. This attempt is never completely successful. It was possible to demand that the government commit itself to a vigorous program of underground tests as a price for support of the partial Test Ban Treaty. But it is not possible to prevent the Secretary of Defense and the Soviet Defense Minister from looking more favorably upon reductions in expenditures because the treaty ratification has changed the international atmosphere. Treaties will change government perspectives on the threats they face. This is one of the *opportunities* as well as one of the risks of agreements.

Finally, the formal treaty, but not the tacit agreement, will reduce the incentives to procure weapons that may exist or arise in nonnuclear countries. The prospects for major-power progress in disarmament have become highly relevant to the decision in India, for example, to build or refrain from building a nuclear weapon. These issues have become related in large part because the Indians and others in a nonnuclear role believe that they are. The impression is widespread that progress in major-power disarmament would make Indian weapons unnecessary and that an absence of progress would make Indian weapons inevitable. Whatever strategic merit this position may have, it must be treated with the respect due to a self-fulfilling prophecy; a treaty might therefore be useful in slowing the spread of nuclear weapons by enhancing the impression of imminent disarmament.

For the reasons just provided, the freeze treaty could be useful even if strategic weapon procurement were likely to come to a halt without it. Even on the basis of this assumption, however, these reasons do not provide a sufficiently strong motivation to catalyze a consensus for the treaty at the appropriate levels of government. That the treaty is more stable is interesting, but it does not resolve a pressing problem. That the treaty will affect incentives to procurement is also interesting, but controversial in its implications. Nonproliferation is a problem that might be resolved in other ways. And the prospect of spending a few to several billions of dollars in several years is not very frightening. In short, the arguments for a formal treaty do not present the freeze as a resolution to pressing problems involving large costs, and therefore they may not provide the necessary motivation for its negotiation.

In any case, offensive weapon procurement is *not* coming to a halt without a treaty. Over the next five or ten years it is certain that one side will make, or appear to make, enough progress in defensive weapons to encourage the other to procure additional offensive weapons. (This is certain because it is already happening.) The defenses of one side will encourage the other to procure bombers, nonballistic missiles, additional ballistic missiles, and new penetration aids. This is really the major objection to viewing the freeze treaty as "unnecessarily" formal. The tacit agreement will not work.

The last point of view puts the freeze in an appropriate perspective. Shall we have a freeze, or buy ABM systems? Shall we have a freeze, or a new round in the arms race? These are the pressing problems that underly the choice between a freeze and inaction.

The Freeze and Ballistic Missile Defense

Both major powers have based their hopes for a world without nuclear war on the efficacy of retaliatory weapons. In principle, these weapons could cease to be a reliable deterrent to attack if they could themselves be easily attacked or easily defended against. There is at present no real prospect of either of these destabilizing possibilities coming to pass. But one of them, ballistic missile defense, still retains the power to excite emotions and to galvanize the further procurement of strategic weapons. The prospect of an effective missile defense will be with us, I believe, throughout our lifetime. No one can be confident that such a defense will or will not be achieved over the coming decades.

It seems that the other possibility — that weapons might be effectively attacked — has been made sufficiently unlikely by the development of missile-firing submarines that it will soon cease to be a motive for procurement of additional strategic weapons. However, we have noted the possibility that land-based missiles might become suddenly and dramatically more vulnerable, and in the long run, sea-based weapons might also appear to be threatened.

At present, however, the key to a halt in strategic weapon procurement lies in the prospects for missile defense. It can probably be put quite unequivocably. If a defense against ballistic missiles were inconceivable, the procurement of ever greater numbers and ever more modern types of strategic weapons would gradually cease of its own accord. On the other hand, as ballistic missile defenses become more feasible or begin to be procured, then offensive strategic weapons will be bought to neutralize their political or strategic effect. In short, the negotiability of a freeze will depend, from a *strategic* point of view, very directly on the prospects for missile defenses, whether or not these prospects are reflected in treaty provisions.

Probably in both major powers it is also true that the prospects for a freeze depend, from a *political* point of view, on the prospects for missile defense. For example, assume that the United States considered it fairly likely that it would buy a ballistic missile defense during the late sixties. How would it treat the freeze proposal? First of all, if the freeze were to be taken seriously, the prohibition on defensive systems would have to be removed lest it compromise the later decision. But even so, if the agreement were ratified, the United States would be strongly pressured not to risk disrupting the treaty by introducing a defensive system. Just as we would consider a Soviet defense to be tacitly prohibited by a freeze on offensive weapons, the Soviets would claim that our defense violated the spirit of the agreement. This view would find support in the United States. In addition, the relaxation of tension associated with the treaty would further fragment the agreement to procure an expensive defense. In short, if we wanted a missile defense, the last thing we should wish to get involved with would be a partial or total freeze of strategic weapons.

What if we did not want to buy a defense? In this case, we should want to negotiate for a freeze — at least insofar as strategic factors are concerned; in the absence of a freeze we should eventually find ourselves buying the missile defense that we did not want. It only takes one "yes" to get the system started and, considering our general tendency to want to stay ahead in all aspects of the arms race, a Soviet decision to buy missile defenses would also spark our own. Hence one leadership group in either major power can start the process.

United States support for a defense can come from technical improvements, from unwillingness to rely upon our ability to deter potential Chinese missiles, from Soviet unwillingness to build offensive systems that would probably make our prospective defensive systems ineffective, and so on. Indeed, the government might simply yield to demands that it "do more" in national security and might find no other area in which to do it.

Soviet support for missile defense is also probably easy to anticipate: the Soviets always spend money on defenses. They may be unwilling to rely on their ability to deter Chinese missiles or those of France. They may fear our procurement and wish to be "first." And the Soviet government may also yield to internal pressures that it "do more" for defense.

Speaking generally, it is hard to believe that a tacit understanding not to procure defenses could so effectively withstand these shifting considerations that no decision to go ahead with procurement would be made in either major power for, say, ten more years.

Therefore the lines are very clearly drawn. If we want to try to fashion a defense against nuclear bombardment, we should avoid comprehensive freezes. If we do not want a defense, we need to strengthen the hands of those in both major powers who do not wish to spend the resources and disturb the present balance with all of its implications.

What, in brief, are the implications of the choice? The cost of procuring, improving, and maintaining a missile defense over ten or fifteen years could easily reach $50 to $75 billion. The cost of complementary improvements in air defenses — including a new interceptor — in antisubmarine defenses, and in fallout shelters (possibly with some blast shelters) could run into some additional tens of billions of dollars. Finally, the Soviets — who are rarely more than five years behind us — would produce a defense modeled after our own. This would necessitate continued improvements in our offensive weapons at a cost of some further additional tens of billions of dollars. The total cost during ten or fifteen years alone could easily be more than $100 billion. And during this time, we may, if we are unlucky, find ourselves emphasizing or worrying about relative advantages in defenses much as we previously competed in numbers of missiles. The defense gap could rival the missile gap, if things went badly.

If, on the other hand, we indulge in a freeze, we suffer none of these economic and political costs. Assuming that the defenses would work — something no one will really know until a war occurs — they might save some tens of millions of lives over and above those that would be saved without a defense. Because a general nuclear war is especially unlikely, we may not want to pay such costs for this potential but far from guaranteed protection.

Because this choice, these costs, and these risks completely overshadow the problems of maintaining a short-run relative advantage or of forestalling the procurement of only offensive weapons, the strategic *purpose* of the freeze can be said to be the avoidance of a new round in the arms race.

Why is it so important to try to determine a single "purpose" for the freeze? Because we must not make the mistake of committing ourselves or our efforts to the *wrong* kind of freeze. We must know what we are after if we are to maximize our chances of getting it. A freeze designed to prevent a new round in the arms race may be far more feasibly negotiated than one designed for another purpose. And it will be designed in quite a different way, as is discussed next.

Design of the Pause Treaty

This section discusses, in general terms, how a freeze treaty might be made consistent with the preceding conclusions. The discussion almost certainly leaves out certain considerations that are important, but it should nevertheless give an indication of the kind of treaty that might be suitable to the purpose. In addition, it should indicate the kind of reasoning that is appropriate in designing the treaty provisions. But it should also be mentioned that many crucial decisions about the contents of a freeze require political judgment. Here, especially, there is room for disagreement. And it should be understood that the design of a freeze is far more sensitive to small details, which may often depend upon secret information, than are other aspects of arms control and disarmament. The drafting of a suitable instrument must be done very carefully and with the best and most recent information.

The design of the pause treaty to follow is based on two important principles, simplicity and purpose. If the treaty has a very low probability of successful negotiation — which it certainly does — then we must not ask too much of it. If the treaty is to constitute an alliance between political leaders on both sides who wish to avoid expenditures, then it must be readily understood by them, and they must be able to argue for it against a hostile opposition — including at least some military leaders. If the treaty is to be unpopular with some of the military leadership, then it must not be *too* unpopular. Speaking very generally, if the military leadership in each major power would prefer to be unrestrained, even at the cost of having the adversary unrestrained, the treaty must not be too restrictive.

As a result, the treaty discussed below buys off its critics by permitting a continuation of the arms race through the modernization of forces, the procurement of bombers, and in other ways. But it insists upon (1) maximizing the chances for getting some kind of treaty; (2) seeming to have ended the arms race; and (3) preventing those costs and problems associated with the large-scale procurement of defenses.

The Negotiator's Pause

In the United States, discussion of the freeze has tended to assume that the treaty would be of indefinite duration. Although the treaty was to contain withdrawal clauses and the right of either party to call occasional or periodic meetings for renegotiation, it was not to be a treaty that lapsed automatically. (We shall refer to the government's proposal as "the Freeze.")

There seems to be merit, however, in designing a treaty so that it will indeed lapse in the absence of renewed agreement. Such an agreement might call for a treaty to last for a fixed period of years — for instance five or eight — during which intensive negotiations went forward with a view to achieving substantial disarmament. If these negotiations were unsuccessful, the treaty could be renewed — perhaps on different terms. If neither further agreement nor renewal were possible, the agreement would lapse, and a return to unrestricted procurement would ensue. This agreement could have a variety of political and strategic advantages over the Freeze.

First, the Pause treaty to a greater extent than the Freeze, would give the appearance, and have the appeal, of being a document oriented to disarmament. Since those most sympathetic to disarmament either have little influence in the U.S. government or would be satisfied to get any comprehensive arms control agreement — at least after a closer look at the obstacles — this advantage may be most important in providing the Soviets with an excuse for accepting a proposal that otherwise seems all "arms control" with no "disarmament."

Perhaps more important than its appeal to those sympathetic to disarmament is its ability to placate those who are hostile to disarmament. As a more limited commitment than an indefinite freeze, the Pause may be thought to be less drastic in its implications. For example, it might have less impact in inhibiting research and development. For the Soviets, the agreement might be portrayed internally as a potential "breathing spell" rather than as a decision to acquiesce permanently in an inferior posture.

Second, technical objections to an indefinite freeze will be vitiated by focusing the discusssion on a five-year period — the strategic implications of such a period are often fairly well understood — and many inspection requirements and related restraints might be thus simplified.

Third, because of its limited duration the Pause is less likely than the Freeze to end in an embarrassing abrogation; instead, parties anxious to terminate the treaty are likely to be willing to let it lapse automatically. While the specter of lapsing agreements is bound to be disturbing, it is hard to believe that the presuppositions of even a loose long-term freeze treaty would not change over a period of five to ten years. Hence the only question may be how changes are made in the treaty. It may be better to have modifications in the treaty go forward, under the threat of a lapsing agreement, than to have each power force the other to choose between outdated bargains and abrogation. Perhaps the fear of a return to the arms race, which the Pause treaty evokes, is the strongest, and politically the easiest, guarantee that we or the Soviets can give to negotiations in good faith.

Finally, specific political problems in one or both major powers, concerning the procurement of heavy bombers, for example, might be circumvented if it could be shown in advance, as it might, that the issues would not arise during the particular five-year period in question.

Numbers of Missiles

The treaty must control numbers of strategic missiles. Whether or not these numbers possess important strategic significance, the treaty can appear to have ended the arms race only if levels of missile inventories cease to grow or are precluded from growing past specified levels. For some years, the general perception of the arms race has been as a race in numbers of missiles; halting the race is therefore much the same as halting increases in numbers. In addition, the control provisions associated with limiting numbers of missiles are relatively simple, and it is hard to imagine restraints on other aspects of offensive capability in treaties that did not control numbers of missiles. It may be desirable to discuss limitations on numbers of missile launchers as well. It is possible that numbers of launchers could be inspected unilaterally if satellite observation were efficient enough.

The choice between freezing numbers of missiles and numbers of launchers has its parallel at sea where restraints could be based on submarine-launched missiles alone, or on missile-firing submarines *and* submarine-launched missiles. Again this could be subject to negotiation, and as before the important political issues would probably call for the freezing of missile numbers.

The restraints on missile-launcher ratios would be important if the purpose of the treaty were to freeze our advantage, but it has no particular importance for the three criteria mentioned earlier: getting a treaty, seeming to have ended the race, and preventing ballistic missile defenses. In justifying a loose treaty we need constantly to repeat: "What is it that the other side can do under this treaty that he could not do in its absence?"

Indeed, the looser treaty, focusing on missile numbers, would permit us many advantages. We could rearrange our land-based Minuteman force if deployment were not fixed. Thus we could substitute numbers of mobile missiles for the fixed-site Minuteman missiles. And we could also dilute the number of missiles per submarine to achieve greater numbers of missile-launching submarines.

Applying the principles of simplicity and purpose, we assume that the limitation would be only on missile numbers rather than on numbers and deployment. (Numbers would be frozen in the following separate categories: ICBM's, IRBM's, MRBM's, and submarine-launched missiles.) Obviously, however, a detailed study of the implications of this choice is necessary.

Similarly we leave unrestrained the characteristics of missiles that are very difficult to control without inspection that neither side would permit. Indeed, some of the characteristic improvements that might be made under our treaty would render defenses against missiles less feasible. Since a purpose of the treaty is to inhibit the procurement of defensive systems, there is some merit in permitting such missile improvement as would weaken the incentive to buy defenses.

Antiballistic Missile Systems

While the prohibition on increases in numbers of missiles would be the important part of the treaty from the public's point of view, the prohibition on missile defenses would be the crucial part of the treaty from an economic and strategic point of view. Despite its importance, there is some question about how it should be incorporated into the treaty.

At one extreme, it could be left out completely. The treaty could refer only to numbers of missiles, and both sides could perceive that the procurement of ABM defenses would so promptly destroy the presuppositions of the treaty that it would become a justification for withdrawal. (Alternatively the treaty could mention the fact that gross changes in strategic posture related to the treaty would justify withdrawal.) Probably if the understanding were to take this form, it should be framed not as a treaty but as a set of simultaneous announcements in which the Soviet Premier and the U.S. President stated their intention of holding down the numbers of weapons. As a treaty, an agreement on numbers alone might lack sufficient strategic substance. It might be *too* simple. Perhaps, if defensive systems were not to be mentioned, a somewhat more stringent control over offensive weapons, such as a freeze on deployment, would be appropriate.

If defensive systems were referred to in the treaty, either a freeze on ballistic missile defensive systems or a limitation on numbers of defensive launch sites might be appropriate. The latter would permit some deployment and relax the pressures associated with fear of Chinese threats to the larger cities of each major power.

The explanation for controlling defensive missile systems is the one given by the United States in including such restraints in its Freeze proposal — that a failure to restrict defensive systems would be "destabilizing." This term is, of course, more correctly applied to the stability of the treaty than to the tendency of the strategic situation to erupt into war.

Bombers and Bomber Defenses

Probably neither major power will procure heavy bombers in the future, and even if they do these bombers will have little important strategic effect. What effect they do have will tend to make missile defense systems less valuable if the bombers can elude the defenses. Hence there is merit in permitting the maintenance of bombers so as to support the central purpose of the treaty — to discourage the purchase of defenses. In addition, in this country, the political problems associated with preventing the procurement of new bombers are substantial. And any restraints on bombers would have to distinguish between our heavy bombers and our F-111 (TFX) aircraft, which it might be hard to do to the satisfaction of the Soviets. Finally, eliminating bomber restraints will simplify the treaty.

If bombers are not to be restrained, little need be said about bomber defenses. These are difficult to control, not likely to absorb much money in the absence of procurement of missile defenses, and unlikely to become a political issue.

Antisubmarine Defenses

U.S. and Soviet antisubmarine warfare capabilities do not lend themselves to control, for a variety of reasons. The defenses are composed of many different types of weapons and sensors. Some of these are highly secret, some are used for other purposes. Finally, to a great extent, the capabilities and methods of the two sides are not symmetrical. In addition, it seems likely that the failure to freeze antisubmarine warfare activities would not destroy the presuppositions of the rest of the treaty for the foreseeable future — certainly not until the period of the Pause lapsed. Thus the treaty can be simplified by permitting submarine defenses to be unrestrained.

Prospects in the Absence of a Pause

At the present time Soviet procurement may well be more significant in determining future weapon procurement in the United States than are U.S. policies in determining Soviet procurement. By our standards the Soviet Union ought to be less satisfied with its force posture and more likely, on military grounds, to indulge in adjustments of it that, in turn, could motivate corresponding changes in the U.S. force posture.*

Thus a large Soviet buildup in numbers would probably lead to large increases in the numbers of Minutemen or to the development of a new mobile missile in the United States. A new Soviet bomber could lead to changes in our air defense policies and to increased pressure for a new follow-on bomber of our own. An increased number of Soviet submarines would probably lead to greater ASW expenditures. Soviet antiballistic missile expenditures could lead to a decision in favor of our Nike-X or a nonballistic missile, and so on. In each of these cases, the U.S. decision is considerably less likely in the absence of Soviet encouragement. For example, *The New York Times* noted, after referring to the high cost and low efficiency of ABM: "A third factor [encouraging delay in decision mak-

---

* But U.S. standards are generally inappropriate to predict Soviet actions. In October 1964, R. Fryklund noted that missile predictions had been cut again for the year and remarked: "Since the wild days of the missile gap predictions, the Soviet Union never has built the force expected."[4]

ing] is the resistance in the Administration against undertaking a major strategic weapon development at a time when relations with the Soviet Union have reinforced hopes in ultimate disarmament agreements." [5]

Which Soviet decisions will be made is difficult to predict. Soviet decisions on strategic force procurement depend on a variety of factors: ideology, decisions already made, internal political considerations, costs, decisions concerning resource allocation, committed resources, personalities, Soviet vested interests, U.S. responses to Soviet actions, and so on. Even from our vantage point, our own procurement has little "inevitability" associated with it. The number of Minuteman procured, the emphasis on submarines, bombers, or defenses, are all the result of intense controversy and negotiation inside the Pentagon between those of differing views.* The outcome of similar Soviet discussions is even harder to predict than the outcome of our own discussions would be.

Indeed, there is wide disagreement as to the general Soviet attitudes underlying strategic force procurement. Soviet actions sometimes seem to be preparations to fight a sort of World War II with nuclear weapons — preparations that would presumably be the product of doctrinal lag or of vested interest. Alternatively, they may be acting as if security would be assured if only Europe were kept hostage to massive Soviet retaliation. Perhaps they believe that very few nuclear weapons, and fairly uncertain delivery capabilities, are sufficient to deter; perhaps they want badly to economize on offensive weapons; or, perhaps, they are simply confused.† Still further possibilities include an exaggeration — from the present standpoint — of the utility of secrecy, a desire to buy

---

* For example, the U.S. Air Force first proposed, in June of 1961, that 2,500 missiles be placed in silos and railroad cars over a five-year period from fiscal 1962 to fiscal 1967. This five-year plan was cut to 1,000 silo-based missiles in the fiscal 1963 budget, and Congress approved 800.[6]

† According to the Swedish spy, Colonel Stig. E. C. Wennerstrom, Russian leaders, "because of an inherent leaning toward landbased strategy," would not readily accept his report that American bombing of targets in the Soviet Union was unrelated to invasion.[7]

large numbers of weapons only when they are both cheap and reliable, or a desire to buy only those weapons that might "leapfrog" U.S. capabilities.

The most common fears of a Soviet military breakthrough in the absence of some kind of halt in procurement involve antiballistic missile systems; reports of Soviet ABM activity tend to support a common expectation that the Soviets will emphasize defense against missiles as they have emphasized defense against aircraft. Whether or not the next ten, fifteen, or twenty years could produce a new and effective Soviet defense, Soviet pretenses to a defense in the forthcoming years could have an extensive effect on U.S. procurement encouraging both the nonballistic missile and the follow-on bomber. Whether the Soviet Union will pretend to make substantial progress in this field is not completely clear.* But that an effective Soviet antiballistic missile system is not an immediate prospect seems quite clear. The Secretary of Defense has asserted that he sees "no possibility of any Soviet anti-ballistic missile system in any way eroding our present advantage" over the next five years at least.[9]

What are the Soviet choices in weapon procurement? The Secretary of Defense has made them apparent, in a statement quoted earlier. He noted that significant quantities of fully hardened land-based missile sites and submarines on station are required to neutralize U.S. capabilities for threatening a counterforce attack. The Soviet Union might elect to procure one or the other, both, or neither of these capabilities. Each possibility would lead to quite a different strategic context and to different responses by the United States. For instance, in early 1964, the Secretary reaffirmed previous comments and said: "As I pointed out last year, the Soviets are hardening

---

* Unquestionably, however, such pretensions give rise to concern in this country. Hanson Baldwin wrote in 1964 under the title, "New Soviet Anti-ICBM Site Seen as Increasing Pressure on Pentagon": "The apparent installation of a second Soviet anti-ballistic missile site near Moscow is expected to increase political pressure in the United States for the deployment of an American defensive system against ballistic missiles." [8]

some of their ICBM sites and are building missile-launching submarines." [10] But the following excerpt from a column by Richard Fryklund in the *Washington Star* shows our uncertainty:

> New intelligence figures indicate that the Soviet Union once again has failed to build the number of ICBM's predicted in the annual American estimates. As a consequence, officials say, American missile plans probably will be adjusted downwards. . . . The new long range predictions, which will be completed toward the end of this year, are expected to concede the Russians several hundred — but well under a thousand — ICBM's by 1970. [11]

The next general possibility for Soviet procurement would be one in which the Soviets elected to build high-quality Polaris-type submarines and to put them on station but not to make major changes in their land-based missile force. The Secretary of Defense has called the possibility of high-quality Soviet submarines "entirely probable" and one of the "major factors" in his conclusion that "given the size and kind of strategic offensive forces we project for the Soviet Union and for ourselves — great damage to both sides in an all-out nuclear exchange could not be avoided under any conceivable set of circumstances." [12] There are reports that Soviet submarines are, indeed, being procured at the rate of 7 to 10 a year, but there are also many indications that Soviet submarines are not now of high quality in their reliability, their range of firing, and their capacity to fire under water. It certainly seems possible from the available evidence that for a combination of political, technological, strategic, and cost-effectiveness reasons, the Soviets might not develop this capability for some time. The following are a few of the factors that might dissuade them: they might not possess the technology or resources necessary to provide easily handled missiles with light but high-yield warheads, with accurate submarine guidance capabilities, or with worldwide radio directional-signaling stations; they might be discouraged by U.S. antisubmarine warfare capabilities; they might fear defection or confrontation;

and the geography of Soviet submarine bases — in conjunction with a relatively small number of missiles per submarine — might make the cost per submarine on station seem prohibitively high. (Our submarines have 16 missiles per submarine and, from overseas bases, clearly travel much less distance to reach on-station positions.* A submarine base in Cuba, now somewhat improbable, would greatly improve the cost effectiveness for the Soviets of keeping submarines on station.)

If the Soviets were to procure high-quality submarines, the United States would logically increase its antisubmarine warfare capability but probably not its own Polaris fleet, unless and until the Soviet fleet challenged our own numerically. This last response is, of course, motivated by political rather than strategic concerns, since the two fleets of ballistic missile firing submarines do not interfere with each other's functions.

Secretary McNamara has noted the "highly tentative" nature of the U.S. ASW force structure, which depends upon a "number of uncertainties" concerning Soviet submarine capabilities.[14] Hence increases in ASW expenditures are a likely response to Soviet submarines.† But for the most part, the

---

* We probably should be cautious in evaluating estimates of the projected Soviet submarine threat, since two different influential sets of expectations would be realized if the threat materialized. First, the Navy might tend to believe in the likelihood of such a threat, because it would wish to be conservative in estimating an enemy threat and because our antisubmarine expenditures are in large part based on such estimates. Second, the widespread view that U.S. counterforce capabilities are waning and (hence) should be de-emphasized in favor of attempts to restrict the arms race is derived in no small measure from anticipated Soviet submarine forces. According to the *Washington Star*, the Soviet submarine-launched missile force is "lagging behind American intelligence estimates." [13]

† However, the extent of increases in antisubmarine warfare expenditures probably depends primarily on the effectiveness of the measure rather than upon the extent of the threat. For instance, in discussing the need to include antisubmarine warfare capabilities in any "damage-limiting" program, Secretary of the Navy Nitze remarked: "The nature of the threat would warrant spending additional billions. Yet, today, until we can provide improved ASW performance, I cannot in good conscience recommend large additional forces for this single purpose." [15]

procurement of ASW forces is one of the responses least likely to exacerbate the arms race or to interfere with the possibilities for a freeze. Much of the new activity would be secret or would be closely related to nonstrategic naval capabilities. Virtually none of it would be involved in hypothetical plans for a freeze because, for a variety of reasons, ASW does not lend itself to formal restraints. And if, as predicted, ASW continued to be relatively ineffective, our activity would not be especially likely to influence Soviet procurement. Finally, the response to Soviet submarines would be dampened by the relatively poor cost effectiveness of ASW.

Hence ASW preparations would not be likely to interfere with a Pause, which thus might be technically feasible immediately after the Soviet submarine buildup. In short, it would seem that the procurement of Soviet missile-firing submarines would have a relatively significant effect in decreasing Soviet vulnerability without a correspondingly significant effect on force procurement in the United States. It would be more likely to postpone than to prevent a tacit or negotiated halt.*

A third possibility for Soviet force procurement in the absence of a halt would be a few hundred land-based ICBM's. If immobile but fully hardened, they would, as noted, increase Soviet invulnerability. But, compared to Soviet submarines, they could encourage U.S. force procurement more substantially. In the first instance this would be because fixed-site ICBM's can be targeted, if they can be located, while submarines cannot. The Secretary of Defense testified in 1963: "The increasing strategic nuclear power in the hands of the Soviets has acted to increase our costs because it has been our

---

* This assumes that the appearance of missile-firing submarines off our shores would not have a more decisive impact on the U.S. tendency to buy an antiballistic missile system than did a few hundred Soviet ICBM's. Note also that the most immediate threat posed by the submarine-launched missiles, which is an almost warningless threat to air bases, has already been discounted in the anticipated nonprocurement of a follow-on bomber. (That is, if no new bomber is procured, the destabilizing impact of the submarine-launched missiles will be greatly diminished.) In any case, "pessimistic" Department of Defense estimates for the later sixties may already assume that no heavy bombers survive.

policy to endeavor to target those weapons for destruction to the extent they can be destroyed under assumed sets of circumstances." [16] Considering the existing numerical preponderance of the United States, it seems reasonable to assume that everything that can be located permanently has been targeted. The temptation to continue to target even fully hardened Soviet ICBM's should not be underrated. It would probably require a difficult-to-justify change of procedure to do otherwise. In the absence of a Soviet submarine buildup, the case for the inevitability of Soviet retaliation would be weakened and the argument for targeting land-based missiles would be strengthened.

But second, the Secretary noted earlier that it was "at this time" that we could not envisage the destruction of fully hardened land-based missiles. The argument that pay load, accuracy, and yield might eventually "beat" hardening would further encourage missile procurement by the United States.*

The justification for this procurement might be substantially reduced if the fully hardened missiles could be launched readily in salvos, as they presumably could be.† In this case the argument that targeting Soviet missiles would reduce damage if war occurred would be substantially undercut. Such a procedure would reduce damage only if the United States struck the first strategic blow, and this possibility would seem increasingly remote as the fears of an invasion on Western

---

* If an ICBM would be rendered unusable if its site were within two and a half times the radius of the apparent crater — the plastic zone — then accuracies for a 1-20 MT warhead would have to be between .25 and .75 miles.[17] Improvements in kill mechanisms or methods, increases in yield-to-weight ratios, pay load, etc., could also help change the balance.

† That Soviet missiles may not now be launched readily in salvos has been widely asserted in the press on more than one occasion. Most recently, for instance, an article in *Missiles and Rockets* under the title "USSR Can't Salvo ICBM's," suggested: "because of certain Soviet command and control arrangements, it is believed that a U.S. second strike could destroy a number of Soviet ICBM's before they got off the ground." The article speculated that these arrangements resulted from a deployment pattern of 6 to 8 missiles combined with a single launch-control center that could handle only 1 missile in the air at a time.

Europe dissipated. Nevertheless, the residual political pressures to maintain a sizable preponderance, the need to target the missiles on something, and the problem of determining where to draw the line in targeting targets that can be located, might well combine to produce a continuation of existing doctrines. Although from the U.S. point of view this would be considered politically desirable rather than strategically meaningful, the Soviets might not believe that they had achieved a high degree of security against a strategic attack. Hence the procurement "race" might not be a suitable stopping point.

If the Soviet Union then proceeded to build several hundred, rather than a few hundred, missiles, it is hard to believe that the United States would not return to procurement of at least a few hundred land-based missiles. These would be purchased in response to political pressure to stay further ahead and as a result of strategic concerns over the vulnerability, to a larger Soviet force, of Minuteman silos. If the Soviet pattern of development followed our own, the expensive liquid-fuel missiles, procured in relatively small numbers, would be followed by much larger numbers of solid-fuel missiles procured at a rate of one per day. (The gap between development and initial deployment of the Minuteman solid-fuel missiles was about five years.)[18] However, the Soviets have shown no signs of desiring to procure a large force of land-based missiles. The Secretary of Defense testified in 1963:

> It is clear that the Soviets do not have anything like the number of missiles necessary to knock out our Minuteman force, *nor do they appear to have any present plans to acquire such a capacity.* If they were to undertake the construction and deployment of a large number of very high-yield missiles, we would probably have knowledge of this and would have ample time to expand our Minuteman force, or to disperse it more widely.[19] (Italics added.)

A final possibility is that in the absence of a freeze, the Soviet Union would, indeed, buy many high-quality missile-launching submarines and a few hundred fully hardened launch sites. This combination would coincide with what seem to be present qualitative predictions and hence would tend to reinforce the conclusion drawn from these predictions that nothing can be done about a growing Soviet retaliatory capability. The impulse to target locatable ICBM's effectively would be diminished by the observation that submarines could not be targeted. In turn, the difficulty of targeting hardened ICBM's would diminish enthusiasm for strenuously tackling the difficult problem of antisubmarine warfare.

In summary, the Soviets can buy, or pretend to buy, an antiballistic missile system, make relatively slight changes in their missile force, procure a high-quality submarine force, or a relatively invulnerable land-based force, or both. The degree and extent of the response by the United States will be based primarily on three factors: the extent to which the Soviet action can be effectively neutralized; the extent to which it undercuts, or seems to undercut, the U.S. deterrent; and the extent to which it challenges the U.S. preponderance of forces. Applying these and other criteria to possible weapon systems that a forthcoming Soviet force might emphasize, a list of them, leading from most likely to gain a response to least likely, would read: (1) antiballistic missile systems, (2) large numbers of vulnerable, locatable, and slow-to-fire land-based missiles, (3) substantial numbers of fully hardened land-based missiles that can be salvoed, and (4) high-quality missile-firing submarines. The United States seems unlikely to permit Soviet ICBM's to exceed in numbers some fraction of our own missiles — much less to have a force exceeding our own in size. And in politically sensitive characteristics such as yield, the development of new types of nuclear explosives, new types of missile fuels, and so on, there would also be a tendency for the United States to try to maintain a competitive position.

Relation to Other Agreements

Nonaggression Pact

As always, the Soviets are likely to want to include a nonaggression pact, and as always the United States is not likely to wish to do so. The reasons go well beyond arms control, involve European politics, and occasionally verge on the scholastic.

Nonproliferation Treaty

It seems unlikely that the Pause could be negotiated in the absence of conditions suitable to a nonproliferation agreement. Hence nonproliferation might be part of the agreement.

Fissionable Material Cutoff

If the Soviets were willing to permit inspection of delivery-vehicle production centers as part of a Pause, they might be willing also to permit inspection of fissionable material production. Hence a formal agreement on a fissionable material cutoff might be conjoined with the Pause treaty.

Relation to an Underground Test Ban

For much the same reasons, the Soviets might be willing to permit a few on-site inspections for tests if inspection of production centers was also going on. Hence a complete Test Ban Treaty might be achieved in conjunction with a five-year Pause. Whether or not this attempt should be made is not clear. A prohibition of underground testing is, in and of itself, not very important, and the five-year Pause is a much bigger "first" step. On the other hand, the Test Ban has achieved a certain priority.

Nuclear Test Ban Treaty and the Pause

Presumably the abrogation or violation of either one of these agreements would provide justification for the other party to withdraw from both commitments. Nevertheless, it might be well to reaffirm and seek Soviet reaffirmation of the Test Ban Treaty if the Pause were to break down after ratification.

Other Parties

Chinese Procurement

While a major-power renewal of procurement does not effectively threaten the Chinese — they are so far behind anyway — the existence of the Pause treaty would increase the possibility of joint U.S.-Soviet action against them. The Pause in procurement would not affect the offensive weapons likely to be involved in Chinese conflicts. The major powers would retain many weapons, and the Chinese would presumably be most interested in relatively short-range missiles and rockets suitable for deterring the Soviets and for threatening nearby Asian countries.

Negotiation with the Chinese poses still further problems. It is not clear what the United States could offer that would be acceptable to the Chinese as an inducement to halt Chinese procurement. Moreover, the Soviet Union and the United States can neither negotiate separately nor jointly with China. To negotiate together poses complicated problems so long as the Soviets and the Chinese are formally bound by ideology against the United States. But to negotiate separately poses military problems. Neither major power separately can hope to undermine the Chinese military incentives for procurement, because the Chinese perceive potential military threats from *both* major powers.

French Procurement

The military problems associated with French strategic weapons arises from their tendency to induce Soviet defensive procurement. French procurement might be slowed through political mechanisms with the emergence of a Pause treaty; but it is hard, as it is with the Chinese, to see military mechanisms through which it could be discouraged. During the transition from aircraft to land-based and sea-based missiles, French procurement may, on military grounds, be especially difficult to interrupt.

Multilateral Force

The multilateral fleet is a more serious obstacle to a Pause agreement than either French or Chinese procurement. As far as the Pause agreement is concerned, it would be useful if the multilateral fleet were not established at all or, if established, were composed of as few ships as possible — and these built or converted as quickly as possible. And if the proposal should no longer be actively pushed, it would be useful if it were, in one sense or another, formally withdrawn.

Current Prospects

In early 1964, when the United States first proposed the indefinite freeze of strategic weapon procurement it seemed to do so with very little previous thought. Indeed, the United States did not really propose an agreement but only its consideration.

Quite obviously we learn more and more concerning the nature, purpose, and design of a freeze over time. To this extent, the prospects for a freeze improve. However, the technical problems associated with certain freezes may, in combination with political problems, make them obviously nonnegotiable. In addition, there are a wide variety of world events, political attitudes, or attitudes of particular decision makers that would prevent the negotiation of the treaty. A formal freeze treaty is, by its nature, of low probability.

On the other hand, it is also unlikely that the procurement of weapons on each side will continue at the same pace as it has in the past, and it is possible that this slowing down will eventually be supported by some kind of understanding. This understanding could be expressed in simultaneous announcements from the U.S. President and the Soviet Premier, in an exchange of speeches in which each tries to deter the other from expanding the arms race, or in a very loose executive agreement. Certainly, some kind of freeze is far more likely than any agreement on reductions.

It is hard to expect a much better team for effective negotiation of a freeze treaty than that of President Johnson and Secretary McNamara. They combine relatively firm control over both the military and political aspects of the problem with a relatively high degree of sympathy for the objectives of arms control, including especially economy.

The Soviet leadership may find a freeze more desirable as time goes on if its economic problems become more difficult, if its failure to reach a rapprochement with the Chinese becomes more obvious, if it establishes itself more firmly, and, most important, if it begins to perceive the necessity of an agreement to forestall further U.S. expenditures that will stir up the arms race.

Whether or not these conditions are sufficient to induce a formal treaty, it is clear that the period between 1966 and 1968 may be relatively opportune, politically and strategically, for a freeze, if the war in Vietnam is resolved. Assuming, as is likely, that the Soviet Union would not have agreed to a freeze before developing its own nuclear weapons, and that to forestall the development and procurement of intercontinental missiles would have been impossible, this may be the first period since World War II in which a freeze agreement could be plausibly conceived.

How long it will remain feasible is unclear. Once the purchase of antimissile systems is begun, a freeze must either interrupt plans for procurement of defenses or acquiesce in them. This is likely to be difficult on many political, technical, and strategic grounds. Once contracts are let and work begun, it is no simple task to halt the process. Probably neither side would find it politically feasible suddenly to decide to defend only one-half as many cities as it had planned, after the deployment of a few batteries had begun. By this time, the procurement of the later batteries would be well under way.

It is not so obvious, but may also be true, that a freeze would be very difficult to design once missile defenses had been deployed around the major metropolitan areas. Treaty designers could not freeze effectively the penetration capability of missiles, because neither side would be willing to permit the necessary inspection. Hence, they could not justify freezing either the numbers of missile interceptors or their efficiency. In turn, if the capability of the defense could not be controlled, then even the numbers of offensive weapons might not be suitable for restraint in a feasible treaty. In short, it might not be possible to freeze the missile defense contest while it was being played out through the procurement of weapons. Any restraints that were imposed might upset the balance or appear likely to do so. These restraints might decide the contests rather than freeze them.

If an offense-defense race could not be frozen in its course, the prospects for a freeze after the United States had begun to procure Nike-X would be poor for a long time. Soviet procurement would follow our own, and for an indefinite period the defenses of one or both sides would be of some effectiveness. We would then have to wait until the offense-defense contest was decided or superseded in both major powers before we could reach agreement. It is as if we had determined in the early fifties that a freeze was impossible so long as bombers and bomber defenses were in delicate balance: we should then have had to wait until the missile age made the bomber versus bomber-defense contest irrelevant. At the present time it is unclear what new weapon system might eventually make irrelevant the contest between ballistic missiles and ballistic missile defenses. Whatever it turned out to be — perhaps nonballistic missiles — it might take ten years or more before it came upon the scene. And, at that time, the situation might or might not lend itself to a freeze. It should also be mentioned that, once the initial down payment has been committed for missiles defenses, much of the motivation for avoiding a new round may be diminished. Finally, the impetus for a freeze is presently encouraged by the general belief in both major powers that it would be helpful in coping with nonproliferation problems.

For these reasons it may not be an exaggeration to speculate that the present strategic situation is more likely to produce a freeze agreement than at any other period between 1945 and 1980 at least; by the latter date the missile-ABM race might cease to occupy the center of the strategic stage.

Those most responsible in the governments of both major powers would undoubtedly like to avoid the expenses and headaches associated with a new round of procurement. Each would also, undoubtedly, like to avoid the painful process of trying to negotiate a comprehensive arms control treaty with the other. But it seems that both sets of problems cannot be avoided. How much will each major power spend, and what will each undergo, in an effort to avoid a formal agreement? This seems to be the question posed jointly by the freeze and the ballistic missile defenses.

DEVISING FURTHER ARMS CONTROL PROPOSALS

WHILE MANY would argue that the plans put forward are too conservative, they are unlikely to be negotiable in their present form — almost all arms control proposals are; the ideas they present need to be further watered down. To those who do not find this obvious from the exposition of the plans and the arguments made for them, it may be useful to point out that the benefits of arms control or disarmament are equivocal. For every advantage perceived by some, disadvantages will be seen by others. If resources are saved by both sides, some will complain that we are not exploiting our economic advantage in the arms race. If weapons are to be destroyed in agreement with the Soviets, many will think the bargain — whatever it is — a poor one, and many others will believe that no bargain can be a good one. Reductions in weapons, even obsolete weapons, are not supported by everyone, even in principle. The "Hot Line" has, or had, many who opposed it for one reason or another; and a less controversial arms control agreement would be hard to find.

For these reasons, and for other institutional and bureaucratic ones, it is most unlikely that we shall be able to trade very substantial losses for very substantial gains even when that trade may seem highly favorable to one, or a few, or even a great many of us. From the perspective of an arms controller, the government seems a conglomeration of vetoes, a process fraught with inertia. And vetoes can arise from allied foreign governments as well, and from our perception of their concerns.

Especially important, we get little or no help from the Soviets. Their plans and proposals generally reflect even less wisdom and preparation than our own. Their initial responses to our suggestions are almost invariably negative and discouraging — at least until they think the matter over. And while we may put too much emphasis on technical matters, their emphasis on political issues has become an obstacle to technical discussions of details. This has contributed to a continuing Soviet ignorance both of strategic "realities" (as we see them) and of our point of view — perhaps these are the same. And their use of arms control proposals for political purposes is far more marked than our own. None of this helps, and it contributes to a general confidence, in those Western circles unfriendly to arms control, that the Soviets can be depended upon to save us from the consequences of our own suggestions. In this regard, the Soviet willingness to sign the Test Ban was a shock to many in the West.

There are many other obstacles. Recurrent elections in the West make planning difficult. Every Soviet governmental transition induces a slowing down. Vietnam is a dramatic example, but not a unique one, of the perturbing impact of events outside the area of direct confrontation. Even plans like that for the multilateral force can prevent arms control proposals from being considered; more startling is our inability to pronounce them obsolete after they are virtually dead. Changing technology and new strategic concepts also have a conflicting effect. It is very difficult for the Secretary of Defense to predict his position on issues even a few years hence, and most far-reaching disarmament proposals require him to take such a position. The net effect of these, and many other restraints, is to place most current proposals for formal arms control well below the threshold at which the government can be forced to consider them seriously.

But if we consider all of the restraints in order to avoid cutting across them, if we mold plans as closely as possible to the shape of things, and if we seek the support of many influential groups, the proposals we produce are very much less significant than we could wish. Perhaps it would be better to hammer away at the "system" independently of the chances for success. The hammering process might be useful in itself and, perhaps, some President will change all of these "realities" through the force of his dedication and the power of his office. This is the approach of many concerned with arms control; it is reflected to some extent in the proposals just supplied, but I am not sympathetic to it and grow less so with time.

There is a long history of arms control efforts; it provides little that is hopeful and positive and much that is neither. In the light of that history, it is better to settle for the possible than to seek the improbable. This is not a bad rule simply because it is being applied to an area in which much that is desirable is most unlikely. It is no solution to insurmountable difficulties to ignore them.

Fortunately, the possible may be more powerful than at first it appears. A little arms control can go a long way if it exploits the attention focused on the subject and the symbolic significance that now attaches to every agreement. Within limits, arms control agreements can be made to mean or signal whatever both sides want them to. Nonaggression pacts can preclude military maneuvers; destruction of obsolete bombers can undermine the prospects for new weapon systems; and a ban on war propaganda can substitute the arms race for the adversary as the villain of the mass media. Therefore, there is merit in trying to seek agreements in the substance of which we are little interested. The form of an agreement and the fact of its ratification may go further than its substance. It may become more than the sum of its intended parts. It may interact with unanticipated political factors to provide new opportunities or new successes. The very meaning of the agreement may change. With time, its sanctity, its importance as a precedent, and the field of application of its provisions may grow.

If so, perhaps we should not try to do too much. Perhaps our proposals should seek to achieve goals in subtle ways or to seek goals that are themselves rather subtle; perhaps they should seek ends not clearly related to their substance; perhaps they should anticipate favorable effects that are not easily opposed because they are not clearly indicated. This is not to suggest that we and the Soviets should attempt to deceive each other, or ourselves, with proposals that have "small type" or deceptive clauses. It does mean that we should attempt to use agreements less to dictate, and enforce, desirable changes, and more to encourage them gently and to increase their probability. Our proposals should be part of a process rather than a series of ends in themselves. This process should be easier to achieve because it is designed to be encouraged rather than to be suddenly ratified. Perhaps we want to shape an atmosphere rather than destroy a weapon system; perhaps we want to show and encourage rapprochement or a common understanding.

In a sense, we want to expand the notion of a withdrawal clause. If none of our agreements are *really* binding, perhaps they should be much looser so as to be more susceptible to whatever kind of ratification they require, while still signifying whatever they wish. In the last analysis, it is often much easier to agree that certain acts should, and therefore will, signify progress than it is to achieve a comparable formal advance. A formal agreement is better in a world under law but not clearly necessary in a world without it.

We may be approaching a rather important opportunity to apply these considerations. Perhaps it would be well to conclude a book of specific proposals with a concrete approach to the design of their successors. If so, attention might be directed to the question, "After Vietnam what?" As this is being written the war in Vietnam approaches a crisis; but eventually it must end or cease to be such an obstacle to U.S.-Soviet arms control activities. As the war subsides U.S. and Soviet officials may be anxious to make progress, perhaps quick progress.

Impatient with the delay in improving U.S.-Soviet relations, eager to improve the damage now being done to those relations, conscious of many events that could abruptly arise to forestall progress, freshly reminded of the dangers of U.S.-Soviet opposition, and released from the pressures of the crisis, both sides may engage in a coordinated search for something that will signal a change in heart, a new attitude, a fresh start, a beginning, or an end. There is more than a slim chance here. Perhaps in arms control, it will be darkest before the dawn. What should we make of this possibility?

Perhaps we should prepare an act, or pair of acts, that to most (uninformed) persons would signal the end of the arms race itself. In mechanical terms it may be easy to do this. Perhaps all that are required are the right *statements* on both sides made in an appropriately dramatic setting. The pronouncements could be embedded in a communiqué after a Presidential visit to Moscow, in a set of parallel coordinated announcements by governments, in a couple of good speeches exchanged on television, or even in a new disarmament effort with new faces and new terms of reference. These statements would not signify that the cold war was over, but only that the procurement contest in strategic weapons, the numbers game with missiles, and the efforts to achieve a strategic advantage were all past. Maybe we want to say that we both have enough missiles; that there is no merit in pushing onward in this direction; that we both recognize this fact; that some kind of halt, freeze, or pause is inevitable; that the world is faced with overkill; that the President of the United States and Premier of the Soviet Union should instruct their negotiators to clean this mess up and to stamp "finis" on something already expiring.

It may be that this sort of thing would achieve much that we desire. There is, after all, very little that we can realistically hope to achieve that will not follow quickly and easily from a *détente* and a general realization that the arms race has run its course. Perhaps we should forget arms control that emphasizes and presupposes a military relationship with an adversary. Instead, measures that signal, and hence effect, a political change in the relationship itself may produce more arms control than either side could ever ratify in any fixed atmosphere of suspicion. It may be easier to thin out troops in Europe, to dampen the incentive to embark on new and expensive weapons, to avoid constructing additional missiles, and to cut military budgets, if we simply work for a set of acts that will tell people the present contest is over. And these acts might have a much easier time passing through the bureaucracy than would a comparable set that, in itself, *legislated* an end to the arms race through comprehensive and detailed agreement.

Furthermore, the acts may benefit from timing. Opponents of arms control and *détente* could not oppose the Test Ban on the grounds that the Soviets and the Chinese had just had a particularly angry exchange; nevertheless the extent to which such a proposal may have relaxed U.S.-Soviet tension was certainly influenced by its temporal proximity to signs of feuding. Thus, if political events throughout the world lent themselves to a convincing Presidential declaration that the acts to be undertaken reflected a (post-Vietnam) "new start," the agreement would be enormously enhanced but no more easy to oppose.

In devising further proposals we want to consider these kinds of possibilities carefully. Whatever we do, arms purchases will continue in one form or another — we shall be replacing old tanks with new ones for at least a few hundred more years. No formal agreement, no matter how comprehensive, can stop everything. Nor need it. If, after Vietnam, we announce that the arms race is over, we shall have begun where eventually the competition must end — in the minds of men.

POSTSCRIPT

AS THIS VOLUME goes to press, in February 1966, Secretary McNamara's statement in support of the fiscal '67 budget has not been issued; the first hearings have not yet been held. On January 25th, however, he testified before a Bomber Subcommittee of the House Armed Services Committee, which was exercised about his decision to phase down the bomber force and his failure to order a new strategic bomber. His statement could not be restricted to bombers alone since decisions concerning them must be related to the other strategic forces. As a result, judging by its form and content, his prepared remarks were the larger part of his annual statement on strategic forces yet unreleased to the full committee. It permits us to bring this book precisely up to date.

The main surprise in the budget is not a surprise to the reader. The decision to scale down the heavy bomber forces, while a variant of TFX is phased in, has now been made. Potentially more important is the evidence that ballistic missile defenses are becoming even more effective. And underlying the significance of these changes are signs of a continuing failure or inability of the Soviet Union to achieve forces that are highly secure against attack — a failure that may have far-reaching consequences in time.

The defense statement actually listed the following as a major issue: "Should a manned bomber force be maintained in the 1970's; if so, what aircraft should be selected for the force?" Its answer, for now, was to propose to discard 345 of the 600 B-52's left (Models C through F) and to replace them over the 1967–1971 period with 210 FB-111A's (a bomber

223

version of TFX). Newspaper reports say that the FB-111A will have a speed range from 100 miles per hour to 1,700, will weigh 10–20,000 pounds more than the fighter (which weighs 60–70,000 pounds), have a range of 4,000 miles empty, and the ability to carry fifty 750-pound bombs as does the B-52 operating in Vietnam. The budget contains provisions for the modification of the other 255 operational B-52G-H's to keep them in a "satisfactory operational status" at least through fiscal year 1975. This switch from B-52's to FB-111A's was not hard; there was nothing else ready and the cost of substitution was somewhat smaller than the cost of modifying the older B-52's. The Air Force was persuaded to propose the replacement and the Chiefs to support it. We noted in early 1964 (see the top of page 77) that the distinction between fighter bombers would be clouded by TFX. Now two years later, a version of it is programed to substitute for a heavy bomber, and it is referred to as a "truly effective strategic bomber" for the next five-year period. With this substitution, the distinctions — real or apparent — which encouraged considerations of *heavy* bomber disarmament are further weakened.

Missile Defense

The missile defense questions are much more important, and they are becoming more urgent. The testimony speaks of a new kind of missile defense that seems to have been a breakthrough of 1965. It uses missile interceptors, variously referred to as "long-range," "new extended-range," and "exoatmospheric." Such defense would permit an "area" rather than a "point" defense. One supposes that enough batteries of such weapons might cover the United States as a whole rather than only a few tens of metropolitan centers. This breakthrough, combined with on-going progress, has produced a number of surprisingly optimistic statements. For example, "An ABM system employing long-range exoatmospheric interceptors in addition to lower altitude interceptors could complicate even a sophisticated attacker's ballistic missile penetration problem." Or, "it now appears to be technically feasible to design a defense system which would have a reasonably high probability of precluding major damage to the United States from an *N*th country nuclear threat, e.g. Communist China in the 1970's." And this optimism is reflected also in a related concern: "We now propose to carry [our work on penetration aids] forward on an accelerated basis, particularly with regard to the development of new penetration aids, which would be needed to defeat an area ABM defense employing exoatmospheric missiles."

While it is admitted that there are still "many unresolved questions" about the design and performance of such a system, the development of long-range methods of destroying incoming missiles may eventually turn out to be the breakthrough — or a prelude to the breakthrough — that so many feared might sharply modify the balance between offense and defense. Certainly a few more years of progress like this could be unsettling. One numerical signpost, important mainly in reflecting a change in attitude, is revealed in the following comparison between McNamara's statements.

In early 1965:

> There is no defense program within this general range of expenditures which would reduce fatalities to a level much below 80 million unless the enemy delayed his attack on our cities. . . .

In early 1966:

> Against likely Soviet postures for the 1970's [even at] substantial additional cost to the U.S., . . . against a massive and sophisticated Soviet surprise attack on civil targets, there would be little hope of reducing fatalities below 50 or more million.

If the debate remains focused on a "light" ABM system for Chinese missiles, and if the debate really reflected the Pentagon interest in a ballistic missile defense, the decision to go ahead could wait five to ten years. This report says the Chinese could "possibly" deploy a small force of ICBM's by the "mid to latter part of the 1970's." By this measure a four-year-lead-time ballistic missile defense would have to be started only between 1971 and 1976. Unfortunately, the Defense Department has its own unique brand of political science — which is really applied war-gaming — and it shows a naïve tendency to believe that missile defenses might deter the construction of Chinese missiles. (The statement asserts that the "prospect" of an effective U.S. defense might possibly weaken the incentives to produce and deploy such weapons altogether.) But in the end, many in the United States will ignore the distinction between "prospect" and "existence," and make a still-anticipated Chinese missile an excuse for action. (In fact, atomic-submarine warfare capabilities in the Pacific may be the real answer to a more plausible Chinese threat.)

The fact that the exoatmospheric missile defense system is an "area" defense can hardly be overestimated in importance. The statements assert that it would, "for the first time, give hope of achieving a high confidence defense against a light ICBM attack not just for a few selected cities but for the entire nation." One particular consequence of importance is that it weakens the link between missile defense and fallout shelters. This statement suggests that "against small unsophisticated attacks," something less than a "full fallout shelter program" might be appropriate. If, eventually, fallout shelters are to cease to be a presupposition of missile defense, the prospects for missile defense will improve. More generally, an area defense element in the posture weakens — without completely eliminating — a great many points against missile defense, some unreal but all complicating the debate. The capacity of the Russian attacker to strike undefended cities disappears, the calculated attempt to create fallout outside defended areas is less plausible still, and the political question as to "whom to defend" is removed from the debate.

What does all this cost? The light system will cost $2 billion a year for the first five years. The system designed overtly against Soviet forces would cost $5 to $6 billion a year over the early 1970's and $4 to $5 billion thereafter. The smaller system could be augmented to increase its effectiveness. For this reason, it is still likely to be the first step — a step not yet taken. (In December, *The New York Times* reported that the long lead-time items for a missile defense system would be bought, but this quiet and ambiguous beginning seems to have become a victim of the Vietnamese war expenditures.)

That ballistic missile defenses are evidently showing more promise will not have a dramatic effect on the standard war-outcome computations so long as U.S. and Soviet missiles are hard to attack on the ground; an ABM defense against an un-damaged enemy missile force is not likely to seem promising even on paper. Unfortunately it is getting easier to destroy hardened missile silos with incoming missiles. In 1964, the Secretary's statement said:

> Neither could we count, with any reasonable degree of assurance, on destroying all or almost all of the Soviet's hardened missile sites, even if we were to double or triple our forces.

Two years later, it reads:

> Feasible improvements in missile accuracy and re-entry vehicles could greatly increase the efficiency of our offensive forces against Soviet hard targets. However the effectiveness of offensive forces in the damage-limiting role, is sensitive to the timing of a nuclear exchange.

In other words, the safety of Soviet forces may eventually depend a good deal more than we had expected on who strikes first.

We discussed in Chapter Four the very sizable improvement that Minuteman II will be over Minuteman I as we phase it in over the next few years. The Secretary now announces that he will begin in fiscal 1967 to buy a model of Minuteman so much improved that it warrants being called Minuteman III. According to the *Washington Star* (January 24, 1966), it has improved guidance devices and multiple warheads; the latter improve the prospects for destroying targets. Since the Soviet submarine-launched missile force is not growing especially rapidly, and since the Soviet Union has only just begun to show the new missiles that are capable of greater protection in deep underground silos, we may speculate that we are in a period in which our capacity to strike Soviet forces is growing

227

more rapidly — perhaps much more rapidly — than their capacity to defend them.

Speculating freely now, we may be faced with the following possibilities for the medium run. It may be that Soviet land-based forces cannot, without great effort, be protected beyond the capacity of our forces to find and destroy them with high certainty. Our missiles, in numbers and accuracy, may have made it pointless, or useless, for the Soviets to follow our pattern of replacing the early and unprotected liquid-fuel missiles with the newer, solid-fuel ones in fixed silos. And it may be that, for any number of reasons such as costs, technology, geography, traditions, and bureaucracy, the Soviet forces will never include large numbers of submarine-launched missiles on station. Then, especially, we should retain for a long time an incentive to use ICBM's first if war broke out in Europe.

These incentives pose two kinds of problems. There is first the problem that a missile war might indeed seem imminent, that a President might in fact be persuaded during a local conflict to try to disarm the Soviet Union for the safety of Europe and ourselves. True, the probability of U.S.-Soviet war seems so low, and so nicely declining, that these fears seem to be nightmares only. But partly because this is true, the Soviet Union may devote its resources to other problems. And a great imbalance may last for a long, and hence risky, period. Our own dynamic for retaliatory weapon production is now so well established as to be almost independent of the real likelihood of war; it will not falter. Hence the differences in U.S. and Soviet capabilities could conceivably get even larger as we continued to exploit one breakthrough after another. And if we achieve successes in one area of weaponry, we may be tempted to devote other resources to complementary weapons. A great success in the capacity to destroy land-based missiles would induce us to spend additional funds on antisubmarine warfare. So also would a lag in the Soviet development of submarines. We have a compulsive urge to achieve whatever strategic superiority is possible, and only resistance on the part of technology or of the Soviet government can prevent us from achieving it.

On the other hand, Soviet resistance also tends to encourage our efforts. The numerical growth of their missile force would encourage ours, and the development of a Soviet ballistic missile defense would encourage us to build one also. It is hard to know which one prefers: sufficient Soviet efforts to achieve a secure deterrent force, or a continued Soviet apathy. When we thought there was a simple solution to the problem of building invulnerable weapons — land-based missiles and submarines — such secure forces on both sides seemed to be the thing to wish for. Neither side's effort to achieve secure forces of this type would have encouraged the other to buy more: more would not help an attack, and would not be necessary to prevent an attack on one's own. But if there is no simple Soviet counter to our efforts, we might learn to hope that they would acquiesce, as they have so far, in a degree of U.S. superiority that is, after all, not very relevant to real issues. We might hope that the Soviet leadership would not lose its nerve; that it would continue to ignore irrelevant computations; and that it would muzzle those of its military officers who might complain. We might hope that the Soviet government would prefer to forget about the race than attempt to shift the balance more nearly toward parity — a parity that may be further from achievement than it was two years ago.

But if parity is desired, the best Soviet strategy is ever more clearly defined by McNamara's statement. The Soviet government should first quietly persuade the United States government to continue to put off ballistic missile defenses in return for comparable Soviet restraint. It should then set about building submarine-launched missiles. The first is absolutely critical; if the Soviet Union fails to dissuade us from ballistic missile defenses, the case for improved U.S. strategic forces will be improved across the board. Every single new weapon system will be encouraged, some of them very substantially, by our effort to achieve a "balanced" defense, and by our encouragement in the notion that the effects of nuclear war can be minimized. To our Defense Department these days the whole is more than the sum of its parts. Each individual part of a defense against Soviet strategic forces is, in effect, too inadequate to be worth buying; but the total is thought to be meaningful, and ballistic missile defense batteries are most of the total. They will lead promptly to the purchase of the rest.

The case for Soviet submarines is equally clear. No land-based system can complicate the problems of defense and surprise attack with as high a level of confidence as can sea-based forces. If Minuteman II is eight times as effective as Minuteman I; if Minuteman III is comparably improved; if reconnaissance has improved at a rate to challenge science fiction; if the United States is going to retain a 3 or 4 to 1 preponderance in missile numbers; and if the capacity of these missiles to be retargeted will make it unnecessary to fire several at once at each target, then Soviet land-based missiles may become vulnerable as fast as they are built. The Secretary's statement practically shouts this assertion and it is impossible to believe that elements in the Department are not just as happy to let the Russians know — most of them in the interests of slowing the arms race, perhaps some in the interests of persuading the Russians to lie back and relax.

The submarines are not the only answer, only the best one. No one knows what we will be able to do in detecting and destroying submarines ten years from now. But submarine warfare will never lend itself to the nice computations associated with land-based missiles, just as "bomber wars" have not. There are uncertainties associated with submarine warfare that are very unlikely to be eliminated. No one can now imagine how even a few Soviet submarines could be destroyed simultaneously and by prearranged plan. And in the long run, when submarines have global missiles that can hit any target from any point, the problem of surprise attack will be reduced to the ultimate problem of trailing submarines through the waters of the globe.

If this is what the Soviet *should* do — if they want to buy weapons at all — what they *will* do is another matter. As likely as not, the Russians will buy a small ballistic missile defense (the main effect of which will be to induce our own) and then fail to buy secure retaliation forces — lacking either the resources or the conception of how to go about it. Such a blunder would be most un-Bolshevik — a pointless provocation leading to unnecessary weakness. Nevertheless, their bureaucracy may be capable of it. And the mistake would be easy to make both because defensive systems seem harmless and also because in the fifties, secretaries of defense, arms controllers, and the budget-minded, all *slowed* U.S. procurement by arguing that high estimates of Soviet procurement of offensive weapons were *not* accurate. Now the argument *against* U.S. weapons purchases is based on expectations that they would be wasted if the Soviets *did* fulfill high estimates. This is why the Secretary of Defense continually emphasizes the potential growth of Soviet forces in a future that sometimes fades further and further away. And this is why arms controllers have emphasized the real possibility of a dramatic Soviet response to U.S. construction of a ballistic missile defense. Whether this peculiar reversal of attitudes will be made clear to the Soviet Union before it plays into the hands of those most hostile to it, and fearful of it, is unclear.

In general, the Defense Department statements are getting blunter in talking about some strategic computations that do in fact influence our military decisions to some extent. One column of a table of U.S.-Soviet war outcomes is even entitled "U.S. first strike." (It assumes "that events leading up to the nuclear exchange develop in such a way that the United States is able to strike at the Soviet offensive forces before they can be launched at our urban targets.") Part of this frankness is simply the culmination of an evolution permitted by a presumed decline in Soviet sensitivity and an increasing familiarity with the real issues on all sides. Part of it is a desire to be frank where frankness will disarm Soviet fears: the column entitled "U.S. first strike" claims that, even in this case, we would suffer very large numbers of U.S. casualties.

But part of the greater frankness is an attempt to discourage China. The statement actually refers to the possibility that our missiles might engage in "pre-emptive countermilitary strikes" upon them; the phrase would have been eschewed in earlier years. It is presumably related to the President's assertion, after the first Chinese detonation, that this nuclear device could "only increase the sense of insecurity of the Chinese people." All this represents a strain of government thought that is devoted to the veiled threat. It is not necessary to inform the Chinese that their forces might be attacked in a pre-emptive strike: this is what they expect of us. Such references reshape only our expectations about ourselves. And when statements read like this, they encourage those elements among us, and in us, that are superficial, impulsive, and obsessed with unreal military solutions to unreal military threats.

This budget is McNamara's sixth. He has at most six more to present, at least as part of a Johnson administration, and since no ballistic missile system has yet been begun, any created will be only barely completed by about 1972. Thus we are now talking about systems for Johnson's successor, or successors, and about periods during which others will have to make the decision to push ahead with them or halt. And we are talking in terms that may seem as foolish in 1972 as terms of six years ago, such as "Sino-Soviet bloc" and "Cold War," have begun to sound today. The phases of our political competitions now occur as rapidly as we can build new weapon systems. We must therefore try to avoid fighting today's political problems with tomorrow's weapon systems. We ought to try to avoid estimating unconsciously the worth of weapons systems in terms of today's enmities. And we ought, out of respect for the opinions of Presidents and secretaries of defense to come, to try not to saddle them with the dead weight of avoidable programs — programs that it will be their job to finance or quietly dismantle. Whether considerations such as these will receive appropriate weight in today's atmosphere is not clear.

BIBLIOGRAPHICAL NOTES

INTRODUCTION

1. Ware Adams, "On Regulation by Law or Agreements" (Typescript, 1964).
2. Donald G. Brennan and M. H. Halperin, "Policy Considerations of a Nuclear Test Ban," in *Arms Control, Disarmament, and National Security,* Donald G. Brennan, ed. (New York: George Braziller, 1961).
3. McGeorge Bundy, "The Presidency and the Peace," *Foreign Affairs,* Vol. 42 (April 1964), p. 362.
4. Allen Dulles, *The Craft of Intelligence* (New York: Harper & Row, 1963). See also "Swedish Spy Details Soviet ICBM Gamble," *Aviation Week and Space Technology* (December 14, 1964).
5. Dulles, *The Craft of Intelligence.*

CHAPTER 1

1. For this quotation and an interesting discussion by Congressman Gerald Ford and Secretary McNamara, see U.S. Congress, House, Subcommittee of the Committee on Appropriations, *Department of Defense Appropriations for 1964* (88th Cong., 1st sess., 1963), Part 2, pp. 312 ff. Cited hereafter as *House Hearings on Defense,* by year.
2. V. D. Sokolovskii (ed.), *Soviet Military Strategy,* trans. RAND Corporation (Englewood Cliffs, N.J.: Prentice-Hall, 1963), p. 316.
3. U.S. Congress, House, Committee on Armed Services, *Hearings on Military Posture and H.R. 2440* (88th Cong., 1st sess., 1963), p. 613.
4. Maxwell Taylor, *The Uncertain Trumpet* (New York: Harper and Brothers, 1959), p. 68.
5. *House Hearings on Defense, 1964,* Part 1, p. 434.
6. *Ibid.,* p. 435.
7. U.S. Congress, Senate, Committee on Armed Services, *Military Procurement Authorization Fiscal Year 1964* (88th Cong., 1st sess., 1963), p. 150. Cited hereafter as *Senate Hearings on Military Procurement,* by year.
8. U.S. Congress, House, Committee on Armed Services, *Hearings on*

Military Posture and H.R. 9637 (88th Cong., 2nd sess., 1964), p. 7016.

9. U.S. Congress, Senate, Subcommittee of the Committee on Appropriations, *Department of Defense Appropriations for 1964* (88th Cong., 1st sess., 1963), p. 133. Cited hereafter as *Senate Hearings on Defense,* by year.
10. J. S. Butz, Jr., " 'Super' Guns for Missile Defense," *Air Force and Space Digest,* Vol. 47 (November 1963), p. 51.
11. *House Hearings on Defense, 1964,* Part 1, p. 439.
12. U.S. Congress, Senate, Committee on Foreign Relations, *Nuclear Test Ban Treaty* (88th Cong., 1st sess., 1963), p. 163. Cited hereafter as *Nuclear Test Ban Treaty.*
13. "Remarks of Secretary of Defense Robert S. McNamara before the Economics Club of New York; November 18, 1963," Department of Defense Press Release No. 1486-63 (November 13, 1963).
14. *The New York Times,* February 6, 1963.
15. *Senate Hearings on Military Procurement, 1964,* p. 60.
16. *Nuclear Test Ban Treaty,* p. 531.
17. See *House Hearings on Defense, 1964,* Part 1, p. 115; and *Senate Hearings on Military Procurement, 1964,* p. 45.
18. *Senate Hearings on Military Procurement, 1964,* pp. 67–68.
19. *House Hearings on Defense, 1964,* Part 1, pp. 433–437.
20. *House Hearings on Defense, 1965* (88th Cong., 2nd sess., 1964), Part 4, pp. 187, 351.
21. *Senate Hearings on Military Procurement, 1965* (88th Cong., 2nd sess., 1964), p. 44.
22. *House Hearings on Defense, 1965,* Part 4, pp. 187–188.
23. *The New York Times,* January 19, 1965.
24. *Nuclear Test Ban Treaty,* p. 543.
25. Sokolovskii (ed.), *Soviet Military Strategy,* p. 315.
26. *The New York Times,* April 18, 1963. See also *Nuclear Test Ban Treaty,* p. 778.
27. *Senate Hearings on Defense, 1964,* pp. 132–133.
28. *Senate Hearings on Military Procurement, 1964,* p. 149.
29. *John F. Kennedy, January 1 to December 31, 1962,* Public Papers of the Presidents of the United States (Washington, D.C.: GPO, 1963), p. 188. Cited hereafter as *Kennedy Papers.*
30. Nelson A. Rockefeller, "Background Memorandum — Nuclear Test Ban Treaty" (Press Release, August 12, 1963). The second sentence may be found in *The New York Times,* August 12, 1963.
31. *Nuclear Test Ban Treaty,* p. 30.
32. *House Hearings on Military Posture and H.R. 2440* (88th Cong., 1st sess., 1963), pp. 308–309.
33. *Senate Hearings on Military Procurement, 1964,* pp. 89–90.
34. *The New York Times,* June 24, 1963.
35. *Senate Hearings on Military Procurement, 1964,* p. 89.
36. *Ibid.,* pp. 103–104.
37. See, for instance, McNamara, "Remarks before the Economics Club of New York."

38. *Nuclear Test Ban Treaty*, p. 163.
39. *House Hearings on Defense, 1964*, Part 2, pp. 32, 131, 314, 586; *House Hearings on Military Posture and H.R. 2440*, p. 1234.
40. Taylor, *The Uncertain Trumpet*, p. 68.
41. See *The New York Times*, November 8, 1963.
42. *House Hearings on Military Posture and H.R. 2440*, p. 1192.
43. Matthew Meselson, "Possible Efforts towards Missile Defense and Their Effect on International Relations" (Typescript, 1964).
44. *Nuclear Test Ban Treaty*, pp. 784, 788.
45. Sokolovskii (ed.), *Soviet Military Strategy*, p. 345.
46. Speech of October 22 on Soviet arms buildup in Cuba, in *Kennedy Papers*, p. 807.
47. U.S. Congress, House, Subcommittee of the Committee on Government Operations, *Civil Defense, 1961* (87th Cong., 1st sess., 1961), p. 216.
48. *Senate Hearings on Military Procurement, 1964*, pp. 40–41.
49. *Nuclear Test Ban Treaty*, p. 104.
50. U.S. Congress, Joint Economic Committee, *Dimensions of Soviet Economic Power* (87th Cong., 2nd sess., 1962), Annex, p. 21.
51. *House Hearings on Defense, 1964*, Part 1, p. 112.
52. *Nuclear Test Ban Treaty*, p. 568.
53. *American Foreign Policy, 1950–1955*, General Foreign Policy Series 117; Basic Documents, Vol. I, Department of State Publication 6446 (Washington, D.C.: GPO, 1957), p. 82.
54. Stewart Alsop, "Kennedy's Grand Strategy," *Saturday Evening Post* (March 31, 1962), p. 14.
55. *The New York Times*, October 23, 1962.
56. *Ibid.*, March 28, 1962.
57. Press conference, Washington, D.C., September 28, 1962, cited in *The New York Times*, September 29, 1962.
58. *The New York Times*, November 9, 1963.
59. See Sidney G. Winter, Jr., *The Sources of Economic Collapse*, RM-8662 (U.S. Air Force PROJECT RAND, 1961), p. 169.
60. *Nuclear Test Ban Treaty*, p. 30.
61. *Ibid.*, p. 117.
62. *Ibid.*, p. 859.
63. *Senate Hearings on Defense, 1964*, p. 196. See also U.S. Congress, House, Committee on Armed Services, *Hearings on Military Posture and H.R. 9751* (87th Cong., 2nd sess., 1962), p. 3217.
64. *House Hearings on Military Posture and H.R. 2440*, p. 544.
65. *Senate Hearings on Military Procurement, 1964*, p. 80.
66. See "Gun Launches Show A-ICBM Potential," *Missiles and Rockets*, Vol. 13, No. 1 (July 1, 1963); Butz, Jr., " 'Super' Guns for Missile Defense"; and Butz, Jr., "Soviets May Have Ultimate ABM," *Missiles and Rockets*, Vol. 13, No. 12 (September 16, 1963).
67. Sokolovskii (ed.), *Soviet Military Strategy*, p. 419.
68. *Nuclear Test Ban Treaty*, p. 531.
69. *Ibid.*, pp. 588, 377.
70. *Philadelphia Inquirer*, February 1, 1965.

71. *Statement of Secretary of Defense Robert S. McNamara before the House Armed Services Committee on the Fiscal Year 1966–70 Defense Program and 1966 Defense Budget* (Washington, D.C.: House Armed Services Committee Secretary, 1965), p. 46. The table of estimated casualties was taken from this source.
72. *Ibid.*, pp. 62–63.
73. *Ibid.*, p. 49.
74. *The New York Times*, February 18, 1965.
75. *Ibid.*, February 28, 1965.

CHAPTER 2

1. *The New York Times*, January 29, 1964.
2. *Ibid.*, January 29, April 3, and June 20, 1964.
3. U.S. Congress, Senate, Subcommittee of the Committee on Appropriations, *Department of Defense Appropriations for 1964* (88th Cong., 1st sess., 1963), pp. 191–193. Cited hereafter as *Senate Hearings on Defense*, by year.
4. *Senate Hearings on Defense, 1963* (87th Cong., 2nd sess., 1962), p. 977.
5. U.S. Congress, Senate, Committee on Armed Services, *Military Procurement Authorization Fiscal Year 1964* (88th Cong., 1st sess., 1963), p. 475. Cited hereafter as *Senate Hearings on Military Procurement*, by year.
6. This information is taken from Institute for Strategic Studies, *The Military Balance, 1963–1964* (London, 1963); International Aerospace Specification Tables, issued by *Aviation Week and Space Technology*; Hanson W. Baldwin, "Strategic Air Outlook," *The New York Times*, November 21, 1963; and *Senate Hearings on Defense, 1962* (87th Cong., 1st sess., 1961), pp. 862–863.
7. U.S. Congress, House, Subcommittee on Committee on Appropriations, *Department of Defense Appropriations for 1960* (86th Cong., 1st sess., 1959), Part 1, p. 800. Cited hereafter as *House Hearings on Defense*, by year.
8. *Senate Hearings on Military Procurement, 1964* (88th Cong., 1st sess., 1963), p. 47.
9. *Senate Hearings on Defense, 1964*, p. 356.
10. U.S. Congress, Senate, Subcommittee on the Air Force of the Committee on Armed Services, *Air Power* (84th Cong., 2nd sess., 1956), Part 2, p. 83. Cited hereafter as *Air Power*.
11. See *Senate Hearings on Military Procurement, 1964*, p. 96; and *House Hearings on Defense, 1962* (87th Cong., 1st sess., 1961), Part 5, pp. 467–469.
12. *House Hearings on Defense, 1962*, Part 5, p. 465; Part 6, p. 192.
13. *House Hearings on Defense, 1960*, Part 1, pp. 330–331.
14. *House Hearings on Defense, 1964* (88th Cong., 1st sess., 1963), Part 2, pp. 530–531.
15. Herman Kahn, *On Thermonuclear War* (Princeton, N.J.: Princeton University Press, 1960), p. 373.

16. *Statement of Secretary of Defense Robert S. McNamara before the House Armed Services Committee on the Fiscal Year 1965–69 Defense Program and 1965 Defense Budget* (Washington, D.C.: House Armed Services Committee Secretary, 1964), p. 50. Cited hereafter as *McNamara Statement.* See also *Senate Hearings on Military Procurement, 1963,* p. 67.
17. *Senate Hearings on Defense, 1964,* p. 191.
18. *McNamara Statement,* p. 33; *House Hearings on Defense, 1961* (86th Cong., 2nd sess., 1960), Part 7, p. 100.
19. *Air Power,* Part 2, p. 146.
20. *McNamara Statement,* p. 37.
21. *House Hearings on Defense, 1964,* Part 1, p. 318.
22. *McNamara Statement,* pp. 37–38.
23. *House Hearings on Defense, 1960,* Part 1, p. 836.
24. *Senate Hearings on Military Procurement, 1964,* p. 93.
25. *House Hearings on Defense, 1964,* Part 1, p. 114.
26. *Ibid., 1963* (87th Cong., 2nd sess., 1962), Part 2, p. 15.
27. *Ibid., 1960,* Part 2, p. 378.
28. *Senate Hearings on Defense, 1964,* p. 192.
29. J. S. Butz, Jr., "The Future of Manned Bombers," *Air Force and Space Digest,* Vol. 46 (March 1963), p. 29.
30. *Senate Hearings on Military Procurement, 1964,* p. 932.
31. *Ibid.,* p. 85.
32. N. S. Khrushchev, "The Present International Situation and the Foreign Policy of the Soviet Union," report at session of U.S.S.R. Supreme Soviet, December 12, 1962, cited in *Current Digest of the Soviet Press,* Vol. 14 (January 16, 1963), p. 5.
33. *The New York Times,* May 17, 1960.
34. Hans Speier, *Divided Berlin* (New York: Praeger, 1961), p. 109.
35. *House Hearings on Defense, 1964,* Part 2, p. 527.
36. *McNamara Statement,* pp. 31–32.
37. Stewart Alsop, "Our New Strategy: The Alternative to Total War," *Saturday Evening Post* (December 1, 1962), p. 18.
38. Quotations from *House Hearings on Defense, 1964,* Part 1, p. 317; *Senate Hearings on Military Procurement, 1964,* p. 77.
39. Baldwin, "Strategic Air Outlook."
40. Figures may be found in Baldwin, "Strategic Air Outlook"; *House Hearings on Defense, 1964,* Part 1, p. 114; and *Senate Hearings on Military Procurement, 1963,* p. 17.
41. See *House Hearings on Defense, 1964,* Part 2, p. 530; and Baldwin, "Strategic Air Outlook."
42. *The New York Times,* February 7, 1964.
43. Butz, Jr., "The Future of Manned Bombers," pp. 31–32.
44. Hanson Baldwin, "France's A-Bomb Deterrent Power," *The New York Times,* January 25, 1963; *Air Power,* Part 3, p. 269.
45. This information is taken from Institute for Strategic Studies, *The Military Balance, 1963–1964;* and the International Aerospace Specification Tables, issued by *Aviation Week and Space Technology.*

46. *Senate Hearings on Defense, 1964,* p. 192.
47. "Statement on U.S. Military Strength," Department of Defense Press Release No. 308-64 (April 14, 1964).
48. The information in this paragraph comes from comments of H. S. Dinerstein, L. Gouré, and T. W. Wolfe in their annotation of V. D. Sokolovskii (ed.), *Soviet Military Strategy,* trans. RAND Corporation (Englewood Cliffs, N.J.: Prentice-Hall, 1963), pp. 351–352.
49. *Ibid.,* pp. 346–347.
50. *House Hearings on Defense, 1964,* Part 2, pp. 529–530.
51. U.S. Congress, House, Committee on Armed Services, *Hearings on Military Posture and H.R. 2440* (87th Cong., 2nd sess., 1963), p. 1192.
52. See Stuart Symington, "Where the Missile Gap Went," *Reporter,* Vol. 26 (February 15, 1962).
53. "Remarks of Secretary of Defense Robert S. McNamara before the Economics Club of New York; November 18, 1963," Department of Defense Press Release No. 1486-63 (November 13, 1963).
54. Institute for Strategic Studies, *The Military Balance, 1963–1964.*
55. *Air Power,* Part 3, p. 255.
56. *Ibid.,* p. 294.
57. *House Hearings on Defense, 1963,* Part 2, p. 250.
58. Kahn, *On Thermonuclear War,* p. 345.
59. *Air Power,* Part 2, pp. 332–333.
60. For McNamara, see *Senate Hearings on Military Procurement, 1964,* p. 63; for Brown, see *Senate Hearings on Defense, 1964,* p. 1243.
61. *McNamara Statement,* pp. 44–45.
62. Institute for Strategic Studies, *The Military Balance, 1963–1964.*
63. See *Aviation Week and Space Technology* (January 14, 1963), p. 30; W. Root, "France Explodes A-Bomb Readiness against an Enemy by the End of the Year," *Washington Post* (January 23, 1963).
64. Baldwin, "France's A-Bomb Deterrent Power."
65. *Documents on Disarmament, 1945–1959,* Department of State Publication No. 7008 (Washington, D.C., 1960), Vol. II, pp. 1230–1243.
66. P. M. S. Blackett, "Steps Toward Disarmament," *Scientific American,* Vol. 206 (April 1962).
67. *The New York Times,* August 21, 1963.
68. U.S. Congress, Senate, Committee on Foreign Relations, *Nuclear Test Ban Treaty* (88th Cong., 1st sess., 1963), p. 978.
69. *House Hearings on Defense, 1964,* Part 1, p. 115.
70. *McNamara Statement,* pp. 33, 36.
71. *Aviation Week and Space Technology,* Vol. 79, No. 13 (September 23, 1963), p. 39.
72. *Senate Hearings on Military Procurement, 1965,* p. 33.
73. See *The New York Times,* August 18, 1964 (picture).
74. McNamara, "Remarks before the Economics Club of New York"; *Senate Hearings on Military Procurement, 1964,* pp. 125, 147.

75. *McNamara Statement*, p. 35.
76. *Documents on Disarmament*, Vol. II, p. 990.
77. *Senate Hearings on Military Procurement, 1964*, p. 47.

CHAPTER 3

1. U.S. Congress, House, Subcommittee of the Committee on Appropriations, *Department of Defense Appropriations for 1965* (88th Cong., 2nd sess., 1964), Part 5, p. 50. Cited hereafter as *House Hearings on Defense*, by year.
2. Richard Fryklund, "Manned Bomber Plan Offered by Air Force," *Washington Star*, August 24, 1964.
3. U.S. Congress, Senate, Subcommittee of the Committee on Appropriations, *Department of Defense Appropriations for 1965* (88th Cong., 2nd sess., 1964), Part 2, p. 452.
4. Address by Secretary of Defense Robert S. McNamara before the American Legion, Dallas, Texas, September 22, 1964; cited in *The New York Times*, September 23, 1964.
5. *House Hearings on Defense, 1965*, Part 5, p. 50.
6. U.S. Congress, Senate, Committee on Armed Services, *Military Procurement Authorization Fiscal Year 1962* (87th Cong., 1st sess., 1961), p. 336. Cited hereafter as *Senate Hearings on Military Procurement*, by year.
7. *Washington Star*, October 9, 1964.
8. *Senate Hearings on Military Procurement, 1965*, p. 714.
9. U.S. Congress, House, *Additional Views on H.R. 9637 of Messrs. Stratton, Cohelan, Pike, and Nedzi, To Accompany H.R. 9637* (*Authorizing Defense Procurement and Research and Development*) (88th Cong., 2nd sess., 1964), Union Calendar 471, Report 1138, Part 2.
10. Roswell Gilpatric, "Our Defense Needs: The Long View," *Foreign Affairs* (April 1964), p. 373.
11. J. Atwater, "Last Stand of the Big Bomber: Debate Between McNamara and LeMay," *Saturday Evening Post* (June 20, 1964).
12. *Senate Hearings on Military Procurement, 1965*, p. 47.
13. *Washington Star*, October 9, 1964.
14. *House Hearings on Defense, 1962* (87th Cong., 1st sess., 1961), Part 3, p. 11.
15. *The Christian Science Monitor*, November 30, 1963.
16. See *Washington Post*, November 18, 1963; *New York Herald Tribune*, November 17, 1963.
17. *The New York Times*, August 21, 1964.
18. *Senate Hearings on Military Procurement, 1965*, p. 65.
19. *Ibid.*, p. 715.
20. *Washington Star*, October 9, 1964.
21. Fred C. Iklé, *How Nations Negotiate* (New York: Harper & Row, 1964), p. 21.
22. U.S. Congress, House, Committee on Armed Services, *Hearings on*

Military Posture and H.R. 9637 (88th Cong., 2nd sess., 1964), p. 6986; *New York Herald Tribune*, March 16, 1964.

23. United Nations, *Verbatim Records of the Conference of the Eighteen-Nation Committee on Disarmament* (U.N. Secretariat, 1964), Document ENDC/PV. 163, February 4, 1964, p. 19.

24. *Senate Hearings on Military Procurement, 1965*, p. 52.

25. *Ibid., 1964* (88th Cong., 1st sess., 1963), p. 77.

CHAPTER 4

1. Vannevar Bush, *Modern Arms and Free Men* (New York: Simon & Schuster, 1949), p. 128.

2. U.S. Congress, Senate, Subcommittee on the Air Force of the Committee on Armed Services, *Hearings on Study of Airpower* (84th Cong., 2nd sess., 1956), Part 1, p. 38. Cited hereafter as *Senate Hearings on Airpower*.

3. Quotations from, respectively, "Remarks of Secretary of Defense Robert S. McNamara before the Economics Club of New York," Department of Defense Press Release, No. 1486-63 (November 18, 1963), p. 7; and U.S. Congress, Senate, Committee on Armed Services, *Hearings on Military Procurement Authorization, Fiscal Year 1965* (88th Cong., 2nd sess., 1964), pp. 30–31. Cited hereafter as *Senate Hearings on Military Procurement*, by year.

4. Quoted from Herbert Ritvo, "Internal Division on Disarmament in the USSR," in *Disarmament, Its Politics and Economics*, Seymour Melman, ed. (Boston: American Academy of Arts and Sciences, 1962), p. 212.

5. U.S. Congress, House, Subcommittee of the Committee on Appropriations, *Hearings on Department of Defense Appropriations for 1960* (86th Cong., 1st sess., 1959), Part 5, pp. 636–637. Cited hereafter as *House Hearings on Defense*, by year.

6. U.S. Congress, Senate Subcommittee of the Committee on Appropriations, *Hearings on Department of Defense Appropriations for 1964* (88th Cong., 1st sess., 1963), p. 1241. Cited hereafter as *Senate Hearings on Defense*, by year.

7. U.S. Congress, House, Committee on Armed Services, *Hearings on Military Posture, Fiscal Year 1965* (88th Cong., 2nd sess., 1964), p. 7414. Cited hereafter as *House Hearings on Military Posture*, by year.

8. *Senate Hearings on Military Procurement, 1962* (87th Cong., 1st sess., 1961), p. 386.

9. U.S. Congress, Senate, Preparedness Investigating Subcommittee of the Committee on Armed Services, *Hearings on Inquiry into Satellite and Missile Programs* (85th Cong., 1st and 2nd sess., 1958), Part 1, p. 826. Cited hereafter as *Satellite and Missile Inquiry*.

10. *Documents on Disarmament 1945–1959*, Department of State Publication 7008 (Washington, D.C., 1960), Vol. II, p. 920.

11. *Satellite and Missile Inquiry*, pp. 822–823.

12. *Ibid.*, p. 6.
13. *Ibid.*, p. 58.
14. *House Hearings on Defense, 1960*, Part 1.
15. *Ibid., 1958* (85th Cong., 2nd sess., 1957), Part 2, p. 371.
16. The information in this table is well known and comes from the following sources: *House Hearings on Military Posture, 1963* (87th Cong., 2nd sess., 1962), p. 3960; *ibid., 1965*, p. 6949; *House Hearings on Defense, 1962* (87th Cong., 1st sess., 1961), Part 1, p. 372; *Senate Hearings on Military Procurement, 1962*, p. 45; *ibid., 1964* (88th Cong., 1st sess., 1963), pp. 962–963; *ibid., 1965* (88th Cong., 2nd sess., 1964), pp. 34, 71; *Senate Hearings on Defense, 1960* (86th Cong., 2nd sess., 1959), p. 738; Institute for Strategic Studies, *The Military Balance, 1963–1964* (London, 1963), p. 35.
17. *Senate Hearings on Military Procurement, 1965*, p. 54.
18. U.S. Congress, Senate, Committee on Foreign Relations, *Hearings on Nuclear Test Ban Treaty* (88th Cong., 1st sess., 1963), p. 102. Cited hereafter as *Nuclear Test Ban Treaty*.
19. *Ibid.*, pp. 529–530.
20. *Senate Hearings on Military Procurement, 1965*, p. 754.
21. *Nuclear Test Ban Treaty*, p. 102.
22. Quotations from *Senate Hearings on Military Procurement, 1964*, p. 151; and *Senate Hearings on Military Procurement, 1965*, p. 53.
23. *The New York Times*, August 18, 1964.
24. *House Hearings on Defense, 1958* (85th Cong., 1st sess., 1957), Part 1, p. 1033.
25. *Senate Hearings on Military Procurement, 1964*, p. 96.
26. *House Hearings on Defense, 1961* (86th Cong., 2nd sess., 1960), Part 6, p. 420; "State of the Union Address," *The New York Times*, January 8, 1960.
27. *Senate Hearings on Military Procurement, 1964*, p. 52.
28. McNamara statement from *House Hearings on Military Posture, 1965*, p. 6941; Zuckert testimony from *Senate Hearings on Military Procurement, 1965*, p. 724.
29. Hanson W. Baldwin, "Russian Missiles Guarded by Concrete Installations," *The New York Times*, July 26, 1962; Stewart Alsop, "Our New Strategy: The Alternatives to Total War," *Saturday Evening Post* (December 1, 1962); Baldwin, "Strategic Air Outlook," *The New York Times*, November 21, 1963; Baldwin, "Soviet Bomber Threat," *The New York Times*, February 14, 1964.
30. Institute for Strategic Studies, *The Military Balance, 1963–1964*, p. 35.
31. Baldwin, "Russian Missiles Guarded by Concrete Installations."
32. *Ibid.*
33. McNamara statements from *Senate Hearings on Military Procurement, 1965*, pp. 31, 30.
34. *House Hearings on Military Posture, 1962* (87th Cong., 1st sess., 1961), p. 398.
35. Institute for Strategic Studies, *The Military Balance, 1963–1964*, p. 3.

36. "Preventive War, Nuclear Suicide," *International Affairs*, No. 9 (1962), p. 18.
37. *House Hearings on Defense, 1961*, Part 2, pp. 388 (White), 277 (Power).
38. *Senate Hearings on Military Procurement, 1965*, p. 721.
39. *Address by N. S. Khrushchev at World Congress for General Disarmament and Peace, July 10, 1963* (New York: Crosscurrents Press, Inc., 1963).
40. *Satellite and Missile Inquiry*, p. 378.
41. *Nuclear Test Ban Treaty*, p. 102.
42. *Aviation Week and Space Technology*, Vol. 76, No. 3 (May 14, 1962), p. 26.
43. Herman Kahn, *On Thermonuclear War* (Princeton, N.J.: Princeton University Press, 1960), pp. 468–469.
44. Glenn A. Kent, *On the Interaction of Opposing Forces under Possible Arms Agreements*, "Occasional Papers in International Affairs," No. 5 (Cambridge, Mass.: Harvard University Center for International Affairs, 1963), p. 36.
45. *House Hearings on Defense, 1965* (88th Cong., 2nd sess., 1964), Part 4, p. 537.
46. Information in this paragraph from *House Hearings on Defense, 1962*, Part 3, p. 8, and Part 5, p. 302; *Senate Hearings on Military Procurement, 1964*, p. 45.
47. See *House Hearings on Defense, 1964*, Part 1, p. 115; *Senate Hearings on Military Procurement, 1965*, p. 34; *House Hearings on Defense, 1963* (87th Cong., 2nd sess., 1962), Part 2, p. 15.
48. *House Hearings on Defense, 1962*, Part 3, p. 8.
49. Information in this paragraph from *Senate Hearings on Military Procurement, 1963*, p. 20; *ibid., 1964*, p. 53; *ibid., 1965*, p. 35; *House Hearings on Defense, 1960*, Part 5, p. 306; *House Hearings on Military Posture, 1964*, p. 1078.
50. *House Hearings on Defense, 1962*, Part 3, p. 325.
51. *Senate Hearings on Military Procurement, 1964*, pp. 71–72.
52. *House Hearings on Defense, 1962*, Part 3, p. 326.
53. *The New York Times*, February 16, 1964.
54. *House Hearings on Defense, 1962*, Part 1, p. 452.
55. *Ibid., 1963*, Part 5, p. 238.
56. *Ibid.*, Part 4, p. 152.
57. *Nuclear Test Ban Treaty*, p. 380.
58. *House Hearings on Military Posture, 1964*, p. 1081.
59. *House Hearings on Defense, 1965*, Part 4, pp. 660, 676.
60. *House Hearings on Military Posture, 1964*, p. 1081.
61. *Senate Hearings on Military Procurement, 1962*, p. 81; *House Hearings on Defense, 1965*, Part 2, p. 398.
62. *House Hearings on Defense, 1965*, Part 4, p. 704.
63. Information in this paragraph is from *Senate Hearings on Military Procurement, 1965*, p. 35; *House Hearings on Military Posture, 1965*, p. 6955; *House Hearings on Defense, 1965*, Part 2, p. 392; *Missiles and Rockets*, Vol. 14, No. 1 (January 13, 1964), p. 18.

64. Quotations in this paragraph are from *House Hearings on Defense, 1960*, Part 5, p. 280; *Senate Hearings on Defense, 1962* (87th Cong., 1st sess., 1961), p. 932; *House Hearings on Defense, 1965*, Part 2, p. 400. See also *House Hearings on Defense, 1965*, Part 2, p. 416.
65. *House Hearings on Military Posture, 1964*, p. 612.
66. Institute for Strategic Studies, *The Military Balance, 1963–1964*, p. 35.
67. *House Hearings on Military Posture, 1965*, p. 7569 (Brown); *Senate Hearings on Defense, 1964*, p. 544 (Anderson).
68. *The New York Times*, March 3, 1964.
69. The proposals named in this paragraph have been garnered from *Aviation Week and Space Technology*, Vol. 77, No. 2 (October 15, 1962); *Missiles and Rockets*, Vol. 12, No. 2 (April 29, 1963), p. 9.
70. Institute for Strategic Studies, *The Military Balance, 1963–1964*, p. 6.
71. U.S. Congress, House, Committee on Armed Services, *The Fiscal Year 1965–69 Defense Program and 1965 Defense Budget* (88th Cong., 2nd sess., 1964), p. 74.
72. Information in this paragraph is from "Statement on U.S. Military Strength," Department of Defense Press Release No. 308-64 (April 14, 1964); *Aviation Week and Space Technology* (May 6, 1963), p. 36; Baldwin, "Soviet Missiles."
73. V. D. Sokolovskii (ed.), *Soviet Military Strategy*, trans. RAND Corporation (Englewood Cliffs, N.J.: Prentice-Hall, 1963), p. 348.
74. See, for example, U.S. Department of Commerce, *Military Strategy USSR: A Comparison of the 1962 and 1963 Editions* (Washington, D.C.: Office of Technical Services, 1963).
75. *House Hearings on Defense, 1964* (88th Cong., 1st sess., 1963), Part 1, p. 342.
76. *Ibid.*
77. Hanson W. Baldwin, "Soviet Submarine Lag," *The New York Times*, April 18, 1963; *Senate Hearings on Military Procurement, 1964*, p. 665.
78. *Satellite and Missile Inquiry*, Part 2, p. 1979.
79. *Senate Hearings on Defense, 1962*, p. 936.
80. *Satellite and Missile Inquiry*, Part 1, p. 651.
81. *House Hearings on Defense, 1958*, Supplemental Appropriations, p. 243, and Part 2, p. 241.
82. *Ibid., 1961*, Part 2, p. 37.
83. *Senate Hearings on Defense, 1964*, p. 1285; *House Hearings on Defense, 1962*, Part 4, pp. 320–321.
84. *House Hearings on Defense, 1962*, Part 3, pp. 257–258.
85. *Ibid., 1960*, Part 1, p. 746.
86. *Ibid., 1961*, Part 6, p. 15.
87. *House Hearings on Defense, 1960*, Part 2, p. 318.
88. *House Hearings on Defense, 1962*, Part 4, pp. 320–321; *Aviation*

Week and Space Technology, Vol. 78, No. 3 (May 27, 1963), p. 19.
89. *House Hearings on Defense, 1962,* Part 3, p. 258, and Part 4, pp. 320–321.
90. *Ibid.,* Part 4, p. 321.
91. *Senate Hearings on Military Procurement, 1962,* p. 73.
92. *Aviation Week and Space Technology,* Vol. 76, No. 3 (May 14, 1962), pp. 292–293.
93. *House Hearings on Defense, 1965,* Part 4, p. 693.
94. *Senate Hearings on Military Procurement, 1962,* p. 74.
95. *Ibid.,* p. 73.
96. *House Hearings on Defense, 1961,* Part 2, p. 23.
97. *Ibid., 1963,* Part 2, p. 539.
98. *House Hearings on Military Posture, 1965,* pp. 7569–7570.
99. *Aviation Week and Space Technology,* Vol. 79, No. 13 (September 23, 1963).
100. *Senate Hearings on Military Procurement, 1964,* p. 147.
101. *Nuclear Test Ban Treaty,* p. 102.
102. U.S. Congress, House, *Report No. 1561 To Accompany H.R. 11998* (86th Cong., 2nd sess., 1960), p. 32.
103. Roswell Gilpatric, "Our Defense Needs," *Foreign Affairs* (April 1964), p. 373.
104. *Documents on Disarmament, 1962,* U.S. Arms Control Agency Publication No. 19 (Washington, D.C., 1963), Vol. I, p. 353.
105. United Nations, *Verbatim Records of the Conference of the Eighteen-Nation Committee on Disarmament* (U.N. Secretariat, 1964), Document ENDC/PV. 163, February 4, 1964, p. 32.
106. *The New York Times,* December 3, 1963. See also C. L. Sulzberger, *The New York Times,* March 4, 1964.
107. *House Hearings on Military Posture, 1964,* p. 571.
108. ENDC/PV. 163, pp. 33–35.
109. *House Hearings on Military Posture, 1964,* p. 409.
110. *Senate Hearings on Military Procurement, 1965,* p. 44; *Nuclear Test Ban Treaty,* p. 163.
111. ENDC/PV. 163, p. 37.
112. Quotations from Department of Commerce, *Military Strategy USSR,* p. 6; and ENDC/PV. 163, p. 22.
113. *Documents on Disarmament, 1945–1959,* Vol. II, p. 1283.
114. *Senate Hearings on Defense, 1963;* Department of Commerce, *Military Strategy USSR,* p. 92.
115. Sokolovskii (ed.), *Soviet Military Strategy,* pp. 384, 398.
116. *Documents on Disarmament, 1962,* Vol. I, p. 136.
117. *Ibid.,* p. 501.
118. *Ibid.* (Statement by Foreign Minister Gromyko, March 15, 1962), p. 94; Department of Defense, *Statement on U.S. Military Strength.*
119. ENDC/PV. 165, February 11, 1964, p. 41.
120. *Ibid.*
121. *Nuclear Test Ban Treaty,* p. 856.
122. Figures obtained from Nuclear Bomb Effects Computer, a cal-

culating device issued in conjunction with Department of Defense, *The Effects of Nuclear Weapons,* Samuel Glasstone, ed. (Washington, D.C.: Atomic Energy Commission, 1962).

123. *Senate Hearings on Military Procurement, 1965,* pp. 34, 38.
124. *Ibid.,* p. 316; *House Hearings on Defense, 1965,* Part 2, p. 392.
125. *Senate Hearings on Military Procurement, 1964,* p. 52.
126. *Ibid., 1965,* p. 34.
127. Institute for Strategic Studies, *The Military Balance, 1963–1964,* p. 35.
128. *Izvestia,* September 9, 1961.
129. ENDC/PV. 163, pp. 21–22.
130. *House Hearings on Defense, 1964,* Part 1, p. 105.
131. *House Hearings on Military Posture, 1962,* p. 511.
132. Gilpatric, "Our Defense Needs."
133. ENDC/PV. 163, p. 22.
134. *International Affairs,* No. 3 (March 1964).

CHAPTER 5

1. United Nations, *Verbatim Records of the Conference of the Eighteen-Nation Committee on Disarmament* (New York: U.N. Secretariat, 1964), Document ENDC/PV. 157, January 21, 1964, p. 11.
2. *Ibid.*
3. Adrian S. Fisher, in a statement made at the Conference of the Eighteen-Nation Committee on Disarmament, April 16, 1964.
4. Richard Fryklund, "Missile Output of Reds Falls under Estimate," *Washington Star,* October 1, 1964.
5. *The New York Times,* June 13, 1964.
6. *Aviation Week and Space Technology* (November 26, 1962), p. 27.
7. *Aviation Week and Space Technology* (December 14, 1964).
8. *The New York Times,* July 24, 1964.
9. *Ibid.,* May 7, 1964.
10. U.S. Congress, House, Subcommittee of the Committee on Appropriations, *Department of Defense Appropriations for 1965* (88th Cong., 2nd sess., 1964), Part 4, p. 27. Cited hereafter as *House Hearings on Defense,* by year.
11. Fryklund, "Missile Output of Reds."
12. *House Hearings on Defense, 1965,* Part 4, p. 57.
13. Fryklund, "Missile Output of Reds."
14. U.S. Congress, Senate, Preparedness Investigating Subcommittee of the Committee on Armed Services, *Hearings on Military Procurement Authorization Fiscal Year 1964* (88th Cong., 1st sess., 1963), p. 665.
15. Speech at Forty-sixth Annual Dinner of the American Ordinance Association, Chicago, May 19, 1964; quoted in *The New York Times,* May 31, 1964.
16. *House Hearings on Defense, 1964* (88th Cong., 1st sess., 1963), Part 1, p. 328.

17. Roswell Gilpatric, "Our Defense Needs," *Foreign Affairs* (April 1964).
18. U.S. Congress, Senate, Subcommittee of the Committee on Appropriations, *Hearings on Department of Defense Appropriations for 1963* (87th Cong., 2nd sess., 1962), p. 194.
19. U.S. Congress, Senate, Committee on Foreign Relations, *Hearings on the Nuclear Test Ban Treaty* (88th Cong., 1st sess., 1963), p. 102.

INDEX

ABM (antiballistic missile), area defense, 224–227
 cost of U.S., 24, 29, 30, 52, 163, 163n, 165
 disarmament of, 66, 165, 200–201
 effect of deployment of, 6, 14, 47–48, 50, 63–64
 for Europe, 63
 exoatmospheric, 224–227
 restraints on procurement, 26, 50, 51, 54–55
 Soviet, 16, 33, 34, 35, 38–49, 67–68, 204, 210
 terminal-intercept systems, 28, 38, 55–56, 61–63
 U.S. procurement of, 27, 31–39, 70–72, 153, 165
 see also Nike-X; Nike Zeus
Accidents, 10, 58–59
Adams, Ware, 3n
Advanced manned precise-strike system, see AMPSS
Advanced manned strategic aircraft, see AMSA
AEC (Atomic Energy Commission), 129
Alsop, Stewart, 134
AMPSS (advanced manned precise-strike system), 108
AMSA (advanced manned strategic aircraft), 108–112
Anderson, George, 1, 42, 144, 148
Antiballistic missile, see ABM
Antisubmarine warfare (ASW), 24, 95, 146–149, 151, 201–202, 205–207
Arms Control and Disarmament Agency, 20, 39, 184
Artemis, Project, see Project Artemis

ASROC, 150
Assembly of the Western European Union, 160n
ASW, see Antisubmarine warfare
Atlas, 29n, 130, 132, 133, 136, 163n
Atomic Energy Commission, see AEC
Australia, 111n

B-36, 110
B-47, characteristics of, 78
 disarmament of, 75, 76n, 91, 100, 100n, 101, 102, 104, 107, 118
 operations of, 82, 118n
 phasing out of, 79, 89, 106, 111
B-52, characteristics of, 77–78, 79, 83, 90, 100n, 128
 disarmament of, 76, 76n, 107–112, 114, 118–123
 operations of, 6, 76n, 78–79, 81–82, 102, 103n, 104n
B-58, 102, 110
 deployment of, 62
 number of, 79, 82
 range of, 78, 100n
B-70, 80n, 90, 108
Badger (Tu-16), 75, 76, 91, 92, 96, 98, 100, 100n, 101, 102, 104, 106, 118
Baldwin, Hanson, 99, 134, 135, 145, 147, 204n
Ballistic missile defense, see ABM
Ballistic Missile Early Warning System, see BMEWS
Bambi, 56
Beagle (Il-28), 98, 107
Bear (Tu-20), 76, 92, 100n, 107, 108

PUBLICATIONS WRITTEN UNDER THE AUSPICES OF THE CENTER FOR INTERNATIONAL AFFAIRS HARVARD UNIVERSITY

Created in 1958, the Center for International Affairs fosters advanced study of basic world problems by scholars from various disciplines and senior officials from many countries. The research at the Center focuses on economic and social development, the management of force in the modern world, and the evolving roles of Western Europe and the Communist bloc. The published results appear here in the order in which they have been issued. The research programs are supervised by Professors Robert R. Bowie (Director of the Center), Hollis B. Chenery, Rupert Emerson, Samuel P. Huntington, Alex Inkeles, Henry A. Kissinger, Edward S. Mason, Thomas C. Schelling, and Raymond Vernon.

Books:

The Soviet Bloc, by Zbigniew K. Brzezinski (jointly with the Russian Research Center), 1960. Cambridge, Mass.: Harvard University Press.

The Necessity for Choice, by Henry A. Kissinger, 1961. New York: Harper & Brothers.

Strategy and Arms Control, by Thomas C. Schelling and Morton H. Halperin, 1961. New York: The Twentieth Century Fund.

Rift and Revolt in Hungary, by Ferenc A. Váli, 1961. Cambridge, Mass.: Harvard University Press.

United States Manufacturing Investment in Brazil, by Lincoln Gordon and Engelbert L. Grommers, 1962. Boston, Mass.: Harvard Business School.

The Economy of Cyprus, by A. J. Meyer, with Simos Vassiliou (jointly with the Center for Middle Eastern Studies), 1962. Cambridge, Mass.: Harvard University Press.

Entrepreneurs of Lebanon, by Yusif A. Sayigh (jointly with the Center for Middle Eastern Studies), 1962. Cambridge, Mass.: Harvard University Press.

Communist China 1955–1959: Policy Documents with Analysis, with a Foreword by Robert R. Bowie and John K. Fairbank (jointly with the East Asian Research Center), 1962. Cambridge, Mass.: Harvard University Press.

In Search of France, by Stanley Hoffmann, Charles P. Kindleberger, Laurence Wylie, Jesse R. Pitts, Jean-Baptiste Duroselle, and François Goguel, 1963. Cambridge, Mass.: Harvard University Press.

Somali Nationalism, by Saadia Touval, 1963. Cambridge, Mass.: Harvard University Press.

The Dilemma of Mexico's Development, by Raymond Vernon, 1963. Cambridge, Mass.: Harvard University Press.

Limited War in the Nuclear Age, by Morton H. Halperin, 1963. New York: John Wiley & Sons, Inc.

The Arms Debate, by Robert A. Levine, 1963. Cambridge, Mass.: Harvard University Press.

Africans on the Land, by Montague Yudelman, 1964. Cambridge, Mass.: Harvard University Press.

Counterinsurgency Warfare, by David Galula, 1964. New York: Frederick A. Praeger, Inc.

People and Policy in the Middle East, by Max Weston Thornburg, 1964. New York: W. W. Norton & Company, Inc.

Shaping the Future, by Robert R. Bowie, 1964. New York: Columbia University Press.

Foreign Aid and Foreign Policy, by Edward S. Mason (jointly with the Council on Foreign Relations), 1964. New York: Harper & Row, Publishers.

Public Policy and Private Enterprise in Mexico, by M. S. Wionczek, D. H. Shelton, C. P. Blair, and R. Izquierdo, ed. Raymond Vernon, 1964. Cambridge, Mass.: Harvard University Press.

How Nations Negotiate, by Fred C. Iklé, 1964. New York: Harper & Row, Publishers.

China and the Bomb, by Morton H. Halperin (jointly with the East Asian Research Center), 1965. New York: Frederick A. Praeger, Inc.

Democracy in Germany, by Fritz Erler (Jodidi Lectures), 1965. Cambridge, Mass.: Harvard University Press.

The Troubled Partnership, by Henry A. Kissinger (jointly with the Council on Foreign Relations), 1965. New York: McGraw-Hill Book Company.

The Rise of Nationalism in Central Africa, by Robert I. Rotberg, 1965. Cambridge, Mass.: Harvard University Press.

Communist China and Arms Control, by Morton H. Halperin and Dwight H. Perkins (jointly with the East Asian Research Center), 1965. New York: Frederick A. Praeger, Inc.

Pan-Africanism and East African Integration, by Joseph S. Nye, Jr., 1965. Cambridge, Mass.: Harvard University Press.

Problems of National Strategy, ed. Henry A. Kissinger, 1965. New York: Frederick A. Praeger, Inc.

Deterrence before Hiroshima: The Airpower Background of Modern Strategy, by George H. Quester, 1966. New York: John Wiley & Sons, Inc.

Containing the Arms Race, by Jeremy J. Stone, 1966. Cambridge, Mass.: The M.I.T. Press.

Occasional Papers, Published by the Center for International Affairs:

1. *A Plan for Planning: The Need for a Better Method of Assisting Underdeveloped Countries on Their Economic Policies*, by Gustav F. Papanek, 1961.
2. *The Flow of Resources from Rich to Poor*, by Alan D. Neale, 1961.
3. *Limited War: An Essay on the Development of the Theory and an Annotated Bibliography*, by Morton H. Halperin, 1962.
4. *Reflections on the Failure of the First West Indian Federation*, by Hugh W. Springer, 1962.
5. *On the Interaction of Opposing Forces under Possible Arms Agreements*, by Glenn A. Kent, 1963.
6. *Europe's Northern Cap and the Soviet Union*, by Nils Örvik, 1963.
7. *Civil Administration in the Punjab: An Analysis of a State Government in India*, by E. N. Mangat Rai, 1963.
8. *On the Appropriate Size of a Development Program*, by Edward S. Mason, 1964.
9. *Self-Determination Revisited in the Era of Decolonization*, by Rupert Emerson, 1964.
10. *The Planning and Execution of Economic Development in Southeast Asia*, by Clair Wilcox, 1965.
11. *Pan-Africanism in Action*, by Albert Tevoedjre, 1965.
12. *Is China Turning In?* by Morton H. Halperin, 1965.

Do Nothing &
Do Everything

Do Nothing & Do Everything

An Illustrated New Taoism

Written and Illustrated by

Qiguang Zhao

PARAGON HOUSE
St. Paul, Minnesota

Published in the United States by
Paragon House
1925 Oakcrest Avenue, Suite 7
St. Paul, MN 55113

Library of Congress Cataloging-in-Publication Data

Zhao, Qiguang, 1948-
  Do nothing and do everything : an illustrated new Taoism /
written and illustrated by Qiguang Zhao. -- 1st ed.
     p. cm.
  Includes bibliographical references and index.
  Summary: "This introduction to ancient Taoism utilizes stories
and illustrations to convey the subtle ideas that go beyond language
as the author applies the Taoist Wu Wei (do nothing) and Wu Bu
Wei (do everything) to modern life"--Provided by publisher.
  ISBN 978-1-55778-889-4 (hardcover : alk. paper)
  1. Taoism. I. Title. II. Title: Illustrated new Taoism.
  BL1920.Z452 2010
  299.5'14--dc22
                                        2009038970

Manufactured in the United States of America

The paper used in this publication meets the minimum requirements of American National Standard for Information Sciences—Permanence of Paper for Printed Library Materials, ANSIZ39.48-1984.

10 9 8 7 6 5 4 3 2 1

For current information about all releases from Paragon House,
visit the web site at http://www.paragonhouse.com

Table of Contents

Table of Contents

to Litao

The stars of wisdom shine over us.
The winds of humor dance between us.
The seas of knowledge carry us to the land of miracle.

Acknowledgements

I would like to express my gratitude to my family for their loving support. I thank my parents for teaching me culture, literature, and life philosophy through a scientific approach. With a wise sense of humor, my father, Professor of Physics Zhao Jingyuan, gives me a love of Chinese tradition and its application to modern life. Also a professor of physics, my mother, Wang Shuxian, loved and wrote Chinese classical poems. We had discussed some of the ideas and illustrations in the book a few months before she passed away. My deepest thanks go to my other family members, especially Zhiming, who edited some of my writings and provided numerous technical supports, Qizheng, who encourages me to present my ideas to a broad audience, and Qida, from whom I learned drawing pictures while telling stories.

I thank Carleton College for the financial and academic support for the project. Beautiful lakes and forests on campus, together with thought-provoking faculty, staff, and students, provide a most serene environment for talking, writing, and thinking. I greatly appreciate my students' support and involvement. Through the years, students in my course "Taoist

Way of Health and Longevity: Tai Chi and Other Forms" spoke intelligently in crowded classrooms and performed Tai Chi on campus islands. Sophie Kerman organized primary materials. Jessica Taylor edited the writing and scanned the illustrations. Kaitlin Justin, Jane Caffrey, and Zheng Zhu enthusiastically helped me to complete the final manuscript and gave me wise input.

Dr. Andrew Weis was enthusiastic about my manuscript and shared ideas on Taoism with me. He carefully read through the manuscript and gave me valuable comments and suggestions. My thanks extend to Mr. Roger Lasley, who read my manuscript and gave me helpful advice. I am deeply grateful to my colleague Professor Hong Zeng, who offered consistent support.

Many of the opinions in this book were formed when I was featured on a talk show series about Lao Tzu, aired on Shanghai Television in 2007. I thank Professor Qian Wenzhong of Fudan University for recommending me for the series. Producer Yu Yongjin, anchorman Jin Bo, and director Xia Ning of Shanghi Television made the show come to life for an audience of millions.

It is impossible to mention all of the people who have helped and inspired me. To all of them, I give my sincere thanks.

Preface

When I was completing this book, my mother passed away. She was a professor of physics, a poet, an athlete, and a great mother. Suddenly life and death stand in front of me not as a theoretical discussion in the classroom but as a challenge to reality. It is so difficult for us to accept the deal that life offers us. It seems unfair and crazy. We are given life, and then life is taken away without our agreement. Without a wise mother to protect me, I feel I have an immediate call to figure out the puzzle of life and death.

We do not get to choose when we are going to die or how to die. Yet we can decide when we are going to live. The time is *now*. Seize today and trust not in tomorrow. Eternity does not begin after death, it extends to all of the time in our lives. We are in it now. We can have it if we give up—give up our imagined ability to control life. The moon shines over snow; a planet swings around a star; a black hole devours a constellation. We cannot affect these big phenomena, and we let them be. Our daily life is part of the universe, as every small drop of ocean water reflects the enormous sun. If we cannot change the orbit of the sun, we cannot decide everything in our life either. Therefore, we should accept the pain, treasure the joy, and appreciate life now.

Nowadays, people do not live fully, and they get only about 20 percent out of their lives. This hard-to-get 20 percent of life follows the accepted standards of success and failure. The other 80 percent can be reached effortlessly. Just follow the course of nature, and life will reward you generously. Between your house and your shop, there are numerous little spots of happiness: a squirrel running away from you, a raindrop falling on you, and a stranger greeting you. Just acknowledge them. They always come to you. You do nothing, and nothing is left undone.

A life of reaction is a life of bondage. I believe that one must strive for a life of nonaction or action, not one of reaction. Doing nothing leads to courageous liberation. We should act effortlessly, without anxiety and hesitation. Sitting on the beach quietly is doing nothing. Swimming in the ocean bravely is doing everything. There are no forbidden walls between doing nothing and doing everything. We are free, as long as we cross between the two without anxiety or hesitation.

Do not hesitate when crossing. Do not be bothered by the opinions of others. Hear the call of nature, and act for yourself. You do not want to come to the last moment of your life and find that you have simply lived life's length. You should also have lived the life's width. So when you leave the world, you will not say, "I didn't do this" or "I did that wrong." You are going to say, "I regret nothing. I came. I did nothing. I did it all. As a happy guest, I leave now."

Introduction

This book is based on a course I have taught since 1997, "The Taoist Way of Health and Longevity: Tai Chi and Other Forms." It started out with only six students; by 2006, it had grown to about 60. The class has become one of the most popular courses at Carleton College. In this class, the students and I get lost in the mysterious and serene atmosphere of Taoism. With Lao Tzu, we ride green bulls through Hangu Pass; with Zhuangzi, we watch the fish from the bank of a river; with Liezi, we ride on the wind; with Zhang Sanfeng, we perform Tai Chi by the Cannon River. We promise to meet again in 200 years at the legendary mountain, Dahuang Shan.

On the islands in the campus's two lakes, the students and I get along well. The generational and cultural gaps disappear before the ancient philosophical giants. We even use the first paragraph of the *Tao Te Ching* as our class password. The first student says, "The Tao that can be said..." The second student answers, "...is not the eternal Tao." The first student says, "The name that can be named..." The second student says, "...is not the eternal Name." When they meet again in two hundred years, they may not recognize each other, but they will know each other by this password.

Could you tell us where to find the Tao?

One year, on the last day of our class, some students jumped into the lake and performed Tai Chi to show their Taoist love of water. I realized that American students can really appreciate Taoism, even though their textbook was written in English. This gave me confidence in the cross-linguistic and cross-cultural power of Taoist thought. Thought does not belong only to its birthplace; it belongs to anyone who studies and understands it. Anyone can drink from the source and gain inspiration, health, and longevity.

About the spelling of the Chinese terms: I use the old system for important names and words like *Taoism*, *Lao Tzu*, *Confucius*, and *Tai Chi*, because they have become part of the English language. I have moved to the modern pinyin system for less familiar names and words, such as *Zhuangzi*, *Liezi*, and *Xiang Yu*. The mixture of the old and the new romanization systems reflects the rapid cultural changes that have taken place in China during the past 50 years.

Unless otherwise noted, all quotations from Lao Tzu are from: *The Tao Te Ching: A New Translation and Commentary*, Ellen M. Chen (St. Paul: Paragon House, 1989).

Let's get another perspective on things.

A Manifesto of
Modern Taoism

Students: Are you a Taoist?

Qiguang Zhao: I refuse to be named. Ancient Taoist thinkers and their works are ancient history. I am influenced by Taoism, but I keep my spiritual freedom and my right to fly without confines.

Students: What is Applied New Taoism?

Qiguang Zhao: Applied New Taoism seeks to discover the spiritual state between sleeping and waking; between life and death; between present, past, and future; and between Wu Wei and Wu Bu Wei.

Wu Wei, doing nothing, and Wu Bu Wei, doing everything, are our answers to the challenges of modern life. We question the existence and importance of time. *Wu* means "no" and *Wei* means "action," so *Wu Wei* can be translated as "nonaction" or "do nothing." For Wu Bu Wei, the translation is "do everything," because *Bu* means "not," and its combination with *Wu* creates a smart double negative. Thus, *Wu* and *Bu* cancel each other, and *Wu Bu Wei* can be simplified to *Wei* only, with an emphasis on doing all things or leaving nothing undone.

Wu Wei, "do nothing" or "doing nothing," is to follow the course of nature. It is confidence in the universe. Since everything happens within the universe, if you follow the wonder of nature, wonders will occur around you every day.

Wu Wei is wisdom. You tell life, "I trust you; do whatever you want." Life will always reward you with everything surprising. Wu Wei is habit.

Wu Bu Wei, "doing everything," is the creativity to build a good habit. We do not have to solve every basic question of life. We just follow the established good habit, as a mathematician follows established equations without having to prove it every time.

Wu Wei is modesty, knowing that each person has his or her own ambition, each thing has its own owner, and nature and society have their own rules. Wu Bu Wei is courage to navigate through the rules.

Wu Wei is a delight in knowing that everything will be all right. It is not refusing to do anything, it is refusing to do insignificant things. Wu Wei is efficiency. It is the precondition of Wu Bu Wei. Wu Wei requires giving up secondary matters and aiming for the key matters. You can only Wu Bu Wei because you Wu Wei.

Wu Wei is the secret of health. Only if you abandon anxiety can you do anything with a healthy mind and body.

We respect but do not totally agree with ideologies. We do not agree with anyone's opinions: we have opinions of our own.

We gaze at the stars and compare them with ourselves. We do not gloat at our neighbors, envy their successes, or become angry at our differences.

We are alone. We shut the world out as we think, feel, and move. We talk to the world, we listen, we observe, we join, but

The modern meets the ancient.

we keep Tao at the core, like a cliff hanging above the surging ocean. Let the world make ripples, waves, or storms on the ocean; our cliff stays high and grows higher.

We think with our bodies. Usually, the body is directed by the mind. Yet when we move with uniform motion, our bodies give us a message, a biofeedback, which brings the mind closer to the uniform motion of the universe.

We create a surreal world. We fly in the clouds, we ride rainbows.

The world has waited too long for a voice with fresh ideas and new approaches to life. We hope to create such a voice by echoing an old tune, a voice that soothes the heart and strengthens the mind in a new established form. We want to create a mode of communication between humans that is beyond language.

We are not scholars who make every effort to understand books. We are artists who apply our knowledge to our lives. I invite you to creation, a forging of the missing links between ancient worlds and our life. Let us go through the thorns of elite scholarship, through the bushes of vulgar devices, and visit a quiet, forgotten land.

Let us find love, in a broad sense, a love whose object is not one person called *Lover*, not a group of persons called *Class* or *Nation*, but rather a concept of ultimate beauty that extends to the ends of the universe. I want to inform you, coach you, inspire you, and then ask you to meet the challenges of the world, to form healthy, balanced ways of thinking, living, approaching, and existing.

We know how to relax and do nothing, or Wu Wei, because without doing anything, the stars twinkle quietly numerous light-years from earth, and the earth rotates on its axis once every 24 hours. If the universe can, so can we; we know how to do everything without worrying, because we only belong to this world for a short while.

2 Many Thinkers, One Tao

In a culture dominated by Confucianism (which represents, among other things, the moralistic, the official, and the respectable), these lonely thinkers echo each other with an individualistic, unconventional, and spontaneous voice.

Lao Tzu was the author of the *Tao Te Ching* and an older contemporary of Confucius in the Spring and Autumn period (722–481 BCE). He was born in Zhou State and was the librarian of the Zhou Emperor. We are not certain whether he was one person or many; it is possible that a number of people wrote the *Tao Te Ching*. However, as with Shakespeare, the exact identity of the author is less important than the content of the works. According to legend, Lao Tzu was born with gray hair and left China riding backwards on an ox; at the gate of China, the gatekeeper persuaded him to write the Tao Te Ching as a last record of his philosophy.

Zhuangzi lived in the fourth century BCE. He was a rival of Confucianism and a follower of Lao Tzu, and in his writings, he often satirized the popular Confucianist and Mohist philosophies of the time. Together, Lao Tzu and Zhuangzi are considered the fathers of Taoist philosophy (as distinguished from Taoist religion).

Liezi was another representative Taoist. The teachings of Liezi were close to those of Zhuangzi. He was supposed to have lived during the early part of the Warring States Period (476–221 BCE). However, the extant version of his works reflects the thinking and writing style of later scholars.

Confucius (551–479 BCE) has been the dominant Chinese philosopher both morally and politically. In the Warring States Period, Mencius (c.390–305 BCE) extended and systematized Confucius's ideas. With the Han Dynasty's (206 BCE–220 CE) adoption of Confucianism as the official moral and political doctrine of the State, the Confucian tradition became so broad that "scholar" became all but synonymous with "Confucian." Confucius discusses the Tao quite often, but his Tao is entirely different from that of Lao Tzu and Zhuangzi. He is in many ways a rival, in opposition to Taoism, though he had a great respect for Lao Tzu and his ideas. The six main Confucian principles are loyalty, filial piety, ritual, righteousness, honesty, and shame. The Confucian emphasis on ritual and obligation is in strong contrast to Taoist philosophy.

Confucius asked in the *Analects*:

> Is it not a great pleasure to study and to practice what you
> have learned?
> Is it not a happiness to have friends coming from far away?
> Is he not a gentleman who is not bothered by people who
> do not recognize him?[1]

Compare this with Lao Tzu's three questions after he suggested "Abandon learning and put an end to your troubles":

Is there a difference between yes and no?
Is there a difference between good and evil?
Is it not nonsense that I must fear what others fear?

There were 200 years between Lao Tzu and Zhuangzi; there are over 2000 years between Zhuangzi and us.

Here, we gather to answer Zhuangzi as he answered Lao Tzu.

If we cannot, who can?

If we won't, who will?

We heard your voice, 2000 years ago.

We saw your banners, 15,000 miles away.

Together, we go rambling without a destination. We even things out. We find what matters in life.

I learned the following comical poem from my father, who often recited it during the Cultural Revolution. It is a few lines from a Peking opera, recited by a robber who, sword in hand, stops the traveling hero and roars:

> I opened this road
> I planted this tree
> You want to go ahead
> Leave money to me
> It will be too bad
> If you do not agree
> I will chop your head
> You cannot flee

The hero just mocks the robber and announces, "I would give you my money, but I have two friends who do not agree."

"Which two friends?" the robber demands.

The hero raises his right fist. "This is the first friend of mine." He raises his left. "This is my second friend."

"Ah ya-ya!" The robber yells as he jumps on the hero. They fight fiercely, and the hero eventually wins.

We can have two friends in our lives: Confucius and Lao Tzu. Following just one would leave us incomplete. We can be practical and spiritual, awake and dreaming. With a balance between direction and nondirection, between action and inaction, we will follow a middle path.

3 Take It Easy and Take Care

Confucianism and Taoism can be seen as two opposite responses to social pressures. While Confucianism is concerned with social relations and conduct, Taoism has a much more individualistic and carefree character and is greatly influenced by nature.

Two American expressions reflect these opposite attitudes. Both expressions mean "goodbye" but can be seen as standing for Confucian and Taoist life philosophies. When I first came to the United States for graduate school in the early 1980s, I found that Americans say goodbye differently than what I learned in my textbooks in China. In those days, students learned only formal British English in China. There were several ways to say goodbye, even including "Cheerio" or "Farewell until we meet again."

When I finished my first class in an American classroom, I walked up to the professor and tested my textbook sentence: "Farewell until we meet again," I said. He answered with a smile, "Take it easy." I took the expression literally, as advice, thinking I must look too nervous in class. So I tried to loosen up a bit in the next class meeting and even ventured to chime in with my opinions. At the end of the next class, I walked up to him again and bade him adieu. "Take care," he advised. Instead of urging me to take it easy, he warned me to "take care!" I thought I was being admonished for my carelessness, thought I might have been relaxed to a fault. Indeed, I should take care of my performance.

After several cycles of taking it easy and taking care, I realized that Americans just say to "take care" or "take it easy" as a casual way of saying goodbye, without meaning to give advice or warning. Now when I hear people say to "take care" or "take it easy," I cannot help smiling, because the casual parting expressions remind me of when I first came to the United States.

These expressions also reflect the opposed attitudes of Confucius and Lao Tzu. A Confucian would say, "Take care" and a Taoist would say, "Take it easy."

Lao Tzu counseled people to turn away from the endless river of human care and return to their natural wellspring. According to Confucius, the process of learning the names used in the classics helped one to make distinctions between good and evil, beautiful and ugly, high and low, "being" and "nonbeing." According to Lao Tzu, to abandon knowledge is to abandon names, distinctions, tastes, and desires. This would result in nonaction, doing nothing, or spontaneous behavior (Wu Wei) and lead us to spiritual freedom.

When they face the world, Confucians take care, while Taoists take it easy. Confucians worry about future consequences, while Taoists enjoy the present harmony. Confucians hold life and names dear. They climb on the mountain of life and see that the path to glory is always rugged. They counsel caution and warn fellow climbers, "Take care."

Taoists know that life comes and goes. They deny none of their natural penchants, repress none of their desires, and never feel the spur of reputation. They saunter through life, gathering its pleasures as the whim moves them. Since they shun personal fame and gains, they are beyond care and fear. Name and gain are temporary visitors, not permanent residents of the world. They climb the mountain of life, see the setting sun gild the sky, and announce triumphantly: "Take it easy."

Take it easy and enjoy the scenery. Take care and do not tip the boat.

4 Take It Easy, but Take It

A Confucian Taoist would say "Take it easy, but take it." If you cannot take care as a Confucian, and will not take it easy as a Taoist, you can take it easy, but take it. This is probably closest to our concept of Wu Wei and Wu Bu Wei. Wu Wei is not passively doing nothing, but rather doing everything effortlessly, as bamboo shadows sweep the terrace without stirring any dust, as moonlight pierces a marsh but leaves no traces. There is a Chinese idiom, "Push the boat with the current," meaning to use an opportunity to go forward, or to give judicious guidance according to circumstances.

Push the boat with the current.

Ronald Reagan was the only American president to quote Lao Tzu in a state of the union address: "Govern a great nation as you would cook a small fish," he said. That is, when you cook a small fish, you should not flip it too much or overdo it. He was promoting the conservative ideology of the free market as an engine of economic progress, but he also revealed this basic idea in his approach to world affairs.

Some people credit Reagan for destroying the Soviet Union. His voice, with his actor's rhythmic tone, still echoes today: "Mr. Gorbachev, tear down that wall!" Lo, the Berlin Wall fell in no time: the Iron Curtain fell, and America became the only superpower. The whole Western world stood up and roared, "Well done, Big Ronny!" Who is this Ronny guy? A magician? A Solomon? A First Emperor of the Qin Dynasty? What magic did he perform to change the color of the "Evil Empire"? What wisdom won him such loving respect? What power did he possess to destroy the supposedly invincible adversary?

His cheerleaders could not rationalize the sudden fall of the "Evil Empire," nor could they figure out how Reagan contributed to it. So they surmised that Reagan lured the Soviet Union into an arms race, which dragged the Soviet economy down. While Reagan took afternoons off for golf on weekdays, the Empire spanning six time zones worked itself to death. As a matter of fact, the arms race between the Soviet Union and the United States had already been going on for 70 years before Reagan and Gorbachev, and every American president had tried to beat the Soviet Union in that race. Nobody needs to lure anybody to do something both have already been doing wholeheartedly for 70 years.

The Soviet Union collapsed under its own weight. President Reagan's magic, his wisdom, and his power were Wu Wei, or doing nothing. Reagan did nothing to destroy the Soviet Union. He just left the fish alone and let it cook itself. The Soviet Union fell because of its own internal faults.

When we say he did nothing, we are not discrediting him. Quite the contrary, America should be grateful to this president. If he had done something, such as invade that country, the Soviet Union would have lasted a few more decades at least. Both Napoleon and Hitler found that they could not defeat Russia by invading it; in fact, their attacks only made it stronger. The power of American presidents is limited domestically because of the constitutional division of powers, but as commanders in chief, presidents are almost unlimited decision makers in international affairs. If they want to leave a presidential legacy, or if they want to test the clout of the military, aggressiveness can be very attractive. The tragedy of the leaders of the great powers is that they do not know how to stand and do nothing.

We are often put in an unfavorable condition or circumstance. However, unfavorable circumstances can also give us opportunities. In addition, the world is more complex than we understand, and we do not really know what a situation means for us. When we are unsure, the best strategy is to accept the situation and go with the flow. Lao Tzu said, "Misfortune is the root of good fortune; good fortune gives birth to misfortune." When an unfavorable situation arises, we must first

Wu Wei: accept and understand its possible potential, and gracefully turn the tables. If it works, we are happy. If it does not work, we at least have avoided doubling our misfortune by going in a wrong direction.

5 Wu Wei

Wu Wei is a basic principle of Taoism. *Wu* can be translated as "no"; *Wei* can be translated as "do" or "accomplish." The literal meaning of *Wu Wei* is "nonaction" or "without action." Why Wu Wei? And if we are not to do anything, what should we do?

Wu Wei means to follow the course of nature. It means to break the chain of worries and realize that not everything leads to your goal in life; it means to give yourself a break realizing that the process is more beautiful than the goal.

Nonaction is building a habit. That habit leads your life. You cannot make a decision every day or every minute. Should I get up now or at 7:30 AM? Should I smoke or not? Should I be an optimist or a worrier? When a habit is built, you are liberated from hourly, daily, weekly, or yearly action. You do not have to solve every problem from the very beginning. You do not have to agonize over the question of whether to be or not to be, because "to be" is already a habit. We should have seven, seventy, seven hundred, and seven million good habits, but we do not have to rebuild them or rationalize them every time. With good habits, we are free from making "much ado about nothing." A sparrow flies in the azure sky, seemingly without effort. Hundreds of muscles are working, but the sparrow does not have to think about each one. It simply has a good habit, a habit so natural and serene that it is effortless, like bamboo that grows by a stream, the boat that floats on a river, and the clouds that slide on the sky.

A good habit, like a boat anchored in a quiet harbor after a storm, is established by doing nothing after a lot of doing everything.

Wu Wei is frequently misunderstood. In modern China, if you tell a person you follow Taoism, sometimes you will receive a comment like, "Oh, is it the philosophy of Wu Wei? Why do you follow the philosophy of idleness?" As a matter of fact, Wu Wei is not passively doing nothing, but rather knowing when to act and when not to act. It is often included in the paradox Wei Wu Wei, or acting nonaction. The goal of Wu Wei is to achieve a state of spontaneous alignment with the Tao, and, as a result, obtain a perfect form of supple and invisible power.

The Sage is occupied with acts without effort, messages without speaking, and successes without exertion. Lao Tzu teaches without wordiness, produces without possessing, and creates without regard for result. Not overdoing things and doing them at the proper time is the key to success. Taoism recognizes that the universe works harmoniously in its own ways; as humans put forth their will against the world they interrupt the existing harmony. This is not to say that we ought not to exert our will to act. Rather it is knowing whether, when, and how to act in relation to natural processes.

Wu Wei has also been interpreted as the art of letting be, or creative quietude. This does not mean a laziness of action or a dullness of the mind; rather it is an alert and effortless determination to obey the rules of the Way. One way of thinking of Wu Wei is through Lao Tzu's words about how to govern a big nation. The advice is to govern a big nation as you would fry a small fish: too much flipping and the fish is ruined.

Lao Tzu said:

> To pursue learning one increases daily.
> To pursue Tao one decreases daily.
> To decrease and again to decrease
> Until one arrives at not doing.
> Not doing and yet nothing is not done.
> Always take the empire when there are no businesses.
> If there are businesses,
> It is not worthwhile to take the empire.
> (Chen: *The Tao Te Ching*, Chapter 48)

In learning, we always pick up more. In Taoism, we drop things. Since our infancy, we have learned many things that separate us from the universe. We worry about trivial matters, like wealth and prestige. Now we want to return to our origins, to be more like a baby and forget these distractions. We want to do nothing. This is Wu Wei.

By choosing nonaction, we choose to empty ourselves and go with the flow rather than fight the current. Nonaction does not mean not doing, stopping the natural progression of events; instead, nonaction means to follow nature's course without fighting, striving, or resisting change. We are like water, like the empty vessel, formless and nameless; and in so being, we cannot act: we must accept what challenges the universe throws at us. At the same time, by fulfilling our purpose and allowing ourselves to be empty, we are doing all that we need to do. We do nothing and, in so doing, accomplish everything.

Wu Wei is an act of spontaneity and effortlessness. Zhuangzi refers to this type of existence as *xiao yao,* or "purposeless wandering." It should not be considered laziness or mere passivity. Instead, it is the practice of going with nature, or swimming with the current. The Chinese expression *"ting qi zi ran,"* "let nature take its course," and the English axiom "Go with the flow" are close approximations of this fundamental Taoist principle.

Perhaps the most glorious and prosperous period in China was the Rule of Wen and Jing (180 BCE–141 BCE) of the Han Dynasty, known for the benevolence and thriftiness of the rulers. These two emperors reduced taxes and other burdens on the people, practiced pacifism, and preserved general political stability. The Rule of Wen and Jing was marked by Taoist influence on its political theory due to the influence of Empress Dou, who was the wife of Emperor Wen and mother to Emperor Jing. Unfortunately, when she died during the reign of her grandson, Emperor Wu, the Taoist leadership came to an end. The Rule of Wen and Jing was exceptional and is viewed as the Golden Age of Chinese history. The country was so rich that the coins in the treasury piled up into mountains. The strings that held them together rotted and broke, and many coins fell out of the building, along with piles of extra grain from the government granaries. Almost no emperors in Chinese history have reached as high a level of peace and prosperity as these two emperors and their strong Wu Wei wife and mother.

The problem with other emperors is that they did too much. Take, for example, the First Emperor of the Qin Dynasty (221 BCE–206 BCE). He could not stop after he unified China and went on to undertake some Herculean construction projects, including building the Great Wall. He built an enormous mausoleum for himself, including an underground terra cotta army of 8,000 soldiers. He burned almost all existing books and buried 460 scholars alive. He could not be satisfied with doing nothing. But public works and attacks on those who opposed him were too great of a burden for the population. Qin rule, supposedly the strongest in Chinese history, came to an end shortly after his death. It lasted only 15 years. The Qin emperor's problem was that he was not able to do nothing. When his power and desire combined, ferocious fire burned his dynasty to ashes. I am not saying that he should have been dormant in his throne, but he should have known where to stop.

Fortunately and unfortunately, most of us do not have the power of emperors. However, we can become Wu Wei emperors of our own territory. Let us spend one day as free as water, as nature, and not be thrown off track by every petty noise of the world. We can rise early, gently, and not be upset by the terrible rapids and whirlpools we encounter. Let us sit quietly by the window, watch the clouds float over the horizon, watch the leaves fall, the flowers bloom, and the seasons come and go. Then we can say we have brought peace to our reign. Our land is small, and our power is limited; but with our limited power to rule our limited territory, we can create a place. Peace is the first form of serenity and happiness. If everyone has found peace within, there will be peace everywhere.

In this world, life is eating everyone up. People are pressed to act, sometimes irrationally. Let us set aside a serenity into which the world cannot intrude. There is an ancient Wu Wei that we carry in our hearts. Sometimes we are trapped in a corner and forced to make decisions. We often assume that if we do not decide, our little world will fall apart. As a matter of fact, the two decisions may be both right and wrong. We only find out what was right after the decision is made and the consequences have unfolded. So it is better not to worry, but to be at peace.

Lao Tzu sometimes puts the verb *Wei* (to act or practice) before *Wu Wei* (no action). He said:

Do when there is nothing to do,
Manage affairs when there are none to manage,
Know by not knowing.
Regard the great as small, the much as little.
Repay injury with *te*.
Plan the difficult while it is easy.
Accomplish the great when it is small.
(Chen, *The Tao Te Ching*, Chapter 63)

Doing nothing is hard work. Keeping the status quo is as difficult as creating change. Being still requires effort. This is true for anything, from humans to stars.

If each person has peace in his or her heart,
there will be peace in the world.

When a star gets sufficiently dense, the repulsion caused by the Exclusion Principle would be less than the attraction of gravity. The Nobel laureate astrophysicist Chandrasekhar calculated that a cold star of more than about one and a half times the mass of the sun would not be able to support itself against its own gravity. This mass is now known as the *Chandrasekhar limit*.[2]

Maintaining our present position is a hard job. Just as the star supports itself against its own gravity, Lao Tzu said "Wei Wu Wei," or "act nonaction." So nonaction is an action: just as a star maintains its own gravity, a human attains longevity and humankind protects the environment. Many people cannot support themselves; they destroy themselves with gambling, drugs, and smoking. Maintaining a healthy life is both Wu Wei and Wu Bu Wei. Not having a bad habit takes as much work as having a good habit.

NOTES

1. Stephen Hawking, *The Theory of Everything* (Beverly Hills: New Millennium Press, 2002), 50.

6 Wu Bu Wei

Taoism is not a passive philosophy; it advocates adventures, as long as you enjoy the adventure for itself and do not focus on the aim.

> Tao everlasting does not act,
> And yet nothing is not done.
> If kings and barons can abide by it,
> The ten thousand things will transform by themselves.
> If in transforming desire is aroused,
> I shall suppress it by the nameless uncarved wood.
> With the nameless uncarved wood,
> There shall be no desire.
> Without desire there is thus quietude.
> The world shall be self-ordered.
> (Chen, *The Tao Tè Ching*, Chapter 37)

In the pursuit of learning, every day something is acquired.

> To pursue Tao one decreases daily.
> To decrease and again to decrease,
> Until one arrives at not doing.
> Not doing and yet nothing is not done.
> Always take the empire when there are no businesses.
> If there are no businesses,
> It is not worthwhile to take the empire.
> (Chen, *The Tao Tè Ching*, Chapter 48)

Remember when we discussed Lao Tzu's Chapter 48 in the context of Wu Wei, doing nothing? The story is a little more complicated than that.

In both Chapter 37 and Chapter 48, Lao Tzu twice uses the words *Wu Wei* (literally, "no do" or "doing nothing") and *Wu Bu Wei* ("no no do," or "not doing nothing," or "doing everything"). *Wu Bu Wei* is traditionally translated as "nothing is left undone." *Wu Bu Wei* is a consequence clause, an upshot of Wu Wei, as if Lao Tzu is saying, "If you do nothing, then everything will be done."

However, in the original Chinese, Lao Tzu uses the conjunction *er* between Wu Wei and Wu Bu Wei. *Er* most closely translates to "but" or "and," not "therefore." Wu Wei and

When you play chess, you can do nothing on a cliff and
do everything while you are flying.

Wu Bu Wei are parallel clauses, not expressions of cause and effect.

Lao Tzu thunders the most important message to us from 2,500 years ago: Do nothing and do everything. Not only does this change the meaning of our philosophy, it changes our roles in life. We are not passive objects, waiting for everything to "be done" through our nonaction; rather we are the subjects of our own lives. We use both Wu Wei and Wu Bu Wei; we do nothing and do everything.

The Tao abides in nonaction *and* in action: we do everything by doing nothing. Since man follows Tao and Tao follows nature, we should do nothing against nature. To understand Wu Bu Wei, think of the Uncertainty Principle of physics. According to Stephen Hawking:

> The uncertainty principle implies that the more accurately one knows one of these qualities, the less accurately one can know the other. So in empty space the field cannot be fixed at exactly zero, because then it would have both a precise value, zero, and a precise rate of change, also zero. Instead, there must be a certain minimum amount of uncertainty, or quantum fluctuations, in the value of a field.[3]

Therefore, absolute Wu, absolute negation, is impossible. There must be something in the Wu; you must have something to negate. Absolute Wu Wei is also impossible, because one cannot make absolutely zero change. In the "field" of action and nonaction, the demarcation line between Wu Wei and Wu Bu Wei is uncertain. We travel between Wu Wei and Wu Bu Wei, usefulness and uselessness.

Our key figure for Doing Nothing and Doing Everything.

Here is a story told by Zhuangzi:

Zhuangzi was walking in the mountains and saw a huge tree lush with leaves. All the woodcutters left it alone. Zhuangzi asked a woodcutter why. The woodcutter answered, "That tree is useless." Zhuangzi commented, "This tree is useless and can live out its life."

Zhuangzi left the mountain and went to stay at a friend's house. The friend was very pleased to see him and asked a boy to kill a goose in Zhuangzi's honor. The boy said, "One goose can honk and the other cannot. Which one should I kill?" The friend said, "Kill the one that cannot honk."

The next day, a student asked Zhuangzi, "The other day, we saw a tree that could live out its life because it was useless. Just now, we saw a goose killed because it was useless. What do you choose, master? Usefulness or uselessness?"

Zhuangzi smiled. "I will stay between usefulness and uselessness. This position looks useful but is useless, and we cannot avoid the burden. It is different to drift with the Tao; there is neither praise nor blame. Sometimes you're a dragon, sometimes you're a snake, floating with time, never focusing on one thing, up and down, using harmony as measurement. Swimming with the ancestor of the ten thousand things, taking things as things, not being taken as a thing, how can you be burdened?"[4]

We have spoken about nonaction: staying weak, staying low. On the other hand, when the time comes, do not hesitate to go high—just so long as you know that it is temporary. In your life, you can be successful or unsuccessful: it doesn't matter, as long as you flow with the time. Your purpose will be the realization that you are part of the universe.

When a triumphant general returned to Rome, he would ride through the street, and the crowd cheered on both sides. Yet he always had a slave sitting in the carriage, to whisper in his ear: *"Respice post te! Hominem te esse memento! Memento mori!"* ("Look behind you! Remember you are only a man! Remember you will die!") The general would smile.

According to the Uncertainty Principle, there is much in life that we cannot control. Since we cannot control the universe, we do nothing. Since we cannot control the universe, we can also do everything, just for the fun of it. The earth moves, but we do not feel its motion. We do nothing, but we do it all.

Our temple is supported by separate pillars: Wu Wei and Wu Bu Wei. We cannot say that today our temple will lean on only one of them. We cannot say, "Today I do nothing; tomorrow I will do everything." We live in the vague domain between doing everything and doing nothing. We shift between Wu Wei and Wu Bu Wei, just as modern binary systems shift between 0 and 1. Making ourselves artificial obstacles to the transition between doing nothing and doing everything causes mental pain and operates against the Uncertainty Principle.

Cause and effect are not as they seem. We can do nothing, we can do everything: the result is the same. In time, everything in the universe will end. Even when we achieve our goals, we cannot own them, and they may not turn out as we had planned. Our expectations may betray us, and when all is said and done, all of our actions will be lost in the flow of nature.

NOTES

2. Stephen Hawking, *The Theory of Everything* (Beverly Hills: New Millennium Press, 2002), 82.

3. Stories from *Zhuangzi* are translated by the author, unless otherwise noted.

7 The Universe and Us

The best show in the universe is the universe. Look at the starry sky. What a show!

The best show of the world is the world.

The universe is big, and we are small. When we are small, so are our problems. Let the starry sky lead us to a time that is neither the past nor the future nor the present. Let the stars lead us to a space beyond life and death. The best show in the universe is the universe!

"What a piece of work is a man," Hamlet says. "How noble in reason, how infinite in faculties; in form and movement, how expressive and admirable; in action, how like an angel, in apprehension, how like a god." This is why he is crazy. He thinks human beings are larger than the world, and his problems grow out of his control. The self-centered people will be punished by the world.

Who agrees that humans are so great? Do birds agree? Do ants agree? Do monkeys agree? Even cats do not agree. Only dogs, our sole companions after 15,000 years of domestication, might agree that we are "the beauty of the world, the paragon of animals!" Only dogs look at us and try to understand us as if we were a piece of Shakespeare's poetry. The problem is, if your best friend was the only one to call you "the beauty of the world," it might be wise not to believe him. So I urge you not to watch men only, but to watch, as Hamlet said, "the air, look you, this brave o'erhanging firmament, this majestical roof fretted with golden fire."

Many people ignore the beauty of the world and the splendid show of the universe. Hamlet noticed the beauty of the world and of humanity, but his problems grew so big that he could not draw strength from this. Renaissance humanism, as represented by Hamlet, put humanity at the center of the universe, which during the Middle Ages had been God's place. Humans took up the burden of to do or not to do, or in Hamlet's case, to be or not to be. According to Taoism, everything that bothers us is small compared to the vastness of time and space. When you realize how small you are, you no longer believe you are a god; without that pressure, you can move freely with the universe with no illusions of grandeur.

We cannot claim to be gods, but how much more freedom we have in the knowledge of our insignificance!

We are not the center of the world,
although our best friend may think so.

Zhuangzi told a story to explain our limitations:

The autumn flood came; the Yellow River swelled with water from its hundred tributaries. You could not tell a horse from a cow on the opposite bank. The river god was contented and thought he had swallowed every beautiful thing. He followed the current to the east and reached the North Sea. He looked east and did not see the limit of the water. He looked around and sighed to Ruo, the ocean god. "As the saying goes, 'One who has heard a hundred truths thinks he's the best in the world.' This is me. Now I know you are infinite. If I had not come to your door, I would be in great danger of being loved by all people."

Ruo said, "You cannot tell a frog in a well about the ocean, because it is limited by space. You cannot tell a summer insect about ice, because it is limited by time. You cannot tell a bookish scholar about the Tao, because he is limited by education. Today, you have broken out of your cage and watched the ocean, and you know your own pettiness. Now we can talk about great wisdom."

Like the river god and the frog in the well, our abilities of perception are tiny compared to the vastness of the universe. We are just small creatures, and we are only here for a short visit. Let nature take care of the order of things.

Nature heals our wounds, gives us freedom, and offers us help we cannot give to each other. Zhuangzi told another story:

> When a spring dries up, and the fish are stranded on the land, they keep each other moist with their own bodies and with the foam they spit at each other. They would be better off if they could forget each other in the rivers and lakes. Rather than praising the sage king Yao and denouncing the cruel tyrant Jie, we could forget both of them and let their Ways dissolve.

Although they spit foam at each other during a drought, the fish would rather be able to forget each other in the joy of swimming. We would rather forget the trivial events of our time and lose them in the vastness of the universe. Forget these distinctions, forget these anxieties; they are all small compared to the Tao.

There is a story recorded by a Warring States statesman, Lu Buwei:

A man of Chu State lost a bow but decided he would not look for it. "A Chu man lost it, and a Chu man will find it," he said. "Why bother to look for it?"

Confucius heard this story and commented: "The word 'Chu' can be dropped."

Lao Tzu heard the story and commented, "The word 'man' can be dropped."

(Qiguang Zhao heard the story and commented, "The words 'lost' and 'found' can be dropped.")

The Chu man is patriotic: whether the bow is his or not does not matter to him, as long as it still belongs to a citizen of Chu.

Confucius is a humanitarian: it does not matter what country the bowfinder belongs to, as long as the bow belongs to a human being.

Lao Tzu is a Taoist: it does not matter if the bow belongs to a human being or to a mound of dirt; it belongs to nature. (Lu Buwei said Lao Tzu is the most selfless among the three.)

Qiguang Zhao says the bow is not ours anyway. In the year 2007, astronomers demoted Pluto, but it doesn't matter to Pluto whether or not we call it a planet. The bow is itself; the "lost" and "found" only create an illusion of attachment to things.

楚人失弓，楚人得之

A person of Chu loses it; a person of Chu finds it.

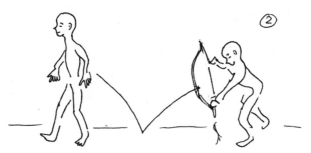

A person loses it; a person finds it. —Confucius

失之，得之

It is lost; It is found. —Lao Tzu

It. —Qiguang Zhao

What does it matter if it is lost or found? It is all part of the universe. As words reduce, our view enlarges.

8 Reversing

Returning is the movement of Tao.
Weak is the functioning of Tao.
The ten thousand things under heaven are born of being.
Being is born of non-being.
(Chen, *The Tao Te Ching*, Chapter 40)

If it does not work, just try reversing it.

The universe began from a very small point. The density of the primordial universe was so great that millions of tons were concentrated in a point as big as the tip of a needle. It is now expanding, and there are three theories of what its ultimate fate will be. The first is that it will continue to expand forever, spreading all its matter and energy so thin that no life of any kind will survive. The second is that the expansion will continue, but will slow down and eventually stabilize. The third possibility—which is my favorite, because it is the most Taoist—is that once the universe has stopped expanding, it will begin to contract again. It will contract back to the size of a needlepoint. When this happens, gravity will become so strong that everything will stop moving. Wu Wei triumphs in the end. All life, information, and history will be lost; it will return to the great emptiness. Then why shouldn't the Big Bang happen again?

The universe is moving in a cycle, expanding and condensing between two extremes. Because we live in the universe, whatever we do is a part of the universal cycle of reversal. Everything will eventually transform and become its opposite, and we can learn this best from watching the universe.

A student once asked me, "What is the opposite of time?"

Without thinking, I answered "space."

What is time? We think of time as the years, days, hours, and minutes that make up our lives. Superficially, it is also a measurement of movement through space: the sun rises, the sun sets, the earth rotates around the sun. Neither time nor space exists without the other; they are complementary, like the Taoist yin and yang.

Most people agree that the universe is expanding, and many say that at some point, it will begin to shrink. Everything transforms into its opposite: the universe will become smaller and smaller, and then it will shrink to a single point.

That is to say someday, everything in the universe will stop. Time and space can become each other, and someday they will both disappear. The law of the unity of opposites is the fundamental law of the universe. Everything is a unity of opposites; everything exists because of its opposite. There is yin because there is yang; there is up because there is down; there is white because there is black; there is male because there is female.

Everything exists because of its opposite, and everything will become its opposite someday. What expands must shrink. The universe, when it stops expanding, will contract into a black hole. The hardest tree, when blown over by a strong wind, will decay and become soft.

反者道之用
Reversing is the
motion of the Tao

Qiu zhu
2006

Reversing is the motion of the Tao. Turn this book upside-down. Just as these drawings show different faces when you look at them upside-down, the world looks different when you look at it in reverse. Try standing on your head: It really changes your perspective on things.

Reversing does not mean that you must change between just two opposites; often, there is a whole new dimension you have to consider. This is what we call "thinking outside the box."

In the following ancient Chinese story a man and his elderly advisor consider different options but get stuck in only two dimensions:

A man from Lu carrying a long pole tried to enter the city gate. First, he held the pole upright, but it was too tall, and he could not get it through the gate. Then he tried holding it

Sometimes the correct solution is the simplest.

horizontally, but the pole was too wide, and it still could not pass through. He was stumped. An old man came along and said, "I am not a sage, but I do have a lot of practical experience. Why not cut the pole in two at the middle?" So the man cut the pole in two at the middle.

The best way to go around a barrier is to go through it.

Benjamin Franklin was certain of two things: death and taxes. Taoists are simpler. We are certain of only one thing: change, in all dimensions. Do not worry that your answer may be too simple. The simple answer usually works better than the complex one.

Lao Tzu was respected for his dialectical understanding of change—everything changes to its extreme, hence the paradox that to achieve a goal, one should begin with its opposite. To be yang, one must retain yin. To have strength, one must retain weakness. Because things develop to their opposite, when they reach the extreme, one should interfere as little as possible with nature. The best sovereign does not exercise active rule. Everything exists because of its opposite, and everything changes towards its opposite. If you have life, you will develop toward death. Because everything moves toward its opposite, if you want to be strong, you need weakness. The wise, the heroic, and the strong must be foolish, cowardly, and weak.

9 Naming

> Tao that can be spoken of
> Is not the Everlasting Tao.
> Name that can be named
> Is not the Everlasting name.
> Nameless, the origin of heaven and earth;
> Named, the mother of ten thousand things.
> (Chen, *The Tao Te Ching*, Chapter 1)

Lao Tzu tried to distinguish between the namable and unnamable in the world. The former included the specific things, and the latter included the eternal, limitless, and primitive universe. Thus, the unnamable is the beginning of heaven and earth and the mother of all things. The Tao is unnamable because it is the beginning of all beginnings and never ceases to be. It is all embracing, infinite, and the source of all specific shapes. Words are not enough to define the Tao; it is greater than a single word and cannot be confined to language. Expression goes beyond words. The Tao encompasses the universe; how can the infinite be expressed in a single name?

The first chapter of *The Tao Te Ching*, quoted above, is like a knock on the door. When we open the door to the concept of the nameless, we begin to experience a wider meaning to the universe.

When we refuse to name the Tao, we perform our first act of Wu Wei, or nondoing. We do not fight to confine the Tao within one name or category. In letting the principle of our lives remain nameless, we are embracing the freedom of the Tao, which includes the expanse of the ocean, the boundlessness of the starry sky, and the depth of the human spirit.

Without names, we are undefined; without definition, we have no meaning; without meaning, our borders are limitless. We are not defined by others: we define ourselves. To do that, we need a beginning. We choose to begin nowhere, with the emptiness that came before the modern world gave us names.

10 Emptiness

Tao is a whirling emptiness,
Yet in use is inexhaustible.
Fathomless,
It seems to be the ancestor of
ten thousand beings.
It blunts the sharp,
Unties the entangled,
Harmonizes the bright,
Mixes the dust.
Dark,
It seems perhaps to exist.
I do not know whose child it is,
It is an image of what precedes
God.
(*Tao Te Ching*, Chapter 4)

Thirty spokes share one hub to
make a wheel.
Through its non-being,
There is the use of the carriage.
Mold clay into a vessel.
Through its non-being,
There is the use of the vessel.
Cut out doors and windows to
make a house.
Through its non-being,
There is the use of the house.
Therefore in the being of a
thing,
There lies the benefit.
In the non-being of a thing,
There lies its use.
(*Tao Te Ching*, Chapter 11)

The house exists because of the space inside, not because of the beams and materials. The bowl itself is not useful; the empty space within a bowl is useful. Like the house and the bowl, we are no longer useful if we have no internal space. We find this physical space by exhaling, but we also must empty ourselves of the weight of the world, which we have wrongly placed upon our own shoulders. We must rid ourselves of anxiety, preconceptions, greed, and false ambitions. As humans, and not gods, we have no need for these worries, which we ultimately cannot control. We must become the empty vessel, nameless and receptive to the beauty of nature.

The usefulness of emptiness.

Water

A person with superior goodness is like water,
Water is good in benefiting all beings,
Without contending with any.
Situated in places shunned by many others,
Thereby it is near Tao.
(Chen, *The Tao Te Ching*, Chapter 8)

Water is the essence of Wu Wei, nonaction. As water flows downhill, it takes the path of least resistance and follows the contours of the land. It takes many shapes and adapts itself to the form of its surroundings. Though many may not wish to venture into the low places of the world, there is nothing undignified about water. Though it is humble enough to enter into dark places, the humility and weakness of water is its greatest strength: by not striving, it carves away caves and smoothes the most jagged of rocks. Behave like water, take on its nature: I invite you to swim in the world.

The Chinese dragon flies in the air, but it primarily behaves like a water god. It is believed to descend into the water at the autumn equinoxes; at the vernal equinoxes, it leaves the water and ascends into the sky. It rises on the wind and the clouds, and its very breath condenses to form the rain—not only the gentle rains of the spring and autumn, but the fierce storms that make rivers overflow their banks. The dragon's spiral path to the highest heavens forms tornadoes, whirlwinds, and waterspouts. Here, dragons are the symbol of water, the symbol of life. In contrast, the Western dragon is the dragon of fire. The one ability all Western dragons have in common is their ability to breathe out smoke and fire. Their eyes, too, are usually red and furious. Because of its union with fire, the Western dragon is associated with death and the subterranean world.

Just like the free and elegant flow of water, the Chinese dragon has the Taoist freedom to do nothing gracefully and do everything elegantly. Confucius once compared Lao Tzu with the dragon, a symbol of mystery and sagacity, of aspiring deep thought and high nobility, the combination of water's flexibility and the sage's ability.

> Nothing under heaven
> Is softer and weaker than water,
> Yet nothing can compare with it
> In attacking the hard and strong.
> Nothing can change place with it.
> That the weak overcomes the strong,
> And the soft overcomes the hard,
> No one under heaven does not know,
> Though none can put it into practice.
> Therefore a sage said:
> "One who receives the filth of a state

Is called the Master of the Altar of the Soil and Grain;
One who shoulders the evils of a state
Becomes the king under heaven."
Straightforward words appear to be their reverse.
(Chen, *The Tao Te Ching*, Chapter 78)

The Qing Dynasty Cloud Dragon playing with a pearl.

We have only one moon, and no rings, but we have water.

No celestial bodies that we know of have liquid water. Intelligent beings from other planets that have no water must think we are mad with happiness to be surrounded by blue oceans and rushing rivers.

Very few people realize how fortunate we are and enjoy this beautiful world full of water. Even though Lao Tzu didn't have the knowledge of the earth's uniqueness as a ball covered with water, he finds that water represents all aspects of goodness and happiness. He believes that "the highest good is like water. Water gives life to the ten thousand things and does not strive." If we behave like water, we will be happy.

The great ocean sends us drifting like a raft, the running river sweeps us along like a reed. We do not tell the ocean to stop its tides, and we do not tell the river to flow slower. We just join them to celebrate the existence of happiness and freedom. We let water carry us to a new adventure.

12 Calm Down

How high is your blood pressure? Some people have been found to suffer from what doctors call "white coat hypertension." The doctor, believing that the hospital environment makes some people nervous enough to artificially raise their blood pressure, will help the patient to calm down, perhaps telling the patient to sit quietly and do nothing for a few minutes, or even sending the patient to rest in a darkened room. The second blood pressure reading will, of course, be lower. So which measurement represents the real blood pressure? Can patient and doctor really ignore the first, high reading? Are you usually as tense and nervous as you might be when you first enter the doctor's office? Or do you really "do nothing" all day, like the doctor had you do to calm you down? White coat hypertension notwithstanding, the first high measurement is probably closer to your true blood pressure, because most people do not allow themselves to calm down in daily life.

Unfortunately, we do not allow ourselves to do nothing during the day, even for a little while. We are constantly restless, which leads to higher blood pressure. We endlessly act and worry all our lives, except for some special moments, such as when we are checked for blood pressure. If we know that this calmness, this doing-nothing, can help us during the physical examination, why do we not perform it from time to time: not for the doctor, but for our arteries? In our daily life, we can relieve our stress-induced hypertension by creating a quiet inner corner—a self-created serene environment. We may let the day become a flowing meditation. Why do we only lie down and do nothing while sleeping during the night? We may have a short nap or powernap during the day. Why can we only calm down while listening to music? We may let the music from heaven echo through our soul. Why do we realize our humble limitations only while listening to sermons? We may give up the desire to control and let the divine universe take its course. Why do we not take time to do nothing when we have nothing to do? Rabindranath Tagore said, "Let my doing nothing when I have nothing to do become untroubled in its depth of peace like the evening on the seashore when the water is silent."[5]

You are not likely to have high blood pressure if, after a busy working day, you can see the afterglow of sunset at the margin of starry silence, if you can smell the fragrance of flowers after a bad storm, and if you can listen to honking geese head south for the winter after a busy autumn. The relaxation can be as short as ten minutes every day, or one minute every hour, or one second during a ten-minute task. The world will be different, because you are different after the relaxation.

Year in and year out, your body becomes a walking autobiography, telling acquaintances and passersby alike of the trivial and major stresses of your life. Stress can come from many places—finances, health, job, or family issues. Salt, fat, and lack of exercise will raise your blood pressure; physical or emotional stress only add to that.

High blood pressure was the necessary response of our primitive ancestors to pump extra oxygen to their vital organs when they faced predators or cold weather. In the age of hunting and gathering, our ancestors led a quiet life. They picked berries, drank water, hunted rabbits during the day, and slept peacefully under the stars at night. However, when another tribe or a saber-toothed tiger invaded their territory, they were faced with life-or-death decisions. Primitive man had two instincts when faced with danger: to fight or to run. In either case, he didn't have the time or necessity to consider whether or not to act. There was no obstacle between stimulus and response. He belonged to nature.

We are not too different from our ancestors.

Modern man still has the same two instincts, but he is not always able to act on them. When his boss yells at him for a wrong report, he cannot kick him (although tempting) or jump out of the window (also tempting).

Modern man's response to stress is just like the caveman's. His pancreas cranks out a lot of insulin, his blood pressure rises very high, and his blood sugar shoots up to prepare for an action that he ultimately cannot take. He cannot fight or fly; he cannot kick his boss or jump out the window. Instead, he usually responds by becoming frustrated, angry, and maybe depressed.

Most of our problems do not merit the full fight-or-flight response. The high blood pressure to heighten physical alertness is not as necessary in modern life as it was in prehistoric times. If your mind continually feels stressed out, your body may maintain an abnormally high level of responsiveness, creating an artificially induced state of high blood pressure. Modern life needs a third mode, beyond the first one (fight) and the second one (flight). This third mode is nonaction. Instead of punishing ourselves for the mistakes of others, we should do nothing. That is, we should either ignore the situation, because we cannot control it, or do everything by following the course of nature.

Instead of worrying, modern man can walk out of his cramped office and watch the flowers grow, hear the birds sing, or gaze at the stars shining. He can do everything as nature does, because he is in this world for only a short visit. He does not have to solve the problems of his immediate surroundings, a limited environment that temporarily constrains him, just as he cannot solve the problems of the explosion of stars or the disappearance of a black hole. Yet he can fly with the stars, float with the clouds, and swim with the fish. If you cannot defeat the universe, you can join the universe. This is doing everything while doing nothing.

Your doctor tells you to calm down while you have your blood pressure measured. Relax, think nothing and do nothing, the doctor orders. You follow the doctor's order and can really bring your blood pressure down for the sake of the measurement. In this short period of time, you isolate yourself from the daily reality of your finances, health, job, and family. You give yourself a spiritual Shangri-la because you want to see your "real health situation." As a matter of fact, what you see is not your normal situation but your potential. Your real health situation is the first measurement, before you calmed down, when you were under the daily pressure. The measurement once you have calmed down shows your potential: you can create a Shangri-la among the daily sound and fury by taking a break or doing nothing for a moment. Unfortunately, many of us have not realized our potential to think of nothing. We think of our life as an unbroken chain: Every link in the chain is supposed to be connected to our ultimate goal in life, such as the American Dream of a house with three garages. A single error in daily life—a forgotten number, a missed appointment, an overcharged bill, a supercilious look by the boss, an awkward joke by a colleague, or a low school grade—would all supposedly impact the goal in our blueprint of life. Therefore, any event—big or small, real or imagined—causes us tension and raises our blood pressure.

One of my favorite American sayings is, "Give me a break." By saying this, we ask to be left alone from repeated pressures. "Give me a break" is an urgent plea for a pause, a rest, a cherished bit of respite. Unfortunately, while we often urge others, we do not give ourselves a break. We cannot break the self-designed chain linking everything together. We cannot pause, even for a minute, because we connect every minute with our daily bread, our life's goal, or our personal identity. We do not have the courage to take a link out of the chain. We do not have the confidence to give ourselves a hiatus in which we can stop thinking and ease our hypertension. We are not able to hold back the wheel of life to smell the fragrant flower by the road, watch the blue sky above, or talk to a passing dog, because we assume these pauses would cause us to lag behind and let our competitors pass us. We hear a cold, inimical voice reverberating: "All eyes to the front as you pass the other competitors! You do not deserve a break!"

We believe this voice. It seems we do not deserve a break as long as we have a dream. Ironically, another American dream is to retire at 50. In order to have a long break, or reside permanently in the Shangri-la of doing nothing at 50, many workers refuse to give themselves a break any time before the goal is realized. As a result, between the ages of 30 and 50, their systolic blood pressure rises 3 mmHg per year, their diastolic, 1 mmHg per year. They retire at 50, if they are lucky enough to live that long, with a blood pressure of 180 over 100.

We know how to calm down when we have our blood pressure measured. Instructed by the doctor, we can practice focusing on feeling calm. We can produce a state of relaxation that reduces heart rate, slows breathing, and lowers blood pressure. Yet we often shy away from practicing calmness because it feels artificial. We just calm down for a moment to cheat the blood pressure meter. Why do we not do ourselves a favor and have a lucid awareness of calmness a few times during the day? Why do we not pause to have a minute meditation every hour, involving deliberate breathing and sitting quietly, not for the blood pressure meter but for ourselves, not for the doctor but for our dear ones. The earth will not stop rotating if we focus on a pleasurable image, sound, or mantra, just to give ourselves a break and try to let all thoughts, feelings, sounds, and images just pass through our minds.

Many of the ways people control their stress or mask it— like eating, drinking alcohol, and smoking—contribute to the development of high blood pressure. You may wish to exercise to manage your stress. Exercise is a healing break from the chain of life. It provides your body with well-controlled physical relief. Since we usually cannot fight or fly in modern society, we use exercise as a physical substitute. However, we should also remember nonaction in this beneficial physical action. Pause and moderation are a matter of life and death for exercisers. Excessive physical stress does not benefit your circulatory system. Rather it increases your risk of illness and even death. Exercise is a marvelous antidote to pressures. However, excessive doses of an antidote can also result in injury to health. Every man is the builder of a temple: it's called a body. We should not pollute it with smoke or junk food, but neither should we overburden it and let it collapse prematurely.

In the past decade, I have been saddened by the sudden and premature deaths of my "proactive" friends. Their lives may have been entirely different. It struck me that they had one thing in common: they enjoyed strenuous or competitive exercise. Many of them were men who did sports such as marathons, lap swimming, mountain climbing, and baseball. Many of them overdid their favorite athletic activity, sometimes days or hours before their death. Many of them could have lived years longer if they had known how to exercise in moderation. It is correct to say life depends on movement. As Confucius said, "Going too far is as bad as not going far enough." Similarly, Lao Tzu said:

> Nature speaks little.
> Hence a squall lasts not a whole morning,
> A rainstorm continues not a whole day.
> What causes these?
> Heaven and earth.
> Even [the actions of] heaven and earth do not last long,
> How much less [the works] of humans?
> (Chen, *The Tao Te Ching*, Chapter 23)

Let us bellow to our middle-aged friends: Stop, pause, idle, do nothing on the edge of fatigue. Even engineers describe how metal reaches its limit and becomes stressed. You are humans of flesh and blood. Mind your "hypertension"—the word says it all.

NOTES

4. Rabindranath Tagore, *Stray Birds*, (Old Chelsea Station, NY: Cosimo Classics, 2004) poem #208.

13 Serenity and Health

The best way to let nature follow its course is to be healthy. Every day, you replace a certain percentage of your cells. When you are optimistic, your body releases specific substances that move through your blood, telling your cells to grow and reproduce. A serene and merry mind seems to do nothing, but it sends out signals telling the cells to do everything. Exercise is like thinking with the body. Instead of receiving signals from the mind, exercises—especially noncompetitive exercises like swimming, Tai Chi, and Yoga—make your body send back healthy signals to the mind.

We are built to move, and emotion reinforces our system. Exercise triggers the signaling system that tells our mind to be calm, to stop agonizing. As a result, the mind sends "go ahead" signals to cells for the daily processes of cell replacement. Thus, the sound mind builds on a sound body, and the sound body on a sound mind. Together, they create a healthy balance of doing nothing and doing everything. So to a certain extent, your mind decides whether your cells will be healthy.

As I see it, good signals tell your cells that living is worthwhile, and healthy cells are in demand; bad signals tell your cells that reproduction is not necessary, and the existing cells can decay. Stress is the suppressed intention to act, the mentality of not allowing yourself to do nothing in the face of dangers that threatened your physical security in the past or your financial or social safety now. Long-term stress, worry, and regret produce a steady trickle of chemicals that cause your cells to neglect their long-term health to keep you wired for short-term action, in effect telling your cells to decay over time. Depression threatens your life not only through suicide but also with the cell-damaging effects of worrying. Most suicidal people do not physically commit suicide, but a suicidal mentality can terminate the body just as effectively. The mind can kill the body slowly and subconsciously. This slow dying can be reversed.

To be healthy, follow the course of nature, find a better way of living, and liberate yourself from the chains of imagined responsibility. Be generous with yourself. It is not a crime to do nothing when you do not know what to do. A typical theme in traditional Chinese painting is the fisherman returning home. His boat may be full or empty, but he is serene and healthy because he has done his day's work, and he will have nothing to do now, except let the ripple touch his boat, the breeze caress his face, and the sun set.

Nature is the great healer. Stare at it with curious eyes and know your limitations; breathe it with an empty belly, and immerse yourself in limitlessness, contemplate it with humble appreciation, and liberate yourself from unnatural bonds. Tell nature, "I trust you," and nature will not fail to give you surprises. Allow nature to embrace you, and nature will take your unhealthy mentality away and return you a calm mind and a rejuvenated body.

A day's work is done, a fisherman returns to his cottage
behind the willow trees.

14 Eating

> To pursue learning, one increases daily.
> To pursue Tao, one decreases daily.
> To decrease and again to decrease,
> Until one arrives at not doing.
> Not doing and yet nothing is not done.
> Always take the empire when there are no businesses.
> If there are businesses,
> It is not worthwhile to take the empire.
> (Chen, *The Tao Te Ching*, Chapter 48)

The Taoists see food as an essential key to achieving health and longevity. They have a tendency to reduce and simplify food (Wu Wei) and another tendency to explore the world to find the healthiest food and herbs (Wu Bu Wei).

Taoists "do everything" by seeking out all kinds of natural herbs to preserve life. We can find a hermit's practice of gathering herbs in the beautiful Tang poem by Jia Dao (779–843 CE):

Seeking but Not Finding the Hermit

Under pine trees
I ask the boy;

he says: "My master's gone
to collect herbs.

I know that
he's on this mountain,

but the clouds are too deep
to know where."

Hidden deep in the cloudy and misty mountains, ginseng, ginger, and flowers join together to give us endless blessings for health and longevity. Healthy food may not always be delicious. Bitter and dry ginger may not be as tasty as a thick and juicy Big Mac. However, Mark Twain was right: "The only way to keep your health is to eat what you don't want, drink what you don't like, and do what you'd rather not." Lao Tzu tells us to "regard the great as small, the much as little" (*Tao Te Ching*, Chapter 63). The small, the few, and the tasteless can make life more healthy and tasteful.

Besides gathering herbs, the ancient Taoists created mineral medicines through alchemy, using a combination of pharmacological and spiritual techniques. Alchemy, the extreme example of doing everything, was originally an attempt at longevity in China, but it became a mysterious practice to create gold in Europe during the Middle-Ages and later transformed into chemistry during the Industrial Revolution. This practice of Wu Bu Wei is the ancestor of modern chemistry and pharmacology. The Taoists did everything imaginable to find an elixir to extend life.

Chinese emperors were notorious for having everything in life, but they had a common fear of everything that represented death. The first emperor of the Qin Dynasty defeated all his enemies in rival kingdoms and unified China in 221 BCE. After all this, he began to be haunted by his last and invincible enemy—death. When the court sorcerer, Xu Fu, persuaded him that there was elixir for life in the East, the Emperor sent him to the eastern seas twice to look for the magic drug. Xu Fu's two journeys took place between 219 BCE and 210 BCE. It was believed that his fleet included 60 ships and around 5,000 crew members, plus 3,000 virgin boys and girls. Xu Fu never returned after he embarked on a second mission in 210 BCE. Historical records suggest that he may have landed and later died in Japan. Despite his convincing argument for an elixir, Xu Fu died. The Japanese built a temple in his honor.

The first Emperor may have been too greedy and Xu Fu too cunning, but the ambition to live forever has never died in China. The Chinese Taoists are probably the people most stubborn in their belief that human beings can challenge death and disease by doing everything as well as nothing. We should adopt this spirit of persistence to achieve health and longevity. The secret was already discovered by the ancient sages: you are what you eat. You can be healthy if you consume healthy food and healthy medicine.

In Taoism, food and medicine are interchangeable. People should absorb nutritious food—such as fish, fruit and vegetables—in their bodies, supplemented by healing herbs, Tai Chi, and meditation. Traditionally, Taoist and Buddhist hermits ate very little or stopped eating at noon. Some of them ate wild berries and drank from clear springs (and fairies only sipped dew). It is a Taoist ambition to someday give up food and avoid the contamination from the "red dust" of the earth.

Zhuangzi imagined that on the mysterious mountains, there live divine immortals whose skin is white like snow, whose grace is like that of a virgin, who eat no grain and live on air and dew. They ride on clouds with flying dragons, roaming beyond the limits of the mortal realms. When time matures, the immortals can ward off corruption from all things and yield nourishing crops. We understand that people cannot live on air and dew. However, this ancient idea reveals an early awareness of the danger of overeating, even in a time when food was not as plentiful as it is today.

Lao Tzu realized the danger of luxury in eating and drinking:

> The five colors blind a person's eyes;
> the five musical notes deafen a person's ears;
> the five flavors ruin a person's taste buds.
> Horse-racing, hunting, and chasing
> drive a person's mind to madness.
> Hard-to-get goods
> hinder a person's actions.
> (Chen, *The Tao Te Ching*, Chapter 12)

Therefore, Taoism, while incorporating Wu Bu Wei to lengthen life with healthy food and medicine, also advocates constraint, or Wu Wei, in eating.

Lao Tzu said, "In Tao, you should reduce something every day." Generally, modern people become obsessed with accumulating and only apply the philosophy of reducing when they want to lose weight. Modern people hate to lose anything; the only thing that they like to lose is weight. Unfortunately, the crusade to lose weight has not been successful in creating healthy eating habits.

When bored or depressed, people tend to eat too much; they do this to kill time, but in doing so, they also kill themselves. Our bodies should be sacred temples; food should be a holy sacrifice. Yet the sacred temple of the body is often offered garbage. People accumulate, and they put more and more stuff in the temple. Modern Americans have a dream: to have a house with a two- or three-car garage. However, if you walk down the street of a typical American town and peep into an open garage, you see that two thirds of that garage is filled with junk. This is like the modern person's body: commercial fullness replaces the Taoist emptiness.

As a result, two thirds of Americans are overweight or obese. I have a friend who is both nearsighted and forgetful. Every time he flies to America, he forgets his eyeglasses at home and cannot read the flight information. Luckily, he can always find the line of Americans in the airport. He just looks for the lines composed of tall, heavy ladies and gentlemen. He always identifies the correct line.

The World Health Organization (WHO) says that

Americans are the most obese people in the world. This may be because most Americans have not heard of the Taoist philosophy of constraint or Lao Tzu's saying, "In the pursuit of Tao, every day something is dropped." At the same time, many Chinese have simply forgotten their ancestors' teachings. The Chinese are catching up very quickly in their economy and, unfortunately, in their eating style as well. By 2008, more than 25 percent of the Chinese were declared overweight. It would be a nightmare if the traditional image of a slim, old Chinese sage sitting on an anchorless boat was replaced by a middle-aged, fat businessman driving a huge, Chinese-made Buick. Modern Chinese and Americans both should heed the ancient lessons, echoing from 2500 years ago, and control their desires for excessive amounts of food.

On the other hand, according to the WHO, one third of the world population is underfed and another third is starving. In such a dire and ironic situation, Lao Tzu's wisdom is like an arrow hitting the center of the target:

> The way of heaven,
> is it not like stretching a bow?
> What is high up is pressed down,
> what is low down is lifted up;
> what has surplus is reduced,
> what is deficient is supplemented.
> The way of heaven,
> it reduces those who have surpluses
> to supplement those who are deficient.
> (Chen, *The Tao Te Ching*, Chapter 77)

May the Tao of heaven conquer the way of men, and may the spirit of health and fairness permeate each corner of our unbalanced earth.

In the hunting, gathering, and farming eras of human history, people had to accumulate food, because they consumed a lot for hard labor, and they did not know when the next meal would be. This lack of food reliability is still a fact for one-third of the world's population, living in poor countries today. On the other hand, another third of modern people, who live in consumerist cultures, do not require as much food in their sedate lifestyles. Their habits lag behind their improved conditions, as they still maintain the mentality of accumulating food for hard labor and the future. For them, Lao Tzu's philosophy is again useful: "To hold and fill (a vessel) to the full, it had better not be done. To temper and sharpen a sword, its edge could not be kept long" (Chen, *The Tao Te Ching*, Chapter 9).

You will not die of thirst if you do not fill your cup to the brim. Instead, if it is too full, you may spill everything. Those who have too much must pour some of their fortune into the cups of those who have not enough to benefit the health and longevity of all. Food, the miracle cause of both life and death, should manifest itself as an equalizer between the hungry and the overfed, the meeting place for Wu Wei and Wu Bu Wei.

15 Sleeping

One thing closely related to eating is sleeping. When we sleep, our subconscious examines our daily activities, including our eating habits, because during sleep we are more alone, sensitive, and vulnerable. In my hometown there is an old folk saying: "One less bite of supper gives you a whole night of comfort." If the farmers found such a truth when food was scarce, this saying will surely be more applicable to the present world, where one third of the population overeats.

Eating both rewards and punishes sleep. The best time to know whether you are eating the right amount is usually when you half wake up at midnight or dawn. You will realize then if you have eaten too much, because this is the time of day that you are most sensitive to your previous day's behavior. Unfortunately, the feelings at this time are often depressed into the subconscious, and when the daytime comes again, we may repeat the excessive lifestyle by forgetting our body's sensitivity. Remembering the message of Wu Wei during sleep is good guidance during the daytime.

When we talk about life, we focus on our waking lives, but sleep takes up one third of our time. Shakespeare said that sleep is the chief nourisher of life's feast. In his eyes, sleep is the preparation for our waking life. As a matter of fact, sleep itself is a part of life.

In sleep, one has an endless depth of blackness to sink into. Daylight is too shallow; it will not be able to bear the heavy burden of sleep. Quality of sleep is as important as the quality of waking time, and the health of sleep is just as important as health when we are awake. People enjoy or suffer a lot during sleep, just as much as during the day, even though they do not always remember it. Sleep, doing absolutely nothing, allows the body to rejuvenate and repair itself for tomorrow's work, the work of doing everything.

It takes a lot of effort to enter the realm of doing nothing. Half of the population suffers from insomnia. In most cases, insomnia is just anxiety against doing nothing. They are worried that they are wasting time by lying awake. Most people cannot do nothing while awake and keep worrying about their daytime life. Some people feel that it is a disaster to enter the realm most close to death. They fight with the pillow and cannot kick their worries out of bed. When asked about a cure for insomnia, Mark Twain said, "Try lying on the edge of the bed, then you might drop off." There is wisdom in this pun: when we go to sleep, we need the courage to let go, even with the risk of falling off the edge. We should be like Huck Finn drifting down the Mississippi River, and say firmly to life, "I believe in you. Just give us what you have."

In most languages, sleeping like a baby is the best kind of sleep. At the same time, when we sleep, we allow ourselves to do everything—such as flying, chasing or being chased by a monster, saying what we would not dare to say, and experiencing what we would not dare to experience. That is dreaming. Deep sleep, deep nonaction, lets us dream and allows us to cleanse our nervous system of toxic stress and anxiety. Sleep is the best expression of doing nothing. An unknown author called consciousness "that annoying time between naps."

We do not understand our existence, but we can acknowledge the limits of our understanding. As long as you understand your limitations, you are able to surpass them. Zhuangzi often writes about withdrawal from the numerous into the one as a detachment from the whole world of multiplicity. One's mind ventures into a lonely place beyond the reach of life and death. It is the Taoist dream to find a kingdom between life and death. An active sleep, a positive meditation, is closest to this realm, a land where one can move freely between doing nothing and doing everything and reach a kind of liberation from selfhood that triumphs over death. Joy and sorrow are alternatives, like day and night, like birth and death. There is an ecstasy between life and death that can be experienced as we fall asleep every night. When we go rambling without a destination, enjoying the joy of soaring above the realm of conventional concerns and practical judgments, the universe expands, the world goes on; somebody creates goodness somewhere, and someone commits an evil somewhere, but we have found the courage to sleep and solve our problems later.

Zhuangzi once dreamed he was a butterfly. In shape and in mood, he really felt like a butterfly. He did not know Zhuangzi at all. Suddenly he woke up, and really felt he was Zhuangzi. He did not know whether he was Zhuangzi dreaming that he was a butterfly or a butterfly dreaming that he was Zhuangzi.

Nevertheless, sleep is not that easy for everybody. Every night, a billion people in the world will stop breathing during sleep, some for a few seconds, some for a few minutes. Snoring results from the repetitive closure of the airway. These people suffer from a sleep disorder called sleep apnea, but unfortunately, 90 percent of those who have it do not know that they suffer from it, and even fewer seek treatment. There are many treatments for this disease, from air-pumping machines (CPAPs) to dental devices to surgery. People should do everything to find a treatment in order to be able to do nothing—and sleep.

Sleep apnea causes fatigue, damages the cardiovascular system, and disrupts family harmony. Sleep, for those who suffer from sleep apnea, is a nightmare. The victims forget it the next day, but their fatigue, irritation, and clumsiness during waking hours tell the world how they have suffered. When Edgar Allen Poe said, "Sleep: those little slices of death! How I loathe them!" he revealed that he might have suffered from sleep apnea. For sleep apnea patients, falling asleep is like falling dead with suffocation every night, but fortunately, most of them do not remember the experience the next morning.

Since the transition between sleep and waking is like that between life and death, we often feel very lonely when we fall asleep. In most languages, sleeping with someone means having sexual relations with them. However, to sleep with somebody requires more love than sexual relations, because in falling asleep, you enter an unknown world. This voyage requires the best company you can find. In the Peking opera "Legend of White Snake," a boatman sings to a couple who are falling in love. He sings, "You have to have ten lives of good behavior for you to take the same boat together once. You have to have 100 lives of good behavior to share the same pillow."

The moon's beams dance, the stream's ripples sing a lullaby,
and the time to sleep has come.

16 Do Nothing, Only Breathe

In bringing your spiritual and bodily souls to embrace the One,
Can you never depart from it?
In concentrating your breath to attain softness,
Can you be like an infant?
(Chen, *The Tao Te Ching*, Chapter 10)

The first thing you did in life was what? Breathe. The last thing you will do before you leave this world is what? Breathe. Lao Tzu often says to forget everything, so we must relearn how to breathe.

The best things in life are free. Air, so far, is free. Breathwork is not only the least expensive activity, it is also the most effective healing exercise. Breath represents the movement of energy in the body. Life begins with breathing and ends with breathing. Unfortunately, most people perform this birthright in the wrong way: too shallowly, too passively, too irregularly, and too unconsciously.

Proper breathing is the key to self-healing and anxiety control, providing astonishing cures by our mind for our body. There is not much you can do to control your heart or stomach or bowels, but you can use your lungs either consciously or unconsciously, deliberately or automatically.

Lungs are double-directed; they're the link between the conscious and the unconscious. The most beautiful places in the world are the places where two phenomena meet: the seashore, where the ocean splashes the sand, the riverbanks, where water splashes the earth. Breathing can be the most beautiful function of our body, because in breathing, the conscious touches the unconscious. You can establish ways of breathing that make your voluntary nervous system affect your involuntary nervous system. In breathing, the two worlds of doing everything and doing nothing touch each other and produce transparent sparks, shining over our often dark and anxious minds. You can do everything to change the rhythm and depth of your breath; you can do nothing and let the universe breathe through you.

In Chinese, breath or qi (chi) represents energy, spirit, and life. The Confucian philosopher Mencius declared, "I am prone to nurture my broad breath." Taoist philosopher Zhuangzi, advocating the deepest breath possible, imagined immortals who could breathe from their heels. They all believed that breathwork can lift your spirit.

Your breath is the most important tool you have to control your mind. Emotional stress can constrict muscles all over your body, including your neck, shoulders, and chest. The constriction can limit your lungs' capability to expand when you inhale, so you take quick and shallow breaths that fill only the upper part of your lungs. This leads to a shortage of oxygen, as if you were at the top of a high mountain. Lack of oxygen causes stress, irritation, and anxiety. The converse is also true: when you are stressed, irritated, or anxious, you breathe fast and shallowly. The faster you breathe, the more upset you are; the slower you breathe, the more tranquil you are; the deeper you breathe, the calmer you are. Shallow and quick breath is the invisible assassin of your mind and body.

Many people know how to relax at any given moment: take a few long, deep breaths in and out. However, few know a more effective remedy: breathe abdominally when you breathe in. In belly breathing, when you breathe in, you still lower the diaphragm, but the ribs stay still, instead of going up. When you inhale, expand your belly rather than your chest. You still expand your lungs, but your focus is lower.

When we were more like other animals, we used four limbs to move around. Four million years ago, we stood up and walked on two legs: we became different from every other animal. Everything human is vertical and tall. We must look very funny to other animals! Now, when we belly-breathe, we reverse; everything is lower. We are returning to our origins, to a lower space that is closer to the earth, as when we walked (crawled) on our four limbs. The lower focus of belly breathing will reverse the human tendency to grow higher all the time. The more advanced, higher, and straighter position has

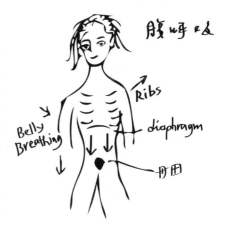

some side effects, such as high blood pressure, and back and neck pain.

To learn belly breathing, place a hand on your abdomen and take a slow and deep breath, imagining that your belly is an empty lake that you are filling with clear water through the river that flows through your respiratory tract. Your hand should rise when you inhale and fall when you exhale.

Belly breathing is how people normally breathe when they are relaxed; when people are stressed, they resort to laborious chest-breathing. For too many people, relaxation is not the normal state of mind; for them, chest breathing has become the "normal" way to breathe. Through practice, you can train yourself to breathe from the belly, even when you do not pay attention to it. You can return to natural and healthy breathing. Breathing this way will massage your spine from the inside; no massage from the outside will be able to do that. If you can breathe like this even when you are stressed, you reach the goal of doing nothing while doing everything. You beat the stress.

Prolonged stress contributes to many different illnesses. Stress depresses your immune system, raises your blood pressure, and strains your sanity. By learning to center the mind and make our breathing work more effectively, we can neutralize stress so that it will not damage our bodies. To relieve stress, some people indulge in smoking, gambling, and illegal drugs. By doing these things, people wish to center the mind and do nothing. Actually, they are doing something—something that is damaging to health and economically unrewarding, something that they will regret later. Proper breathing, on the other hand, is healthy, free, and impossible to regret.

In breathing, emptiness is more important than fullness. People seem to think and behave otherwise. They fill and overfill everything, including a practice as simple as a breath. Watch how people breathe. You will find most of them make efforts to inhale but none to exhale. Common sense seems to support that exhalation is passive and inhalation is active. When you breathe with this "common sense," you do not move enough air in and out of your lungs. Remedy: put emptiness above fullness. Squeeze out more air and empty your lungs. You take care of the exhale part; let inhale take care of itself. Most swimming coaches tell their swimmers to exhale thoroughly before they inhale. Try to make your exhalation as long and smooth as possible. Combine this exhaling with belly breathing. Your hand on the belly should feel the belly fall deeply while you exhale and rise high while you inhale, just as tides rise and fall. "What are you doing?" people may ask you. "Nothing," you answer. People still breathe while doing nothing, do they not? You really do nothing between exhale and inhale.

A yawn extends the transition between inhale and exhale: it's a deep breath with the mouth open, a stretch of the body, a contraction of the tongue, a pause against the process of life, a break against daily boredom. It's a demonstration of our body's wish for Wu Wei. Belly breathing, like yawning, is nonaction, giving your body a break; but this time, it is nonaction of the chest.

During the transition, you take a brief pause between breathing in and breathing out. You may extend the transition to give your respiratory system a break. As a matter of fact, you are also doing everything: you find the breath of the universe, you resume the cycle of life, and you wander in the world of infinity.

Changing from chest breathing to belly breathing is a reversal. Everything reversed is a new opportunity. Your ribs have been moving the wrong way all your life, but now they can rest.

17 Learning

In the present world, we drown in information and starve for knowledge. We drown in expertise and starve for wisdom. Information includes facts and data; knowledge makes facts and data relevant. Expertise seeks answers to every question; wisdom rests at the juncture between us and our question. Rainer Maria Rilke warns us, "Do not seek answers, which cannot be given to you. The most important thing is to experience everything. Live the questions now." We should be patient towards all that is unanswered in our heart, and to try to love the questions themselves.

An ancient wise man's knowledgeable discovery on an innocent stone.

From knowing to not knowing,
This is superior.
From not knowing to knowing,
This is sickness.
It is by being sick of sickness
That one is not sick.
The sage is not sick.
Because he is sick of sickness,
Therefore he is not sick.
(Chen, *The Tao Te Ching*, Chapter 71)

Confucius said something similar: "To know something is to know it; not to know something is not to know it. That is knowledge." Socrates also said: "I'm more intelligent than others simply because I know that I am ignorant."

Assuming to know what you do not leads to evil. Recognize your ignorance and know your limits. When a common person thinks he is knowledgeable when he is ignorant, he is funny or even adventurous. When a person with power thinks he is knowledgeable when he is ignorant, he can cause terrible destruction. Evil is ignorance plus power.

It would seem, then, that the best way to avoid evil is to learn. Confucius believed this, and traditional Chinese culture seems to be built on the idea that the only people qualified to lead are the scholars. Lao Tzu dared to challenge this tradition:

Eliminate learning so as to have no worries.
Yes and no, how far apart are they?
Good and evil, how far apart are they?

What the sages fear,

I must not not fear.

I am the wilderness before the dawn.

The multitude are busy and active,

Like partaking of the sacrificial feast,

Like ascending the platform in spring;

I alone am bland,

As if I have not yet emerged into form.

Like an infant who has not yet smiled,

Lost, like one who has nowhere to return.

(Chen, *The Tao Te Ching*, Chapter 20)

Lao Tzu promotes contradiction and reversal, but is he really against knowledge?

We can understand him on three levels:

First, some scholars say that "give up" is the wrong translation from the Chinese. They prefer: *With extreme studies, you will have no worries.*

Second, some see studies as referring to established, Confucian forms of learning: *Give up scrupulous studies, and you will have no worries.*

The third is a more literal understanding: *Give up all learning, and you will have no worries.*

The second translation, the compromise, is easier for us to understand, but Lao Tzu is clearly saying that we should give up knowledge completely. Our troubles start from knowledge: when we analyze things, when we try to control our fate, when we play the ruler of the universe, we get into trouble. Can we really give up all study? Not really. Lao Tzu is overcorrecting.

These graduates follow *Tao Te Ching* literally
and have abandoned learning.

In the following picture, a little girl is running towards the target. Every direction she takes is wrong. First, she aims too far to the left—that is wrong. She runs too far to the right—wrong again. In the end, she reaches the target because she keeps correcting herself: left to right, right to left. Each correction helps her to approach the target. We do this kind of thing every day of our lives. To drive straight, we must turn the wheel a few degrees to the left, a few degrees to the right, and back again every moment.

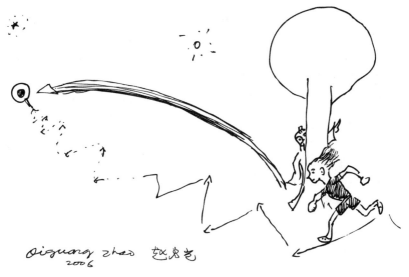

Every direction is wrong,
but every correction brings you closer to the goal.

When our car slips on ice and swerves to the left, we turn the steering wheel hard to the right, even though we only want to keep going straight. If we refused to do this, we would drive into a ditch. We cannot help it if we do the wrong things, say the wrong words, and get the wrong ideas. Yet we keep correcting our deeds, words, and ideas to reach our goals. To "stay the course" and refuse to correct ourselves would be disastrous! We move in numerous sub-directions that keep going to their opposites. Every direction is wrong, but we correct ourselves by reversing, self-denying, or self-correcting. When we are facing in the right direction, we must turn the wheel back to the left again and straighten out. We reach our goals by a series of mistakes, a series of continuous, self-reversing mistakes.

When a bike rider turns left at the edge of a gulf, we shout "Right!" although the correct direction is front. When Lao Tzu tells us to abandon learning, he's pointing us in the wrong direction. He is still right—just make sure that you do not take his advice too far and fall off the other edge. Like the girl's zigzag path toward her target, or the back-and-forth motion of steering a car, the "correct direction" is really a series of wrong directions that cancel each other out. Lao Tzu tells us to give up all knowledge so that when we turn away from our rigid studies, we will be pointed in the right direction.

Be aware of the master's wise overcorrection
and do not fall over the other edge.

Knowledge can help us, but it can also allow us to be manipulated. When we only follow what we know, and forget to follow what we feel, we can easily be led down the wrong path. Let go of the arguments and counterarguments that confuse the matter, and make your own path.

> The five colors blind a person's eyes;
> The five musical notes deafen a person's ears;
> The five flavors ruin a person's taste buds.
> Horseracing, hunting, and chasing
> Drive a person's mind to madness.
> Hard-to-get goods
> Hinder a person's actions.
> Therefore the sage is for the belly, not for the eyes.
> Therefore he leaves this and chooses that.
> (Chen, *The Tao Te Ching*, Chapter 12)

There are too many colors in the world that distract us. Trust your mind and instincts, not superficial first impressions or artificial knowledge.

Zhuangzi told the story of a cook famous for his skill at carving oxen. He was so skilled that his movements were like a dance and the sound of his knife was like music. Prince Wenhui asked him how he could perform this task so beautifully. The cook put down his knife and answered:

I follow the Tao, and the skill follows me. When I first began carving oxen, all I saw was the whole ox. Now, three years later, I do not see the whole ox at all. I use my spirit to see instead of my eyes. My senses may wish to stop, but the spirit will keep going. I just follow Heaven's law.... A good cook changes his knife once a year because he cuts; a common cook changes his knife every month because he hacks. I have used my knife for nineteen years, having cut thousands of oxen, and my knife is as sharp as it was when it was new.... My knife is thin; the oxen's joints are wide. The thinness enters the wideness, and my job becomes effortless.

The cook cuts the ox so effortlessly because he understands it in pieces, and not as a whole ox. He lets his knife follow a natural course and does not care for "skill." Skill can be taught; the spiritual, the instinctive, cannot. This is also nondoing or nonlearning, because the cook does not use the knife to carve the ox; he uses nature to carve the ox. What Lao Tzu wants is to abandon the common cook's carving by fixed skills and learn the effortless talent demonstrated by the super cook. This is the true learning.

We have tons of how-to books, but we should not let them smother us. You cannot learn how to lead your life; let nature guide you, and your knife will always stay sharp.

Zhuangzi echoes Lao Tzu:

> The skillful toil, the clever worry,
> Have no abilities and you'll have no ambitions.
> Eat your fill and stroll as you please,
> Adrift like a boat loose from its moorings.[6]

Oiguay Zhao 4/2/2006

Drift like a boat loose from its moorings.

This is not to say that all skills are bad, but we should allow ourselves to wander from the fixed path. We should allow ourselves to gaze at the sky and accept that the current will shift, and our boat may not travel in the direction we first expected. When we cut ourselves loose, we are free to see the beauty around us without worrying about which harbor our boat will eventually come to rest in. When we have created a peaceful mind, it will lighten our hearts and open the door to knowledge; the light of wisdom will shine around us. If you want the world to be happy, start with being happy yourself. This is the hardest thing to learn.

> When a superior person hears Tao,
> He diligently practices it.
> When a middling person hears Tao,
> He hears it, he doesn't hear it.
> When the inferior person hears Tao, he roars.
> If Tao were not laughed at,
> It would not be Tao.
> (Chen, *The Tao Te Ching*, Chapter 41)

Taoism is for everyone, not only for us; but we are the ones who chose to grab it and make it ours. Does that make us wise students? Perhaps.

If Lao Tzu's teachings were nothing more than "common sense," nobody would laugh. However, Lao Tzu's thoughts were provocative and original; they made people uncomfortable. Conventional minds laughed Taoism off as ridiculous, but their laughter shows that Lao Tzu hit a sensitive spot. Lao Tzu called them foolish, but he knew that we need "foolish" people. His Tao would not exist without them.

Understanding is elusive. Life is short, the universe goes on, and there is a lot you will not understand. If you play the game of life well, you can make it a comedy, even if the whole thing is tragic.

NOTES

5. Zhuangzi, *The Inner Chapters*, trans. A.C. Graham (Indianapolis: Hackett Publishing Company, Inc., 2001), 142.

18 Justice

> Govern a state by the normal;
> Conduct warfare as the abnormal;
> Take the empire when there is no business.
> (Chen, *The Tao Te Ching*, Chapter 57)

According to Lao Tzu, the concept of justice incorporates elements of surprise. When you play chess, you attack by surprise. This is Wu Bu Wei, or doing everything. In your daily life, if you work under justice and fairness, you can still make surprise moves. At the same time, your soul should abide by nonaction. You understand that whatever happens may not be what you initially expect. You understand that you should not be confined by worry about the past, the present, and the future. They are beyond your control. Keep a just strategy, surprise moves, and a calm mind.

> What is at equilibrium is easy to maintain;
> What has not emerged is easy to plan;
> What is fragile is easy to dissolve;
> What is minute is easy to disperse.
> Act when there is yet nothing to do.

> Govern when there is yet no disorder.
> A tree whose trunk is of a man's embrace,
> Begins from something extremely tiny.
> A tower of nine stories high
> Is built from a heap of earth.
> A trip of a thousand miles
> Begins right at one's feet.
> (Chen, *The Tao Te Ching*, Chapter 64)

I once said in class, "Do not interfere too much with the world." A student asked me, "But what do we do with evil? Do we sit around and let it happen?"

Of course, we cannot always avert disaster. When we see evils in the world, our first response is to do something. We want to take an eye for an eye and a tooth for a tooth. We consider this just and fair. We think that through action, we will quickly solve our problems. Instead, our first response should be to strengthen our sense of goodness and to ask ourselves whether violently eliminating the "evildoer" really solves the problem. We do not know that the "evildoer" is the real source of the problem, and the chain reactions to our first "Empire Strikes Back"–style response may cause chaos or retaliation. If we act without thinking, we will have to remedy all the problems we created by our action. Ideally, we should keep evil from happening at the very beginning; trouble is easily overcome before it starts.

It is often unclear whether we should meet injustice with action or with nonaction. Action is commonly considered the strong, moral option, while nonaction is thought to be weak or immoral. As a matter of fact, nonaction can be equally moral and may demand more strength and respect for justice.

After 9/11, most Americans came to see Saddam Hussein as an evil person, but the link between Saddam Hussein and 9/11 was unclear and the Iraq invasion put Iraq in turmoil. Political analysts argue about whether the United States should or should not have removed him from power, but in the future, we should consider that nonaction can be just as ideologically and morally fair as action. If we do not take action, it does not mean that we are sympathetic with evil. We should not be considered weak if we do not take immediate action. Nonaction means not to take action against nature. Human rights are one aspect of nature, so when we act for justice, we follow the course of nature. We must be sure that if we act for justice, we are not creating more problems through our actions than we would create through inaction.

19 Work and Leisure

"Never be afraid of the moments," announces the voice of the eternal. "Never be afraid of doing nothing," announces the voice of doing everything.

Let me do nothing when I have nothing to do. Let me be when I do not do. Let leisure and guilt never stroll hand in hand. Let work and pain never stride shoulder to shoulder.

Take the leisurely route and follow the course of nature.

Zhuangzi said, "To regard accumulation as deficiency, and to dwell quietly alone with the spiritual and the intelligent—herein lie the techniques of the Tao of the ancients." To earn bread is important; to taste its sweetness is more important. Richard Layard, an economist at the London School of Economics, provides one important example of work and happiness. He argues that unemployment is no longer Britain's biggest social problem. While there are many Britons unemployed, there are as many receiving disability benefits because depression and stress have left them unfit to work. Policy-minded economists such as Lord Layard are no longer satisfied with raising the rate of employment. They want to lift the rate of enjoyment too.

We like to fantasize that hard work will lead to leisure. John Keynes, the supporter of capitalism, anticipated that wealthier societies would become more leisured ones, liberated from toil to find pleasure in the finer things in life. Karl Marx, the adversary of capitalism, also predicted that the owners of productive property would enjoy leisure in culture and education. If our lives together prove half as rosy as they predict, we will be well content. Today, people work harder and more willingly to afford possessions they hope will make them happy. Ironically, people seem to overwork, especially in the United States, where Keynes is popular, and in China, where Marx is respected. People work by all the means they can, in all the ways they can, in all the places they can, at all the times they can, and as long as they can, only to discover that the fruits of their labor sour quickly. Everybody wishes for a higher place in society's pecking order, and they force others in the rat race to climb faster to keep up. As a result, everyone loses. Americans are still much like Alexis de Tocqueville discovered them in 1835: "So many lucky men, restless in the midst of abundance." The reason? They have more, but so do their neighbors. The Chinese in the twenty-first century have much more material wealth than they had decades ago, but more people become victims of "red-eye disease" (in Chinese) or "the green-eyed monster" (in English), because they see that their neighbors have more than they do.

Many of us cannot simply mind our own business; we cannot help minding other people's business either. Doing well is not sufficient. We want to beat our peers. This status anxiety runs deep in our nature. Monkeys at the top of the tree enjoy more mates and more bananas. The monkeys in the lower branches have mates and bananas, too, but they are restless, because the top monkeys have more. To occupy a higher position in the tree, many people are willing to work overtime every day. They gain in rank at the expense of their own and their colleagues' leisure time. In making that sacrifice, they also hurt anyone else who shares the status anxiety. Their coworkers must give up their free time to keep up. Many people wish to work less, if only others would do so. Yet a bargain cannot be reached unilaterally. On the contrary, the little guys are afraid of falling behind in the race, knowing that if they do not work harder, they will lose their rank to somebody who does.

Rabindranath Tagore believes that, "Leisure, in its activity, is work" (see his poem, *Stray Birds*).

Even Alan Lakein, after speaking of "mastering your time and mastering your life," suggests that we find time to relax and do nothing; we will have more fun and get more done doing it.

People could work shorter hours and commute shorter distances, even if that means living in smaller houses with cheaper gadgets. Modern people have become like Kua Fu in the ancient Chinese story. It is said that in antiquity a giant named Kua Fu was determined to have a race with the Sun. So he ran like an arrow in the direction of the Sun. Finally, he was too thirsty and hot to continue. The Yellow River came into sight, roaring on in front of him. He swooped upon it earnestly and drank up the whole river. Then he drank all the water of the Wei River. He still felt thirsty and hot, so he marched northward for the lakes. Unfortunately, when he was halfway there, he fell down and died of thirst and heat. This is the origin of the Chinese idiom, "Kua Fu chasing the Sun." It applies to someone who does something courageous but impossible to accomplish, just like Icarus, the Greek mythological figure, who flew too close to the sun with his wings of wax.

Unfortunately, there are numerous Kua Fus in the modern world. They chase the suns named Prosperity and Success without stopping. These modern sun-chasers are even more miserable than Kua Fu. While Kua Fu chased the sun alone, pausing and drinking deliberately, modern sun chasers are pressured by their fellow runners. While Kua Fu could only aim at the target in the sky, his modern followers have to aim at the same target, while also looking backward over their shoulders. Even though they are thirsty, hot, and exhausted, they cannot stop, because they see the sun moving above and

Kua Fu, the sun chaser.

the competitors catching up. In addition, many people say, "I will retire when I have worked this many years and saved this much money." Some fortunate people really reach their goal, ready to enjoy the years of leisure they have worked for all their life. Unfortunately, many die or lose their health before they can fully enjoy the fruits of their labor. Some people even die before they can retire, and some people never save that much money when they have worked that many years. The sun is still moving, but the chasers are not anymore.

Not that we should love ease and detest work. On the contrary, work is a lasting joy. Insight, ingenuity, and vigor lie in our work. The most happiness a man ever feels is the happiness of finishing his work. People are happy while reading, listening to music, and wandering around the garden, but lucky people also get satisfaction from losing themselves in their work, "forgetting themselves in a function," as W.H. Auden put it. In Auden's poem, surgeons manage this by "making a primary incision," and clerks do it when "completing a bill of lading." This state of losing oneself is just doing nothing while doing everything.

While losing ourselves in work, we take work seriously but we do not take ourselves seriously. This kind of work saves us from depression. We are invigorated by the work itself,

Mr. Lee finally moves from a cubicle to an office with a view. Unfortunately, the beauty of mountaintops reminds him of the NASDAQ charts.

instead of feeling wasted by worries about personal gains and losses. Work should provide a process instead of a goal, a sense of control instead of submission, and harmony instead of confrontation. Therefore, jogging under the rising sun gives us carefree and joyous invigoration, while chasing the sun can cause untold suffering.

20 Fame and Fortune

Your name and your body, which is dearer?
Your body and material goods, which is more abundant?
Gain and loss, which is illness?
Therefore in excessive love, one necessarily goes to great expenses,
In hoarding much, one necessarily loses heavily.
Knowing contentment, one does not suffer disgrace,
Knowing when to stop, one does not become exhausted.
This way one may last long.
(Chen, *The Tao Te Ching*, Chapter 44)

Liu Zongyuan, a great Chinese writer of the Tang Dynasty, was once the governor of Liuzhou. He recorded this anecdote:

The people of Liuzhou were good swimmers. One day, there was a flood, and five or six people tried to cross the river. When they were in the middle of the river, their boat began to leak. Everybody jumped into the river and started to swim. One man swam very hard, but not as well as usual. His companions yelled, "You're the best swimmer, why are you lagging behind?" He said, "I have a thousand coins wrapped around my waist. They're very heavy." His companions said, "Why do not you let them go?" He would not answer, but only shook his head. A little later, he was exhausted. Some of his companions had already reached the shore. They jumped up and down, yelling, "You idiot! You're drowning! If you die, what will you need money for?" He shook his head again and drowned.

The fish: "I hope there are more idiots like him."

Liu Zongyuan commented, "I was very sad to hear this story. He was drowned by a small fortune, but many important people are killed by bigger fortunes."

Shakespeare said in *Timon of Athens:* "Gold? Yellow, glittering, precious gold? ...Thus much of this will make black white, foul fair, wrong right, base noble, old young, coward valiant." I would like to add that it can also make alive dead.

Robbers all over the world, without having to be taught, know how to use this line: "Your money or your life?" Most people would choose their life in this critical moment, but when there is no robber holding a gun to their head, they do not realize that they are facing the same life-or-death question. Like the drowning swimmer, they cannot answer Lao Tzu's question: "Self or wealth: Which is more precious?" In daily life, money lovers may not drown immediately, but the heavy load, little by little, drags them under.

If we think that the man in Liu Zongyuan's story was foolish because he would not throw away the heavy copper coins around his waist, think again: many great men in history have made exactly the same mistake. They were dragged under the water by the heavy burden of wealth and something similar: fame. As a matter of fact, there is a Chinese word that combines the concepts of fame and wealth: *mingli*. Lao Tzu severely criticized those people who sacrificed their life for *mingli*. In one breath, he asked, "Fame or self: Which matters more? Self or wealth: Which is more precious? Gain or loss: Which is more painful?"

Xiang Yu was a well-known tragic hero who lived during the end of the Qin dynasty (221 BCE–207 BCE). He was from the kingdom of Chu, which was conquered by the Qin. Taking advantage of the turmoil against the cruel Qin emperor, Xiang Yu rose to be the mightiest of the rebels who overthrew the Qin Dynasty. Among the rebel leaders was another well-known general, Liu Bang. Xiang Yu was from an aristocratic family that loved fame and ritual. Liu Bang was from a common family and was crafty and shameless. Their competition for the crown of China became a favorite topic of Chinese literature and theater.

Xiang Yu had many opportunities to capture or eliminate Liu Bang because, in the beginning, Liu Bang was much weaker. Again and again, Xiang Yu let Liu Bang go, because he did not want to look like a bully. During the most famous of these missed opportunities, Hongmen Feast, Xiang Yu forced Liu Bang to visit his camp to have a banquet with him. When Xiang Yu's mentor and chief advisor raised a jade decoration to signal Xiang Yu to arrest Liu Bang, Xiang Yu looked away. Finally, he let Liu Bang leave safe and sound, and Liu Bang grew stronger and stronger, until he drove Xiang Yu into a corner.

Ultimately, Xiang Yu was surrounded at Gaixia. His soldiers were few and his supplies were exhausted. From the top of a hill, Xiang Yu saw only lines and lines of enemy camps. At night, he heard the enemy soldiers sing the folk songs of the kingdom of Chu, his native land. He exclaimed, "Has the enemy conquered my kingdom and enlisted my young men?" Then he began to drink his last cup of wine with his concubine, Lady Yu. She was a brave woman, who had followed him from battlefield to battlefield up until that moment. He untied his favorite steed and tried to get it to leave, but it would not go away. Lady Yu said, "You often ask me to dance, and I've always refused. Now I'll do my first and last dance for you." Xiang Yu said, "I'll accompany you with my song." This song became one of the most famous Chinese poems. Its heroic and tragic tone has touched millions of people through the years:

I am strong enough to uproot the hills,
I am mighty enough to shadow the world.
But the times are against me,
And my horse will not leave.
When my horse will not leave,
What then can I do?
Oh Lady Yu, my Yu,
What will become of you?

Xiang Yu was defeated by his love of fame.

At the end of the dance, the concubine killed herself with his sword. Xiang Yu escaped to the shore of the River Wu, chased by the army of Liu Bang. A village head, who was waiting with a boat on the riverbank, said, "I beg you to make haste and cross the river, and you can raise an army to counterattack from your original base."

Xiang Yu laughed bitterly and replied, "It is Heaven that is destroying me. What good would it do me to cross the river? Once, with eight thousand sons from the land east of the river, I crossed over and marched west, but today not a single man of them returns. Although their fathers and brothers east of the river should take pity on me and make me their king, how could I bear to face them again? Though they said nothing of it, could I help but feel shame in my heart?"[7]

Raising his head, he saw the enemy marching close to him. He dismounted and drew his sword for his last fight; he killed hundreds of soldiers. Exhausted, he found an old acquaintance among the marching enemy. "I heard that Liu Bang will pay a thousand ounces of gold for my head," he said to his former friend. "I will give the honor to you." And with that, Xiang Yu cut his own throat.

Xiang Yu blamed heaven and the times for his failures, but he forgot to blame himself. He was so attached to his fame that he let his archenemy go, so attached to his fame was he that he would not return to his home town lest his countrymen should laugh at him. His attachment to fame was as solid and heavy as that of the sinking swimmer to the money around his waist.

In our daily life, we also have attachments; we take them as part of our identity and forget that we can free ourselves from the burden. We are so afraid of peer pressure and gossip that we sink and kill ourselves without knowing it. We are afraid of being criticized, and we worry about our images. Am I too fat? Am I too inefficient? Is my car fancy enough? Do people like me?

Outside material things have become an inseparable part of our ego. Faced with the alternatives Lao Tzu offers us—wealth or self, fame or self—we often make the wrong choice unknowingly. Let Lao Tzu's prescription cure our attachment:

> Therefore in excessive love, one necessarily goes to great expenses,
> In hoarding much, one necessarily loses heavily.
> Knowing contentment, one does not suffer disgrace,
> Knowing when to stop, one does not become exhausted.
> This way, one may last long.
> (Chen, *The Tao Te Ching*, Chapter 44)

Modern people have more attachments than ever, such as cars, houses, and cell phones. They do not know these attachments rob them of a meaningful life. I had a friend in business who lost his cell phone containing thousands of numbers. This was a disastrous thing, because people in modern China all depend on their *guangxi*, their business and social network. If you want to get anything done, you have to know someone in your guangxi either directly or indirectly. Without guangxi, you are nobody, so naturally he was panicked, pacing up and down "like an ant on a hot wok." He did nothing the whole day. When he returned home, he walked toward his apartment building and a miracle happened: Something caught his attention that he had totally ignored before. There was a tree in front of the building that had grown tall from a sapling. He had never noticed it, because he was always calling someone on the cell phone. He entered his apartment, sat with his family for dinner, and for the first time, he was not calling someone. He looked around—who was this lady with fair gray hair around her temples? Who was this lanky teenager who used to be a toddler? They were his wife and his daughter; he had not looked at them carefully for the past 10 years. Now he stared tenderly at his family, and they looked back with smiles. A harmonious chi rose among them, like an auspicious cloud bringing back 10 years lost among thousands of telephone conversations.

For the first time he "did nothing" at home. No socializing with his friends, no negotiating with his partners, and no conspiring against his opponents. As a matter of fact, in doing nothing, he had done everything that was necessary to reconnect with his family and redefine himself. Here, gain and loss occur simultaneously. As Lao Tzu said, "Thus things are either decreased so as to be increased, or increased so as to be decreased" (*Tao Te Ching*, Chapter 42). He lost his cell phone, but he regained something he did not realize he had lost: his family, his happiness, and his life. The whole family also regained what was lost before. Doing nothing is returning to the present, liberating oneself from the fantasy of potential gains and losses.

You do not have to throw your cell phone away to do nothing. You can do something very simple that is unconventional, something you have never done before: leave your cell phone at home, read a book in the forest, write a note to leave at the tree, stand with your arms upward for a few minutes, and look at the shining stars. There is courage in not caring what others think about your uncommon action, when you find that the greatest show in the universe is the universe. Today, you are not going to miss this show. This time, you are going to watch the stars—the great doing nothing and doing everything.

In doing nothing (but actually doing everything) in this manner, you lose the greed, you gain freedom. You have nothing to lose but your chains. You have a whole world to win.

NOTES

6. Cyril Birch, ed. *Anthology of Chinese Literature,* trans. Burton Watson (New York: Grove Press, 1965), 121.

21 Beauty

> Mao Qiang and Li Ji were beautiful in the eyes of men, but
> when the fish saw them, they sank deep. When the birds saw
> them, they flew high, and when deer saw them, they dashed
> away. Who among them can see real beauty in the world?
>
> —*Zhuangzi*

Philosophers and thinkers all over the world have talked
about beauty for thousands of years. Beauty has become a
sphinx; we think that if we can resolve the meaning of beauty,
we can save our spiritual world. For a Chinese peasant in times
of drought, a black cloud over the land is the most beautiful
thing in the world. A medieval knight might say that a lock of
his lady's hair is the most beautiful thing in the world. A Wall
Street trader may see a rise in the NASDAQ as the most beautiful thing in the world. A mathematician sees beauty in a perfect equation or an elegant proof. In reality, these people are
not talking of beauty but of their need for satisfaction. Beauty
is not a need, not a thirsty lip or an outstretched hand, but
a spiritual experience, a burning heart and a hungry mind.
Beauty is not the achievement of a goal.

When he was in Qi, Confucius heard the music of Shao, and he was so moved that for three months, he didn't taste meat. He said, "I did not imagine that any music existed which could reach such perfection as this."

—*Confucius,* Analects

Confucius experienced real beauty. He did not have an intimate need for this music, his survival did not depend on it, but he could not deny that he had a thirsty heart, humiliated and hurt by the world. When he observed this music, it overcame his need for meals. Beauty is nature. Emerson once said, "A nobler want of man is served by nature, namely, the love of beauty."

As an opposite, success meets our needs. From success, you get lots of things, but not that great, inner feeling that beauty brings us. Beauty is a process without a goal. Beauty is Wu Wei, because it cannot be possessed.

You will not be able to have everything in the world. If you did, where would you put it? You cannot have all the success in the world. If you did, how could you bear it? However, you can have the most beautiful thing in the world, because you do not possess it, and you do not move it into your property from somewhere else. You see it, you experience it, and you feel it, but you do not keep it to yourself. The beauty of beauty is that it is not yours; you cannot take beauty from the universe and deny other peoples' access to it. Success is limited, but beauty is limitless.

Lao Tzu said, "When all under heaven know beauty as beauty, there is then ugliness." (*The Tao Te Ching,* Chapter 2)

The high and nonpossessive beauty.

When people see beauty, they try to possess it. The struggle for beauty has become an ugly nightmare. Only if you do nothing, and let beauty observe you, soak you, and bring you to a world beyond yourself, have you found real beauty.

Those who believe in nature—bred under the starry sky, their minds cultivated by its vastness—will not lose the inspiration during the day in the sound of cities or the fury of crowds. Amidst the disturbances of daily life—the chaos of war, the anarchy of revolution, the death of relatives, with all the accompanying pain and suffering—the starry sky will talk to you, telling you ancient stories, comforting your mind, and soothing your pains. It will say, "Everything is temporary." Again, the Milky Way glimmers, the nightingale sings, the meteors fall, the moon shines, and the stars twinkle. The night grows quiet from the day's noise, and all action takes a rest. The tide rises up and becomes low again. The high wind passes, and the sea becomes calm again. The moonlight shines on the calm water. Waves ripple in the shadows of the willow. It is the way of nature to return to its stillness. With these scenes, the spells of calmness, the keys of strength, are put into our hands. We will forget our temporary worries, because a voice from far away will whisper, "These will also pass."

Beauty is eternally viewing itself in the mirror of the universe. As long as you become a part of the mirror, you will be a part of beauty. You will walk in a garden ever in bloom, but you do not pick the flowers. You fly with a flock of angels without ever fighting with them. You dance with a dragon without slaying it.

Beauty is freedom: freedom from world affairs, from the consequences of efforts and success. When given the choice between success and beauty, Zhuangzi chose beauty.

> Zhuangzi was fishing at the River Pu. The king of Chu sent two ministers to tell him that he intended to give him his entire kingdom. Zhuangzi did not put down his fishing pole. He did not even turn his head. "I heard that in Chu there is a divine tortoise that has been dead for three thousand years. The king put it in a box and set it on the shrine to his ancestors. Would the tortoise rather be dead, having its bones worshipped, or alive, dragging its tail in the mud?" The ministers answered, "It would rather be alive dragging its tail in the mud." Zhuangzi said, "Then go away and let me drag my tail in the mud!"

In 1976, I experienced one of the greatest natural disasters in human history. An unprecedentedly strong earthquake shook the Tangshan area, very close to where I attended school. This earthquake killed 260,000 people—more casualties than any earthquake ever recorded. During the night, we felt the whole world was shaking. It was like we were sitting in a boat, tossed up and down in the ocean. We raced from our dorm like mad, and all the students stood on the central sports grounds. We stayed outside for many days without being able to enter the building. A few days later, a strong aftershock came and moved our tall dorms and all the classroom buildings like weeds in the wind. We all stood, watching nature reveal its power.

A classmate of mine named Yuan suddenly said, "That's beautiful." Everybody was quiet. Nobody punched her in the nose, nobody called her a counterrevolutionary, and nobody even called her cynical. Everyone was lost in deep thought.

Her words haunted me for many years, especially when I heard that she committed suicide ten years later. What beauty had she seen in this disaster? This was our building, this was our campus, this was our dorm. That evening, we would have nowhere to sleep, no classroom to go to. How could that be beautiful?

Maybe what she saw was nature revealing its power. Maybe what she saw was that our daily life, which we take for granted, could be torn to shreds. Maybe she saw death. Maybe she saw the figure of human logic against natural disaster. Maybe, for her, beauty had no consequences; it was detached from daily interests, isolated in an unknown world.

My classmate Yuan might have agreed with Zhuangzi, in that there is also beauty in the destructive work of the creator. Master Si, Master Yu, Master Li, and Master Lai were talking to each other: "We'll be friends to those who can take nothingness as the head, life as the spine, and death as the rump." The four people looked at each other and smiled. They agreed with each other in their hearts, so they became friends.

Sometime later, Master Yu got sick, and Master Si went to see how he was doing. "Marvelous!" said the sick man. "The creator has squeezed me into such a shape. My eyes, nose, and mouth are facing up, my back is bent double, my cheek touches my navel, my shoulders are higher than my head, and my neck bones point to the sky. Yin and Yang are all awry. But my heart is at ease, and when I go to the well and look at myself, I say, 'Wow! What a shape the creator has squeezed me into!'"

Four friends who agree with each other in their hearts.

Master Si said, "Are you disgusted?"

"Disgusted? What should I be disgusted with? If my left arm becomes a rooster, I'll crow to greet the dawn. If my right arm becomes a slingshot, I can use it to shoot owls. If my buttocks become wheels, my spirit will ride them. Then I won't need to harness another team of horses. When the opportunity comes, you gain; when the opportunity is gone, you lose. Follow the opportunity, and sadness and happiness will not disturb you. This is what ancient people called 'untying the knot.' If you cannot untie the knot, things will tie you up, and things never beat heaven. Why should I be disgusted?"

Later, Master Lai got sick and was dying. His wife and children surrounded him, crying. Master Li went to visit him and told the wife and children, "Go away. Do not bother him." He leaned on the door and said to Master Lai, "Great is the creator. What will it do for you next? Where will it send you? Maybe it will make you into a mouse's liver or an insect's arm."

Master Lai said, "When parents tell their children to go north, south, east, or west, the children obey. When Yin and Yang give orders to human beings, they should obey too. If I was ordered to die, and I refused to do so, I would be disobedient. There is nothing wrong with the order-giver; the universe carried my body, made me work all my life, nurtured me to old age, and is about to send me to death. That which can give me my life can also give me my death. Suppose a blacksmith was hammering iron, and the iron jumped up and spoke with a human voice: 'I want to be the best sword in the world!' The blacksmith would be shocked. If a human being yells, 'I want to be a man again!' the creator would also be shocked. Now heaven and earth are a big furnace, and the creator is a blacksmith; it can do whatever it wishes."

My classmate Yuan's voice sank into our silences like a dim light that quivers in fear of the shadow. In normal situations, she would be condemned for antisocialist gloating. Yet during that moment in front of that scene, everybody was shocked into silence. She had seen nature distort itself, just as Zhuangzi saw nature turn healthy people into cripples. She was not a philosopher, but her mind rubbed against Zhuangzi's mind, and the sparks flew across the space of 2,500 years.

Here, beauty was doing everything. Nature has the power to do everything. It can build a universe and destroy it. It can transform the order we take for granted into nonexistence. When we see this doing everything, we see that our part is to do nothing. When we see the contrast between doing everything and doing nothing, we have a catharsis. Our anxiety, anticipation, and regret all turn out to be futile. The contrast between doing everything and doing nothing is beautiful.

The real beauty is the beauty that we do not understand. Artists create beauty in color, lines, and shapes. They point out what we see but do not understand in forms that cannot be expressed in words. In traditional Chinese painting, you can always see a high mountain shrouded in mist and a zigzag stream with an idle fisherman. Nature is huge, and the human is small. These paintings also often present images of snow, pavilions, streams, and mountains. Snow, instead of representing bitter winter, symbolizes the coming of the spring. A Chinese saying goes, "Timely snow promises a bumper harvest."

A pavilion is a retreat, a place to rest and appreciate the scenery. The pavilion is a window, opened wide, connecting the heart and the universe. The stream is water, and in Taoism, water is the highest good.

As for the mountains, Confucius said, "The benevolent love mountains. The wise love waters." The mountain symbolizes our solid humanitarian base. When stream and mountain combine, Taoism and Confucianism merge to create harmony. Wang Wei, a Tang dynasty poet, gives the following description: "Fresh rain has fallen on the vacant mountains; autumn's evening approaches. The bright moon is shining through the

An ever-present image in traditional Chinese paintings:
high mountains.

pines, the clear stream flowing over the stones." All the images present a calm, hopeful, and harmonious mood, as if to say to us, "Time changes, water flows, and mountains stay calm. Rest a bit here—you deserve it. The future will be all right. Do nothing now."

In the West, especially in Renaissance art, humans are the center of the picture. In the *Mona Lisa*, the human face occupies most of the canvas. Nature, if it exists, is pushed into the corner. For Westerners, beauty is in humans revealing themselves through the face and the body. When the human body is tested with pain, it can be even more beautiful. Jesus Christ, for example, is tortured on the crucifix. Beyond its symbolic meaning, this is a beauty of mind at its climax. Jesus sacrifices himself with his unspoken suffering, but his face and body keep the beauty of unselfishness and hope. His hope can spread among us, as if we, the human, the center of the world, could defeat any evils, slay any dragons, and recover from our sickness.

This image of human suffering contrasts sharply with traditional Chinese paintings, which usually focus on landscapes. The two different focuses—on nature and humans—show two different approaches to life. The Chinese invented gunpowder to make firecrackers; the Europeans used it to make weapons. The Industrial Revolution started the human process of conquering nature, which is against the Taoist principle of leaving nature alone. Now we are eating the bitter fruits of pollution. Conquering nature and accepting nature contrast but also complement each other. We cannot say which is better; we need both. We should walk on two legs.

We should understand and appreciate nature, but we can also change it. *Do nothing* and *do everything* can be two basic tunes of the song we sing in our universe.

This is the world. We should live in it happily forever, like princes and princesses in fairytales. Someday the world will distort the harmony we take for granted. Yet this distortion can be equally beautiful, so long as we realize that we do not play the role of gods, so long as we do not try to make the world into what we wish it to be. This is art. Only when we realize that we are part of the universe, instead of vice versa, can we say to life calmly and firmly, "I have confidence in you. Go ahead and do what you have to do." In the end, life has its own way of responding to your wishes.

22 Love

Suppose a man loves a woman. When he marries her, there is a 50 percent chance of divorce and a 99.9 percent chance that one spouse will die before the other. The surviving spouse's sadness will be equal to the happiness they had. This does not mean that the couple should not have been married and that they should not have enjoyed the journey of their time together. However, they should realize that their present happiness will someday be lost.

Listen to the story of Duke Ye, told by Liu Xiang of the Han Dynasty:

> Duke Ye loved dragons. He decorated his house with everything and anything dragon: the curtains were embroidered with dragon patterns, the pillars had dragons carved into them. The real dragon in heaven was touched by his affection and decided to pay Duke Ye a visit. He descended to the duke's house. His tail coiled around the backyard, and he stuck his head in the window. When Duke Ye saw the real dragon, he was scared out of his mind by the dragon's size and power. He ran out of his house in great confusion and was not heard from again.

When love peeps in, Duke Ye runs away.

Wealth, marriage, and status can be the real dragon. When we have them, they are not what we imagined. We can still work toward them and be successful just for the fun of it, not for the essence we have imagined. We often fail to understand the relationship between cause and effect. The effect is often against our original intention, and the goal is not always reached. The reason we act is for the bliss of the intention and the beauty of the process. The intention is nobler than the result; the process is more beautiful than the goal. As long as we follow nature, we can do nothing and do everything. Anxiety comes from our self-assigned roles as "god." It is as hard to control our own fortune as it is to control the motion of the universe. Love is attachment; wisdom is detachment. I believe there is plenty of room to maneuver between the two, just as there is between doing everything and doing nothing.

"Rapunzel, Rapunzel, let down your hair." This time, Rapunzel sends her hair *up* to the dragon. Unlike Duke Ye, she is not afraid of the real dragon.

To love is to risk not being loved in return, because love is not a trade. To hope and dream is to risk disappointment, because the dream and the nightmare are twin sisters. As Lao Tzu advocated, the two opposite parts should combine and support each other. Risk is necessary, because the greatest risk in life is to risk nothing. By clinging to our so-called security, we are denying life.

Everybody loves love, but can they really handle it? Many lovers are like Duke Ye, because they love the illusion of love, not love itself. Love is one of the most beautiful emotions humans can have. Love is two souls joined together to support each other through sorrow, to strengthen each other in difficulties, to share with each other in gladness, to merge into each other in silent memories. Love is not doing; it is being there. Love says to the loved, "Dear one, I'm here to support you, to strengthen you, to share with you, to merge with you." If you love someone, you want the one you love to be there when you feel happy, or when you see the most beautiful sunset. If your heart can really say, "I wish you were here with me," you know you love this person, because you want to share the moment with him or her, to be there with him or her. The essence of love is silence or Wu Wei.

If you love someone, let them go.

The worst line for love is, "You are mine." This is the destroyer of love; the act of owning someone is the opposite of the nonaction of love. In many romantic songs, people compare their lover to the sun or stars. You admire the beauty of the sun and stars, but you do not want to, and cannot, own them. This is the beauty of nonaction, and it should be the beauty of love.

The worst proverb for love is, "All is fair in love and war." War is Wu Bu Wei, doing everything, to conquer your enemies. When love follows the example of war, sound and fury overwhelms serenity and beauty. Conquest and submission become the name of the game. No wonder love and death are the eternal themes of romantic literature.

When possession gets in the way, a happy homecoming becomes
a miserable reunion for warriors, their wives, and their dogs. Only the
couple who does not believe they own each other can find happiness.

23 The Intercourse between Yin and Yang

Yin and yang are the basic Taoist dialectical approaches, which can refer to all opposites from negative and positive, back and front, and good and evil. However, the original meaning of yin and yang is female and male. The intercourse of these two opposites is the origin of life.

What is the opposite of death? Many people would say life. Yet in order to continue life from generation to generation, human beings must have sex. Therefore, the opposite of death can be sex. Death pronounces the end of an individual, while sex ensures the continuity of the community. If we understand the tremendous fear of death, we can understand the magnificent attraction to sex. Shining and dark, puzzling and clear, reassuring and dangerous, sex draws poets, dragon slayers, and commoners to climb to the unknown climax, where the two adventurers join together to create a two-person world. They announce their independence and freedom from the world, at least for the moment. The couple has become the god and goddess on Olympus. They have stopped time, eliminated space, and denounced death.

Philosophers, prophets, and gurus have competed to explain this unique phenomenon. Some of them try to oppress the intercourse between yin and yang, while others see it as a form of liberation. Most of them approach it from political or moral perspectives. In China, Confucian puritanism made sex a taboo topic, although hypocritically, traditional Chinese society allowed concubines. Confucius said, "It is hardest to deal with women and petty men. If you are too close to them, they lose their humility. If you keep a distance from them, they resent it." For Confucianists as well as Christians, sex has been seen as a necessary evil that is practiced by unequal partners. Art and literature dealing with sexual relationships was often banned, suppressing the celebration of yin and yang.

Contrarily, Taoists view sex as an action that follows the course of nature and allows for the equal combination of yin (female) and yang (male). For them sex is a topic of health, but not politics; a topic of universal harmony, but not a social pact. Lao Tzu said, "Tao gives birth to one, one gives birth to two, two gives birth to three, three gives birth to ten thousand beings. Ten thousand beings carry *yin* on their backs and embrace *yang* in their front, blending these two vital breaths to attain harmony" (Chen, *The Tao Te Ching*, Chapter 42).

Having realized the harmonious and equal combination between yin and yang, Lao Tzu is probably the earliest feminist. He said, "The female always wins the male by stillness, by stillness it is low-lying" (Chen, *The Tao Te Ching*, Chapter 61). For him, women are equal partners to men in their relationships. With figurative and revealing speech, he proclaims that the female can overcome the male by lying low in stillness, based on his argument that the weak will overcome the strong as dripping water wears holes in stone. Together, man like rock and woman like water create harmony, pleasure, and health. Lao Tzu reached this conclusion not only from his observation of society, but also from his understanding of nature. In nature, the sky and the earth complement each other; fire and water contrast to each other; and male and female support each other.

Men and women were considered the equivalent of heaven and earth, but they became disconnected from one another. While heaven and earth are eternal, men and women suffer a premature death. Heaven and earth touch each other through rain, snow, and rainbows. Men and women should do the same. Each interaction between yin and yang has significance, like the caress between heaven and the earth. Numerous Taoist texts discuss the varying skills and moods in the bedroom. The male and female should follow the natural course of Wu Bu Wei, and do everything to make their encounter harmonious.

The Tang writer Bai Xingjian (776–826 CE) describes how the male and the female should imitate the harmonious beauty of nature during the four seasons. The private movements inside the chamber mirror the seasonal changes outside the window. In the spring, the husband should be tender and frisky, while the wife should be humble and coy. They mimic the playful spring light outside, while the golden orioles sing beak to beak, and the violet swallows fly wing to wing. In the summer, the male and female retreat into a deep, red bed curtain, giving generously and accepting humbly, like the shadows from the sunshine that dance on the bamboo mattress and the willows that touch the lotus pond. In the fall, the couple feels a nostalgic love, just as the hand-fans are stowed away and the autumn fragrance penetrates the bed curtain. During the winter, the couple seeks shelter in a warm chamber, under a thick, embroidered quilt. The husband creates spring sunshine over the wife's snow-like body, which mirrors the pure snow outside.

This most poetic and lusty description of intercourse between yin and yang is from Bai Xingjian's text "Tiandi Yin Yang Da Jiaohuan Yuefu" ("The Grand Ode to the Intercourse between Heaven and Earth, Yin and Yang").[8] The text was lost for a thousand years (maybe because of its bold comparison between sex and nature in four seasons), until the French explorer Paul Pelliot found it in a secret chamber in the mysterious Dunhuang Desert in 1908. This unique discovery should not be wasted and should be applied to our lives today. Our sexual relations will be more harmonious if we align ourselves with the picturesque scenery in nature and the soul-touching chorus of the universe.

Most people consider sex as private, even shameful and guilty. For them, it should be performed in a secret chamber, under a fallen curtain, because the world does not approve of it. Maybe the human world does not, but the natural world always approves. A human combination echoes the natural intercourse between yin and yang. A moment like this should be accompanied by the tenor arias, *"Nessun dorma!"* "None shall sleep! Even you, O Princess, in your cold bedroom, watch the stars that tremble with love and with hope." Since you can perform Wu

Bu Wei, you can do two things at the same time. You may turn off your light, but watch the twinkling stars. You may listen to the gurgling stream and tremble with love. Raise the curtain and let the moon peep in and cheer for you. Nature is your fan forever. Open your heart to nature, and the natural world will stand up and sing its most triumphant opera. With nature, you and your partner defeat the whole world.

While the intercourse between yin and yang can be fascinating, it can also be dangerous. As Lao Tzu warns us, misery lurks beneath happiness. Zhuangzi discusses the danger that lurks in sex on the bed and food on the table: "If people knew of a dangerous road, where one in ten would be killed, they would warn their family and friends, and gather a lot of people to go to this road. Isn't this knowledgeable? Yet there are more dangerous places—beds and tables. People indulge themselves on both of them. This is a big mistake."

Ji Xiaolan (1724–1805 BCE) told a story in *Yuewei Caotang Biji*, his well-known collection of strange anecdotes. A man stayed in a house in the mountains. One evening, he was sitting in the courtyard when he saw a beautiful woman peeking over the yard's wall. He could only see her alluring face. It seemed that she was smiling and flirting with him. The man fixed his eyes on her pretty face. Suddenly, he heard some children crying outside, "A huge snake is coiled around a tree, and it is putting its head on the wall!" The man suddenly realized that the woman was actually a transformed demon with a beautiful human face and a snake body, and she intended to suck his blood. Had he approached her, his life would have been put at great risk.

This story strives to show the hidden consequences of debauchery, which can ruin a person's health and life. As Zhuangzi points out, there lies great danger in the bed. He was so insightful, especially when we realize that there were no sexually transmitted diseases in China before the sixteenth century. Still, Taoist masters realized the danger behind "matters on the bed." Their reason for abstinence was simply to preserve life energy. Nowadays, we face dangers hundreds of times more serious with the rampant spread of sexually transmitted diseases. HIV/AIDS manifests itself as an unprecedented threat, like a snake-transformed phantom coiling over the globe. Today with HIV/AIDS, the opposing forces of life and death have a chilly meeting, thousands of years after Lao Tzu and Zhuangzi warned us that opposites will finally join.

We should heed Lao Tzu and Zhuangzi's advice: follow the guide of nature, savor the delight, but be aware of the consequences. As in all other aspects of Taoism, Wu Wei and Wu Bu Wei must again come together in perfect harmony, like the intercourse between yin and yang, which will announce the triumph of life and the defeat of death.

NOTES

7. Bai Xingjian, "Tiandi Yin Yang Da Jiaohuan Yuefu" (The Grand Ode to the Intercourse between Heaven and Earth, Yin and Yang), *Daojia Yangshengshu* (Taoist Way of Health and Longevity). Chen Yaoting, ed. (Shanghai: Fudan University Press, 1992), 487-488.

24 Ambition

If somebody has an ambition when she is young, she can work hard to realize this ambition. When she achieves her goals, she may realize they are not what she really wants; her ambition can betray her. Since she will die someday, she cannot avoid being separated from her goals. Her efforts are in vain. She is a part of nature, part of society. She can work toward her goals, and the work itself, the whole effort, is a realization of natural or social beauty. She can enjoy this beauty, this sense of success, but she should not think that she owns this success. The success itself is temporary.

When we set a goal, we often rely on what other people tell us. We have an aim in life, but we have never been there. Since it is not our own experience yet, we do not know how pleasant it can be; we must depend on other people's descriptions without context. Our own motivations are inspired by other people's words. We work toward a goal, but when we really achieve it, it may not be what we dreamed. Liezi told a story:

A man was born in Yan, but grew up in Chu. When he was old, he came back to his native place. Passing Jin on the journey home, his fellow traveler fooled him into believing that the city wall was the wall of his home town, and he looked sad. The other traveler told him that one temple was his native temple for the God of land, and he sighed with nostalgia. When the traveler told him that a house was where his parents and grandparents had lived, he began weeping. When he was told that a mound was the tomb of his ancestors, he wailed. The other man roared with laughter and said, "That is the state of Jin, my fellow. I have been joking." The man felt very ashamed. When at last he arrived at Yan and saw the city wall and its temple for the God of land, as well as the actual abode and tombs of his ancestors, he was no longer that sad.[9]

The man from Yan was moved by the tomb that was not his ancestors', but when he sees the real tomb of his own ancestors, he is not that sad. His feelings are controlled by illusions created by other people.

Confucius, who occasionally reveals a subtle appreciation of the Taoist approach, also realizes that we often have ambitions for the future at the cost of the present. The following classical Confucian story shows some Taoist tendency.

Once when Zi Lu, Zeng Xi, Ran Qiu, and Gongxi Hua were seated in attendance with the Master, he said, "You consider me as a somewhat older man than yourselves. Forget for a moment that I am so. At present you are out of office and feel that your merits are not recognized. Now supposing someone were to recognize your merits, what employment would you choose?"

Zi Lu promptly and confidently replied, "Give me a country of a thousand war-chariots, hemmed in by powerful enemies, or even invaded by hostile armies, with drought and famine to boot; in the space of three years, I could endow the people with courage and teach them in what direction right conduct lies."

Our Master smiled at him. "What about you, Qiu?" he said.

Qiu replied, "Give me a domain of 60 to 70 leagues, or 50 to 60 leagues, and in the space of three years, I could bring it about that the common people should lack for nothing. But as to rites and music, I should have to leave that to a real gentleman."

"What about you, Gongxi Hua?"

He answered, "I do not say I could do this; but I should like at any rate to be trained for it. In ceremonies at the Ancestral Temple or at a conference or general gathering of the feudal princes, I should like, clad in the Straight Gown and Emblematic Cap, to play the part of junior assistant."

"Zeng Xi, what about you?"

The notes of the zither he was softly fingering died away. He put it down, rose, and replied, saying, "I fear my words will not be so well chosen as those of the other three."

The Master said, "What harm is there in that? All that matters is that each should name his desire."

Zeng Xi said, "At the end of spring, when the making of the Spring Clothes has been completed, I would like to go with five or six newly-capped youths and six or seven uncapped boys, person the lustration in the river Yi, take the air at the Rain Dance altars, and then go home singing."

The Master heaved a deep sigh and said, "I am with Zeng Xi." [10]

The process is more beautiful than the goal. Many modern girls dream of being a princess, but the more beautiful thing is the process to get there, and not the position itself. Princess Diana was one of the most miserable people in the world, because she reached the goal without the process. The climax of her glory was her marriage. All of her later life was spent paying the price of being a princess without having gone through the process. Most winners of the lottery have lives full of disappointment because they did not have the enjoyment of the process of becoming rich. Wealth is not a bad thing, if it stands at the end of hard work. Remember, the rainbow is more beautiful than the pot of gold at the end of it.

Appreciate, but do not own, the beauty.

The rainbow, colorfully transparent and surrealistically floating, is beyond anyone's reach. Viewers admire it in the crisp air after the rain, and nobody is so silly as to claim to own it. This is the beauty of the rainbow. The ambition of ownership is the destroyer of beauty.

If you want anything to happen, you must start from the very beginning. No matter how ambitious you are, you cannot build a pagoda from above. Eighty percent of all our energy is spent in the wrong direction. Think before you move forward; sometimes direction is more important than hard work. As a Chinese saying goes, "You cannot lower your head and pull a cart."

Zhanguo Ce (*Comments on the Warring States*), a book published more than 2,000 years ago, records the following story:

A man wants to travel to the Chu State in the south, but his driver goes north. A stranger asks him, "What are you doing? You want to go south!"

"But I have a very capable driver," replies the man.

"But the Chu State is in the south."

"But I have a lot of money!"

"You have a lot of money, but the Chu State is still in the south."

"I have a fast horse!"

"Yes, you do, but the Chu State is still in the south."

Here we can see that if the direction is wrong, hard work does not help at all. The driver works harder and the passenger only moves farther from the destination. When the direction is correct, the unforced effort, Wu Wei in this case, will lead the vehicle forward. Wu Wei is not idling but quietly contemplating, musing, and setting a correct direction. The world should realize that a driven worker is not more respectable than a relaxed thinker. Let us leave the thinker alone, maybe she is a direction setter.

According to Lao Tzu, people usually fail when they are

A lonely thinker, a respectable contemplator,
and maybe a direction setter of the world.

on the verge of success. They become overconfident, arrogant, and careless when success is in sight and take the last, but wrong, direction. This is why Wu Wei is important. When you do not know what to do, do nothing and let your mind rest. The mind is more powerful than you know. Take a break and let it work!

Also, remember that the process is more beautiful than the goal. The most dangerous thing is not that you cannot grab the sword. It is that once you have it, you either break it, find that you do not like it, or use it for destruction. The moment you have achieved your goals is the most dangerous time, because you may waste or even abuse the achievements you have worked for years to achieve.

NOTES

8. Liezi, *Liezi*, trans. Liang Xiaopeng and Li Jianguo (Beijing: Zhonghua Book Company, 2005), 81.

9. Adapted from Confucius, *Analects*. trans. Arthur Waley (Hertfordshire: Wordsworth Editions Limited, 1996).

25 Flying

To fly has been a universal human dream since antiquity, and so have mythical flying creatures, like dragons. Belief in them has prevailed all over China for thousands of years and has attained a certain reality through historic, literary, mythological, folkloric, social, psychological, and artistic representations. Hardly any symbols saturate Chinese civilization so thoroughly as those of the dragon. Among its many symbolic meanings, the dragon represents a powerful liberation from the bonds of the world, riding on the wind and reaching the heavens. In the air, across the sky, and above the ocean, it effortlessly soars on the wind and disappears among the clouds.

The Taoist imagination enabled the ideal man to soar like a dragon with elevated and sublime spirits. According to a legend in *Shiji, Records of the Historian*, Confucius once said this of Lao Tzu: "Birds fly, fish swim, animals run. Animals can be caught with traps, fish with nets, and birds with arrows. But then there is the dragon; I do not know how it rides on the wind or how it reaches the heavens. Today I met Lao Tzu. I can say that I have seen the Dragon." Here Confucius refers to the effortless grace of Lao Tzu, who does nothing and leaves nothing undone.

"How many times do I have to tell you, Billy?
There are no such things as dragons!"

A scene from the most universal dream.

Flying

In modern times, humans really can fly. John Gillespie Magee, Jr., was born in Shanghai, China, in 1922 to an English mother and a Scotch-Irish-American father. He dreamed of becoming a pilot and fighting against Nazi Germany, but the United States had not yet entered WWII. As an American citizen, he could not legally fight. He entered flight training in the Royal Canadian Air Force anyway. Within the year, he was sent to England to fight against the German Luftwaffe. John soon rose to the rank of Pilot Officer. On September 3, 1941, he flew a test flight in a newer model of the Spitfire V. As John climbed to a height of 30,000, he was struck with inspiration. Soon after he landed, he wrote a letter to his parents. In the letter, he wrote, "I am enclosing a verse I wrote the other day. It started at 30,000 feet and was finished soon after I landed." On the back of the letter, he jotted down his poem:

High Flight

Oh! I have slipped the surly bonds of Earth
And danced the skies on laughter-silvered wings;
Sunward I've climbed, and joined the tumbling mirth
Of sun-split clouds and done a hundred things
You have not dreamed of—wheeled and soared and swung
High in the sunlit silence. Hov'ring there,
I've chased the shouting wind along and flung
My eager craft through footless halls of air. . . .
Up, up the long, delirious burning blue
I've topped the wind-swept heights with easy grace
Where never lark, or even eagle flew—
And, while with silent, lifting mind I've trod

The high untrespassed sanctity of space,
Put out my hand, and touched the face of God.

Just three months later, on December 11, 1941—only three days after the United States entered the war—Magee was killed in a midair crash. A farmer testified that he saw the Spitfire pilot struggle to push back the canopy. The pilot, the farmer said, finally stood up to jump from the plane. Magee, the pilot-poet, was too close to the ground for his parachute to open and he died immediately. He was 19 years old.

As a young man, John Magee seems to have done everything that many "have not dreamed of." He flew up, up to the "delirious burning blue...where never lark, or even eagle flew." He tested the limit of ecstasy. The poet here does everything, but

Slipping the surly bonds of Earth.

he does everything with freedom. He "topped the wind-swept heights with easy grace." Magee did nothing, but he reached the height of heroism by liberating himself in the air. He gracefully reached heaven like a dragon.

To "slip the surly bonds of Earth" has long been the dream of Taoism. According to Zhuangzi, Wu Wei, or "doing nothing," refers to the attitude of the Taoist sage or the "ideal person." He is not literally doing nothing, but he engages in transparent and effortless activity. In an ideal realm, the ideal person acts in nonaction, relaxes and wanders, roams away with no particular goal. He flies like a bird, floats like a cloud, swims like a fish, meanders like a stream, blooms into life like a spring flower, and falls to death like an autumn leaf. Just like John the airman, he flies his craft "through footless halls of air" with silent, lifting mind.

Wu Wei is associated with the spiritual flying quality of the free person who has overcome the daily bonds of the ego and is able to experience the totality of things. Magee was like Zhuangzi's sage. He "danced the skies on laughter-silvered wings" and "touched the face of God." He has done Wu Wei, or doing nothing, and Wu Bu Wei, leaving nothing undone, in a heaven at 30,000 feet.

The first rockets were invented in China. The Chinese invented gunpowder and made firecrackers by stuffing it into bamboo tubes. According to legend, the world's first rocket scientist was Wan Hu, a Chinese official of the Ming Dynasty. Five hundred years ago, Wan Hu designed a "flying dragon" by binding two large kites and 47 firecrackers to a chair. He asked 47 torch-bearing assistants to light the firecrackers at the same time. They did so dutifully. A thundering roar and fluttering clouds of smoke followed. The smoke cleared, and Wan Hu was no more.

We do not know whether Wan Hu built his rocket out of a Taoist desire to escape from this world or a Confucian desire to serve his nation by inventing a new mode of transport. I prefer to believe he was a Taoist because of his playful imagination and his burning desire to fly into the great nothingness. Did he fly in one piece into the azure sky? The answer is lost in the smoke of antiquity.

Father, are you sure this is the only way to escape from this world?

In Taoism, flying can be reached by imagination. A soaring mind can also lift us from the binding earth. Zhuangzi told a story of a man named Tian Gen, who once asked Wu Ming Ren (Nameless Man) how to rule the world. Wu Ming Ren reproached him for disturbing his spiritual flying, saying, "Go away, you shallow man! Why do you ask such a vulgar question? I was in the company of the creator. When I get bored, I'll ride on the bird of purity and emptiness, and fly beyond the six ends of the earth, and travel in the realm of nothingness."

"Students, do not look at her. The Witch of the West belongs to another realm. We have our own Taoist way to fly."

26 Do Nothing in this World

Not everybody experiences ecstasy in midair like John Gillespie Magee, but everybody has the same guaranteed ending—death. Should we be afraid of death, that "undiscovered country?" For several thousand years, sages and philosophers have been exploring what we do "over there." Here, an anonymous person knows what we do there—nothing, and she yearns for it:

On a Tired Housewife

Here lies a poor woman who was always tired,
She lived in a house where help wasn't hired:
Her last words on earth were: "Dear friends, I am going
To where there's no cooking, or washing, or sewing,
For everything there is exact to my wishes,
For where they do not eat, there's no washing of dishes.
I'll be where loud anthems will always be ringing,
But having no voice I'll be quit of the singing.
Do not mourn for me now, do not mourn for me never,
I am going to do nothing forever and ever."

—Anonymous

This tired housewife has a great sense of humor, but at the same time, she is profoundly sad. She cooked, washed, and sewed all her life without any help. Now she yearns for a world where she will do nothing forever. All worries and chores will be gone. She has been too tired, unrewarded, and unappreciated. She begs her friends not to mourn for her. Instead, they should give a standing ovation to the departure of this tired housewife. Lord Byron said, "Sweet is revenge—especially to women." The tired woman delivered revenge to the world, which required her to do everything by telling the world that she is happy to be dead and doing nothing in the other world.

Life usually lasts less than a hundred years, but death is eternal. No wonder it can seem so much more serene, more real, even more interesting than life. Death started before life and will last after life. We can achieve the serenity of this infinite world by letting life take its natural course. The world is won by those who let it go. Life is won by those who dare liberate themselves to join the universe and follow the philosophy of Wu Wei in life. The tired housewife does not need to die to find the peace she wants. This can be done in this life instead of waiting for the next world. The sky would not fall if she took it easy.

Wu Wei is a behavior that arises from a sense of oneself as connected to the world. It is not built by a sense of separateness, but rather by the spontaneous and effortless art of living, which a pilot or a housewife can both achieve. Through understanding this principle and applying it to daily living, from doing tiring chores to dancing in the skies on laughter-silvered wings, we may consciously become a part of life's flow. Nondoing is not passivity, inertia, or laziness. Rather, it is the experience of floating with the wind or swimming with the current.

The principle of Wu Wei carries certain requirements. Primary among these is to consciously experience ourselves as part of the unity of life. Lao Tzu and Zhuangzi tell us to be quiet and vigilant, learning to listen to both our own inner voices and the voices of nature. In this way we heed more than just our mind to gather and assess information. We develop and trust our intuition as our connection to the Tao. We rely on the intelligence of our whole body, not only our brain. All of this allows us to respond readily to the beauty of the environment, which of course includes ourselves. Nonaction functions in a manner to promote harmony and balance. In a sense, the housewife's tiresome life can be as pleasant as Magee's glide over the cloud. She did not have to wait until the next world. She can do nothing and everything in this world.

27 Walking

When I first came to Carleton College, I took a walk with no destination in mind on Bell Field, a sunken soccer field. I circled and circled, as many Chinese people will do for a walk. Two students were sitting on the hill nearby, watching me. Finally, they came to me and kindly asked, "Did you lose something?" From their bemused expressions, I read another, unasked question: "Are you crazy?"

"Thank you," I said. "I'm just walking."

As a matter of fact, English does not have a good equivalent for the Chinese word *sanbu*, loose or scattered steps. I realized later that in the English language, you *walk* with a goal. Walking in a circle without a destination or purpose seems crazy and like a waste of time. Yet walking without a goal is the best healing practice for your mind, your body, and your soul. You are imitating the basic movement of the universe: a moon circling a planet, a planet circling a sun. One-way walking is normal on earth, something unique for "earth animals," but it is abnormal in the universe. If we move like the universe, we do as Einstein said: "It is still the best to concern yourself with eternals, for from them alone flows the spirit that can restore peace and serenity to the world of humans."

"Sir, can we offer you directions?"

Lao Tzu said, "Good running leaves no tracks." (Chen, *The Tao Te Ching*, Chapter 27) The skilled walker just floats through the air without physical or mental tracks. I believe that if you walk with anxiety, with mental knots, you leave invisible tracks of contagious anxiety behind you, infecting anyone who comes across them. Unfortunately, the world is full of tracks of troubled minds, like a freeway during rush hour clogged with harried drivers.

We do a lot of things while walking—too many. We have a goal, a target, or an errand for the walking. We pay too much attention to the goal, too little to the process—and what a pleasant and graceful process it is! We do not allow ourselves to pause, to smell the fresh air, to look at the blue sky, or to restore peace in ourselves. As a matter of fact, we cannot walk, we can only go—go *somewhere*: go shopping, go to work, or go on an errand. Nevertheless, we should relearn how to walk going *nowhere*. I call this "meditative walking." When you practice meditative walking, each step calls you back to the present moment. Each step enables you to connect to the eternal and to create a link between your mind and your body.

Meditative walking brings you to the present, undoing knots in your heart, transforming negative energies to positive. It seems that you are not going anywhere, but you are going here and now. You are engaging in a process without a goal, a doing without achieving. This is walking without going.

Swimming without a goal is beautiful and graceful, almost like flying. Lao Tzu said,

> A person with superior goodness is like water,
> Water is good in benefiting all beings,
> Without contending with any.
> Situated in places shunned by many others,
> Thereby it is near Tao.
> (Chen, *The Tao Te Ching*, Chapter 8)

When you swim, you are closest to the Tao; you are a king reigning over the vast territory of water, which includes the water outside of you and the water inside of you. The practice of swimming meditation unites you with the water outside in order to restore peace and harmony. Do not count laps, do not count time, and do not worry if people stare at you like you are crazy. You are establishing peace in yourself in the territory of water to which you belong.

Doing nothing not only helps you to be serene and healthy, it can also help you "win," a word Taoism can playfully accept.

The eagle's flight is a perfect combination of movement and stillness. If we know how to relax in strenuous actions, we can move ahead, like a cloud floating over the mountains, like a river flowing into the ocean, and like a wild swan flying to the horizon.

In college, I was a champion of short-distance running. With 11.2 seconds, I won first prize in the 100-meter race and broke the record of my college. My secret was doing nothing while doing everything. For self-training, I read all available books on short-distance running. I was impressed by an author who wrote that you should relax your body after you begin. The runner should set off at a blistering pace; then they should relax the body, especially the neck and shoulders, for a few steps and take advantage of the momentum. Here, I found the secret of winning. I learned to give myself a few relaxed "centiseconds" during the tense 11 seconds. After setting off, I even yelled to myself *fangsong* (relax), and I let the dash become a float. During these 11 seconds, the wind screamed by my ears, the destination was in view, and my competitors were moving back, while I was trying my best to relax. When my friends congratulated me on my championship, I would say in a humble Chinese way, "I did nothing."

28 Tai Chi Boxing, Doing Nothing

Tai Chi Chuan (Quan), or Tai Chi Boxing or Shadow Boxing, is a Chinese martial art that combines self-defense with healing meditation and breath control. The word *chuan* (Quan) means "fist," emphasizing the lack of weapons or tools in this martial art. Tai Chi Boxing is the most common form of Tai Chi. It is practiced by millions of people for its health benefits, stress relief, and relaxation. The slow, low, and weak flowing movements stimulate the flow of energy, *chi* or *qi*, in the body for health and longevity. By practicing Tai Chi, one's body and mind become integrated. Many people enter a state of Wu Wei. Tai Chi is translated as the "utmost pole," the extreme, the end of the limit. The Tao is beyond the utmost pole. When you reach the end of the limit, you return.

The symbol of Tai Chi is the yin-yang.

The symbol of Tai Chi is the circle of yin and yang, black and white intertwined with each other. In this 5,000-year-old mystifying circle, we do not have a beginning, and we do not have an end. We do not have definition. We do not have a purpose. We do not display.

we are joinly the universe
Tai chi's uniform motion =

With Tai Chi's uniform motion, we are joining the universe.
"A journey of a thousand miles must begin with the first step."
(Chen, *The Tao Te Ching*, Chapter 64)

Tai Chi's motion is Wu Wei, doing nothing, because when we do Tai Chi, we move with uniform motion. Uniform motion, according to Newton's laws, is the same as rest. Newton's first law of motion, also called the Law of Inertia, states that an object continues in its state of rest or uniform motion unless compelled to change that state by an external force. In our daily environment on the earth, objects slow down because they are compelled to change speed by a friction force. In Tai Chi, there is no friction, no resistance. We continue with uniform motion.

When we have uniform motion, it is the same as resting; we have become stars and planets of nonaction.

Learning the basic forms does not mean that you *know* Tai Chi. There is always something to improve; think of this as a beginning to a lifelong journey. Knowing the forms is just the beginning.

Attitude in Tai Chi is very important. Do not let your mind wander; feel your place in the universe. Keep in mind these things:

- In order to truly master Tai Chi Boxing, you must be able to assume the correct body positions and be able to control them.

- Your torso should be upright and perpendicular to the ground. Do not lean forward or backward unless the movement calls for it.

- Your legs should be bent, and you should be low most of the time.

- The arms should stretch outwards, not collapse inwards.

- There should be the form of an empty vessel between your bowed legs and outreaching arms.

- Your transitions must be fluid. Think of the transition as part of the movement. Most importantly, speed must be held constant. Think of the earth rotating in space. Should terrorists be able to speed up or slow down the rotation of the earth, our entire world would cease to exist. The earth moves and yet it does not move. It moves with uniform speed, so it does not move. Your Tai Chi Boxing should strive to do the same thing.

- Be flexible! Flexibility is life; stiffness is death. The tongue is flexible, and the teeth are stiff. Which will fall out first?

- The body should expand. Anxiety makes people shrink and protect themselves from the outside world, but to gain awareness of nature, we should relax and expand.

Tai Chi is not a performance. Performance sacrifices the correct way for the entertaining way. Whenever you perform, since your childhood, you have known you have an audience. When you have an audience, you have to show yourself. When you show yourself, you have to be normal. When you are normal, you do things at a normal speed. If you do things slowly, people will think you are not normal, and you are concerned with what other people think. When you do Tai Chi, you should not be concerned with what other people think. You should relax and build a network with the universe. When you build this network, you are spontaneous. Now you do Wu Wei.

People may think you are strange, since they have not seen a human move like this. In the universe, most celestial bodies move in constant motion, in movements with an even speed. We human beings and other animals on the earth act in sporadic motions—very abnormal from the universal point of view. When doing Tai Chi, we move with an even speed, an imitation of the *real* normal motion of the universe. If others think you are strange, you are performing Tai Chi well.

If you have a dog, perform Tai Chi in front of it. The first time you do it, the dog just barks. It will get annoyed, because dogs do not like abnormal movements. You are not performing well in its eyes, so your dog does not know what to do! Do not worry about your dog, and do not worry about other people. They are both bound to the earth. Tai Chi is not a performance but a return to the natural and universal.

Usually, we change our mindset, and our body language follows. In Tai Chi, we change our bodies, and our minds follow. Grace will follow with the right mindset. When our bodies move like a planet, so will our minds.

In my class, I created an imaginary student whose name was Jenny. Smart and individualistic, she would sometimes challenge my teaching, find the contradictions in my lectures, or over-perform what she had learned. This imagined Jenny became a class joke. Students would start laughing as soon as I said, "Jenny, stop doing that, in Tai Chi 101, we can only float five inches above the ground. How many times does our teacher have to tell you that our motto, opposite to that of the Olympics' Faster, Higher, Stronger, is Slower, Lower, and Weaker?"

We should be slower in Tai Chi, because stillness is the essence of the universe. The earth circles the sun, the moon

"Jenny, how many times does the teacher have to tell you that we
can only float five inches above the ground?"

circles the earth, but we cannot even feel the movement. By
being still, we can be closer to the essence of the universe.

We should be lower in Tai Chi, because by being low, we
come closer to the earth.

We should be weaker, because Tai Chi is not for fighting; it
is for peace. Humans used to need strength to survive, attack,
and kill. In the beginning, Tai Chi was used for fighting, and
we can still see this history in its movements; but it has lost
its martial emphasis. Now we advocate the weak as Lao Tzu
would, and we use our strength to heal, not to wound. We
should be slow, low, and weak—like water. Lao Tzu said:

Low, slow, and weak, Tai Chi brings us back to Nature.

Nothing under heaven
Is softer and weaker than water,
Yet nothing can compare with it
In attacking the hard and strong.
Nothing can change place with it.
That the weak overcomes the strong,
And the soft overcomes the hard,
No one under heaven does not know,
Though none can put it into practice.
Therefore a sage said:
"One who receives the filth of a state
Is called the Master of the Altar of the Soil and Grain;

One who shoulders the evils of a state
Becomes the king under heaven."
Straightforward words appear to be their reverse.
(Chen, *The Tao Te Ching*, Chapter 78)

29 Tai Chi Sword, Doing Everything

Tai Chi can be performed with a sword, but we do not want to fight with our swords. We want to play with the clouds and the mountains! Tai Chi Sword is as peaceful as the movement of Tai Chi Boxing, but the illustrative and the dramatic movement of Tai Chi Sword brings the art of Tai Chi to a new peak. The sword is the king of Chinese short-range weapons. It can be deadly in combat. A sword fight requires a level of violence and a mental alertness that not many peace-loving people would want to have; but paradoxically, this practice aims at self-cultivation, longevity, and peace. As Lao Tzu says, "Everything goes toward the opposite extreme."

A hole in the end of the sword's hilt is used to attach a long, red tassel that balances the double-edged blade, thus forming a combination of yin and yang. Despite the threatening sword, Tai Chi Sword has more elegant, dramatic, dance-like characteristics. In contrast to the uniform speed of Tai Chi Boxing, Tai Chi Sword allows acceleration and pause during the continuity of a performance. The points of the sword move from various directions with surprises and variety. If we say Tai Chi Boxing is peacefully doing nothing, Tai Chi Sword is more dramatically doing everything.

The imaginary student Jenny would say, "Wait a minute! Last week, you told us to go rambling without a destination in Tai Chi. Now you are telling us to have a target in mind with Tai Chi Sword. Which side are we going to settle on?"

Jenny wants to find out if she should do nothing or everything with Tai Chi Sword.

Zhuangzi said, "It is different to drift with the Tao; there is neither praise nor blame. Sometimes you're a dragon, sometimes you're a snake, floating with time, never focusing on one thing, up and down, using harmony as measurement."

My answer to Jenny is this: You, disciples, settle between aim and aimlessness, between being good for something and being good for nothing, between Wu Wei and Wu Bu Wei. Basically, Tai Chi Sword is the same as Tai Chi Boxing in that it brings the mind and the body into harmony. The sword helps the performer make an extension of his body. It is essential to enlarge the mind through the tip of the sword. Energy travels from the earth to the feet and is guided through the whole body, through the torso, and to the tip of the sword. It is often said by the masters of Tai Chi Sword that the waist, not the arms, moves the blade. Beginners who move the arm, or disconnect the movement between the arm and the whole body, demonstrate a lack of understanding of Tai Chi principles. The whole body should remain in flux. While the sword spins easily in the air, the performer flies. The feet feel as if they are dragged up by the sword three inches above the ground. This flying would lead the performer to the arch of the sky, to touch the face of the Supreme Being, whether that is God or Nature.

The hand that is not holding the sword should be held with the first two fingers extended and the ring finger and pinky curled in, with the thumb over the ring-finger knuckle. Some people call this hand Secret Sword or Sword Amulet. The two pointed fingers actively cooperate with the hand that holds the sword. They point at the direction the sword would go to lead the performer's energy and attention to that direction, or deliberately point to other directions to distract the imagined opponents. Thus, the tip of the sword, the tip of the tassel, and the tips of the fingers form three points in a sphere, circling around the body in different directions and balancing the energy. It can be a most elegant image, when a master stands inside these three points with her flexing body changing from standing on her toes to doing a split on the ground. A new dimension, a new magical field is created.

This is an ode to possibilities, to courage, and to doing everything possible.

Zhuangzi offers an extraordinary passage about the art of the sword:

The sword of the Son of Heaven... is designed in accord with the Five Phases, assessed by its punishment and bounty, drawn by means of the Yin and Yang, wielded in spring and summer, and strikes its blow in autumn and winter. With this sword you can

> Thrust and there's nothing ahead,
> Brandish and there's nothing above,
> Press down on the hilt and there's nothing below,
> Whirl it round and there's nothing beyond.

Up above, it breaks through the floating clouds; down below, it bursts through the bottom of the earth. Use this sword once, and it will discipline the lords of the states, the whole empire will submit.

The sword of the prince of a state has clever and brave knights for its point, clean and honest knights for its edge, worthy and capable knights for its spine, loyal and wise knights for its hand-guard, dashing and heroic knights for its hilt. With this sword you will

> Thrust and there's nothing ahead,
> Brandish and there's nothing above,
> Press down on the hilt and there's nothing below,
> Whirl it round and there's nothing beyond.

Use this sword once, and it will be like the quake after a clap of thunder, within the four borders, none will refuse to submit and obey your commands.

The sword of the common man is to have tousled hair bristling at the temples, a tilted cap, stiff chinstrap, coat cut up short at the back, have glaring eyes, be rough of speech, and duel in your presence. Up above, it will chop a neck or slit a throat; down below it will burst lungs or liver. This is the sword of the common man, it is no different than cockfighting. In a single morning, man's fated span is snapped." [11]

We do not fight the natural order of things, nor do we leave our tasks undone. The Common Man will act, but he will act with only his own petty aims in mind. When we carry the Sword of the Son of Heaven, our actions are most effective, because they are done in harmony with the flow of the universe.

Greet people with words, not swords.

I respect you, since you are alive and have a battle to fight every day. But may you stop for a while to smell the flowers between your battles, since you are only here for a short visit. Greet people with words, not swords. Be kind! Everyone you meet on the way has a hard battle to fight.

> The world has no room for cowards. We must all be ready somehow to toil, to suffer, to die. And yours is not the less noble because no drum beats before you when you go out into your daily battlefields, and no crowds shout about your coming when you return from your daily victory or defeat.
>
> —*Robert Louis Stevenson*

A warrior without sword, a hero in daily battlefields.

The distinction between Tai Chi Boxing and Tai Chi Sword represents the contrast of doing nothing and doing everything. Tai Chi Boxing flows with whatever may happen and lets your mind be free. This is Wu Wei, or doing nothing. Yielding is the use of the Tao of Tai Chi. Even in small movements, there is grandeur. Do not hurry, do not worry; you are only here for a short visit. You may not be able to accomplish a grand mission today, but stop by and move along with the ten thousand objects of the universe!

For Tai Chi Sword, you stay centered by completing whatever your sword ventures to do. This is doing everything, or Wu Bu Wei, leaving nothing undone. Reversing is the motion of the Tao of Tai Chi Sword. Beautiful things are all around you: the air is close to you, the sky is above you, and you can even lift your head and see the stars. Your sword cannot touch them, but their beauty is there with you. You can amplify the small and flow with the universe.

The Law of the Unity of Opposites is the fundamental law of the universe. Things that oppose each other also complement each other. Thus, Tai Chi Boxing and Tai Chi Sword complement one another like the two sides of a crystal jade.

NOTES

10. Zhuangzi, *The Inner Chapters,* trans. A.C. Graham (Indianapolis: Hackett Publishing Company, Inc., 2001), 246.

30 Happiness

Happiness is internal. It does not depend on what we have but on what we are. It does not depend on what we get but on what we experience. Our hearts are lifted when we behold a rainbow, but we do not want to own it. Most of us do not even want to travel to the end of it to find the pot of gold. We do not have to, because we see the beauty shining against the clouds, and that is happiness enough for us. We do nothing with it except let it shine in our hearts without trying to possess it.

Liu An of the Han Dynasty wrote a story about a lost horse:

An old man who lived on the northern frontier of China was skilled in interpreting events. One day, his horse ran away to the nomads across the border. Everyone tried to console him, but he said, "What makes you so sure this isn't a blessing?"

Some months later, his horse returned, bringing back with her a splendid stallion. Everyone congratulated him, but he said, "What makes you so sure this isn't a disaster?"

Their household was richer by a fine stallion, which the man's son loved to ride. One day he fell from the horse and broke his leg. Everyone tried to console the man, but he said, "What makes you so sure this isn't a blessing?"

A year later the nomads came across the border, and every able-bodied man was drafted into the army. The Chinese frontiersmen lost nine of every ten men. Only because the son was lame did father and son survive to take care of each other.

This story, first told 2,000 years ago, has become a Chinese axiom: "The old man of the frontier lost his horse." It reminds us that blessing turns to disaster and disaster to blessing; the changes have no end, nor can the mystery be fathomed. Our happiness does not depend on what we own. Things like horses and gold come and go. To be happy, one must understand that the gain and loss of material things is simply an ever-changing flow of the river. There are splashes, rises, and falls, but we should remember a simple axiom that exists in all languages: This also will pass.

Lao Tzu said, "Calamities are what blessings depend on, in blessings are latent calamities" (Chen, *The Tao Te Ching*, Chapter 58). The great ocean sends us drifting like a raft, the running river sweeps us along like a boat; but we do not tell the ocean to stop its tides, and we do not tell the river to flow slower. We just join them to celebrate the existence of happiness and freedom. We let water carry our boat to a new adventure. This is why, when we face real ecstasy, we stop doing everything, even holding our breath.

Poetry is the record of the happiest moments of human life. The poet sees the beauty around her, and she wants to put this beauty into a rhythmic pattern that responds to the sight. Poetry is important for all cultures; it has been the center of Chinese civilization for 3,000 years. Chinese officials were poets because of their literary talents, having passed civil examinations on

Rivers flow, boats sail, and the present becomes the past.
This also will pass.

essay and poetry writing. China was a country ruled by poets, many of whom were Taoists—full-time, part-time, real, and pretending Taoists. Observing nature and interpreting life with natural phenomena, they escaped from political, social, and economic pressures.

One of China's most famous Taoist poets, Li Bai (or Li Bo; 701–762 CE) was known for his carefree lifestyle. Most people agree that he is the best Chinese poet because of his unconstrained and joyous understanding of life against the magnificent background of nature. The magic in his poetry comes from his spontaneous enjoyment of life and nature.

Poem 1: Question and Answer in the Mountains

You ask me why I live in the green mountains.
I smile without answering, but with a heart at leisure.
Peach flowers drift away in the stream;
There is another heaven and earth inside the human world...

If no one else comes to your garden party,
invite the moon as your guest.

Poem 2: Drinking Alone Under the Moon

One pot of wine among flowers
Drinking alone without dear ones
Raising the cup and inviting the moon as a guest.
With the shadow, we have a company of three.

Happiness

The moon cannot take a sip,
The shadow follows me in vain.
For now, I have the moon and the shadow as my companions,
Taking advantage of the spring while it lasts.
When I sing the moon wanders,
When I dance the shadow scatters,
When we are sober, we enjoy each other's company,
When we are drunk, we go our separate ways.
We'll have a cold friendship,
Looking for each other through the clouds in the sky.

Nature is the best company, silent like the bamboo or
clucking like the chicken.

The first poem describes the life of a hermit, an ideal Taoist in Chinese traditional literature. In the mountains, he finds happiness and enjoys himself. "Enjoying oneself" is a wonderful English phrase missing in many languages, including Chinese. Although to "enjoy yourself" means to be happy and enjoy the fun, it literally means finding happiness within yourself. In daily life, many people become burdens on themselves. They need jobs, sports, cards, gambling, and smoking to stay occupied. The Taoists seek a way to enjoy themselves without occupation. They can be alone and be happy by finding company in nature. They are not their own burden.

In the second poem, the greatest Chinese poet is alone and lonely, but in a subtle way, he transforms this loneliness into an ecstasy that merges with the flowers, the moon, and the shadow around him. Using the vocabulary of social life, like "company" and "friendship," he builds a happy trust with nature and liberates himself from the desire to seek happiness from other people. He admires the moon, and he experiences a kind of happiness as cold as the moonlight.

Li Bai reaches freedom in nature. He expresses his ecstasy in poems just like Zhuangzi did in his philosophical stories. They both found their happiness in nature and threw off the shackles of society. They saw dignity and self-respect in the natural world that was only understood by people who shared the same feelings. Li Bai is like the fish described by Zhuangzi:

Zhuangzi and Hui Zi took a walk along the bank of the river. Zhuangzi said, "The fish swim with such ease. They're so happy."

Hui Zi said, "You are not a fish. How do you know they're happy?"

Zhuangzi said, "You are not me. How do you know I do not know the fish are happy?"

Hui Zi said, "I am not you. Of course I do not know if you know. But you are not a fish. You do not know if the fish are happy. So there!"

Zhuangzi said, "Let's go to the root of the matter. You asked me how I know the fish are happy. So you agree that I know they're happy, but you want to find out how I know it? I'm standing here on the bank of the river."

Fish are content because they are doing what they are supposed to do. They swim, bubble, and never dream of being something else. Li Bai with his moon, the horse with its grassland, and the fish with its water all reach the realm of happiness. They do not need other people's approval, so they are not the prisoners of public opinion. Happiness is found within; material pleasure and public admiration come from the outside. The inner happiness always surpasses the superficial enjoyment.

Inner happiness demands a calm and individual environment. This environment liberates us from the anxieties caused by our daily necessities. Anxiety is crucial for survival—but only in quick flashes: It damages one's inner health and society's harmony in the long run. Calmness widens wisdom, expands tolerance, and increases health. Quiet joy strengthens our existence and allows us to make a contribution to the world. When we are frightened, angry, or depressed, we shrink into an invisible shell around us, but at the same time, we project a dark cloud onto others surrounding us. As a Chinese saying goes, "One sad person sitting in the corner makes all the people in the room feel unhappy." In contrast, a happy person spreads the aroma of flowers, the shadows of the rainbow, and the individual calmness to benefit the collective.

A society is composed of individuals, and each individual is responsible for the group status. Philosophers have talked for centuries about altruism—sacrificing oneself for society. While we new Taoists agree with this idea of selflessness, I should add that each individual's mood alone determines the world's collective mindset. It would be very dangerous for an unhappy person to hold power, because he can make the world join his misery. History has proved this again and again. Just like the people in power, each one of us can impact larger humankind. If you make yourself happy and healthy, you will add one happy and healthy grain to the ocean of the world. Sometimes, you feel that you are doing nothing for the human race beyond being happy yourself; as a matter of fact, you are doing everything for its harmony. Your status of cheerful mind will add a colorful band to the multicolored rainbow of the world. This kind of Wu Wei is also a Wu Bu Wei.

Being happy is natural. You will be happy if you let your mind perform Wu Wei. European and American culture is a culture of guilt. People are taught to fear the punishment of an invisible hand. Shrug off the guilt that you have allowed the invisible force to place upon you. You are limitless. There is no happiness that you cannot achieve. Chinese culture is a culture of shame. People are taught to fear losing face. Throw away the shame you have allowed the visible society to place on you. There is no sadness in life that cannot be reversed.

31 | No Regret

Reach the pole of emptiness,
Abide in genuine quietude.
Ten thousand beings flourish together,
I am to contemplate their return.
Now things grow profusely,
Each again returns to its root.
To return to the root is to attain quietude,
It is called to recover life.
(Chen, *The Tao Te Ching*, Chapter 16)

Have no regret; you are not responsible for everything that has happened to the world. You are not responsible for everything that has happened to you and your family. You are a drop of water in the ocean, and your position is decided by the movement of a body trillions of times larger than you. Your best relief is to realize you are not a god. Nobody says that they are a god, but many people believe that they have the ability of God to control everything around them. Therefore, they regret that things do not happen in the way that they would like.

Every night, when you take off your socks, please leave all your problems on the floor with them. Have no fear, your socks will not be lost, and the world will come back to you when you put the socks back on the next morning. Your day is done. You are like a ship drawn to the harbor, like a seagull listening to the evening music of the tide. You are like an autumn leaf falling to the earth, like a homesick child returning home. Be still and be peaceful when you enter the sweet world of doing nothing. You have to leave everything, everybody, and every worry behind you. Lao Tzu said, "Reach the pole of emptiness, abide in genuine quietude. Ten thousand beings flourish together, I am to contemplate their return." (Chen, *The Tao Te Ching*, Chapter 16) When you go to sleep, enter the void, join the stillness and quietness.

The most valuable thing is life; we only get one. At death, a person should be able to say, "I am familiar with this, because I have practiced it every night by leaving everything behind me before going to bed. I did something, and I am going to do nothing. I did not have regret all my life, and I do not have it now."

Regret lurks behind your decisions. Your idea may start out like spring flowers ready to bloom. As soon as the decision is made, there is a crash of thunder. Regret comes in like a summer storm, crashing along with rain so thick that the flowers in your mind are drenched. Then there comes a gentle lament, like an autumn drizzle, that whips the surface of your heart, until repentance, like winter snow, floats down and seals your bleeding wounds.

Lao Tzu said, "No action, no regret." Action causes regret, because no single action can be exactly correct the first time. The only way to do nothing wrong is to do nothing. Lao Tzu's "no action, no regret" reflects his theme of Wu Wei. Wu Wei, in this case, is not to avoid decisions in order to avoid regret, but to flow like a river from one correction to another. *Correct*, as an English adjective, means making no mistake. The English word *correct*, as a verb means to change something in order to make it right. Therefore, to be correct, one should continuously correct oneself, instead of bemoaning past mistakes.

This is, as a matter of fact, doing everything. When we walk, we move one foot forward. Soon the direction is wrong, and we have to move it backward. Do we regret that we moved the foot wrongly first time? No. We just constantly change the direction of our two feet, and the whole body moves forward smoothly. Our feet are doing everything (Wu Bu Wei) by moving in opposite directions, and our body is doing nothing (Wu Wei) by moving forward. Therefore, our minds have no regret, because they allow those contradictions to proceed naturally.

Everything will resolve itself sooner or later. This is the way of the Tao. Walk through life without fear for the future or regret for the past. Practice being nothing. In being nothing, you will turn into everything without fear. Watch the clouds in the dawn. As they pass the rays of morning sun, they are tinged but unruffled, penetrated but undisturbed. When they pass the mountains and gorges, they are neither elated by the mountains nor depressed by the ravines. They seem to do nothing but have actually done everything. The clouds will never fear floating toward the peaks ahead, nor will they regret having passed over a valley. This is the mind of Wu Wei and Wu Bu Wei: never elated nor depressed, but rather always flowing at peace.

Watch the way a stream flows effortlessly and passes over the rocks that get in its way. The rocks on the bottom make the limpid water bubble melodiously. Obstacles, like rocks in the stream, can make the path of life more beautiful, so that James Maurice Thompson can say, "Bubble, bubble, flows the stream, like an old tune through a dream." That is the way of life, unencumbered by little impediments. However, the stream takes a bend or diverges around rocks. Water, as Lao Tzu said, "overcomes but never argues, benefits but never claims the benefits." It makes the best of the situation. Overcoming, giving up, doing nothing, and doing everything, the stream bubbles forward without fear or regret. This is what life should be.

Once I asked my father to write something in my notebook. This is what he wrote:

To Qiguang:

Before I turned 80 years old, I used to have a motto: Be strict with yourself and lenient towards others. Now that I am 80 years old, I have a new motto: Be lenient with yourself and lenient towards others. I do not know whether I can correct myself at this age.

Dad, 1997

A very wise man, a professor of physics, and the dean of a well-known university, my father had spent 80 years learning how to treat himself and others: We should treat ourselves with the same forgiving compassion as we give others. Nothing in the world is without flaws, so be tender and kind to others and yourself when you or others stumble. Let us walk our own way, change the direction of our feet, and let others talk. Correct, change, and live without regret, and let the universe follow its own course.

32 Life and Death

Heaven and earth are long lasting.
The reason why heaven and earth are long lasting:
Because they do not live for self.
Therefore they last long.
Thus the sage puts his body behind,
Yet his body is in front.
He regards his body as external,
Yet his body remains in existence.
Is it not because he is selfless
That he can fulfill himself.
(Chen, *The Tao Te Ching*, Chapter 7)

To achieve longevity, we must join the universe. To join the universe, we must think in reverse. Sometimes the Tao sounds like nonsense, but if we think outside the box, it becomes the greatest sense.

The world is divided into opposites. Everything has two sides that coexist. When one side is denied, it develops into the other side. To go forward, we must go backward; everything requires an opposite. When you walk, one foot moves forward and the other pushes back. It is the back foot that pushes your body forward. In aging, the more you stay behind—acting slowly, staying young—the longer you live. In other words, by staying behind, you get ahead.

This process should be natural, effortless, and not achieved through force. When forms change, they can transform without changing their structure, like clouds or flowers.

> At birth a person is soft and yielding,
> At death hard and unyielding.
> All beings, grass and trees, when alive, are soft and bending,
> When dead they are dry and brittle.
> Therefore the hard and unyielding are companions of death,
> The soft and yielding are companions of life.
> Hence an unyielding army is destroyed.
> An unyielding tree breaks.
> The unyielding and great takes its place below,
> The soft and yielding takes its place above.
> (Chen, *The Tao Te Ching*, Chapter 76)

Lao Tzu's wisdom can be seen in numerous phenomena. Everyone has teeth and a tongue. Which is softer? The tongue, of course. Which falls out first? Of course, the teeth. Have you ever heard of anyone's tongue falling out?

One of Aesop's famous tales, "The Oak and the Reeds," reflects the same concept. A very large oak was uprooted by the wind and thrown across a stream. It fell among some reeds, which it thus addressed: "I wonder how you, who are so light and weak, are not entirely crushed by these strong winds." They replied, "You fight and contend with the wind, and consequently you are destroyed; while we, on the contrary, bend before the least breath of air, and therefore remain unbroken, and escape." We yield and we live. We yield more, and we live longer. However, death will come to us anyway.

Which is more normal, life or death? If life is normal, why have humans not found life anywhere in the universe except the earth? If death is so abnormal, why does the whole starry sky radiate the shining light of nonlife?

If life is normal, why does it belong to you for only 80 or 90 years, while death embraces you for the eternities before your birth and after your death?

The lifeless surface of Mars is normal. Its scenery, waterless and lifeless, is more representative of the universe than the Earth's. The wet surface of the Earth is the anomaly. Life, as far as we know, could not exist without liquid water, which is rare in the universe. No water, and consequently no life, has been found on other planets. Therefore, death is more the essence of the universe. When we die, we just return to normal. We should not cling to the temporary abnormality that is life and refuse the eternal and universal norm.

The person who fears death is like the child who has forgotten the way home. Liezi told a story about Duke Jing of Qi:

Duke Jing climbed up Mount Niu and looked over his capital. He began to cry. "What a magnificent capital! How can I die and leave behind this flourishing town, these verdant forests?"

His two ministers, Shi Kong and Liang Qiuju, also began to weep. "Thanks to Your Highness, we can feed ourselves with our simple food and get around on our humble carriages.

Even though we live only modest lives, we do not want to die! And the thought of our lord dying is unbearable!"

Yangzi stood nearby, laughing into his beard. Duke Jing frowned. Wiping his eyes, he turned to Yangzi. "I am quite sad here, and Shi Kong and Liang Qiuju are weeping with me. Why are you laughing?"

"If a worthy sovereign were to reign forever," said Yangzi, "your grandfather or Duke Huan would still be king. If a brave ruler were to reign forever, Duke Zhuang or Duke Ling would still be our lord. If any of these men were still in power, you would never have succeeded to the throne. Your Majesty might be farming in the fields in a straw coat and bamboo hat, without any time to ponder your death. Reigns have followed reigns until at last your turn came, and you alone lament it. I laugh because I'm looking at an unjust lord and his two yes-men."

Duke Jing was ashamed. He penalized himself with one cup of wine and his attendants with two.

Zhuangzi once told a story:

When Zhuangzi's wife died, Huizi went to console him. He found Zhuangzi sitting cross-legged, drumming on a pot and singing. Huizi said, "You lived with her and she raised your children. Now she is dead. It would be bad enough if you didn't cry. But now you are drumming and singing. Isn't this too much?"

Zhuangzi said, "Definitely not. When she first died, how could I not mourn? Then I realized there was no life in the beginning. Not only no life, but there was no shape. Not only was there no shape, but there was no energy. In the subtle

Should we cry or laugh over the city we will
lose some day because of death?

chaos, changes happened. Energy emerged. Energy became
shape, shape became life, and now life has become death. This
is just the same as the succession of spring, summer, autumn,
and winter. My wife was sleeping calmly in a big hall, and I
followed her wailing and crying. Then I realized that I did
not understand the rules of life. So I stopped crying."

The message of Zhuangzi's story is consistent with that of
numerous Taoist stories: death is a natural return to peace and
eternity. However, if Taoists are so comfortable with this "big
return," why are they so obsessed with longevity and immortality? The Taoist tradition is probably the most famous in the
world for its pursuit of the elixir of life through alchemical

"miracle drugs." If they were not afraid of death, why did they work so hard to avoid it?

You can linger at the top of the mountain and wait for the sun to set, but that does not mean you are afraid of going home to the valley. Taoists love life, but they do not fear death. Their search for immortality comes from a desire to stay a little longer in the lively and familiar realm of life, not from a terror of the unknown and quiet domain of death.

Zhuangzi celebrates his wife's return to Nature.

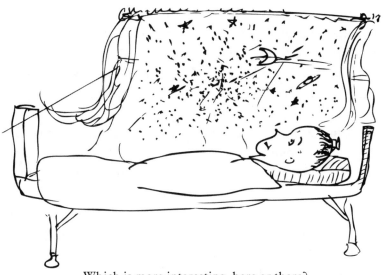

Which is more interesting, here or there?

We will only be in this world for a short time, but we will be in the other world forever. Death must be interesting, because we have never experienced it; but life is interesting, too, because we have been there, done that. We want to enjoy the adventure as long as possible and do everything before we do nothing.

If life is a dream, let us keep the dream long and sweet. If life is a game, let us make it fun. If life is a one-way journey, let us stop, go outside, and enjoy the scenery. Why hurry? Why always ask, "Are we there yet?" With a healthy understanding of death, we can have a long, healthy, and fearless life.

The barrier between life and death is not absolute. Really, we do not understand death at all. Without knowing anything about it, how do we know that it is not better than life? If we understood death, we would not cry over it. We are not afraid of death; we are afraid of the unknown.

In the Jin dynasty (265–420 CE), when Taoism was not only a theory, but was also practiced by many scholars as a way of life, there was a well-known group called "the Seven Sages of the Bamboo Forest." Among the seven sages, Liu Ling was the one least interested in worldly affairs. According to *History of the Jin Dynasty*, Liu Ling was ugly, free-spirited, quiet, and socially awkward. His spirit soared through the universe and did not distinguish between the ten thousand objects of the world. When he met two other sages of the bamboo forest, Ruan Ji and Ji Kang, the three of them were pleasant and carefree and entered the forest hand in hand.

Liu Ling's instructions: "Bury me where I fall."

According to *Shishuo Xinyu,* a book of historical anecdotes by Liu Qingyi (403–444 CE), Liu Ling often took off his clothes and drank wine at home. When people saw him and laughed, he answered, "I take heaven and earth as my house, my house as my trousers. What are you doing in my trousers?" He did not care about property, and often he rode in a small cart with a bottle of wine, followed by a boy carrying a hoe. His instructions to this boy were, "When I die, bury me where I fall." He paraded around with a boy with a hoe to announce that death is not something to be afraid of, but something as normal as life, perhaps even more normal.

Zhuangzi considers death a natural change of small forms in the infinite universe:

A strong man can carry away our boat no matter how deeply
we hide it in the valley.

The huge clump of earth carries my body, puts me to work all my life, nurses me through old age, and lays me to rest with death. Therefore, the one who can give me life can also give me death. You hide your boat in a valley and your fishing tackle in a marsh, and you think it's safe, but at midnight a strong person can carry them away without your knowing it. It's proper to hide a small thing in a big thing, but you still may lose it. If you hide the world in the world, you will not lose it. This is the universal law. People are happy when they get a body, but the changes of the body are endless; therefore, the happiness is limitless.

When the day comes to die, we are very afraid. We want to own, to cling to, this thing we call life, but it is only one of millions of transformations. Leaves fall, the sun sets, stars burn out, and we die. Life and death are different stages of the same process. Therefore, if you think well of life, you must think well of death.

Before I leave this world, I am never going to say,
"I didn't do this"or "I regret I did that." I am going to say:
"I came, I went, I did nothing, I did all."

Appendix A

When the Red Guards Knock

All incoming Carleton freshmen are given a common reading book to discuss when they arrive at college. In 2003, that book was Balzac and the Little Chinese Seamstress, *and Qiguang Zhao was asked to speak at the opening convocation about the book. The following is an excerpt from that speech, given at Skinner Memorial Chapel at Carleton College on September 11, 2003:*

Archimedes once said, "Give me a lever long enough and a fulcrum on which to place it, and I shall move the world." But where should we place this fulcrum?

Physics tells us that the longer the distance between the two objects, the more powerful the lever. We must build our lever on our connections to the unfamiliar world of nature, beauty, and our fellow humans. On that solid ground, we can move the world.

I am a witness to that power of connection. When I was just about your age, I experienced China's Cultural Revolution. The Cultural Revolution was actually a revolution of anti-culture, which attempted to create a proletarian revolutionary culture by cutting all connections between modern China, traditional China, and the rest of the world.

At the beginning of the Cultural Revolution, the Red Guards searched houses for "bourgeois books and objects." The first group who came to my parents' house was a group of college students. They were students of my parents, who were both professors of physics. One evening, the Red Guards knocked loudly at our front door. At that critical moment, I remembered that my mother had a diary which would have been extremely dangerous if it fell into the hands of the Red Guards. I grabbed the diary, and rushed out our back door just as the Red Guards were entering the front door. I ran for a mile and ducked into a public restroom.

The restroom was quiet. The moon and stars shone through a window overhead; I could hear the familiar lyrical chirpings of the crickets and the unfamiliar militant songs of the marching Red Guards. I looked at the well-kept diary. I wanted to keep it alive in my heart before it sank into oblivion. Under the moonlight, I quickly read my mother's diary, then tore it off page by page and flushed it down the toilet. Most of the diary was written in exquisite Chinese calligraphy. Parts of it were written in English, which I could not read at that time. In two hours, I finished the job and learned for the first time how my mother grew from a remote countryside girl into a professor of physics, a very rare success in her time. In a nation full of wars, famine, and revolution, my mother was motivated to connect herself with the world through the pursuit of knowledge. She had found solid ground to stand on in an unpredictable time.

I left the restroom and looked up at the stars in the night sky. They were tranquil, mysterious, and extremely beautiful, forming a sharp contrast to the dark earth. When I returned home, the Red Guards were gone. My parents' house was a mess, but strangely, though their personal and academic writings had been taken away, most of my parents' thousands of books were untouched. My mother was relieved to learn that her diary was destroyed instead of being taken by the Red Guards.

"They are my students in the physics department," my father said. I did not know whether he was rejoicing over the limited damage or lamenting the violation of a sacred Confucian relationship, that between teacher and students. I only understood his comment many years later, after the Cultural Revolution, when my father became the dean of the University. The first policy he suggested was to require science majors to study humanities and humanities majors to study science. The Red Guards had allowed themselves to be led toward destruction because they lacked comprehensive knowledge of the world and a sense of history. These days, we often talk about good and evil. I believe that evil occurs when ignorance and power meet.

This house search was just the beginning; more groups of Red Guards came in the following few days. The newcomers were mostly high school students. They were more violent and burned nonrevolutionary books. My family's decision was probably unique during the Cultural Revolution: when the Red Guards knocked, we would turn off the lights and not open the door. Group after group of Red Guards passed by our dark windows or pounded on our door but left without breaking in. They were not thorough revolutionaries, I guess.

For many nights, while hearing the pounding on the door—the ugliest noise ever made by men—we sat quietly among books written by the most beautiful minds of the world: great books by Li Bai, Confucius, Lao Tzu, Chang Tzu, Einstein, and Shakespeare. We took great risks in order to protect those books. House searches stopped in a few weeks, but the Cultural Revolution was to continue for 10 more years, with schools closed and most books banned. Fortunately, our books remained, and we remained connected to the world. My family defeated the Cultural Revolution in an isolated battle. During China's darkest years, I found comfort and inspiration among those books of science, literature, and history. They were my solid ground for connections.

Even today, I like to stay among books and journals in a library, reading, researching, and writing as if behind the Great Wall: safe against the sound and fury of the world. Sometimes I just sit quietly with a book on my lap, trying to connect myself to the mysterious universe or looking through the window to the horizon, as if there is something between the sky and the earth. (I call it thinking, but my wife calls it wasting time). I like to sit in a sanctuary of learning, where mellow silence reigns and I do not hear the piercing pounding on the door.

But I would like to warn you today, especially after the events of September 11: Please do not take your sense of safety for granted. No culture is immune to disasters. If you allow yourselves to be disconnected from the world, you may hear that ugly knocking at your door.

Appendix B

In Memory of Hai Zi, Who Died for Beauty

Hai Zi (1964–1989) was an ephemeral star among the "obscure poets" that emerged after China's 1979 reforms. He dazzled the world twice: the first time when he was accepted by the prestigious Beijing University at the age of 15, the second time when he committed suicide by laying himself on a railway track at the age of 25. Between these two events, he left a bright trail that is composed of 2 million characters of poetry and prose.

Hai Zi was not my friend when he was alive, but he is now in his death. According to *About the Death of Hai Zi* by his best friend Xi Chuan, Hai Zi carried four books to the railway tracks: the Bible, Thoreau's *Walden*, Thor Heyerdahl's *Kon-Tiki: Across the Pacific by Raft*, and *Selected Novels of Joseph Conrad*. I was saddened and flattered when I saw the title of the last book that Hai Zi took to another world, because I compiled, cotranslated, and prefaced the *Selected Novels of Joseph Conrad*. Before leaving for the United States in 1982, I handed the manuscript to the publisher, and I had scarcely heard anything about it after that. Now I received the most overwhelming feedback that an author or translator can hope for. Hai Zi is no stranger anymore. I did not know I had such a sincere friend and fellow traveler. Together we penetrated the heart of darkness and sailed through a typhoon. We went there together. We both decided we liked the beauty in those places. I left, but he stayed there forever.

Hai Zi died in the line of beauty just as some martyrs die in the line of duty. Beauty's way of treating us is different from duty's way. Ellen Sturgis Hooper's (1816–1841) poem discusses the relationship between duty and beauty:

> I slept, and dreamed that life was Beauty;
> I woke, and found that life was Duty.
> Was thy dream then a shadowy lie?
> Toil on, poor heart, unceasingly;
> And thou shalt find thy dream to be
> A truth and noonday light to thee.

Duty commands, beauty inspires. Beauty is freedom; duty is constraint. Yet our relationship to beauty is the same as our relationship to duty. We can reject beauty's appeal, as we can reject duty's command; yet duty, like beauty, cannot be rebuffed with impunity. Hai Zi rebuffed duty in the name of beauty. He paid for beauty with the dearest price—his life.

Hai Zi is a quixotic hero. He began by testing his mind against the world and ended by destroying his body for spiritual freedom. He believed that he could shape Chinese reality into the foreign images of the Messiah's paradise, Thoreau's Walden Pond, Heyerdahl's raft, and Conrad's ocean. Like Don Quixote, he was doomed to fail heroically. This Chinese knight-errant broke himself against the bars of his self-built prison. He belongs to no world, neither foreign nor Chinese. He focused too much on his spiritual odyssey without preparation of his sailing skills. He loved the ocean, but he could not swim. He loved romance, but he could not dance. He loved the earth, but he could not ride a bike. He loved life, but he could not live. He loved beauty, and he succeeded in creating a unique and original world of words and rhythms. In that sense, he is triumphant.

Hai Zi must have read the following epitaph inscribed on Conrad's gravestone at St. Thomas Church, Canterbury, England. I translated and quoted it in the preface of *Selected Novels of Joseph Conrad*:

> Sleep after toyle, port after stormie seas,
> Ease after warre, death after life, does greatly please.

I believe this poem by George John Spencer did not cause Hai Zi's death but confirmed his desire to find rest in eternity. He chose to die for beauty, just as some people choose to die for truth. Hai Zi's epitaph should be Emily Dickinson's poem:

> I died for beauty but was scarce
> Adjusted in the tomb,
> When one who died for truth was lain
> In an adjoining room.
> He questioned softly why I failed?
> "For beauty," I replied.
> "And I for truth—the two are one;
> We brethren are," he said.
> And so, as kinsmen met a-night,

We talked between the rooms,
Until the moss had reached our lips,
And covered up our names.

Or Tao Yuanming's, "Lament":

What you can say about death
Just identify the body with the mountains

Or, more properly, Hai Zi's own poem; "Spring, Ten Hai Zi":

Spring. Ten Hai Zi all resurrected.
In the bright scene
They mock at this one barbaric and sad Hai Zi
Why on earth do you sleep such a dead, long sleep?
Spring. Ten Hai Zi rage and roar under breath
They dance and sing around you and me
Tear disheveled your black hair, ride on you and fly away,
stirring up a cloud of dust
Your pain of being cleaved open pervades the great earth
In the spring, barbaric and grief-stricken Hai Zi
Only this one is left, the last one
A child of dark night, immersed in winter, addicted to death
He cannot help himself, and loves the empty and cold village
There crops piled high up, covering up the window
They use half of the corn to feed the six mouths of the family,
eating and stomach
The other half was used in agriculture, their own procreation
Strong wind sweeps from the east to the west, from the north to the
south, blind to dark night and dawn

What on earth is the meaning of dawn that you spoke of?[12]

Hai Zi did what he said and killed himself near the starting point of the Great Wall, where the mountains meet the ocean. His death was a gallant and romantic declaration of his passions, devotions, and beliefs. People finally believed he meant what he had "roared" in his poems, when he willingly returned to the mountains and ocean.

Poetry hides behind the opening and closing of a door, leaving those who look through to guess about what could be seen when the door was open. Hai Zi's poems, like the marks left in the snow by goose tracks, are the traces of his life. Now, let us open the door and let our ephemeral star be seen.

Notes

11. Hai Zi, *An English Translation of Poems of the Contemporary Chinese Poet Hai Zi*, trans. Hong Zeng (Lewiston, New York: Edwin Mellen Press, 2006).

Appendix C
Student Contributions

In a recent class, 59 students of Carleton College, all members of Qiguang Zhao's course, The Taoist Way of Health and Longevity: Tai Chi and Other Forms, were divided into six groups and wrote their own manifestos of Applied New Taoism.

Students were also asked to keep a journal of their reactions to the class lectures. The included excerpts from group manifestos and class journals are the products of ten weeks of reflection on both Taoist philosophy and how to apply that philosophy to modern life. The following are their words, either as a group or as individuals.

Student Groups:

Ganbei:
Caitlin Bowersox
David Chin
Rachel Danner
Lianne Hilbert
Craig Hogle
Karen Lee
Matthew Shelton

Like Water:
Naomi Hattori
Aaron Kaufman
Marie Kim
Paul Koenig
Nora Mahlberg
Nelupa Perera
Charles Yi

Old Fishermen:

William Bennett
Philip Casken
Anna Ing
David Kamin
Sophie Kerman
Greg Marliave
Carisa Skretch
Andrew Ullman

The Sorting:

Alex Baum
Jean Hyun
YoonJung Ku
He Sun
Chris Young
Xiuyuan Geoffrey Yu

The Place Where the Water Meets the Sand:

Becky Alexander
Matt Bartel
Elizabeth Graff
Mark Stewart
Aaron Weiner
Kristi Welle
Katie Whillock

The Sound of One Hand Clapping:

Jacob Hitchcock
Anthony McElligott
Lauren Milne
Megan Molteni
Emily Muirhead
Peter Olds
Sam Rober

The concept of Wu Wei is illustrated by the tale of two men stranded in rapids. The first, being too old and weak to fight the current, lets it carry him downstream. By surrendering to the current, he is swept out to calm waters. The second man tries to fight the current and drowns. The old man discovered the nature of water, became water, and was brought to safety. You cannot fight nature; it is arrogant to think that you can change the path of the eternal.

—*The Sound of One Hand Clapping*

By attempting to "return to the source," we are trying to attain a higher state of thinking, a state of nothingness. It is not a state that implies ignorance or pessimism, but a state that rejects attempts to regulate society or go against the natural flow.

—*Ganbei*

Not every problem needs fixing, and not everything that looks wrong is broken.

—*Alex Baum*

We are like a drop of water in a river. We do not notice that we are moving, because the rest of the water drops are also moving. We strive to move ourselves when all we really need to do is rest and move with the flow of the universe.

—*Dan Edwards*

We are on a rambling path; we should pay attention to the present. There should be a balance between understanding that we are part of a whole, stretching across time and space, and realizing that we are limited in some regard to our time and space. To ignore this is to ignore where our rambling path has taken us.

I consider it like a great mural: for example, the Sistine Chapel. Certainly Michelangelo had a sense of the work as a whole, but at the same time, each individual part needed special care and attention in order for the whole to succeed.

—*Greg Marliave*

It's a marvelous moment when you see a constellation clearly, or see a tree in bloom in the spring, but it also makes you think, "Why didn't I notice it earlier?"

—*Jenny Oyallon-Koloski*

The most stunning aspects of the universe are effortless—the planets, moons, and stars move with majestic ease. The beauty of the water flowing, birds flying, and trees waving in the wind all occur without effort.

—*Mark Severtsgaard*

Through Taoism, I have realized that my role in the universe is not one of great importance. In so doing, I become a part of the universe and a master of the universe as well. I do not understand the universe yet, because I do not know myself fully, but the goal is not the destination. The goal to know myself lies in the journey, for in the journey lie beauty and knowledge.

—*The Sound of One Hand Clapping*

I've noticed in my travels that in places where there is a lot of space (the great outdoors or small towns), time seems to slow down and stop at times, but when space is limited (in a big city) time stops for no man.

—Kristi Welle

We are now unable to instinctively understand [Taoist] concepts, for our minds have been crowded with materialistic worries. Taoism is not looking to transform us into a brand new being; rather, it seeks to return the being back to its original state at the beginning of time, away from the corruption that society has instilled upon humans. In this state, one will be yielding, free, and effortless.

—Karen Lee

Everything needs its opposite to exist. Without an opposite, you cannot define yourself.

—Peter Olds

The moon leads, and the tides follow.
For what does the moon care for the tides?
The tree grows and sprouts new leaves.
But what do the roots know of blooming?

Erase distinction and the roots feed the leaves,
The tides move with the moon.

The sages see good in simplicity:
The ocean at war with the moon, who would think it?
In ebbing and flowing as one, they feed us all.
If the roots forgot the tree, both would die.

—Old Fishermen

To illustrate the principle of reversal, let us consider the motion of water. First, we have waves. Waves flow toward the shore, but when they arrive there, they recede. Second, and on a grander scale, we have the tides. Over a period of hours, the water on a beach will move up the shore until it reaches the high tide point, and then it reverses. When we consider that the tides are caused by the moon, it seems almost certain that reversal is a cosmic principle.

The principle of reversal is also evident in our daily lives. When we realize that we have made a mistake, we correct that mistake by changing our actions to the opposite of what we had been doing. That is, we must reverse. The principle of reversal also plays out over the course of our lives. We are born completely dependent upon others for our survival. As time passes, our demands on others lessen until we reach independence. However, as we continue to age, we become dependent upon others for more and more until we cannot survive without them.

—Like Water

When we discussed reversing today, I was reminded of the first art class I ever took. For the first six weeks of class, we weren't allowed to use erasers when we drew. Our teacher told us that this exercise would teach us how to trust our instincts. More often than not, the first line you draw is better than any other you draw in its place. Whenever I erase over and over again, I usually just end up either starting over or coming back to the original line! It seems it is better to trust your instincts than to keep drawing and drawing, only to end up back at the same place you started.

—Marie Kim

The sage makes cryptic remarks,
He speaks in generalities.
By naming one thing,
He names all of the ten thousand things.
By naming nothing,
He names that which escapes all words.
He calls it Tao.
When speaking of it, he does not define it.
When asked to define it, he does not speak.

—*Old Fishermen*

If I name something, I am separating it from other things. But the Tao is not separable; one cannot take a knife to the universe and cut out a slice that is Tao. In the words of Bruce Lee, "It is like a finger pointing at the moon. Do not look at the finger, or you will miss all of that heavenly glory." Here, language is our finger. Lao Tzu is pointing at the Tao, but if one looks too hard at the words, one misses the point entirely.

—*Will Bennett*

When thinking about naming things, I think about Shakespeare: "What's in a name? That which we call a rose by any other name would smell as sweet." People get wrapped up in names: when a mother is with child, the first question is, "Have you thought of names?" When something new is created, we wonder what to call it, but in the end, it doesn't matter.

—*Kristi Welle*

Perhaps the idea of an empty vessel is an encouragement not to save anything for later. Do not save your cute underwear for a special day; make today your special day.

—*Becky Alexander*

To someone living in the wealthiest nation in the world, it has been difficult to come to terms with the idea of not filling to the brim. We live in a world of "all-you-can-eat-for-$6.95," far from the concept that fully stretching oneself is actually detrimental to one's health and state of mind.

—*Megan Molteni*

We live in a consumer economy that, through regular and repeated advertising, leads us to believe that the only way to achieve happiness is through money and material possessions. We live in a world where we must super-size to get our money's worth. If we look toward modern culture in order to find happiness, we will most likely find ourselves feeling unfulfilled. No matter how much we try to fill our lives to the brim, we still long for something more.

Instead, look inward. Just as the Tao is an empty vessel, we must look to rid ourselves of our dependence on material objects. It is not our possessions that determine our worth. True usefulness does not come from the container that is filled to the brim but the container that is empty. Only when we are empty can we put our own materials in, not what others tell us we should have.

—*Ganbei*

The water carries the boat.
If the fisherman is restless, the boat will tip.
If he does nothing, he will forever drift.
But if he guides his boat with the current,
He will find what he seeks.

—Old Fishermen

What there is now is all that there is.
Thoughts of what was, or what could be,
Bring nothing but worry and remorse.
If we rid our mind of what is not,
We are left only with happiness of what is.

—Old Fishermen

Is escape always good? Shouldn't we face the trials of life rather than running from them? Doing nothing isn't the same as avoiding everything.

—Sophie Kerman

Riding the tides of nocturnal oblivion, one can reflect upon the Tao. Only in sleep can this truly happen, because one cannot coherently think; one can only be guided by the cycles of the mind. Only when you release all aspirations, all goals, all feelings of being, when through living you come closest to death, can one meet the Tao.

—The Sorting

None of us knows if we are ourselves. I cannot tell, when I close my eyes at night, if the world exists while I am sleeping. Each of us may be a butterfly dreaming—reversing each night as we go to sleep.

—The Place Where the Water Meets the Sand

If we cannot tell what is real and what isn't, we may as well make beauty where we can, and hope the ugliness is part of the illusion.

—*Sophie Kerman*

We fill our bellies with breaths so that we can empty our hearts of thought. In breathing with our whole bodies and seeing beyond the fragmentation of our own bodies, we may begin to see beyond the superficial fragmentation of the universe.

—*The Place Where the Water Meets the Sand*

I've written 20-page papers and solved complex mathematical problems. But to return to my roots, to completely relearn how to do something I've known since birth, to relearn how to breathe was the most complicated obstacle by far.

—*Karen Lee*

If you ignore your own ignorance, you will be unable to further your learning. You will remain ignorant and will only think you know all.

—*Anthony McElligott*

The eventual understanding of your own spirit is the greatest pursuit of knowledge we can and should be engaged in. Scholastic learning may seem impressive, but when compared to enlightenment, it is nothing.

—*Aaron Kaufman*

You have to learn something in order to unlearn it. Is that what Lao Tzu means, that the goal isn't learning but rather unlearning?

—*Sophie Kerman*

Do you not have to learn Taoism? Can you not learn from the world? How can you change if you do not learn? Humans seem to have to learn everything—it's part of our nature; that's how we grow. How can we refuse our nature?

—*Lauren Milne*

I wonder if this alludes less to the meaning of learning and more to our concept of worry. Worry is a learned reaction. Could Lao Tzu mean to say, "Forget how you learned about worry, for I wish to teach you a new way to process the events that would have caused you worry?"

—*Kristi Welle*

We need to return to our roots: eat when we're hungry, sleep when we're tired, scratch where it itches, without rudeness or reservations.

—*Becky Alexander*

Taoists *do* do everything backwards. Everyone else cannot wait to grow up. Taoists say no; we will return to infancy. We will feed our bellies and not worry about the tiny trials in our own lives. We will be the blank slate.

—*Megan Molteni*

The Taoist path is rambling,
The path cannot be planned.
Dwell in the future or the past,
And you will never be prepared.
Go forward with no presumptions about the future,
And you will always be prepared.
Remember that the present happens only once,
Do not waste your opportunity.
The future will always be on the horizon,
Do not let it distract you from the present.

—Greg Marliave

What do we do with real and immediate conflict? We can carry the Tao internally, but when someone faces us with an egregious wrongdoing, what do we do, from a Taoist standpoint? Should we let people be killed, because there are no distinctions between wrong and right? Because they'll just die later anyway?

—Sophie Kerman

A rose is not pretty to become pretty, but its design for itself makes it beautiful.

—Gregory Ely

Life is about expression and passion. Without the two you cannot live. You may live, but unperceived by others, unacknowledged by the future. This is like life without life, an eternal death. We can do nothing about death, but we can make life the true opposite of death through expression.

—Peter Olds

In music, the beauty comes from both the notes and the spaces between the notes. The opposites are united, and in synthesis form something greater than themselves.

—*Andrew Ullman*

I think the best art captures a moment of universality, one moment that is made eternal. Why would we need to immortalize the look in one person's eyes, or the fall of a leaf from a tree, if these things weren't constantly escaping us?

Could we say that art reverses the deteriorating process of time? Yet at the same time, art ages and deteriorates, and its meaning always changes, even to the same person (who is different the next time they see it). Art encapsulates both life and death.

—*Sophie Kerman*

We are completely dependent on the universe. But in that dependency we find the freedom not to worry.

—*Sophie Kerman*

Life and death are not interchangeable for those whom we care for. Even if time is not well defined, I still have to live my life with someone I care about. That alone is worth ensuring that we value life.

—*Craig Hogle*

Sometimes we need to stop being cosmic, come back down to earth, and realize that we are all human, and we all need some simple human pleasures: music, love, friendship, playfulness, good food, dancing, whatever you like.

—*Mark Stewart*

If we are not trying to win, we cannot lose, and thus, there is never an outcome unless there is one of "winning."

—*Mark Stewart*

Be spontaneous
Go where the winds will take you
The Tao will find you

Let the quick fox jump
I will be the lazy dog
Yet achieve my goal
Leave time in your day
The work you do is valued
The peace is priceless

—*Becky Alexander*

Is it better to do great things with knowledge and ability, or to lead a simple life without ambition? Is there a way to lead a "great" and Taoist life?

—*Matt Bartel*

There is no purpose in life. We have made ourselves a purpose, because we cannot deal with life without it.

—*Caitlin Bowersox*

I am who I am: who are you?

—*Rachel Danner*

What makes us more special than a pine tree? At least the pine is content with itself and does not envy the flowers growing nearby. At least the pine does its job its whole life, without whining and complaining. Humans are flawed in so many ways that we are unaware of.

—*Calvin Lieu*

As we move into the future, we create technological innovations at increasing rates. We are like the man with the great wagon, the great horse, and the great driver. Now, our wagon is even better; it is a jet plane. We have made the horse obsolete, for it is too slow. Our pilots are better; they attend flight school for years. However, it is of no use to have these things if we move in the wrong direction. As we continue to get higher and faster, we must not forget the lessons that can be learned from going slower, lower, and weaker.

—*Old Fishermen*

If you have any goals, you are not free to renounce things.

—*The Sorting*

Taoism sometimes makes me think of the Robert Frost poem, "The Road Not Taken." Most people think that Frost was glad he took the road less traveled by, but that's not what he said. He said that it made all the difference. Who knows what that difference was? I suppose Taoism would have me take the path that leads downhill. But if you always go downhill, you'll never get to see the sunrise over the trees.

—*Matt Bartel*

If we did not have an end to strive for, would we even bother taking the journey? I'd like to think we would, but I'm a bit doubtful.

—*Jenny Oyallon-Koloski*

Tai Chi under the stars is very calming. In one way it is like being left alone in the world. When no one else is awake or outside, you can truly be alone. On the other hand, everything that is not out during the day comes out during the night, so you can connect with the other half of the world.

—*Emily Muirhead*

"You don't need a badge on your sleeve to have honor." —*A Few Good Men*

—*Becky Alexander*

Hatred and rancor are poisonous. Times I've been filled with them—and they've been few, thank God—I've ended up literally feeling physically ill! If that's not evidence, I don't know what is.

—*Paul Koenig*

One who practices moral conduct will share the happiness of others and experience the pain of those who are suffering. They will be humble and not envy or act in anger. By following moral conduct, they will help maintain the rhythm of nature, which in turn leads them to the way of the universe.

—*Nelupa Perera*

When we are kind to people and greet everyone we meet with positive, free flowing energy, with smiles, we are creating a new kind of uniform motion! Perhaps warmth will flow from one person to the next. Nothing will be lost, and everyone will gain.

—*Eleni Schirmer*

If you own nothing, you will lose nothing.
If you desire nothing, you will never be left wanting.
The pain of loss is self-inflicted.
The joy of contentedness is self-protecting.
Accept what is now as perfect
And you will never be unhappy.

—Old Fishermen

My birth was not my beginning, because I am unborn, and my death will not be my end, because I am ever-living.

—Andrew Ullman

One can love both life and death. Not being afraid of death doesn't mean one can't work to prolong life.

—Alex Baum

If someone wants to party all night long, it doesn't necessarily mean they're afraid of going to bed.

—Jessica Taylor

We don't cry for people when they die; we cry for ourselves because we are alone.

—Caitlin Bowersox

If we always fear death, then we can never enjoy life. People who live in fear of death will rarely do anything that may pose a risk. Rather than fearing the end, we should think in the reverse and take comfort in the fact that we are aware of our limited time on earth. With this knowledge, we can try to live every moment to the fullest.

—Naomi Hattori

Why do we fear the unknown? Is the known always worth holding onto?

—*Paul Koenig*

In modern life, we try to physically ward off death by quitting smoking or wearing a seatbelt. We are always fighting someone outside of ourselves. In Taoism, the true enemy is one's traditional mindset. When Zhuangzi's wife died, he played the drums. He defeated death not through action, but through a change in perspective.

—*Lauren Milne*

Really being accepting of death and suffering at any moment means one must be content with life.

—*Kristi Welle*

About the Author

Qiguang Zhao is Burton and Lily Levin Professor of Chinese at Carleton College, Northfield, Minnesota. He was born in Beijing and grew up in China. He has an MA in English and American literature from the Chinese Academy of Social Sciences and a Ph.D. in Comparative Literature from the University of Massachusetts, Amherst.

He started the Chinese Language program at Carleton College and has been teaching courses in Chinese language and literature, comparative literature, and Taoism for 20 years. He leads a study-abroad program in China every other year. His teaching method, *huajiang,* supplements lecture with the lively cartoons that he draws on the board. His favorite course, The Taoist Way of Health and Longevity: Tai Chi and Other Forms, is one of the most popular courses at Carleton College. It has moved to larger and larger classrooms from term to term. In this course, students learn how Taoism and Tai Chi can improve the quality of modern life.

Qiguang Zhao has frequently appeared on Chinese television, discussing culture and international relations. Recently, he talked about Taoism on Shanghai television in a ten-part series called "The Wisdom of Lao Tzu," which was broadcast in November 2007 and will be published in book form. He has also judged the International Emmy Awards. He has published six books, including a comparative study of Eastern and Western dragons.

Qiguang Zhao in front of a statue of Lao Tzu of Song Dynasty, Fujian Province, China.

Students of Carleton College and Qiguang Zhao perform Tai Chi
on the Great Wall, 2006.

Qiguang Zhao and Students in the class of Taoist Way of Health
and Longevity, Carleton College, 2008.

Bibliography

Birch, Cyril, ed. *Anthology of Chinese Literature*. New York: Grove Press, 1965.

Chen, Ellen. *The Tao Tè Ching: A New Translation with Commentary*. St. Paul, MN: Paragon House, 1989.

Chen Yaoting, ed. *Daojia Yangshengshu* (Taoist Way of Health and Longevity). Shanghai: Fudan University Press, 1992.

Confucius. *The Analects*. Arthur Waley, trans. Hertfordshire: Wordsworth Editions Limited, 1996.

Hawking, Stephen. *The Theory of Everything*. Beverly Hills: New Millennium Press, 2002.

Lao Tsu. *Tao Tè Ching*. Gia-Fu Feng and Jane English, trans. New York: Vintage Books, 1989.

Liezi. *Liezi*. Liang Xiaopeng and Li Jianguo, trans. Beijing: Zhonghua Book Company, 2005.

Tagore, Rabindranath. *Stray Birds*. Old Chelsea Station, NY: Cosimo Classics, 2004.

Zhuangzi. *The Inner Chapters*. A.C. Graham, trans. Indianapolis: Hackett Publishing Company, Inc., 2001.

Index